Introduction to

CORRECTIONS

Cliff Roberson, LL.M., Ph.D.

COPPERHOUSE PUBLISHING COMPANY
901-5 Tahoe Blvd.
Incline Village, Nevada 89451
(702) 833-3131 • Fax (702) 833-3133
http://www.copperhouse.com/copperhouse

Your Partner in Education
with
"QUALITY BOOKS AT FAIR PRICES"

Introduction to
CORRECTIONS

Library of Congress Catalog Number 97-65247
ISBN 0-942728-78-5 Paper Text Edition

2 3 4 5 6 7 8 9 10

Printed in the United States of America.

DEDICATION

To Genny, Nickie, T.J. and Isiah—
and, of course, to Lynne, P.A.

PREFACE

Prison is, in practice, the ultimate power the democratic state exercises over a citizen, yet we lack a jurisprudence of imprisonment.
Norval Morris, *The Future of Imprisonment*

Introduction to Corrections is designed to be comprehensive, yet affordable. This text discusses the stages of criminal justice administration that occur after an individual has been convicted of a crime. The title is really a misnomer. The text is about *punishment* and the use of punishment/sanctions to prevent and/or control crime.

This text is written for an introductory corrections course which focuses on both adult and juvenile court dispositions. The main focus of the book is about how our present correctional subsystems function within the larger umbrella of our criminal justice system. It provides a complete overview to the corrections field and considers all types of custody, including probation and parole. As expected, the text covers everything from historical precedents to the latest programs and practices. Pursuant to our times, special attention is given to elderly inmates, violent juveniles, alternative penalties, and private correctional facilities. In addition, included are articles from leading professional journals on corrections. These articles are designed to provide the reader with insight from different viewpoints regarding critical issues affecting modern corrections.

The state of Texas, along with several other states, has concluded that the term "inmate" is politically incorrect. In fact, in Texas, the state office that I am associated with has changed its name from "Inmate Legal Services" to "State Counsel for Offenders." The problem is that the term "offenders" does not describe an individual who is confined. Most offenders receive probation and therefore are not confined. Accordingly, in this text I have retained the use of the term "inmate" to refer to an individual who is incarcerated.

Textbooks are biased to a certain degree based on the background, experiences, and philosophy of the author. In light of this, I have attempted to remove most biases from this text. My background as a prosecutor, defense counsel and judge has allowed me to research the corrections area from the perspective of three different viewpoints. Additionally, I had the unique opportunity to teach criminological theory courses to inmates in a medium security institution on three separate occasions. This experience provided me with an opportunity to have frank discussions with the inmates on crime causation and correctional policies. Therefore, this text is designed to provide the reader with *real world* insight based on my teaching and practical experiences.

While I am listed as the only author of this text, it could not have been possible without the help, assistance, and guidance of numerous others including Cathy Lowe-Anderson, Lynne Shoecraft, and Professor Harvey Wallace.

Cliff Roberson

TABLE OF CONTENTS

Chapter 1
Corrections: A Subsystem

Chapter 2

The Sentencing Process

Chapter 3

The Correctional Client

Chapter 4

Alternatives to Incarceration

Chapter 5

Probation

Chapter 6
Jails and Misdemeanants

Chapter 7
Doing Time

Chapter 8

Institutional Procedures

Chapter 9
Juvenile Corrections

Chapter 10

Special Applications of Detention and Corrections

Chapter 11

Capital Punishment

Chapter 12

Prisoners' Rights

Chapter 13

Innovations in Corrections

Chapter 14

Corrections as a Career Field

CHAPTER 1

CORRECTIONS:

A SUBSYSTEM

KEY TERMS

Blood feuds

Code of Draco

Code of Hammurabi

Deterrence

Holy Inquisition

Ideology

Incapacitation

Penal servitude

Rehabilitation

Retribution

Trials by ordeal

Values

Wergeld

CHAPTER OBJECTIVES

After studying this chapter, the reader will be able to:

☐ Identify the major subsystems in the criminal justice system.

☐ Explain how the criminal justice system is fragmented.

☐ List the major goals of punishment.

☐ Explain the beginning of legal punishments.

☐ Explain the purposes of punishment.

☐ Contrast the different ideologies based on political beliefs.

☐ Identify and explain the four popular goals of punishment.

☐ Identify the early reformers involved in corrections.

☐ Explain the social purposes of punishment.

☐ Identify the criminogenic factors in society.

The criminal justice system is traditionally considered to have three subsystems: law enforcement, the judicial system, and corrections. This text focuses on corrections. While this text deals only with corrections, it is important to remember that corrections is a subpart of the broader criminal justice system and can be understood only as a subsystem of that larger system. It is also important to remember that before an individual comes under correctional control, he or she has already moved from citizen, to suspect, to arrestee, to defendant and finally to convict.[1] In other words, the individual has already experienced the other two subsystems of the criminal justice system: law enforcement and the judiciary.

Corrections, like other subsystems in the criminal justice field, is fragmented. This fragmentation makes administrative coordination and linkage to the other criminal justice components difficult. The following list illustrates the fragmentation of the subsystem.

- By jurisdiction: federal, state, or local
- By location: institutional or community-based
- By age: adult or juvenile
- By other factors: size of institution, sex of inmates, types of offenses, and special programs

The Justification of Punishment

The problem of punishment causes constant, anguished reassessment, not only because we keep speculating on what the effective consequences of crime should be, but also because there is a confusion of the ends and means. We are still far from the answer to the ultimate questions: What is the right punishment? On what grounds do we punish others?[2]

HISTORY AND PHILOSOPHY

Beginning of Legal Punishments

In ancient societies, the remedy for wrongs committed against one's person or property was personal retaliation against the wrongdoer. Unlike modern society, in the early primitive societies, personal retaliation was encouraged. From the concept of personal retaliation developed *blood feuds*, which occurred when the victim's family or tribe took revenge on the offender's family or tribe. Often, blood feuds escalated and resulted in continuing vendettas between families or tribes. In many cases, for religious reasons individuals were expected to avenge the death of a kinsman. The duty of retaliation was imposed by universal practice upon the victim or in case of death, the nearest male relative.

To lessen the costly and damaging vendettas, the custom of accepting money or property in place of blood vengeance developed. At first, the acceptance of payments instead of blood vengeance was not compulsory. The victim's family was still free to choose whatever form of vengeance they wished. Often the relative power of the families or tribes decided whether payments or blood vengeance was used.

The acceptance of money or property as atonement for wrongs became know as "les salica" or "wergeld." This practice is still used in some countries of the Middle East. The amount of payment was based on the rank or position of the victim. The tradition of accepting money for property damages was the beginning of the development of a system of criminal law.

One problem with the acceptance of payment as complete satisfaction for the wrong was the concept that punishment of an individual wrongdoer should also include some religious aspects. To many, crime was also a sin against the church or the state. Accordingly, the concept developed that punishment in the form of *wergeld* (payment to the victim) should also be supplemented with *friedensgeld* (payment to the church or the crown).

Fines and other forms of punishment replaced personal retaliation as tribal and community leaders began to exert their authority during the negotiations or proceedings concerning the damages caused and the wrongs committed. The wrongdoers were not required to attend the proceedings. If, however, they failed to follow the recommendations of the leaders, they were banished or exiled, and thus considered "outlaws."

Because criminal law requires an element of public action against the wrongdoer, the banishment or pronouncement of outlawry was the first criminal punishment imposed by society.[3] Many present-day researchers consider the development of this custom the beginning of criminal law as we know it today. Subsequent legal codes and punishments for different crimes have either stressed or refined the vengeance principle. The concept that a society express its vengeance within a system of rules was present in the ethics of ancient societies.

The two earliest codes involving criminal punishments were the Sumerian and Hammurabic codes. The punishment phases of these codes contained the concept of personal vengeance. The listed punishments in the codes were harsh, and in many cases, the victim or nearest relative was allowed personally to inflict punishment. Permitted pun-

The end result of criminal justice in Colonial America often meant punishment by simple yet effective devices. (Courtesy of Patterson Smith Publishing Corporation)

ishments included mutilation, whipping, or forced labor. At first, the punishments were applied almost exclusively to slaves and bond servants and indicated a dominating mentality towards those being punished. Later they were extended to all offenders.

Upper part of the pillar upon which the legendary Code of Hammurabi was inscribed.

The use of penal servitude also developed. *Penal servitude* involved the use of hard labor as punishment. It was generally reserved for the lower classes of citizens. Penal servitude included the loss of citizenship and liberty (i.e., civil death). With civil death, the offender's property was confiscated in the name of the state and his wife was declared a widow. Later, the use of penal servitude by the Romans was encouraged by the need for workers to perform hard labor.

The Case Against Socrates

Socrates was charged in 399 B.C. with the offense of impiety (corrupting young minds and of believing in new gods). He was tried before a jury of five hundred members. The trial lasted only one day. He was found guilty by a majority of thirty jurors. The prosecution proposed the death penalty. Socrates had a right to propose an alternative penalty. He stated:

Shall I [propose] imprisonment? And why should I spend my days in prison, and be the slave of the magistrates? Or shall the penalty be a fine and imprisonment until the fine is paid? There is the same objection. I should have to lie in prison, for money I have none, and cannot pay. And if I say exile, I must indeed be blinded by the love of life, if I am so irrational was to expect that when you, who are my own citizens, cannot endure my discourses and arguments, and have found them so grievous and odious that you will have no more of them, that others are likely to endure them.

The jury condemned him to death. He committed compulsory suicide by drinking poison, the Athenian method of execution.

The fact that early punishments were considered synonymous with slavery is indicated by the practice of shaving the heads of those punished as a "mark of slavery." Other marks of slavery used on punished wrongdoers included the branding on the forehead or use of a heavy metal collar that could not be easily removed.

The Greek code, Code of Draco, used the same penalties for both citizens and slaves and incorporated many of the concepts used in primitive societies, e.g., vengeance, outlawry, and blood feuds. The Greeks apparently were the first society to allow any citizen to prosecute an offender on behalf of the victim. This practice appears to indicate that public interest and protection of society had accepted the concept that crimes affected not only the victim, but society in general.

Middle Ages

During the Middle Ages, rapid changes were made in the social structure of societies. In addition, the growing influence of the church on everyday life helped create a divided system of justice. The offender in committing a crime, also committed a sin. Accordingly, he or she had two debts to pay—one to the victim and one to the church. *Trials by ordeal* were used by the churches as substitutes for trials. In a trial by ordeal, the accused was subjected to dangerous or painful tests in the belief that God would protect the innocent and the guilty would suffer agonies and die. The brutality of the trial by ordeal ensured that most would die and thus be considered guilty. The practice of trial by ordeal was not abolished until about the year 1215.

It was also during the Middle Ages that the churches expanded the concept of crime to include new prohibited areas. This concept is still present in our modern-day codes. Sexual offenses were among the new areas now covered by law. Sex offenses which included either public or "unnatural" acts were punished by horrible punishments. Heresy and witchcraft were also included in the new prohibited areas of conduct. The church inflicted cruel punishments and justified the punishments as necessary to save the unfortunate sinners. For example, the zealous movement to stamp out heresy resulted in the Inquisition, which was a tribunal established by the Church with very broad powers to use for the suppression of heresy. The Inquisition searched for offenders rather than waiting for charges to be brought forward.

Whipping was the usual method of punishing persons for minor offenses. Whipping was inflicted on women while kneeling and on men while lying on the ground. Generally the victims were stripped to the waist and the blows inflicted on their backs.[5]

The Holy Inquisition

The word "inquisition" means an inquiry. In one sense, all modern courts of law are inquisitions. The Holy Inquisition was a court set up by the Church of Rome to inquire into cases of heresy. It was later extended to cover crimes of witchcraft and ecclesiastical offenses committed by members of the Church. The idea of a court of inquiry into religious offenses was of very early origin. For example, Jews found guilty of deserting their faith by an inquisition were sentenced to be stoned to death.

The Holy Inquisition flourished in all European countries, but its barbarities were the greatest in Spain and the Spanish dominions. The sentences of the court were generally pronounced on Sunday in a church and consisted of burning, scourging, imprisonment, penances, humiliation, and/or fines.[4]

THE EARLY REFORMERS

Voltaire (Francois Marie Arouet) (1694-1778). Voltaire was one of the most enlightened eighteenth century philosophers and probably the most versatile. His writings alerted the public as to the abuses of criminal law in France. He believed that the fear of shame could be used as a deterrent to crime. He opposed the use of torture. Voltaire was imprisoned in the Bastille in 1726 and released only on the condition that he leave France and never return. Voltaire clearly established by his writings that the pen was mightier than the sword.

Cesare Beccaria (1738-1794). Cesare Beccaria was one of the first theorists to espouse the concept of punishment as a deterrent to crime. Cesare Beccaria wrote an essay on penal reform that was originally published in January 1764. It was first published anonymously, because its contents challenged the cherished beliefs of those in position to determine the fate of people convicted of crimes. The 17-page essay is still regularly quoted over 300 years later. It was, however, his only notable publication.

Both his mother and father were members of the aristocracy, and both had achieved distinction in various fields. His mother, worried that her son could not withstand the rigors of business or commerce, obtained for him a professorship with prestige and yet little responsibility. At the university, he tended to be lazy and easily discouraged. He preferred to drink beer at the local pub and discuss literary and philosophical subjects other than work.

Beccaria's interest in penology and crime was aroused by his discussions and debates with two stimulating and keen brothers, Pietro and Alessandro Verri. They encouraged him to consolidate his ideas and to put them in an essay that was later entitled "On Crimes and Punishment."

According to Beccaria, laws are conditions whereby free and independent men unite to form society. Punishments were established to deal with those who transgress the laws. The right to punish transgressors is an essential consequence of the nature and scope of society. The primary purpose of punishment should be to insure the continued existence of society. Furthermore, the amount and nature of the punishment inflicted against the offender should vary in proportion to the degree to which an act of an individual endangers the existence of society. According to Beccaria, the essential end of punishment is not to torment the offenders nor to undo the crime already committed. It is rather to prevent offenders from doing further harm to society and to prevent others from committing crime. To be effective as a deterrent to crime, punishment should be prompt and inevitable, applied equally to all for similar crimes. It should not be cruel or severe, but the punishment must be certain. According to him, it is the strength of the association of crime and punishment that is the most effective deterrent.[15]

Cesare Lombroso (1835-1909). More has been written about Cesare Lombroso than any other criminologist. He is considered by many as the "father of modern criminology." According to him, criminals are distinguished from noncriminals by the manifestation of multiple physical or psychological anomalies, that the criminal is defective and his or her criminal misconduct is not the result of a rational choice on the part of the criminal. Lombroso contended that punishment should have two objectives—to protect society and to improve the criminal. The fundamental principle regarding punishment should be to study and treat, not so much the abstract crime, but the criminal. Accordingly, punishment should fit the needs of the offender. He also contended that the length of imprisonment should depend on the time needed to improve the criminal.[16]

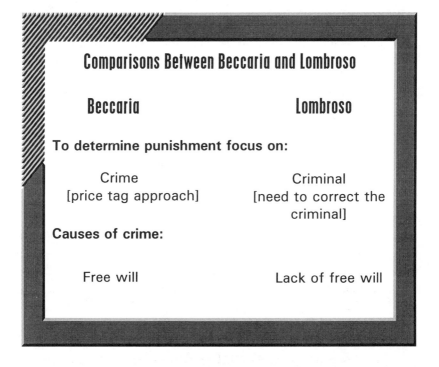

Comparisons Between Beccaria and Lombroso

Beccaria

Lombroso

To determine punishment focus on:

Crime
[price tag approach]

Criminal
[need to correct the criminal]

Causes of crime:

Free will

Lack of free will

Jeremy Bentham (1748-1832). Many consider Jeremy Bentham to be the greatest leader in the reform of English criminal law. Bentham believed that punishments should be designed to negate any pleasure or gain that a criminal would achieve from the criminal act. He advocated a system of graduated penalties that are closely associated with the crime committed. He contended that the main objective of any intelligent person is to achieve the most pleasure and experience the least pain. He applied his "hedonistic calculus" to his efforts to reform criminal law and the punishments used to punish offenders. Included within the concept of hedonistic calculus was the doctrine of utilitarianism. This doctrine holds that the aim of all action should be to obtain the greatest pleasure for the largest number of citizens. Accordingly, the law should be used to inflict enough pain on criminals that they will cease to commit crime and thus "good" would be achieved. Like Beccaria, he advocated that punishment should be used as a deterrent to crime. Bentham became sort of a "crackpot" in his later years.

During those later years, he designed the ultimate prison, the Panoptical. While it was never constructed, the debate over it raged for many years. This prison was designed to be a rational, humane environment for offenders. It was the answer to the human warehouses that existed at the time. The prison was designed as a circular building with a glass roof. Every cell would be visible from a central point. A prison inspector could be kept from the sight of the prisoners by used of blinds. If a prisoner thought that he was fit to be observed, the prisoner could show himself by raising the blinds. The manager of the prison would be liable if too many of his prisoners died. The prisoners could be contracted out, with the manager receiving a percentage of the money earned by the prisoners. In addition, the manager would be held liable if prisoners under his supervision later committed additional crimes after their release.

Bentham died in 1832. According to the instructions in his will, his body was dissected. The skeleton was dressed in his usual attire and is on display at the University College in London. For over 150 years, the fully dressed skeleton has attended the college faculty assemblies. Speakers at the assembly traditionally first voice recognition to Mr. Bentham and then to other members of the assembly and guests.[17]

John Howard (1726-1790). Until he was appointed Sheriff of Bedfordshire, England in 1773, John Howard showed no interest in prisons or prison reform. As sheriff, he was appalled by the conditions of the hulks being used to hold prisoners. *Hulks* were decrepit transport or warships being used to house prisoners in nineteenth century

England. He pressed for legislation to alleviate the abuses and to improve sanitary conditions. In addition, he traveled extensively in France and Italy and wrote about the conditions of their prisons.

As a direct result of Howard's actions, the English Parliament passed the Penitentiary Act in 1799. That act provided four principles for reform: secure and sanitary structures, systematic inspections of the prisons, abolition of fees, and a reformatory regime. The Penitentiary Act resulted in the first penitentiary in England, located at Wyndomhan in Norfolk. Ironically, John Howard died in 1790 of jail fever (typhus) in the Russian Ukraine.

William Penn (1644-1718). William Penn, the founder of Pennsylvania and leader of the Quakers, brought to America, the concept of humanitarian treatment of offenders. William Penn was an English Quaker who fought for religious freedom and individual rights. He obtained a charter from King Charles II in 1681 and founded the Quaker settlement that later became Pennsylvania.

At the time, the American colonies were governed under the codes established by the Duke of York, and earlier, the Hampshire Code. The Quakers advocated eliminating the harsh principles of criminal law in favor of more humane treatment of offenders. The Quakers, though very religious, eliminated most of the religious crimes and created a criminal code that was very secular. The Quaker Code, enacted in 1682, remained in force until its repeal in 1718, the day after the death of William Penn. The code was replaced by the English Anglican Code, which was even worse than the former codes of the Duke of York. The English Anglican Code restored the death penalty for many crimes and restored mutilation, branding, and other brutal forms of corporal punishment.

PURPOSE OF CRIMINAL SANCTIONS

In discussing the purpose of criminal sanctions, various ideologies present themselves. For purposes of studying this chapter, ideology refers to the belief system adopted by a group and consists of assumptions and values. The assumptions are beliefs about the way the world is constituted, organized, and operates. Values, however, are beliefs about what is moral and desirable.[6] There are numerous methods to classify ideologies. Three popular classifications based on political theories that influence our corrections system are conservative, liberal, and radical.

The conservative ideology tends to accept the concept that human beings are rational, possess free will, and voluntarily commit criminal misconduct. Accordingly, criminals should be held accountable for their actions. Punishment should be imposed to inflict suffering on the criminal because the suffering is deserved and because it will deter future crime. The punishment imposed should fit the crime. This ideology, because of its view on the causes of human behavior, generally does not accept the concept of rehabilitation as an attractive objective of punishment.

The liberal ideology tends to view human behavior as greatly influenced by social circumstances including one's upbringing, material affluence, education, peer relationships, etc. Accordingly, human behavior is more than a simple product of free choice. All of the social influences are important factors in shaping our conduct. Viewing criminal behavior as a product of both social circumstances and individual actions, liberals are more likely to support rehabilitation as the proper purposes of criminal punishment. Most liberals tend to be receptive to a wider range of aims for criminal punishment, including deterrence.

The radical ideology rejects both the conservative and liberal ideologies and views crime as a reflection of the status of our present social system. Crime is only a natural consequence of our social system. According to the radicals, fundamental changes in the socioeconomic basis of society are required in order to control crime.

The ultimate purpose of criminal sanctions is generally considered to be the maintenance of our social order. Herbert Packer contends that the two major goals of criminal sanctions are to inflict suffering upon the wrongdoers and to prevent crime.[7] Robert Dawson sees the major purpose of the criminal justice system as to identify, in a legally acceptable manner, those persons who should be subjected to control and treatment in the correctional process.[8] According to Dawson, if corrections does not properly perform its task, the entire criminal justice system suffers. An inefficient or unfair correctional process can nullify the courts, prosecutors and police alike. Conversely, the manner in which the other agencies involved perform their tasks has an important impact upon the success of the process: a person who has been unfairly dealt with prior to conviction is a poor subject for rehabilitation.

The four popular goals of criminal sanctions are retribution, deterrence, incapacitation, and rehabilitation. From the 1940s to the 1980s, rehabilitation was considered by most as the primary goal of our system. Since the 1980s, retribution has received popular support. Each of these four commonly accepted goals are discussed.

Retribution

Retribution generally means "getting even." Retribution is based on the ideology that the criminal is an enemy of society and deserves severe punishment for willfully breaking its rules. Retribution is often mistaken as revenge. There are, however, important differences between the two. Both retribution and revenge are primarily concerned with punishing the offender and neither is overly concerned with the impact of the punishment on the offender's future behavior or the behavior of others. Unlike revenge, however, retribution attempts to match the severity of the punishment to the seriousness of the crime. Revenge acts on passion, whereas retribution follows specific rules regarding the types and amounts of punishment that may be inflicted. The Biblical response of an "eye for an eye" is a retributive response to punishment. While the "eye for eye" concept is often cited as an excuse to use harsh punishment, it is less harsh than revenge-based punishment, which does not rule out "two eyes for an eye" punishment. Sir James Stephen, an English judge, expressed the retributive view by stating that "the punishment of criminals was simply a desirable expression of the hatred and fear aroused in the community by criminal acts."[9] This line of reasoning conveys the message that punishment is justifiable because it provides an orderly outlet for emotions, that if denied, may express themselves in socially less acceptable ways. Another justification under the retribution ideology is that only through suffering punishment can the criminal expiate his sin. In one manner, retribution treats all crimes as if they were financial transactions. You got something or did something, therefore you must give equivalent value (suffering).

Retribution is also referred to as "just deserts." The just deserts movement reflects the retribution viewpoint and provides a justifiable rationale for support of the death penalty. This viewpoint has its roots in a societal need for retribution. It can be traced back to the individual need for retaliation and vengeance. The transfer of the vengeance motive from the individual to the state has been justified based on theories involving theological, aesthetic, and expiatory views. According to the theological view, retaliation fulfills the religious need to punish the sinner. Under the aesthetic view, punishment helps reestablish a sense of harmony through requital, and thus resolves the social discord created by the crime. The expiatory view is that guilt must be washed away, or cleansed, through suffering. There is even an utilitarian view that punishment is the means of achieving beneficial and social consequences through the application of a specific form and degree of punishment deemed most appropriate to the particular offender after careful individualized study of the offender.[10]

Deterrence

Deterrence is a punishment viewpoint that focuses on future outcomes rather than past misconduct. It is also based on the theory that creating a fear of future punishments will deter crime. There is substantial debate as to the validity of this concept. Specific deterrence deters specifically the offender, whereas general deterrence works on others who might consider similar acts. According to this viewpoint, the fear of future suffering motivates individuals to avoid involvement in criminal misconduct. This concept assumes that the criminal is a rational being who will weigh the consequences of his or her criminal actions before deciding to commit them.

One of the problems with deterrence is determining the appropriate magnitude and nature of punishment to be imposed in order to deter future criminal misconduct. For example, an individual who commits a serious crime and then feels badly about the act may need only slight punishment to achieve deterrent effects, whereas a professional shoplifter may need severe fear-producing punishments to prevent future shoplifting.

Often, increases in crime rates and high rates of recidivism cast doubt that the deterrence approach is effective. Recidivism may cause some doubt on the efficacy of special deterrence, but it says nothing about the effect of general deterrence. In addition, unless we know what the crime rate or rates of recidivism would be if we did not attempt to deter criminal misconduct, the assertions are unfounded. Are we certain that the rates would not be higher had we not attempted to deter criminals?

Incapacitation

At least while the prisoner is in confinement, he is unlikely to commit crimes on innocent persons outside of prison. To this extent, confinement clearly helps reduce criminal behavior. Under this viewpoint, there is no hope for the individual as far as rehabilitation is concerned, therefore the only solution is to incapacitate the offender. Marvin Wolfgang's famous study of crime in Philadelphia indicated that while chronic offenders constituted only 23 percent of the offenders in the study, they committed over 61 percent of all the violent crimes.[11] Accordingly, the supporters of the incapacitation viewpoint contend that incapacitating the 23 percent would have prevented 61 percent of the future violent crimes. This approach has often been labeled the "nothing else works" approach to corrections. According to this viewpoint, we should make maximum effective use of the scarce prison cells to protect society from the depredations of such dangerous and repetitive offenders. This approach is present in California's "Three Strikes and You're Out" statute.

There are two variations in the incapacitation viewpoint. *Collective incapacitation* refers to sanctions imposed on offenders, such as violent offenders, without regard to their personal characteristics. *Selective incapacitation* refers to the incapacitation of certain groups of individuals who have been identified as high-risk offenders, such as robbers with a history of drug use. Under selective incapacitation, offenders with certain characteristics or history would receive longer prison terms than others convicted of the same crime. The purpose of incapacitation is to prevent future crimes, and the moral concerns associated with retribution are not as important as the reduction of future victimization.[12] As Herbert Packer states, "Incapacitation is a mode of punishment that uses the fact that a person has committed a crime as a basis for predicting that he will commit future crimes.[13] Packer also states that the logic of the incapacitative position is that until the offender stops being a danger we will continue to restrain him. Accordingly, he contends that pushed to its logical conclusion, offenses that are regarded as relatively trivial may be punished by imprisonment for life.

Rehabilitation

The *rehabilitation* approach pronounces that punishment should be directed toward correcting the offender. This approach is also considered the "treatment" approach. This approach considers the criminal misconduct as a manifestation of a pathology that can be handled by some form of therapeutic activity. While this viewpoint may consider the offender as "sick," it is not the same as a medical approach. Under the rehabilitation viewpoint, we need to teach the offenders to recognize the undesirability of their criminal behavior and make significant efforts to rid themselves of that behavior. The main difference between the rehabilitation approach and the retribution approach is that under the rehabilitation approach the offenders are assigned to programs designed to prepare them for readjustment or reintegration into the community, whereas the latter approach is more concerned with the punishment aspects of the sentence. Packer sees two major objections to making rehabilitation the primary justification for punishment. First, we do not know how to rehabilitate offenders. Second, we know little about who is likely to commit crimes and less about what makes them apt to do so. As long as we are ignorant in these matters, Packard contends that punishment in the name of rehabilitation is gratuitous cruelty.[14]

PURPOSES OF PUNISHMENT

English Statement of Purposes

The United States is not the only country that has had problems determining the proper purposes of punishment. It appears that most other countries have the same problem. An examination of the English Statement of Purposes, below, indicates that the English have similar problems. The English Prison Service has approximately 43,000 confined prisoners. The EPS declares that it "serves the public by keeping in custody those committed by the courts," and that its duty is to "look after them with humanity and help them lead law-abiding and useful lives in custody and after release." The purposes are divided into a series of goals:

- To keep prisoners in custody

- To maintain order, control, discipline and a safe environment

- To provide decent conditions for prisoners and meet their needs, including health care

- To provide positive regimes to help prisoners address their offending behavior

- To allow prisoners as full and responsible a life as possible

- To help prisoners prepare for their return to the community[18]

The Chinese Proverb

There is an old Chinese proverb that states: "It is better to hang the wrong fellow than no fellow." This proverb indicates that certainty of punishment is important. When a crime is committed, someone must be punished.

Guiding Principles

Certain principles are used in guiding the decision as to the proper disposition of a person convicted of criminal behavior. The principles are simple, yet subject to interpretation according to the philosophy of the individuals involved. The generally accepted principles include:

1. **Parsimony.** The least restrictive sanction necessary to achieve the defined purposes should be imposed. The debate regarding this principle centers on what is the purpose of criminal sanctions.

2. **Dangerousness.** Whether the likelihood of future criminal activity should be considered. The controversy on this point is whether

we should use predictions of future misconduct as a basis for present criminal sanctions. Numerous studies which indicate that predictions of dangerousness are unreliable. The studies indicate that we tend to over predict future dangerousness in individuals. There is also the philosophical and due process concerns of punishing a person for conduct not yet committed.

3. **Just Deserts.** Any sanction imposed should not be greater than that which is deserved by the last crime, or series of crimes, for which the defendant is being sentenced.[19]

Early use of the Pillory for punishment.

Social Purposes of Punishment

C. Ray Jeffery, a noted criminologist, contends that the more glaring defect in most analyses of punishments is that the analyses view punishments always in the context of what it means to the individual offender and never in terms of what it means to society. The purpose of punishment, according to Jeffery, should be to establish to the public social disapproval of the act. To him, the use of punishment by society is done for society's sake and not for the individual's. He also contends that punishment serves an important social function in that it creates social solidarity and re-enforces social norms.[20]

CRIMINOGENIC FACTORS IN SOCIETY

Magnitude of the Problem

This section presents statistics regarding prisoners confined in correctional institutions to provide the reader with an understanding of the magnitude of the corrections problem.[21] The total number of prisoners under the jurisdiction of federal or state correctional authorities was 1,053,738 at the end of 1994. During 1994, the states and the District of Columbia added 78,847 prisoners; the federal system, 5,447. Although the 1994 growth rate (8.6%) nearly equaled the average annual percentage increase since 1980, the total increase of 83,294 was the second largest yearly increase on record.

Two states, California and Texas, hold more than one of every five inmates in the nation. Seventeen states, each holding fewer than 5,000 inmates, together hold only four percent of all prisoners. Since 1980, the nation's per capita prison population more than doubled. In addition, the number of sentenced prisoners per 100,000 U.S. residents has more than doubled since 1980.

The states with the highest incarceration rates per 100,000 population are Texas (636), Louisiana (530), and Oklahoma (508). North Dakota (78) had the lowest rate, followed by Minnesota (100), West Virginia (106), and Maine (118). The incarceration rate of blacks is seven times that of whites. There are 1,471 black inmates per 100,000 black U.S. residents compared to 207 white inmates per 100,000 white U.S. residents.

Locations of Confinements

State and federal prisons house two-thirds of all people incarcerated in the United States—the other third are in local jails. The present growth rate of 8.6 percent is greater than the percentage increase recorded in earlier years. The increase translates into a nationwide need to confine an additional 1,602 inmates each week. Fifty-six percent of the increase is accounted for by Texas, California, Georgia, Florida and the federal system. These jurisdictions incarcerate over 40 percent of the nation's prison population. At the end of 1980, only one of every 453 U.S. residents was incarcerated; now, that figure is one of every 189. There are almost 4.9 million people under some form of correctional supervision, including 2.8 million adults on probation and 671,000 on parole. The 10 states with the largest prison populations hold 55 percent of the total prison population nationwide, with California, Texas, and New York accounting for nearly 30 percent.

Demographics

The demographic characteristics of the nation's prison population are changing. Since 1980, the number of female inmates in the nation's prisons has increased at a faster rate (up an average 12 percent per year) than the number of male inmates (up an average 8.5 percent per year). Despite their faster population growth, females still presently make up only about 6 percent of all sentenced prisoners. Oklahoma (with 96 female inmates per 100,000 female residents) and Texas (with 94) led the nation. North Dakota (five per 100,000) and Maine (nine per 100,000) have the lowest female incarceration rates. The national male incarceration rate, 746 per 100,000 male residents, is more than 16 times higher than the female incarceration rate—45 per 100,000 female residents.

Increasing percentages of state and federal inmates are from racial or ethnic minority groups. Since 1980, the percent of sentenced black inmates rose from 46.5 percent to 50.8 percent. Relative to the number of residents in the U.S. population, blacks are seven times more likely than whites to be incarcerated in a state or federal prison.

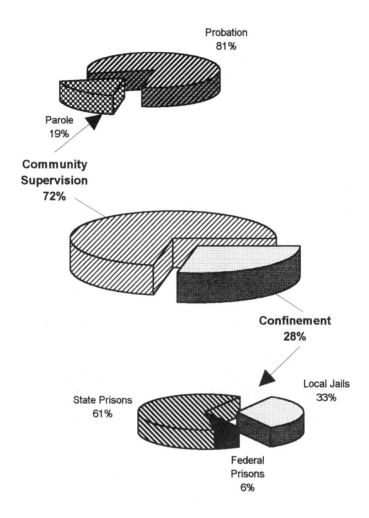

Probation
81%

Parole
19%

**Community
Supervision
72%**

**Confinement
28%**

State Prisons
61%

Local Jails
33%

Federal
Prisons
6%

Hispanics are the fastest growing minority group. Because of variations in record keeping, some states are unable to report data on Hispanic origin; other states report estimates only; a few report only partial counts. Data from past surveys of state inmates, which are based on inmate self-identification during personal interviews, produce higher estimates of the number of Hispanic inmates. Nearly two-thirds of all sentenced prison inmates were black, Asian, Native American, or Hispanic.

Types of Crime

The percentage of state prisoners serving a drug sentence increased almost threefold from 1980. The percentage of federal prisoners serving a drug sentence more than doubled, from 25 percent in 1980 to over 60 percent today. In recent years, although the number of drug offenders in the nation's prisons has grown dramatically, the number of violent offenders has grown the most.

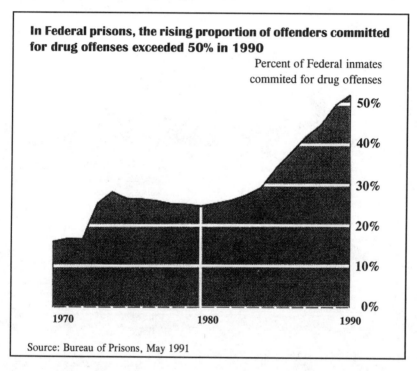

In Federal prisons, the rising proportion of offenders committed for drug offenses exceeded 50% in 1990

Percent of Federal inmates commited for drug offenses

Source: Bureau of Prisons, May 1991

The distribution of the four major offense categories—violent, property, drug, and public-order offenses—changed dramatically in the nation's prison population between 1980 and now. As a percentage of all state and federal inmates, violent offenders fell from 57 percent in 1980 to 45 percent in 1993, property offenders fell from 30 percent to 22 percent, drug offenders rose from 8 percent to 26 percent, and public-order offenders rose from 5 percent to 7 percent.

The rise in the number of drug offenders was the greatest among federal inmates. Prisoners sentenced for drug law violations were the single largest group of federal inmates (60 percent), up from 25 percent in 1980. The increase in drug offenders accounted for nearly three-quarters of the total growth in federal inmates.

The percentage of inmates in state prisons for drug crimes also rose significantly, from 6 percent in 1980 to presently over 22 percent. Nearly 10 times as many inmates are serving time in state prisons for drug offenses than in 1980. In absolute numbers, however, the growth in state inmates was greatest among violent offenders. Since 1980, the number of violent offenders grew by 221,200, while the number of drug offenders grew by 167,000. As a percentage of the total growth in sentenced state inmates during the period, violent offenders accounted for 42 percent of the total growth, drug offenders 31 percent, property offenders 19 percent, and public-order offenders 7 percent.

Time Served

Average sentence length and time served for state inmates has remained relatively unchanged. Data on prison admissions and releases collected annually in the National Corrections Reporting Program (NCRP) suggest that growth in the state prison populations has not been the result of longer sentences. (Each year participating states provide information on sentencing and time served for persons entering or leaving prison. Thirty-eight states and the District of Columbia submitted data, accounting for nearly 93 percent of all admissions and 85 percent of all releases nationwide during the year.) Between 1985 and 1995, years in which comparable data are available, the average (mean) maximum sentences of prisoners actually declined from 78 months to 67 months.

The median sentence length (the fiftieth percentile) of prisoners admitted from court remained constant at 48 months. Moreover, despite the increasing use of mandatory minimums and sentencing enhancements during the period, the percent of inmates who received a maximum sentence of 10 years or longer actually declined (from 19.7 percent in 1985 to 17.7 percent in 1995).

Overcrowding

The extent of crowding in the nation's prisons is difficult to determine because of the absence of uniform measures for defining capacity. Most jurisdictions are operating above capacity. Prisons generally require reserve capacity to operate efficiently. Dormitories and cells need to be maintained and repaired periodically, special housing is needed for protective custody and disciplinary cases, and space may be needed to cope with emergencies. State prisons are generally operating at 17 to 29 percent above capacity, while the federal system is operating at 25 percent above capacity.

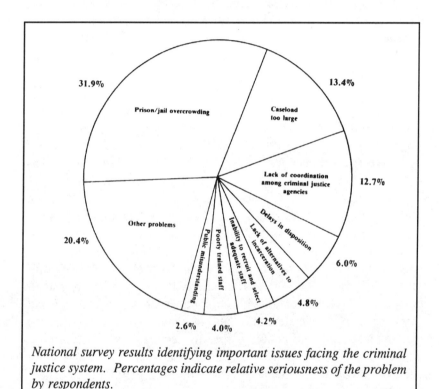

National survey results identifying important issues facing the criminal justice system. Percentages indicate relative seriousness of the problem by respondents.

CHANGES TO THE "JUSTICE" CORRECTIONAL PHILOSOPHY

The Violent Crime Control and Law Enforcement Act of 1994 was one of the most ambitious crime bills in our history.[22] The act allocated over $22 billion to expand prisons, impose longer sentences, hire more police officers, and to a very limited extent, fund prevention programs. The following year, however, the money allocated to prevention programs was eliminated. Such acts have great political appeal, but little support among criminal justice professionals. Most professionals feel that such efforts will do little to reduce crime. This approach has been labeled as the "enforcement model."[23] The popular criticisms of the present "enforcement model approach" are that it is racist, it costs too much, and it fails to prevent young people from entering, and continuing, lives of crime. The popularity of prison as a response to crime has resulted in changes in the public and professional perceptions of the role of corrections.

California Penal Code, Section 1170 (a)

(1) The Legislature finds and declares that the purpose of imprisonment for crime is punishment. This purpose is best served by terms proportionate to the seriousness of the offense with provisions for uniformity in the sentences of offenders committing the same offense under similar circumstances....
(2) Paragraph (1) shall not be construed to preclude programs, including educational programs, that are designed to rehabilitate nonviolent, first-time felony offenders. The Legislature encourages the development of policies and programs designed to educate and rehabilitate nonviolent, first-time felony offenders consistent with the purposes of imprisonment.
[Paragraph (2) added by legislature in 1995.]
[Paragraph (3) omitted.]

The various approaches to correctional philosophy fall into one of three categories: punishment, treatment, or prevention. Often, they overlap as punishment and treatment can be argued as an approach to prevent crime. The 1960s was a period when treatment was the dominant approach. This changed in the late 1970s. Since that time, society in general has preferred the punishment approach. As will be discussed in other chapters, the punishment approach has resulted in overcrowded institutions, budgets are stripped of so-called "frills" needed for treatment and prevention programs. It appears that in the 1990s, the punishment approach may have reached its height, and the future may see the pendulum swing back toward the treatment or prevention emphasis. Note the previous excerpt from the California Penal Code, which indicates a shift away from the punishment approach with its 1995 amendment. It is difficult, however, to predict the future of corrections.

Article

REHABILITATION: HOLDING ITS GROUND IN CORRECTIONS[24]

Introduction

During the Jacksonian era (1820-30s), American penitentiaries failed miserably in their efforts to reform inmates. Yet, rehabilitation was an idea that would not die easily. In fact, prison administrators during the Reformatory era renewed the optimism and benevolence of rehabilitation in the 1870s. Among the many structural alterations that prisons underwent at that time were substantive changes in rehabilitation programs. Prison officials once again embraced the ideals of rehabilitation by offering educational and vocational training, especially at the Elmira Reformatory, where classification was introduced to facilitate individualized treatment (Rothman, 1971, 1980; Welch, 1996a).

It should be pointed out that during the Reformatory era, rehabilitation was not viewed in explicit medical terms. By the turn of the century, however, medical technology was rapidly improving, and it did not take long for corrections officials to take note of medical break-throughs. In an effort to rehabilitate offenders, it made good sense to incorporate advances in medicine into correctional treatment. Taking a genuine medical approach to corrections, prisons began reorganizing programs and introducing a therapeutic staff, psychiatrists, psychologists, clinical social workers, and other specialists. Obviously, the role of the therapeutic staff was to facilitate the process of rehabilitation by transforming the offender into a socially amenable and law-abiding citizen. The newly created Federal Bureau of Prisons furthered efforts to integrate the medical model into corrections in the 1930s. Also during that period, classification became more refined and the medical model provided a state-of-the-art clinical orientation by developing diagnostic and treatment methods.

For decades now, the terms treatment and rehabilitation have been used to refer to a variety of programs that range from educational and vocational training to individual therapy and substance abuse counseling. According to the National Academy of Sciences, rehabilitation is defined as "any planned intervention that reduces an offender's further criminal activity" (Sechrest, White, & Brown, 1979). In this sense, the focus of rehabilitation remains on the psychological causes of crime excluding deterrence strategies (see Kratcoaki, 1994). Although the terms treatment and rehabilitation may have different meanings within the correctional community, in this article these terms are used interchangeably.

The Rehabilitation Controversy

The controversy over rehabilitation generally occurs on two fronts. First, there is discussion over theoretical issues—most importantly, their assumptions and propositions. Second, there remains considerable controversy over program-oriented issues surrounding the ways in which rehabilitation is designed, implemented, and evaluated.

Theoretical Issues

Correctional experts who support rehabilitation programs operate on two basic assumptions. First, that the offender's behavior is related to particular personal defects stemming from the offender's own psychological makeup or adverse conditions (or a combination of both). Second, that the offender can be effectively transformed into a law-abiding human being.

Rehabilitation has been attacked by various critics representing diverse philosophical viewpoints. Conservatives remain skeptical about the assumption that an offender's criminality stems from adverse social conditions or psychological defects (or a combination of both). For instance, if it is argued that living in poverty causes behavior, then why are most impoverished people actually law-abiding citizens? Conservatives question such sweeping generalizations about poverty being a cause of crime (Wilson, 1975).

Critics also question whether offenders can be transformed into law-abiding citizens, thus raising an important issue regarding the medical model in corrections. Prisoners in many ways resemble involuntary patients in psychiatric facilities, because offenders are incarcerated against their will. Conventional wisdom leads us to believe that forcing an offender to become prosocial is problematic. An old tongue-in-cheek riddle among psychologists illuminates this dilemma: How many therapists does it take to change a light bulb? One, but the light bulb must be willing to change (Welch, 1996).

Even in cases where the offender is willing and capable of being rehabilitated, questions remain about the long-term effectiveness of such treatment. This is especially true when we acknowledge that ex-cons (e.g., drug peddlers) eventually return to the community. Typically, the neighborhoods to which they return are impoverished with high unemployment, inadequate housing, high rates of crime and violence, and high concentrations of illegal drug use. Critics argue that the long-term effectiveness of rehabilitation is strained unless comparable changes are also made in society (Currie, 1993, 1985; Reiman, 1995; Walker, 1994). Even so, from a basic logistical standpoint, it is certainly easier to try to correct offenders than it is to alter societal conditions.

Program Effectiveness: "What Works?" v. "Nothing Works!"

Since the 1960s, critics of correctional treatment have referred to the body of evaluation research that reports the weaknesses and limitations of rehabilitation programs. Yet, the evaluation study that delivered the hardest blow to rehabilitation was authored by Lipton, Martinson, and Wilks (1975). In a widely cited spin-off article, Martinson (1974, p. 25) concluded: "With few and isolated exceptions, the rehabilitative efforts that have been reported so far have had no appreciable effect on rehabilitation." Martinson entitled his article "What Works?: Questions and Answers About Prison Reform," but it quickly became known as the "nothing works" report.

Contrary to popular opinion, Lipton, Martinson, and Wilks (1975) did not make the sweeping claim that "nothing works." In fact, they cited positive outcomes in 48 percent of the programs evaluated. In the early 1970s, there had been growing disillusion surrounding rehabilitation, and for several years policy makers were "waiting for the other shoe to drop." The publication of Martinson's article was that "other shoe," and the fact that it became known as the "nothing works" report was testimony that the chapter on liberal-oriented rehabilitation was officially coming to a close. Though conservatives succeeded in driving rehabilitation out of prisons, many liberals also voiced their dissatisfaction with correctional programs. Among other things, liberals pointed to the criminal justice system as the problem, therefore arguing that the effectiveness of rehabilitation was irrelevant. Moreover, radicals also launched resounding attacks on rehabilitation by arguing that rehabilitation strategies represent attempts by those in power to "impose a repressive system of social control over the less powerful" (Michalowski, 1985). In this vein, Greenberg and Humphries (1980) noted that liberal interventions, namely rehabilitation, perpetuated class biases in criminal justice:

> Seen in this light, rehabilitation was not merely a laudable goal that scientific research had failed thus far to achieve, but something more insidious, an ideology that explained crime in highly individualistic terms and legitimated the expansion of administrative powers used in practice to discriminate against disadvantaged groups and to achieve covert organizational goals.

Liberals adamantly defended themselves against charges that rehabilitation represents a form of additional social control and pointed out that the demise of rehabilitation resulted from ideological shifts toward conservatism. Cullen and Gendreau suggested that "the rejection of rehabilitation has less to do with a careful reading of empirical literature and more to do with changes in the social fabric that triggered a corresponding shift in thinking about corrections" (1989, p. 24).

A principal method of assessing the effectiveness of rehabilitation programs was to examine the program evaluation reports. It was assumed that if the evaluation specialists found the program ineffective, their conclusion was uncritically accepted without further investigation. As advocates of rehabilitation programs aptly demonstrated, in many cases the evaluation research was at fault, not the program itself. Indeed, buried deep inside Martinson's (1974) article is the regrettable fact that many researchers had failed to follow rigorous scientific procedures while evaluating these programs.

As we take a closer look at the evaluation research of correctional rehabilitation, it is important to be aware that three outcomes are possible. First, that the program is indeed ineffective. Second, that the program is designed effectively, but suffers from faulty administration (perhaps due to unqualified or incompetent staff). Finally, that research methods used to evaluate rehabilitation programs are flawed. As a result, two types of errors might occur: concluding the program is effective when it is not, or concluding that the program is ineffective when it is not.

In the years leading up to the "nothing works" controversy, several social scientists focused on the research methods of previously published evaluation studies. Overall, most of the evaluation studies that were reexamined suffered from shoddy methodology, therefore, raising questions about their findings and conclusions about correctional programs. Perhaps even more relevant to the current debate on the merit of rehabilitation are the recently published evaluation studies that provide substantial support for the effectiveness of correctional treatment (Andrews, Zinger, Hoge, Bonta, Gendreau, & Cullen, 1990a; Gendreau, 1981; Gendreau & Ross, 1979, 1981, 1987; Greenwood & Zimring, 1985; Halleck & Witte, 1977; Palmer, 1983; Van Voorhis, 1987).

Eventually, even Martinson (1979) recanted some of his earlier conclusions. Moreover, his conversion was based largely on the fact that traditional research designs were too rigid to measure accurately the effectiveness of rehabilitation programs. Martinson later wrote that some programs were indeed beneficial and some treatment programs do have an appreciable effect on recidivism. "It is ironic, but instructive, that whereas Martinson's 1974 nothing works article is one the most cited of criminological writings, his revisionist 1979 essay earned scant attention." Once again, it is helpful to view these developments in the context of important social changes transpiring in the 1970s. The nation was struggling to reestablish the image of a strong government after the turbulent 1960s, and one method of achieving this was to mount a visible "tough on crime" campaign. The "tough on crime" ideology asserted that those who favored rehabilitation were "bleeding heart" liberals—suggesting that liberals were soft on crime.

The implications of this ideological shift are evident. Evaluation reports shape both public opinion as well as public policy, and the two often go hand-in-hand. Therefore, in light of what happened in the wake of the Martinson report, one could argue that rehabilitation was unintentionally sabotaged by evaluation researchers (including many academics), who relied on weak or faulty methodological procedures. In addition, proponents have argued that rehabilitation programs were further sabotaged (intentionally or unintentionally) because they were never fully implemented. The decline of rehabilitation was due to administrative or staff limitations. Yet each of these developments took place in a social context characterized by a shift in correctional ideology from liberal to conservative.

A case in point is the argument presented by conservative retributionist Ernest van den Haag, who asked this question: What is the likely effect of rehabilitation on the crime rate? Van den Haag relied on a set of principles and equations borrowed from econometrics deterrent theorists to support the following contention: because rehabilitation can affect criminals only after their first conviction, even total rehabilitation could reduce neither the rate of first offenses, nor the overall rime rate to the extent to which it depends on first offenses.

Though van den Haag recommends that the criminal justice system assert its emphasis on punishment to deter future crimes, his criticism of rehabilitation shows some valuable insight. With first-time offenders, he notes that rehabilitation comes too late. Indeed, to a certain point he is correct. But the answer does not rest in deterrence and the increased use of punishments. Perhaps a better approach is to prevent such crimes by improving societal conditions (e.g., reducing unemployment) and responding to the offenders' personal problems (e.g., substance dependency and substandard education).

Rehabilitation for the 1990s and Beyond

In light of the ongoing controversy over rehabilitation, we need to address some of the most basic applications of the rehabilitation ideal. Whereas some experts have suggested that various forms of counseling be made available in prison simply to undo the damage that incarceration has on the inmate, there are numerous programs which have become common features within prisons that rarely draw criticism—for example, educational programs. The reason why educational programs are not controversial is because they are based on the conventional wisdom that attributes some types of property crime to inadequate education. Most correctional facilities offer various educational programs ranging from literacy classes, high school equivalency diploma (GED) programs and, in some institutions, college courses. Most correctional facilities also offer vocational training to promote job skills. For example, many correctional systems employ inmates in prison industries, such as bakeries, furniture and sewing shops, cosmetology salons, as well as employing them as telephone operators for the state tourism department.

Educational and vocational programs continue to draw support from mainstream citizens, essentially because education in and of itself is valued in our society. Moreover, educational and vocational programs not only develop practical skills, but they also foster a sense of work-ethic that is central to American culture's emphasis on self-reliance.

However, social services advocates point out the paradox that such programs provide inmates with skills that might have helped to prevent them from turning to crime in the first place. Many social policy and prison experts also note that it is "almost as if Americans have concluded that the problems of the urban poor are intractable and therefore spent their money on a vast network of prisons, rather on than on solutions" (Butterfield, 1992). Again, it is ironic that citizens support the construction of prisons but oppose basic social and educational services for the poor, though such interventions are far cheaper than building prisons. For instance, in 1991 the United States allocated $26.2 billion for building and operating prisons, as well as for supervising parolees and probationers (according to the Edna McConnell Clark Foundation). The same year, $22.9 billion was spent on the main welfare program, Aid to Families With Dependent Children (according to the Department of Health and Human Services). Moreover, we are comparing the social services allocated to 13.5 million women and children on public assistance to the 1.1 million prisoners, mostly men. Critics argue that spending billions of dollars on prisons diverts funds from social services that might prevent crime (Butterfield, 1992).

According to Robert Gangi, the executive director of the Correctional Association of New York, "Prisons are becoming the place where we provide services to our poor people" (Butterfield, 1992, p. E-4). Indeed, "the prison system has become part of the welfare system," says penologist Mark Fleisher. Prisons offer housing that is typically better than that of the inner cities. For inmates from the urban ghettos, meals, medical care (especially for persons with AIDS), substance abuse treatment, and educational and vocational training are generally better in prison than in society at large.

Currently, most inmates lack even the most basic educational and vocational skills. Among the men incarcerated in state prisons, 21 percent have an eighth-grade education or less; roughly 41 percent attended some high school; approximately 27 percent are high school graduates; and barely 11 percent report some college or more. Moreover, in terms of employment, approximately 58 percent of these prisoners were working full-time jobs at the time of their arrest (Bureau of Justice Statistics, 1993).

Ideally, it would make good sense to ensure job placement for those returning to the community. However, such proposals remain unrealistic because we live in a society that does not provide full employment—even for its law-abiding citizens. One can imagine the public outcry if the government gave preference to unemployed ex-cons over the ranks of other unemployed citizens. Nevertheless, educational and vocational programs in correctional institutions remain because they symbolize an important form of rehabilitation.

Another form of rehabilitation that is an integral fixture in most correctional facilities is substance abuse counseling (for both drugs and alcohol). The fact is, the great majority of persons being sent to prison are convicted of drug-related offenses, and many more report drug and alcohol abuse histories. In federal prisons, for example, the number of drug offenders has more than doubled since 1981 and now accounts for 53 percent of the inmate population. It is projected that this figure will increase to 69 percent by the end of 1995 (Mauer, 1992). According to the Johnson Foundation (1993), two-thirds of homicides and serious assaults involve alcohol. Similarly, the Bureau of Justice

Statistics (1993) reports that 31 percent of state inmates committed their offenses under the influence of drugs, and 17 percent committed their offenses to get money for drugs; further, 32 percent committed their offenses under the influence of alcohol.

Naturally, it is important to provide such services to those who are willing to take full advantage of treatment. However, most correctional administrators concede that their substance abuse programs are grossly under-funded by state and federal authorities. This problem is not surprising, because the vast majority of substance abuse programs outside of prison are also neglected by policy makers. A typical response to a drug addict who voluntarily requests treatment at a community substance abuse clinic is: "Come back in four to six months. That's when the program expects the soonest available bed." At this time, 70 percent of federal antidrug funding is still allocated to law enforcement and only 30 percent to treatment and prevention (Mauer, 1992). As a society, perhaps we need to provide more substance dependency treatment to offenders (as well as non-offenders), especially considering what we know about the association between crime, illegal drugs, and alcohol.

In sum, Cullen and Gilbert (1982) cite four reasons why rehabilitation should be reaffirmed in corrections:

1. Rehabilitation is the only justification of criminal sanctioning that obligates the state to care for an offender's needs or welfare.

2. The ideology of rehabilitation provides an important rationale for opposing the conservative assumptions that increased repression will reduce crime.

3. Rehabilitation still receives considerable support as a major goal of the correctional system.

4. Rehabilitation has historically been an important motive underlying reform efforts that have increased the humanity of the correctional system.

Conclusion

By focusing solely on the problems facing rehabilitation, the more basic assumptions of the liberal perspective are neglected. The liberal agenda recognizes the limitations of patching up offenders who have gone astray without seriously examining the deep underlying social and economic problems (Currie, 1985). Indeed, many liberals concede that if rehabilitation means equipping offenders with better coping and survival skills and returning them to their troubled environment (hoping that this intervention would keep them from engaging in future crimes) instead of attempting to alter some basic social conditions, then the foundation of liberalism is virtually ignored. It seems that over the past few decades, liberals adopted an individual-based form of intervention much like the conservatives because of the realization that it is probably easier to try to correct the offender than to alter social conditions. Certainly, this was found to be the case in the 1820s, when the Jacksonians resorted to building prisons because their efforts to reform society failed (i.e., closing brothels and taverns) (Rothman, 1971). Over time, the liberal approach has become more individual-oriented and less society-oriented (see Clear, 1994).

A popular myth today is that most citizens simply support the conservative "tough on crime" proposals to the exclusion of rehabilitation. Politicians have greatly misjudged the complexity of attitudes that citizens hold regarding punishment and rehabilitation. Numerous studies demonstrate that most citizens favor rehabilitation (especially educational, vocational, and substance abuse programs) in addition to a reasonable level of deserved punishment. Furthermore, many citizens have reasonably accurate impressions of the correctional system insofar as they know that prisons do not rehabilitate offenders—even those offenders who probably are good candidates for reform. Nevertheless, the rehabilitation debate is certainly not settled. It is important to note that the rehabilitative approach has proven to be fairly well-received, especially among citizens.

Cullen and Woznik insist that conservatives have enjoyed free reign of the criminal justice system. The conservative "tough on crime" agenda is characterized by liberals as a form of repression of the disadvantaged and less powerful. In reaction to the conservative criminal justice policies, Cullen and Wozniak propose an eight-point counterattack:

1. Expose the irrationality of "getting tough."

2. Punishing doesn't help: do conservatives really care about victims?

3. Oppose all prison construction.

4. Continue the struggle for offender rights.

5. Oppose determinate sentencing reform.

6. Reaffirm rehabilitation.

7. Promote the work ethic as an avenue of penal reform.

8. Appreciate the humane potential of religion.

In sum, the recommendations by Cullen and Woznik are anything but new—indeed, they were introduced nearly 15 years ago. Moreover, since that time, the law-and-order approach to corrections has deepened, even under a Democratic president. According to Currie, "It is painfully apparent that the decade-long conservative experiment in crime control has failed to live up to its promises." Conservatives are now left with the annoying question of why such an enormous investment in punishment has produced such little impact on crime. Perhaps now political leaders ought to reconsider the value of rehabilitation in corrections.

{End of Article}

SUMMARY

The criminal justice system is traditionally considered to have three subsystems: law enforcement, judiciary, and corrections. Before an individual comes under the control of correctional agencies, he or she has already moved from citizen, to suspect, to arrestee, to defendant, and finally to convict.

In ancient societies, the remedy for wrongs done to one's person or property was personal retaliation against the wrongdoer. Blood feuds developed from the concept of personal retaliation. A blood feud occurred when the victim's family or tribe took revenge on the offender's family or tribe. To lesson the costly and damaging vendettas, the custom of accepting money or property developed. This practice is still used in some countries in the Middle East. Later, fines and other forms of punishment replaced personal retaliation.

The two earliest codes delineating criminal punishments were the Sumerian and Hammurabic codes. The punishment phases of these codes were based on the concept of personal vengeance. Early punishments were considered synonymous with slavery. Later, the Greek Code and the Code of Draco used the same penalties for both citizens and slaves.

During the Middle Ages, the growing influence of the churches help create a divided system of justice. The offender, in committing a crime, had two debts to pay. One to the victim, and one to the church. It was also during the Middle Ages that the churches expanded the concept of crime to include new prohibited areas such as heresy, witchcraft, and sex offenses.

While there are numerous methods to classify punishment ideologies, the three popular classifications based on political theories are the conservative, liberal, and radical. The conservative ideology tends to accept the concept that human beings are rational, possess free will, and voluntarily commit criminal misconduct. The liberal ideology tends to view human behavior as greatly influenced by social circumstances, including one's upbringing, material affluence, education, peer relationships, etc. The radical ideology rejects both the conservative and liberal ideologies. To the radicals, crime is a reflection of the status of our present social system.

The ultimate purpose of criminal sanctions is generally considered to be the maintenance of our social order. The four popular goals of criminal sanctions are retribution, deterrence, incapacitation, and rehabilitation. Retribution generally means getting even and is based on the ideology that the criminal is an enemy of society. Retribution is also referred to as the "just deserts" ideology. Deterrence is a punishment viewpoint that focuses on future outcomes rather than past misconduct. It is also based on the theory that creating fear of future punishments will deter crime. The incapacitation viewpoint is often labeled as the "nothing else works" concept. It is based on the concept that prisoners, while in prison, have less chance to commit crimes against the public. The rehabilitation approach emphasizes correcting the offender, and is also considered as the "treatment" approach.

Two states, California and Texas, together hold more than one of every five inmates in the United States. The nation's prison population has more than doubled since 1980. The states with the highest incarceration rates are Texas, Louisiana, and Oklahoma. The states with the lowest incarceration rate are North Dakota, Minnesota, and West Virginia. The incarceration rate of blacks is seven times that of whites. State and federal prisons house two-thirds of all persons incarcerated in the United States. The other one-third are in local jails.

DISCUSSION QUESTIONS

1. Explain how the concept of blood feuds developed.

2. Discuss the functions and purpose of the Holy Inquisition.

3. Compare and contrast the three political ideologies regarding punishment.

4. Compare and contrast the rehabilitation and deterrence approaches to punishment.

5. Explain the contributions to punishment reform of Jeremy Bentham.

6. Describe the demographics of the prison population.

7. List recent changes to the justice correctional philosophy.

ENDNOTES FOR CHAPTER 1

1.Lawrence F. Travis III, Martin D. Schwartz, and Todd R. Clear, *Corrections: An Issues Approach*, 3rd ed. (Cincinnati: Anderson, 1992) p. 50

2. Stephen Schafer, *Theories in Criminology*. (New York: Random House, 1969) p. 291.

3. Albert Kocourek and John Wigmore, *Evolution of Law*, Vol. II, (Boston: Little, Brown and Company, 1915, p. 15).

4. John Swain, *The Pleasures of the Torture Chamber*, (New York: Dorset Press, 1931) p. 157.

5. Ibid., p. 27.

6. Alexis M. Durham III, *Crisis and Reform: Current Issues in American Punishment,* (Boston: Little, Brown and Company, 1994) p. 16-18.

7. Herbert L. Packer, *The Limits of Criminal Sanction* (Stanford, Ca.: Stanford University Press, 1968, p. 33.

8. Robert O. Dawson, *Sentencing: The Decision as to Type, Length, and Conditions of Sentence* (Boston: Little, Brown and Company, 1969).

9. Herbert L. Packer, *The Limits of Criminal Sanction*, (Stanford: Univ. of Stanford Press, 1968) p. 37.

10. Elmer H. Johnson, *Crime, Correction, and Society,* (Homewoood, Ill.: Dorsey Press, 1974) p. 173.

11. Marianne W. Zawitz, ed. *Report to the Nation on Crime and Justice* (Washington, D.C.:, Bureau of Justice Statistics, U.S. Government Printing Office, 1983) p. 35.

12. Durham, 1994:26.

13. Packer, 1963:49.

14. Ibid., pp.55-57.

15. Elio Monachesi, " Cesare Beccaria," in *Pioneers in Criminology*, 2d ed. Hermann Hannheim, editor, (Monclair, N.J.: Patterson Smith, 1973) p.42-49.

16. Marvin Wolfgang, "Cesare Lombroso," in *Pioneers in Criminology*, 2d ed. edited by Hermann Mannheim (Montclair, NJ: Patterson Smith, 1973) p. 232-249.

17. Charles Milner Atkinson, *Jerry Bentham: His Life and Work,* London: Smith, 1905.

18. As reported in *The Oxford History of the Prison*, eds. Norval Morris and David J. Rothman. (New York: Oxford, 1995), p. xi.

19. Norval Morris, *The Future of Imprisonment*, (Chicago: University of Chicago, 1974, p. Xi).

20.C. Ray Jeffery, "The Historical Development of Criminology," *Pioneers in Criminology*, 2d ed. Hermann Mannheim editor (Montclair, NJ: Patterson Smith, 1973) p. 487.

21. The statistics for this section were taken from the NCJRS Report: Prisoners in 1994, NCJ-151654, August, 1995 by Allen J. Beck and Darrell K. Gilliard, BJS Statisticians.

22. Joan Petersilia, "A Crime Control Rationale For Reinvesting in Community Corrections," *The Prison Journal,* Vol. 75, No. 4, December 1995, 479-496.

23. Ibid.

24. Michael Welch, Associate Professor Administration of Justice, Rutgers University. Reprinted with permission from *Federal Probation*, Vol. 59, No. 4, December, 1995.

CHAPTER 2

THE SENTENCING PROCESS

KEY TERMS

Adjudicatory hearing

Deferrred adjudication

Determinate sentence

Disposition hearing

Informal probation

Presumptive sentence

Pretrial diversion

Parole guidelines

Sentence

Sentencing guidelines

CHAPTER OBJECTIVES

After studying this chapter, the reader will be able to:

☐ Identify who has the responsibility for determining the appropriate sentence in a criminal case.

☐ List the restrictions that are placed on judges regarding their sentencing discretion.

☐ Explain the differences between determinate and indeterminate sentences.

☐ Explain the use of sentencing guidelines.

☐ List the duties of the U.S. Sentencing Commission.

☐ Describe the function of good-time laws.

☐ List the conditions under which the Model Penal Code recommends the use of imprisonment as a prison sentence.

☐ Explain the procedures used in juvenile cases.

☐ List the essential components of a presentence investigation (PSI) report.

☐ Explain the two types of suspended sentences

Before the correctional process may be involved, the defendant must be convicted of a crime by a court with proper jurisdiction. In this chapter, we will examine the process by which a citizen becomes a client in the correctional process, i.e., the sentencing process. While there are some variations between the states, generally the processes are very similar. *Sentencing* is the formal process by which the courts deal with defendants convicted of crimes. A *sentence* is an authorized judicial decision that places some degree of penalty on a guilty person.[1] The responsibility for deciding the appropriate sentence is generally delegated to the judges. In a few states, like Texas, the defendant can elect to be sentenced by a jury.

Sentencing involves selecting the appropriate sentence from an array of choices that include incarceration, fine, forfeiture, probation, and alternative corrective programs. Once the sentencing decision is made, the responsibility for administrating the decision is placed with the departments of corrections.

American Bar Association's Standards Relating to Sentencing Alternatives

The sentencing court should be provided in all cases with a wide range of alternatives, with gradations of supervisory, supportive, and custodial facilities at its disposal so as to permit a sentence appropriate for each individual case.

Until recent years, the determination as to whether a convicted defendant went to prison and for how long was left largely to the courts. Judicial decisions were made with few statutory guidelines except for the stated statutory maximum sentence that may be imposed on the conviction of an offense. In the last two decades, however, many restrictions have been placed on the discretion of judges regarding the types of sentences, whether to suspend sentences or grant probation. Concerns regarding disparate sentences and abuses or perceived abuses in sentencing have resulted in six common strategies used by legislatures to maintain control over the sentencing process and reduce the discretion of the judiciary and correctional administrators. The common theme of the six strategies is to "reduce judicial and correctional imperialism." The six strategies are as follows:

1. **Determinate sentencing.** Establishing set sentences whereby, parole boards are also restricted from releasing prisoners before their sentences (minus good time) have expired.

2. **Mandatory prison terms.** Statutes that require the courts to impose mandatory prison terms for convictions of certain offenses or for certain defendants.

3. **Sentencing guidelines.** Guidelines designed to structure sentences based on the offense severity and the criminal history of the defendant.

4. **Parole guidelines.** Guidelines designed to require parole decisions to be based on measurable offender criteria.

5. **Good-time guidelines.** Guidelines that allow for reducing prison terms based on an inmate's behavior in prison.

6. **Emergency overcrowding provisions.** Regulations that allow early release of prisoners based on systematic provisions to relieve overcrowding.

Likelihood of Conviction and Sentencing

percentage by type of felony arrest

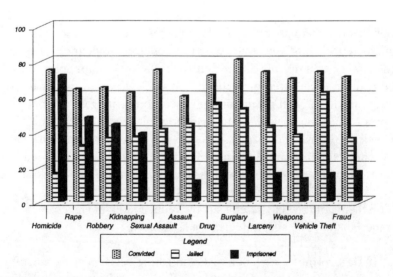

Source: U.S. Dept. of Justice

DETERMINATE AND INDETERMINATE SENTENCING

A *determinate sentence* is a sentence with a fixed period of confinement imposed by the judge of the sentencing court. The determinate sentence is based on the concept that each crime should have a price tag. You commit the crime, you pay the price. Its underlying ideology is based on retribution, just deserts, and incapacitation. A form of determinate sentencing now being used by the federal government and many states is the "presumptive" sentence. A *presumptive sentence* is a sentence suggested by the legislative body based on certain factors regarding the crime and the criminal. The judge is expected to impose the presumptive sentence. If the presumptive sentence is not given, the judge must justify why it was not imposed. Generally, determinate sentencing is used in adult criminal courts.

The *indeterminate sentence* is based on the concept that the sentence should be tailored to the needs of the defendant. Generally indeterminate sentences include the a pronouncement by the judge as to the maximum and minimum terms of confinement. For example, the judge may sentence the defendant to serve a period of confinement of not less than two years and no more than ten. The minimum term establishes the earliest release date (after adjustments for credits such as good time or time previously confined awaiting trial). The maximum term is the maximum length of time that the prisoner will be required to serve. The indeterminate sentence is based on the concept of rehabilitation. The defendant is to be released when he or she is rehabilitated. The decision as to when the defendant is rehabilitated is taken from the judge and transferred to an administrative agency. Most juvenile courts operate on the concept of indeterminate sentencing.

Mandatory Prison Terms

Mandatory prison terms are set forth in statutes that require prison terms always be imposed for convictions of certain offenses or offenders. As of 1996, 48 states have some form of mandatory prison term statutes. The statutes apply for certain crimes of violence and for habitual criminals. These states have eliminated the judges' discretion regarding the imposition of probation in those cases.

Sentencing Guidelines

In determining the appropriate sentence in most states, the judge must follow required guidelines and statutory restrictions. To assist judges in determining the appropriate sentences, most states require that a *presentence report* (PSI) be prepared and submitted to the court. The PSI contains a variety of information, such as statements describing the seriousness of the crime, the defendant's past criminal history, any history of substance abuse, and aggravating or mitigating circumstances.

Sentencing guidelines are being used by the federal government and many states to guide the judges in making their determinations as to appropriate sentences. The guidelines were developed in an attempt to limit disparity and discretion, and to establish more detailed criteria for sentencing. A sentencing commission monitors the use of the guidelines. Written explanations are required when a judge departs from the guideline ranges. Minnesota, for example, provides that while sentencing guidelines are advisory to the judge, departures from the guideline sentences established should be made only when substantial and compelling circumstances exist. In Pennsylvania, failure of the court to explain sentences deviating from the guidelines is grounds for vacating the sentence and resentencing the defendant. In addition, if the appellate court considers that the guidelines were inaccurately or inappropriately applied, the appellate court may vacate the sentence and order a resentencing.

The U.S. Sentencing Reform Act of 1984 advocated the "least restrictive alternative" in sentencing federal prisoners. The U.S. Sentencing Commission has established guidelines that authorize prison terms for all felony convictions. Research indicates that since the adoption of the federal sentencing guidelines, the use of probation and other non-incarcerative sentences have declined.[2]

The *federal sentencing guidelines* were enacted in 1984 and have governed federal sentencing decisions since 1989. The guidelines, which were promulgated by the Sentencing Commission, created 43 offense levels with each level reflecting increased severity of crime. In addition, offenders were divided into six categories based on their criminal history. The net result is a grid containing 258 cells, each of which has a sentencing range expressed in terms of months. The intent was to have the grids serve as advisory to judicial decision making on sentencing. While the stated objective of the federal sentencing reform was to encourage alternative sanctions to prison, the guidelines are constructed in such a manner as to discourage judges from imposing alternative sanctions.

The sentencing court must select a sentence from within the guideline range. If, however, a particular case presents atypical features, the act allows the court to depart from the guidelines and sentence outside the prescribed range. In that case, the court must specify reasons for departure.[3]

In 1984, before the use of the guidelines, approximately 52 percent of felony federal offenders were sentenced to prison. In 1991, the percentage had increased to 71 percent. Since the adoption of the guidelines, there has been widespread criticism of the guidelines among the federal district court judges, who called them unduly harsh and mechanical. Other judges feel that in addition to being harsh, the guidelines are inflexible. Most agree that the guidelines rely too heavily on imprisonment as a sanction.

United States Sentencing Commission

The United States Sentencing Commission is an independent agency in the judicial branch composed of seven voting and two nonvoting, ex officio members. Its principle purpose is to establish sentencing policies and practices for the federal criminal justice system that will ensure the ends of justice by promulgating detailed guidelines prescribing the appropriate sentences for offenders convicted of federal crimes. The guidelines and policy statements promulgated by the commission are issued pursuant to Section 994 (a) of Title 28, United States Code.

Presumptive Sentencing

One alternative used to limit the discretion of sentencing judges is the use of presumptive sentences. Under this system, the state legislature sets minimum, average, and maximum terms. The judges select the term appropriate for the defendant based on the characteristics of the offender and aggravating circumstances. California has used this

Severity Levels of Conviction Offense		Criminal History Score						
		0	1	2	3	4	5	6 or more
Sale of a Simulated Controlled Substance	II	12*	12*	12*	13	15	17	18-20
Theft Related Crimes ($2,500 or less)	III	12*	12*	13	15	17	19	20-22
Theft Crimes (over $2,500) Nonresidential Burglary	IV	12*	13	15	17	18-20	21-23	24-26
Residential Burglary Simple Robbery	V	18	23	27	29-31	36-40	43-49	50-58
Criminal Sexual Conduct 2nd Degree (a) & (b)	VI	21	26	30	33-35	42-46	50-58	60-70
Aggravated Robbery	VII	44-52	54-62	64-72	74-82	84-92	94-102	104-112
Criminal Sexual Conduct, 1st Degree Assault, 1st Degree	VIII	81-91	93-103	105-115	117-127	129-139	141-151	153-163
Felony Murder, 3rd Degree	IX	144-156	159-171	174-186	189-201	204-216	219-231	234-246
Felony Murder, 2nd Degree Murder, 2nd Degree (with intent)	X	299-313	319-333	339-353	369-373	379-393	399-413	419-433

Minnesota Guideline Grid, Presumptive Sentence Lengths in Months

Presumptive commitment to state imprisonment.

* One year and one day

system since 1979. For example, in California, if a defendant is convicted of burglary, the punishment range is set forth in Penal Code 461. That section provides:

> Burglary in the first degree: by imprisonment in the state prison for two, four, or six years.

National Crime Victimization Survey

The annual BJS Bulletin presents the findings from the National Crime Victimization Survey (NCVS), based on an ongoing survey of households, each year interviewing about 100,000 persons in 50,000 households. In 1994, U.S. residents age 12 or older experienced more than 42 million crimes: about 11 million violent victimizations and 31 million property crimes. Violent crimes include rape and sexual assault, robbery, and both aggravated and simple assault (from the NCVS), and homicide (from crimes reported to the police). The violent crime rate has remained essentially unchanged since 1992, following a slight increase between 1985 and 1991. Property crime continued a 15-year decline. Property crimes include burglaries, motor vehicle thefts, and thefts of other property. Victims reported approximately a third of all property crimes. Motor vehicle theft was the most frequently reported crime (78 percent), and theft of other property was the least reported crime (27 percent).

The first decision that the judge would need to make is the "out or in" decision. This decision is whether the defendant should be placed on probation (out) or sentenced (in) to prison. If the judge decides that imprisonment is the correct sentence. The judge would award four years,

Can Society Afford a Zero Crime Rate?

Mark A. Cohen, an economic professor at Vanderbilt University states that our society could not afford a zero crime rate, that it would bankrupt us. He also estimates that crime costs this country about $500 billion a year and that it is a major industry. [Cohen's comments are based on the concept that as a major industry, criminal justice supplies many people with employment (e.g, police officers, lawyers, judges, correctional officers, etc.) and that if this industry is eliminated, unemployment would rise, and with high unemployment, less taxes would be received by governments and more money would need to be spent on welfare. If the crime problem is solved, some economists predict that over 6 million people in the United States would lose their jobs.]

Franklin Zimring, Director of the Earl Warren Legal Institute at the University of California at Berkeley, calls the $500 billion estimate a "phony number." He is worried that by fixing the cost of crime so high, it will make the building of prisons look like a cheap and politically palatable answer to crime. For example, in California in 1996, the state spent more to build and operate prisons than on its public colleges and universities. Prisons are the fastest growing item in almost all state budgets.

John J. Dilulio, professor of public affairs at Princeton University, contends that prisons do pay for themselves. He states that it costs $25,000 a year to keep a prisoner behind bars. He contends, however, that "society saves at least $2.80 in the social costs of crime for every one dollar spent on prisons.

the average sentence, unless there were mitigating or aggravating circumstances. Under aggravating circumstances, the sentence would be six years and under mitigating circumstances, the sentence would be two years. Examples of mitigating circumstances would be that the defendant is a first-time offender, the crime was committed under strong peer pressure, etc. Examples of aggravating circumstances include prior criminal record, great harm to victim, etc.

Parole Guidelines

Parole guidelines are procedures designed to limit or structure parole release decisions based on measurable offender criteria. In some states, the parole board has great latitude in making the parole release decisions. In other states, the parole guidelines are closely prescribed and provide only limited discretion to the parole boards.

States With Statutory Guidelines for Parole Decision

Federal System, Florida, and New York

States With Statewide Policies That Are Not Written Into Statutes

Alaska, California (CYA), District of Columbia, Georgia, Maryland, Missouri, New Jersey, Oregon, Pennsylvania, Utah, and Washington.

States Where Parole Guidelines Are Differently Applied

California (Adults) and Minnesota

Good-time Policies

Good-conduct time (i.e., good-time credit) has traditionally been used by inmates to reduce their time in custody. In most states, by law, good-conduct time applies only to an inmate's eligibility for parole or mandatory release. New York, in 1817, was the first state to pass a good-time statute. By 1916, every state had passed some kind of good-time statute. Most states provide for one day of credit for every two days of good time served. Many states have recently modified their good-time statutes. Generally, good-conduct time is awarded based on the law in effect when the crime was committed. Some states now use programming time or earned time in lieu of good-time credit. The programming time or earned time allows administrators to consider matters other than time in awarding credit. For example, since January 1983, California eliminated automatic time off for good behavior. Prisoners sentenced after that date must earn all their good-time credit through work or school participation. The California approach has been criticized on the basis that it allows the prison guards and other prison personnel to become sentencers. This is based on the fact that the amount of time that a prisoner may earn in California is discretionary and has therefore enlarged the discretionary power of prison officials to affect the duration of confinement.

In most states, good-time credit is awarded based on an inmate's conduct, obedience to rules, willingness to work, and work/school record. Traditionally, good-conduct time is considered a privilege, not a right. Inmates must follow rules to get good conduct time. Some or all of the good conduct time awarded an inmate may be taken away for breaking rules. In some cases, previously forfeitured good-conduct time may be restored to the inmate.

Emergency Overcrowding Provisions

In some states, there are statutes that provide the governor with the authority to release prisoners prior to their normal release date in order to relieve crowded prison conditions. Some states allow parole boards to consider prison overcrowding conditions in determining the release date of certain classes of offenders, and offenders may be released earlier than normal to relieve crowded prison conditions. For example, in the early 1970s, Florida released thousands of prisoners early to make room for newly sentenced prisoners. Since the 1970 release, emergency overcrowding provisions have been used in other states including Texas, New York and Arizona, but not to the extent that it was used in the 1970s.

The sentencing judge should be guided by statutory statements of policy, the criteria in these rules, and the facts and circumstances of the case.

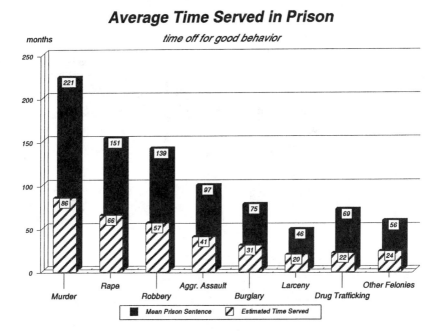

Average Time Served in Prison

Flat Time With Mandatory Supervision

As noted earlier, a determinate sentence is a "flat time" sentence set by the sentencing judge usually based on legislated guidelines. The defendant is given a definite sentence, and once good-time or program-credit calculations are made, the defendant knows his or her expected release date because parole is premised on indeterminate sentencing, which allows the correctional administration to set the release date, the move toward determinate sentencing with mandatory supervision on completion of the sentence is seen by many as the way to eliminate the parole system.

Number of Sentenced Offenders

all correctional populations are growing

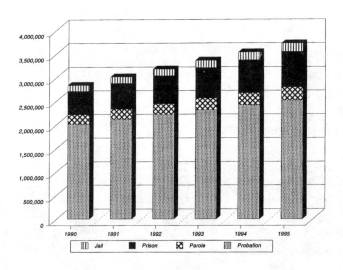

National Conference on Corrections

The National Conference on Corrections held in Williamsburg, Virginia, considered the problems and needs of judges in ascertaining appropriate sentences in criminal cases. The conference advocated eight points with regard to more appropriate sentencing:

California Rules of Court, Rule 410

General objectives of sentencing include:

(a) Protecting society.

(b) Punishing the defendant.

(c) Encouraging the defendant to lead a law-abiding life in the future and deterring him from future offenses.

(d) Deterring others from criminal conduct by demonstrating its consequences.

(e) Preventing the defendant from committing new crimes by isolating him for the period of incarceration.

(f) Securing restitution for the victims of crime.

(g) Achieving uniformity in sentencing.

Because in some instances these objectives may suggest inconsistent dispositions, the sentencing judge shall consider which objectives are of primary importance in that particular case.

1. It should be mandatory that trial judges have presentence reports in all felony cases. These reports should be prepared by qualified probation or corrections officers.

2. Diagnostic facilities should be made available to all judges.

3. Jury sentencing should be abolished.

4. Sentencing judges should be required to record the reasons for each sentence.

5. Sentencing judges should educate their communities on the philosophy of sentencing.

6. Defense counsels and prosecutors should be consulted before imposing the sentence.

7. Probation officers and judges should receive instructions in sentencing and perhaps attend sentencing institutes.

8. Trial judges should be elected or appointed in as nonpolitical a way as possible.

JUDICIAL PROCESS FOR MISDEMEANANTS

Misdemeanants are individuals convicted of minor crimes (misdemeanors). Their sentences are to jails for periods normally not to exceed one year, fines, community service, and/or attendance at some type of behavior modification course. In studying corrections, we rarely consider the roles of our minor courts and their handling of misdemeanants. More citizens, however, get involved at this level than at the felony level. On any given day, it is estimated that approximately 500,000 individuals are confined in local jails. The lower courts of America are truly involved in an "assembly-line" type justice. The operation of jails, jail conditions, and jail problems are discussed in Chapter 5.

JUDICIAL PROCESS FOR FELONS

In most states, sentences to prison or correctional institutions are decided by judges. Several states, such as Texas, allow the defendants to opt for jury sentencing. The incarceration of an individual in a state prison is a dramatic, but all-too-often-used sanction. The Model Penal Code addresses the problems involved in selecting the appropriate sentence. The code also provides that imprisonment should be used only when one of the below condiditions exist:

1. There is undue risk that during the period of probation the defendant will commit another crime.

2. The defendant is in need of correctional treatment that can be provided most effectively by commitment to an institution.

3. A lessor sentence will depreciate the seriousness of the defendant's crime.

Presentence Investigations

In most states, a presentence report is mandatory for felony convictions. The presentence report (PSI) is an important document for trial judges in making their sentence determinations. In most cases, the PSI is prepared by the court's probation office. In some states, such as California, there are private companies that also prepare alternative PSIs for the judges to consider. The alternative PSIs are commissioned and paid for by the defense. Accordingly, they are generally used only in cases where the defendant or defendant's family can afford their costs.

A PSI generally includes the following items:

- A face sheet showing the defendant's name and other identifying data; case number; the crime for which the defendant was convicted; the date of commission of the crime; the date defendant was convicted; the defendant's present custody status; and the terms of any agreement upon which a plea of guilty was based.

- The facts and circumstances of the crime and the defendant's arrest, including information concerning any codefendants and the status or disposition of their cases. The source of the information contained in this section should be stated in the report.

- A summary of the defendant's record of prior criminal conduct, including convictions as an adult and sustained petitions in juvenile delinquency proceedings. Records of an arrest or charge not leading to a conviction generally are not included.

- Any statement made by the defendant to the probation officer, or a summary thereof, including the defendant's account of the circumstances of the crime.

- Information concerning the victim of the crime, including the victim's statement or a summary thereof, the amount of the victim's loss, whether or not it is covered by insurance, and any information required by law.

- Any relevant facts concerning the defendant's social history, including family, education, employment, income, military status, medical/psychological history, record of substance abuse or lack thereof, and any other relevant information.

- Collateral information, including written statements from official source, such as police officers, defense counsels, probation and parole officers, and interested persons including family members.

- An evaluation of factors relating to the sentence, including a reasoned discussion or the defendant's suitability and eligibility for probation. If probation is recommended, a proposed probation plan. If prison is recommended, a reasoned discussion of the aggravating and mitigating factors affecting the sentence length. In addition, a discussion of the defendant's ability to make restitution, pay any fine or penalty which may be imposed, to satisfy any special conditions of probation.

- The probation officer's recommendation, including the length of any prison term that may be imposed, including the base term. The recommendation shall also include in the case of multiple offenses whether the terms for each offense will be concurrent or consecutive.

- Detailed information on presentence time spent by the defendant in custody, including the beginning and ending dates of the period(s) of custody; the existence of any other sentences imposed on the defendant; the amount of good behavior, or work, or participation credit to which the defendant is entitled and whether a hearing has been requested regarding the denying of good behavior, work, or participation credit.

- A statement regarding mandatory and recommended restitution, restitution fines, other fines, and costs to be assessed against the defendant.

The source of all information is listed in the report. Any person who furnished information shall be identified by name or official capacity unless a reason is given for not disclosing the person's identity.

Duty to Provide Corrected Presentence Report

In *State v. Utah* [5], Stephen Thomas Utah pleaded guilty to one count of forgery. At the sentencing hearing, Mr. Utah moved for the presentence report to be thrown out because it contained inaccuracies concerning his prior criminal record.

The district court refused to order a new presentence report. The court stated that it would not consider the disputed items in the report. Mr. Utah appealed. He contended that the district court was required to provide the department of corrections with an accurate presentence report. The state high court disagreed. The appellate court held that the presentence report is used primarily to aid the district court in sentencing. The court stated that any use by the department of corrections is secondary and not grounds for reversal of the sentence.

Suspended Sentences

Suspended sentences are one of two types; suspension of imposition of sentence and suspension of execution of sentence. In cases involving suspension of imposition of sentence, there is a judgment of guilt, but no sanction is imposed. For example, the defendant is found guilty, but imposition of sentence is suspended for a period of three years due to the offender having a clean record. In a case involving the suspension of execution of sentence, there is a judgment and a sentence pronounced, but the execution is suspended. If, within the time frame of the suspension, the dependant remains a noncriminal, the suspension expires along with the court's ability to impose a sanction for the attributable crime(s). If the defendant is rearrested within the suspension time frame, then the court can immediately impose the sentence for the suspended crime.

ALTERNATIVE SENTENCING AND DIVERSION

Alternative sentencing involves the use of nontraditional programs in lieu of fines and custody. One of the most popular alternative sentencing procedures is the use of *deferred adjudication*. Deferred adjudication is a form of probation that is used without a finding of guilt. In deferred adjudication, the defendant pleas guilty and agrees to defer further proceeding. The defendant is then placed on probation or directed to attend counseling, behavior modification courses, etc. After the defendant has successfully completed the requirements, the guilty or nolo contendere plea is withdrawn and the case is dismissed. When the charges are dismissed, the defendant does not have a criminal conviction for this misconduct. If the defendant fails to comply with the requirements, then the court sentences the defendant based on his or her original plea.

Pretrial diversion is a form of probation that is granted prior to trial. Under this process, the defendant agrees to waive time and to complete a program or process. Pretrial diversion is used primarily for offenders who need treatment or supervision and for whom criminal sanctions would be excessive. Like deferred adjudication, there is no finding of guilty and thus no conviction if the program is successfully completed. If the program is not successfully completed, the defendant is then brought to trial on the charges. One of the popular criticisms of pretrial diversion is based on research that indicates that many people are diverted that would not have been prosecuted because of the lack of evidence against them. Accordingly, if this is correct, such action increases the number of persons involved in the criminal justice system.

JUDICIAL PROCESS FOR JUVENILES

Juvenile Court Procedures

In this section, juvenile court procedures and hearing requirements will be examined. In addition, the rules required when a juvenile is taken into custody will be covered.

Generally, the commencement of proceedings in the juvenile court to declare a minor a ward of the court is by a verified petition (signed under oath) and contains the following:

(a) The name of the court to which it is addressed.

(b) The title of the proceeding.

(c) The code section and subdivision under which the proceedings are instituted. Any petition alleging that the minor has committed a crime shall state for each count whether the crime charged is a felony or a misdemeanor.

(d) The name, age, and address, if any, of the minor upon whose behalf the petition is brought.

(e) The names and residence addresses, if known to petitioner, of both of the parents and any guardian of the minor. If there is no parent or guardian residing within the state, or if his or her place of residence is not known to petitioner, the petition shall also contain the name and residence address, if known, of any adult relative residing within the county, or, if there are none, the adult relative residing nearest to the location of the court.

(f) A concise statement of facts, separately stated, to support the conclusion that the minor upon whose behalf the petition is being brought is a person within the definition of each of the sections and subdivisions under which the proceedings are being instituted.

(g) The fact that the minor upon whose behalf the petition is brought is detained in custody or is not detained in custody, and if he or she is detained in custody, the date and the precise time the minor was taken into custody.

(h) A notice to the father, mother, spouse, or other person liable for support of the minor child, that:

(1) State law may make that person, the estate of that person, and the estate of the minor child, liable for the cost of the care, support, and maintenance of the minor child in any county institution or any other place in which the child is placed, detained, or committed pursuant to an order of the juvenile court;

(2) That the person, the estate of that person, and the estate of the minor child, may be liable for the cost to the county of legal services rendered to the minor by a private attorney or a public defender appointed pursuant to the order of the juvenile court;

(3) State law may make that person, the estate of that person, and the estate of the minor child, liable for the cost to the county of the probation supervision of the minor child by the probation officer pursuant to the order of the juvenile court; and

(4) That the above liabilities are joint and several (the costs or expenses may be added together).

(i) If a proceeding is pending against a minor child for a violation of the Penal Code, the parents or legal guardians of the minor will be notified that if the minor is found to have violated either or both of the following provisions that

(1) Any community service which may be required of the minor may be performed in the presence, and under the direct supervision, of the parent or legal guardian pursuant to either or both of these provisions; and

(2) If the minor is personally unable to pay any fine levied for the violation of either or both of these provisions, then the parent or legal guardian of the minor shall be liable for payment of the fine pursuant to those sections. If the minor is ordered to make restitution to the victim, the parent or guardian will be notified that they may be liable for the payment of restitution.

Detention Hearings

Whenever a minor is taken into custody by a peace officer or probation officer, except when such minor willfully misrepresents himself as 18 or more years of age, such minor shall be released within 48 hours after having been taken into custody, excluding nonjudicial days, unless within said period of time a petition to declare him a dependent child or a ward of the court has been filed.

A proceeding in the juvenile court to declare a minor a dependent child of the court is commenced by the filing with the court, by the probation officer, of a petition. Petitions to declare minors wards of the court and criminal complaints are generally filed by the prosecutor, county attorney or district attorney.

In many states, whenever a minor, who has been held in custody for more than six hours by the probation officer, is subsequently released and no petition is filed, the probation officer must prepare a written explanation of why the minor was held in custody for more than six hours. The written explanation is generally required to be prepared within 72 hours after the minor is released from custody and filed in the record of the case. A copy of the written explanation is also sent to the parents, guardian, or other person having care or custody of the minor.

If a minor has been taken into custody and not released to a parent or guardian, the juvenile court shall hold a hearing (which shall be referred to as a "detention hearing") to determine whether the minor shall be further detained. This hearing shall be held as soon as possible, but in any event before the expiration of the next judicial day after a petition to declare the minor a dependent child or ward of the court has been filed. If the hearing is not held within the period prescribed, the minor is required to be released from custody.

If a probation officer or prosecutor determines that a minor shall be retained in custody, he or she shall immediately file a petition pursuant with the clerk of the juvenile court, who shall set the matter for hearing on the detention hearing calendar. The probation officer or prosecutor shall then notify each parent or each guardian of the minor of the time and place of the hearing if the whereabouts of each parent or guardian can be ascertained by due diligence. Each person will be served with a copy of the petition and notified of the time and place of the detention hearing. In some cases, this notice may be given orally and shall be given in this manner if it appears that the parent does not read.

Upon his or her appearance before the court at the detention hearing, each parent or guardian and the minor, if present, shall first be informed of the reasons why the minor was taken into custody, the nature of the juvenile court proceedings, and the right of each parent or guardian and any minor to be represented at every stage of the proceedings by counsel.

In the hearing, the minor, parents, or guardians have a privilege against self-incrimination and have a right to confrontation by, and cross-examination of, any person examined by the court. Upon reasonable notification by counsel representing the minor and the parents or guardians, the clerk of the court shall notify such counsel of the hearings.

Citation

If an officer who takes a minor into temporary custody for a criminal offense and determines that the minor should be brought to the attention of the juvenile court, he or she may release the minor after preparing a written notice to appear before the probation officer. The notice shall also contain a concise statement of the reasons the minor was taken into custody. The officer shall deliver one copy of the notice to the minor or to a parent, guardian, or responsible relative of the minor and may require the minor or his or her parent, guardian, or relative, or both, to sign a written promise that either or both will appear at the time and place designated in the notice. Upon the execution of the promise to appear, the officer may release the minor. The officer then files one copy of the notice with the probation officer.

In determining whether to hold in custody or to release the minor with a citation (written promise to appear), the officer should use the alternative that least restricts the minor's freedom of movement, provided that alternative is compatible with the best interests of the minor and the community.

Venue

Venue refers to the geographical location of the court in which the proceedings will be conducted. Under the U.S. Constitution, an accused in an adult criminal trial has the right to be tried in the county and judicial district where the crime occurred. In juvenile cases, most state statutes provide that in any proceedings involving a juvenile, the proceedings will be held in the county in which the juvenile resides. If the proceedings begin in a different county, the proceedings at the request of the juvenile may be transferred to the county of residence. If a juvenile changes residence during the proceedings, the court may transfer the proceedings to the county of the new residence of the juvenile. For most purposes, a juvenile is considered to reside in the county in which his or her parents or guardian reside.

Intake

The *intake* phase of the juvenile justice case has several purposes. It is used to screen cases in determining whether the juvenile needs the help of the court and to help control the use of detention. It also is used to screen cases in an effort to reduce the courts' caseload. Unlike dependency cases, intake has different functions in different states. In general, intake people exercise a great deal of discretion during this phrase of the proceedings.

One of the first decisions that must be made during intake is whether the case comes under juvenile court jurisdiction. Next, the decision must be made on whether to assume jurisdiction, dismiss the case, or refer the youth to another agency. The court during this phrase may also use informal methods to handle the case such as informal probation. If the youth is in detention and the case is not dismissed or referred, the decision must also be made as to whether the detention should continue until the adjudicatory hearing is held.

During this phase of the case, an intake officer generally reviews the case and makes the preliminary decisions noted above. Generally, the intake officer's recommendations are followed by the judge. In many states, the intake officer's duties are performed by a probation officer. The intake officer will normally recommend dismissal or informal probation for first-time offenders and for minor offenses unless the youth has committed a serious crime.

Under informal probation, the youth is released if he or she agrees to accept certain conditions that are spelled out by the court. Normally, the conditions are that if the youth stays out of trouble for a specified period of time, then the case is dismissed. If the youth violates the terms of the agreement or gets involved in other delinquent acts, the court may recall the case and hold the youth for further adjudication.

Consent degrees are also used in delinquency cases. These degrees are court orders that are agreed to by the youth and accepted by the court. A consent degree removes the need for an adjudicatory hearing. It is similar to a plea bargain in adult criminal court.

Adjudicatory Hearings

After the intake proceedings, the *adjudicatory hearing* is used in those cases not dismissed, referred to other agencies, or subject to consent degrees. The adjudicatory hearing is equivalent to a trial in adult court. While the adjudicatory hearings are less formal that adult trials, as will be discussed in the next chapter, the juvenile has certain due-process rights that must be provided to him or her during this hearing.

Unlike adult trials, the trials are closed to the public and in most states there are no rights to a jury trial. Procedural rights contained in the rules of evidence are required in the adjudicatory hearings and the question as to whether the juvenile committed the crime in question must be established beyond a reasonable doubt.

The order of proceedings during the adjudicatory hearing is generally similar to that of adult criminal cases. The prosecutor puts on the case in chief, followed by the defense, and then any rebuttal by the prosecutor.

Disposition Hearings

The *disposition hearing* is similar to the sentencing phase of an adult criminal trial. In most states, after the court determines that the juvenile has committed the offense, the judge sets a date for the disposition hearing. At the disposition hearing, the rules of evidence are relaxed and the judge is permitted to receive a wide range of evidence regarding the youth. In most states, the probation officer is required to present a pre-disposition report to the court. This report generally contains a written description of the incident, the youth's prior conduct record, information on the youth's family, employment record of the youth, if any, and any other information that may assist the judge in making a disposition decision.

Uniform Juvenile Court Act

The waiver of jurisdiction and discretionary transfer to an adult criminal court provisions of the Uniform Juvenile Court Act are set forth in this section. In addition, at the end of the section are several key court decisions regarding the transfer procedures.

Indiana Juvenile Statutes
(Indiana Juvenile Statutes, 31-6-4-13)

Sec. 13.

(a) This section applies only to a child alleged to be a delinquent child.

(b) The juvenile court shall hold an initial hearing on each petition.

(c) The juvenile court shall first determine whether counsel has been waived ... or whether counsel should be appointed ...

(d) The court shall next determine whether the prosecutor intends to seek a waiver of jurisdiction [for purposes of referral to adult criminal court]. ... If waiver is sought, the court may not accept an admission or denial of the allegations from the child. . .and shall schedule a waiver hearing and advise the child. ...

(e) The juvenile court shall inform the child and his parents, guardians, or custodian, if that person is present, of:

(1) the nature of the allegations against the child;

(2) the child's right to:

    (A) be represented by counsel;

    (B) have a speedy trial;

    (C) confront witnesses against him;

    (D) cross-examine witnesses against him;

    (E) obtain witnesses or tangible evidence by compulsory process;

    (F) introduce evidence on his own behalf;

    (G) refrain from testifying against himself; and

    (H) have the state prove that he committed the delinquent act charged beyond a reasonable doubt.

(h) If the child admits the allegations of the petition, the juvenile court shall enter judgment accordingly and schedule a dispositional hearing.

[Subparagraphs (e)(3) and (4), (f), (g), and (I) are omitted.]

Waiver of Jurisdiction and Discretionary Transfer to Criminal Court

(a) The juvenile court may waive its exclusive original jurisdiction and transfer a child to the appropriate district court or criminal district court for criminal proceedings if:

(1) the child is alleged to have violated a penal law of the grade of felony;

(2) the child was 15 years of age or older at the time he is alleged to have committed the offense and, no adjudication hearing has been conducted concerning that offense; and

(3) after full investigation and hearing the juvenile court determines that there is probable cause to believe the child before the court committed the offense alleged and that, because of the seriousness of the offense or the background of the child, the welfare of the community requires criminal proceedings.

(b) The petition and notice requirements of this code must be satisfied, and the summons must state that the hearing is for the purpose of considering discretionary transfer to criminal court.

(c) The juvenile court shall conduct a hearing without a jury to consider transfer of the child for criminal proceedings.

(d) Prior to the hearing, the juvenile court shall order and obtain a complete diagnostic study, social evaluation, and full investigation of the child, his circumstances, and the circumstances of the alleged offense.

(e) At the transfer hearing, the court may consider written reports from probation officers, professional court employees, or professional consultants in addition to the testimony of witnesses. At least one day prior to the transfer hearing, the court shall provide the attorney for the child with access to all written matter to be considered by the court in making the transfer decision. The court may order counsel not to reveal items to the child or his parent, guardian, or *guardian ad litem* if such disclosure would materially harm the treatment and rehabilitation of the child or would substantially decrease the likelihood of receiving information from the same or similar sources in the future.

(f) In making the determination required by Subsection (a) of this section, the court shall consider, among other matters:

(1) whether the alleged offense was against person or property, with greater weight in favor of transfer given to offenses against people;

(2) whether the alleged offense was committed in an aggressive and premeditated manner;

(3) whether there is evidence on which a grand jury may be expected to return an indictment;

(4) the sophistication and maturity of the child;

(5) the record and previous history of the child; and

(6) the prospects of adequate protection of the public and the likelihood of the rehabilitation of the child by use of procedures, services, and facilities currently available to the juvenile court.

(g) If the juvenile court retains jurisdiction, the child is not subject to criminal prosecution at any time for any offense alleged in the petition, or for any offense within the knowledge of the juvenile court judge as evidenced by anything in the record of the proceedings.

(h) If the juvenile court waives jurisdiction, it shall state specifically in the order its reasons for waiver and certify its action, including the written order and findings of the court, and shall transfer the child to the appropriate court for criminal proceedings. On transfer of the child for criminal proceedings, he shall be dealt with as an adult and in accordance with the Code of Criminal Procedure. The transfer of custody is an arrest. The court to which the child is transferred shall determine if good cause exists for an examining trial. If there is no good cause for an examining trial, the court shall refer the case to the grand jury. If there is good cause for an examining trial, the court shall conduct an examining trial and may remand the child to the jurisdiction of the juvenile court.

(I) If the child's case is brought to the attention of the grand jury and the grand jury does not indict for the offense charged in the complaint forwarded by the juvenile court, the district court or criminal district court shall certify the grand jury's failure to indict to the juvenile court. On receipt of the certification, the juvenile court may resume jurisdiction of the case.

(j) The juvenile court may waive its exclusive original jurisdiction and transfer a person to the appropriate district court or criminal district court for criminal proceedings if:

(1) the person is 18 years of age or older;

(2) the person was 15 years of age or older, and under 17 years of age at the time he is alleged to have committed a felony;

(3) no adjudication concerning the alleged offense has been made or no adjudication hearing concerning the offense has been conducted;

(4) the juvenile court finds from a preponderance of the evidence that after due diligence of the state, it was not practical to proceed in juvenile court before the 18th birthday of the person because:

(A) the state did not have probable cause to proceed in juvenile court and new evidence has been found since the eighteenth birthday of the person; or

(B) the person could not be found; and

(5) the juvenile court determines that there is probable cause to believe that the child before the court committed the alleged offense.

(k) The petition and notice requirements of this code must be satisfied, and the summons must state that the hearing is for the purpose of considering waiver of jurisdiction under Subsection (j) of this section.

(l) The juvenile court shall conduct a hearing without a jury to consider waiver of jurisdiction under Subsection (j) of this section.[6]

SUMMARY

Before the correctional process may be involved, the defendant must be convicted of a crime by a court with proper jurisdiction. Sentencing is the formal process by which the courts deal with defendants convicted of crimes. A sentence is an authorized judicial decision that places some degree of penalty on a guilty person. The responsibility for deciding the appropriate sentence is generally delegated to the judges. Sentencing involves selecting the appropriate sentence from an array of choices that include incarceration, fine, forfeiture, probation, and alternative corrective programs. Once the sentencing decision is made, the responsibility for administrating the decision is placed with the departments of corrections.

Concerns regarding disparate sentences and abuses or perceived abuses in sentencing have resulted in six common strategies used by legislatures to maintain control over the sentencing process and reduce the discretion of the judiciary and correctional administrators.

A determinate sentence is a "flat-time" sentence with a *fixed period* of confinement imposed by the judge of the sentencing court. The defendant is given a definite sentence, and once good-time credit calculations are made, the defendant knows his or her expected release date. The increased use of flat-time sentencing is seen by many as the way to eliminate parole.

A form of determinate sentencing now being used by the federal government and many states is the presumptive sentence which is suggested by the legislative body based on certain factors regarding the crime and the criminal. The indeterminate sentence is based on the concept that the sentence should be tailor to the needs of the defendant. Generally indeterminate sentences, allow the judge a greater degree of flexibility which includes a pronouncement by the judge as to the maximum and minimum terms of confinement. In determining the appropriate sentence in most states, the judge must follow required guidelines and statutory restrictions. To assist judges in determining the appropriate sentences, most states require that a presentence report (PSI) be prepared and submitted to the court. The pre-sentence investigation report is mandatory for felony convictions and is an important document for trial judges in making their sentence determinations. In most cases, the PSI is prepared by the court's probation office.

Good-conduct time (good-time credit) has traditionally been used by inmates to reduce their time in custody. In most states, by law, good conduct time applies only to an inmate's eligibility for parole or mandatory release. In most states, good-time credit is awarded based on an inmate's conduct, obedience to rules, willingness to work, and work/school record. Traditionally, good-conduct time is considered a privilege, not a right. Inmates must follow rules to get good-conduct time. Some or all of the good-conduct time awarded an inmate may be taken away for breaking rules. In some cases, previously forfeitured good conduct time may be restored to the inmate.

In some states, there are statutes which provide the governor with the authority to release prisoners prior to their normal release date in order to relieve crowded prison conditions.

The federal sentencing guidelines were enacted in 1984 and have governed federal sentencing decisions since 1989. The guidelines, which were promulgated by the Sentencing Commission, created 43 offense levels with each level reflecting increased severity of crime. In addition, offenders were divided into six categories based on their criminal history.

Suspended sentences are one of two types: suspension of imposition of sentence and suspension of execution of sentence. Alternative sentencing involves the use of non-traditional programs in lieu of fines and custody. One of the most popular alternative sentencing procedures is the use of deferred adjudication where the defendant is placed on probation or directed to attend counseling, behavior modification courses, etc. After the defendant has successfully completed these requirements, the guilty or *nolo contendere* plea is withdrawn, and the case is dismissed. When the charges are dismissed, the defendant does not have a criminal conviction for this misconduct.

Parole guidelines are procedures designed to limit or structure parole release decisions, based on measurable offender criteria. In some states, the parole board has great latitude in making the parole release decisions. In other states, the parole guidelines are closely prescribed and provide only limited discretion to the parole boards.

Generally, a petition for the commencement of proceedings in the juvenile court to declare a minor a ward of the court is by a verified petition (signed under oath). The intake phase of the juvenile justice case has several purposes: it is used to screen cases in determining whether the juvenile needs the help of the court and to help control the use of detention; it is also used to screen out cases in an effort to reduce the court's caseload. Unlike dependency cases, intake has different functions in different states. In general, intake personnel exercise a great deal of discretion during this phase of the proceedings. After the intake proceedings, the adjudicatory hearing is used in those cases not dismissed, referred to other agencies, or subject to consent decrees. While the adjudicatory hearings are less formal than adult trials, the juvenile has certain due process rights that must be provided during this hearing. Unlike adult trials, the trials are closed to the public, and, in most states, there are no rights to a jury trial.

DISCUSSION QUESTIONS

1. Explain the various restraints imposed on a judge's sentencing discretion.

2. Discuss the problems confronting a judge in determining the appropriate sentence to impose in a criminal case.

3. Explain the purposes of the presentence report.

4. Compare and contrast the different types of suspended sentences.

5. Describe the diversion process.

6. Explain the trial process in juvenile court.

ENDNOTES FOR CHAPTER 2

1. Richard W. Snarr, *Corrections*, (Madison, WI.: Brown & Benchmark, 1996).

2. Elaine Wolf and Marsha Weissman, "Revising Federal Sentencing Policy: Some Consequences of Expanding Eligibility for Alternative Sanctions," *Crime and Delinquency*, Vol. 42, No. 2, April, 1996, pp. 192-197.

3. United States Sentencing Commission, *Guidelines Manual*, (Nov. 1995).

4. American Law Institute, *Model Penal Code*, Proposed Official Draft, (Philadelphia, 1962).

5. Decided by the Supreme Court of Iowa, No. 348/95-107, Dec. 20, 1995.

6. For juvenile procedures described in this section, the rules adopted in the state of California were used. While most states are generally the same, there are some minor variations.

CHAPTER 3

THE CORRECTIONAL CLIENT

KEY TERMS

Career criminals

Prisonization

Professional criminals

UNICOR

White-collar criminals

```
╔══════════════════════════════════════════════╗
║              CHAPTER OBJECTIVES                ║
╚══════════════════════════════════════════════╝
```

After studying this chapter, the reader will be able to:

☐ Describe the concept of prisonization.

☐ Analyze the research on violent criminals.

☐ Explain the problem involved in confining elderly criminals.

☐ Explain the porblems caused by the increase in female prisoners.

☐ Analyze the gender-based problems in the corrections field.

☐ Identify the issues involved with non-citizen prisoners.

☐ List the types of prisoners serving time in federal prisons.

☐ Diagram the organizational structure of the federal prison system.

In this chapter, the various types of individuals who are incarcerated are examined. One of the characteristics of prison populations that should concern us is the increasing absolute numbers and the increases per 100,000 in the rate of incarceration. Included within the prison population are various groups of individuals who need special care and treatment.

PRISONIZATION

Prisonization is the process by which prisoners learn the rules of socialization into the prison culture. Many see it as a criminalization process, whereby a criminal novice is transformed from a prosocial errant to a committed predatory criminal. During the prisonization process, the prisoner learns to exist in the prison community and its depersonalized and routinized life. During this process, the prisoner accepts that his name is replaced by a number, that the warden is all powerful, prison slang, and the other tricks of seasoned prisoners.

THE CAREER CRIMINAL

The term *career criminals* identifies those persons who make or attempt to make a living committing crime.[1] Generally, career criminals are property offenders. Most often they begin their criminal careers early in their juvenile years. Most of them view crime as a safe and enjoyable way to obtain a good life. They expect to return to a life of crime after they are released from confinement. The average career criminal is normally in and out of prison or jail all of his or her life. Most career criminals liv?, however, at or below the poverty level when not confined in prison.

The Rand Corporation conducted several studies on habitual offenders. The first study involved 49 prisoners in California institutions. The second study involved 624 prisoners from five California prisons. The individuals selected in both studies were selected to represent all male prisoners in terms of custody level, age, offense, and race. The studies focused on criminal activities of the prisoners during the three-year period prior to their current incarceration. A third study with a larger sample of prisoners from the states of Texas, California, and Michigan was also conducted.[2]

The first Rand study concluded that most career offenders are not specialized in their criminal activity. They engage in a variety of criminal activities. Most commit crimes at a fairly low rate and the rate of violent crime was low among these inmates. The other two studies tended to confirm these findings. The Rand investigators also concluded that many of the criminals had the self-concept that they could beat the odds, that they were better than the average criminal, that crime was exciting, and that regular work was boring. Most of the individuals involved had started their criminal career at a young age, usually before age 16. Most were unmarried with few family obligations. Most had been employed only irregularly and for short times.

THE VIOLENT CRIMINAL

Banishing young violent males to closed, crowded, and depriving institutions has been a common response to crime in American society.[3]

Researchers have attempted to identify the factors that restrain or encourage inmate aggression. Most of the studies on prison violence deal with characteristics of inmates rather than institutions. The situations in prisons, such as crowding, visiting patterns, involvement in prison programs, and stringency of rule enforcement, have indicated that an association exists between prison conditions and prison violence.

THE YOUNG CRIMINAL

Under current law, prison authorities must keep juveniles out of the "sight and sound" of adult inmates. The definition of juveniles varies by age according to states' definitions. In addition, they must keep juveniles convicted of crimes in the usual sense (e.g., burglary, carjackings, etc.) in different institutions from those that detain youths charged with status offenses, such as truancy, failure to go to school, and incorrigibility. These federal mandates were enacted in 1974 by President Ford. They are administered by the Office of Juvenile Justice and Delinquency Prevention, which is a Justice Department agency that also sponsors research on ways to fight juvenile crime. Each year, however, bills are introduced in the U.S. Congress to remove or eliminate these requirements.

As of July 1996, 40 states were in full compliance with the above mandates. States that are not in compliance are ineligible to receive certain federal grants. In all but one state, Wyoming, status offenders are kept separate from more serious juvenile offenders.

The first efforts to remove juveniles from adult prisons and jails began in 1825 with the founding of the New York House of Refuge, in Manhattan, by a group of reformers. The reformers were appalled by the conditions in the prisons that young prisoners were enduring. According to one reformer, John Pintard, the conditions were designed to make "little devils into great ones and at the expiration of their terms turn out accomplished villains." Later efforts lead to the establishment of juvenile reformatories, followed by the creation of separate courts for juveniles. We still follow these models today.

Hamparian's Research on the Violent Criminal

Donna Martin Hamparian studied 1,222 people born between 1956 and 1960. Her major findings are listed below:

- A relatively small number of violent juvenile offenders are responsible for most arrests for violent offenses.
- Violent juvenile offenders, as a group, do not specialize in the types of crimes they commit.
- Most violent juvenile offenders are repeat offenders.
- Most violent juvenile crimes do not involve the use of weapons.
- The frequency of arrests declines with age.
- Most adult crimes committed by juveniles are not violent crimes.
- Four out of 10 adult offenders were arrested for at least one violent crime.
- Most violent juvenile offenders make the transition to adult offenders.
- Relatively few chronic offenders are responsible for a disproportional number of crimes.
- Incarceration does not slow the rate of arrest, in fact, the subsequent rate of arrest increases after each incarceration.[4]

THE PROFESSIONAL CRIMINAL

Professional criminals or *white-collar criminals* are people of respectability and high social status who commit crime in the course of their occupations.[5] Examples of white-collar crimes include embezzlement by bankers, overcharging by doctors in billing under Medicare programs, and price-fixing in government contracts. It is estimated that white-collar crimes cost our society about $100 billion a year. Many white-collar criminals have extensive financial resources to employ when combating law enforcement efforts to control their activities.

THE ELDERLY CRIMINAL

Violent crime is normally committed by the young. Accordingly, we tend to think of prisoners as being young. All indications are, however, that the number of elderly prisoners will grow. For example in Florida one year, the number of prisoners aged 50 and older increased by 51 percent while the total prison population increased by 25 per-

An elderly inmate looks up from his work while using a sewing machine.

cent. Elderly prisoners need a variety of special care and treatment considerations. Elderly inmates suffer from illnesses such as diabetes, pulmonary diseases, circulatory problems, arthritis, and Alzheimer's disease. By far the greatest number of elderly are arrested for larceny-thefts, mainly shoplifting. In addition, recent studies indicate increasing problems of deviant behavior among the elderly which may be associated with criminal activity. For example, alcoholism and alcohol-related offenses such as drunkenness make up a large portion of the arrests of older people.[6]

Housing requirements differ for elderly prisoners. Many will need housing away from the general population to reduce the risk of victimization. Even the types of recreation programs need to be different to accommodate the elderly. Arts and crafts geared for the elderly are needed. The reading at the end of this chapter refers to a research study regarding the problems of the increasing number of elderly prisoners.

THE FEMALE CRIMINAL

The President's Commission on Law Enforcement and Administration of Justice did not include a single paragraph or statistic on the female offender, nor could any such material be found in its nine supportive Task Force Reports.[7]

Statistics indicate that the growth rate of female inmates has exceeded that for males. For example, the male population in prisons increased by 112 percent in the 1980s, and the female population increased by 202 percent during the same time.[8] Similar growth has been noted for the 1990s. The increases in arrest rates of females for index crimes over the past 20 years exceeds the increases in male arrest rates. Despite the increasing numbers of female offenders, women are still arrested for only about one in five index crimes. Note: index crimes are murder, forcible rape, robbery, aggravated assault, burglary, larceny-theft, motor vehicle theft, and arson. Three-fourths of the female arrests for index crimes are theft-related offenses. Women are also arrested for prostitution. However, the arrest rates for prostitution have decreased in the past 20 years. The most frequent non-index crimes for which women are arrested are driving under the influence, minor assaults, drug-abuse violations, fraud, and disorderly conduct.[9]

A female prisoner sits on a bed in a cluttered cell in a women's prison.

While one in every four people arrested in the United States is female, only one woman out of every 25 is eventually sent to prison. Approximately 70 percent of the women are given probation when convicted. About 10 females out of every 25 arrested serve some time in jails.

The typical female offender is African-American, between the ages of 25 and 34, and unemployed at the time of her arrest. Generally, she is also a high-school dropout with a history of previous involvement in the criminal justice system as a juvenile. In addition, the inmate is in prison for a nonviolent crime. Almost one-third of the female inmates have participated in a drug treatment program. Approximately 40 percent reported that they were either physically or sexually abused prior to incarceration. Approximately 50 percent of the female inmates confined for violent offenses stated they had been abused. Most of the violent offenders were serving time for violence against a relative or male friend.

Approximately 75 percent of the female prisoners were mothers. Most of their children were under the age of 18. Most female prisoners' children were living with relatives, usually the maternal grandmother.

Numerous research studies have indicated that women are more family oriented than men. Accordingly, children typically play a more significant role in female prisoners' lives. Several research studies have indicated that approximately 25 percent of all women entering prison are either pregnant or had given birth to an infant within one year of entering prison. Pregnant prisoners need special diets, medical treatment, lighter work assignments and less stressful environments. Counseling and prenatal care must also be provided.

Unlike the typical male inmate, most female offenders pose little danger to public safety. Hence, the previously discussed high probation rate indicates that the philosophy of reintegration is used when dealing with female offenders substantially more often than when dealing with male offenders.

One of the major problems with female prisoners is the requirement for separate facilities, especially in small jails where facilities for females are usually improvised and there is a lack of qualified personnel and security. Another problem is what to do with the females' children, if they have any. To provide adequate services for children, close coordination with local child protection services is essential.

Another problem with female inmates is the almost total lack of meaningful training programs available to them. Many of the programs available tend to focus on providing what is traditionally considered "female-type" services to the institutions, such as laundry, mending, etc. As recent as 1994, there were only 26 training schools and 127 coed programs for female juvenile delinquents and 75 institutions for women in the United States. In addition, there are approximately 65 coeducational facilities.

The National Advisory Commission on Criminal Justice Standards and Goals made the below recommendations regarding female inmates:

> Each state correctional agency operating institutions to which women offenders are committed should reexamine its policies, procedures, and programs for women offenders, and make such adjustments as may be indicated to make these policies, procedures, and programs more relevant to the problems and needs of women.

1. Facilities for women offenders should be considered an integral part of the overall corrections system, rather than an isolated activity or the responsibility of an unrelated agency.

2. Comprehensive evaluation of women offenders should be developed through research. Each state should determine differences in the needs between male and female offenders, and implement appropriate programming.

3. Appropriate vocational training programs should be implemented. Vocational programs that promote dependency and exist solely for administrative ease should be abolished. A comprehensive research effort should be initiated to determine the aptitudes and abilities of the female institutional population. This information should be coordinated with labor statistics predicting job availability. From data so obtained, creative vocational training should be developed to provide women with the skills necessary to allow independence.

4. Classification systems should be investigated to determine their applicability to the female offender. If necessary, systems should be modified or completely restructured to provide information necessary for an adequate program.

5. Adequate diversionary methods for female offenders should be implemented. Community programs should be available to women. Special attempts should be made to create alternative programs in community centers and halfway houses or other arrangements, allowing women to keep their families with them.

6. State correctional agencies with such small numbers of female inmates as to make adequate facilities and programming uneconomical should make every effort to find alternatives to imprisonment for them, including parole and local residential facilities. For those female inmates for whom such alternatives cannot be employed, contractual arrangements should be made with nearby states with more adequate facilities and programs.

7. Male and female institutions of adaptable design and comparable population should be converted to coeducational facilities. In coeducational facilities, classification and diagnostic procedures also should give consideration to offenders' problems with regard to the opposite sex, and

coeducational programs should be provided to meet those needs. Programs within the facilities should be open to both sexes. Staff of both sexes should be hired who have interest, ability, and training to cope with the problems of both male and female offenders. Assignments of staff and offenders to programs and activities should not be based on the sex of either.[10]

The ABA Standards on the Legal Status of Prisoners provides:

Pending determination of child welfare and placement by courts having appropriate jurisdiction, correctional authorities should ensure:

(a) that accommodations for all necessary prenatal and postnatal care and treatment are available for women prisoners. Arrangement should be made whenever practicable for children to be born in a hospital outside an institution. The fact that a child was born in a correctional institution should not be mentioned in the birth certificate; and

(b) that it is possible for women prisoners to keep their young children with them for a reasonable time, preferably on extended furlough or in an appropriate community facility or, if that is not feasible, that alternative care be promptly arranged. Where the young children remain with the mother in an institution, a nursery staffed by qualified persons should be provided.[11]

As the above standard indicates, provisions for childbirth and child care create special problems for jails and prisons. As noted by the standard, the ultimate determinations of child welfare and placement will be determined by the courts exercising protective jurisdiction. The establishment of a child-care center in a jail or prison undoubtedly will be a controversial issue.

GENDER BIAS

Are men treated more harshly than women in the criminal justice system? This was a question that the Gender Bias Task Force of Texas examined. This task force was jointly sponsored by the State Bar Association, the Dallas Bar Association, the Texas Women's Foundation, the Coastal Bend Women Lawyers Association and others. The final report of the task force concluded that there are disparities in treatment based on gender. They concluded that at every stage of the criminal justice process in all sorts of crimes, from investigation through arrest, bond, indictment, plea bargaining, trial, conviction, punishment, probation and parole, men are treated more harshly than women. This was true even when allowances were made for prior convictions, by tracking only first-time offenders, and for circumstances of the crime by using only similar circumstances.[12]

A similar study in California indicated that for every woman arrested for assault, seven men will be arrested; but by the punishment phases, 25 men will be sent to prison for every woman. For every woman arrested for aggravated assault, 10 men will be arrested, but by the punishment phase, 79 men will go to prison for every woman. The report also indicated that men are nine times more likely to go to prison for the same crime as women.[13]

NONCITIZEN OFFENDERS

The percentage of state and federal prisoners who are noncitizens has increased in the past 20 years. For example, the number of noncitizens in federal prison has increased from 4,088 in 1984 to 18,829 in 1994. The two states with the largest number of noncitizen inmates are Texas and California. While noncitizen inmates are from more than 75 different countries, approximately 50 percent are from Mexico. Approximately 55 percent of them were legally in the United States.

Approximately 35 percent of the noncitizens convicted in state courts were charged with violent offenses and 45 percent for drug offenses. Most convicted in federal court (85 percent) were for drug offenses.

The Immigration and Nationality Act of 1990 authorizes the U.S. Immigration and Naturalization Service (INS) to apprehend and deport criminal aliens. The number of criminal aliens in the United States is unknown. The INS must rely on federal, state, and local law enforcement agencies to notify them when those agencies come into contact with individuals who are believed to be criminal aliens. Once the alien is identified, INS issues a detainer. The alien is then deported after the criminal proceeding or sentence has been completed. In 1995, INS deported nearly 32,000 criminal aliens.

Alien Prisoners

about 1 in 23 inmates are not US. citizens

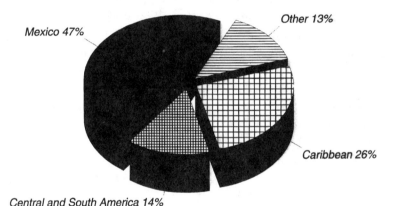

Mexico 47%

Other 13%

Caribbean 26%

Central and South America 14%

over 31,000 inmates

INS has several options for removing an illegal alien (including a criminal alien) from the United States. Fewer than 3 percent of those apprehended are actually deported. Most admit to their illegal status and agree to leave the United States voluntarily. Unlike deportation, voluntary departure does not require adjudication by an immigration judge. Aliens who voluntarily returned, at no expense to the United States, are not prohibited from legally entering at a later time. If, however, they have been convicted of a felony, they are prohibited from returning without special permission.

A deported alien may not be admitted to the United States for five years after deportation. Entry by a previously deported alien within five years of deportation is a felony. Entry by a previously deported alien with a criminal history (felony conviction) is a criminal offense with the maximum term of 20 years imprisonment.

THE FEDERAL INMATE

Federal inmates serve in correctional institutions for the commission of federal crimes. Accordingly, there are generally distinct differences between federal and state inmates. Most federal prisoners are confined for drug violations, tax evasion, and robbing federally insured banks. Because murder, rape, assaults, and other violent crimes are state and not federal crimes, offenders who commit those crimes will generally be in a state, not federal, institution.

The federal prisons are controlled by the Federal Bureau of Prisons, which has a central office in Washington, D.C. and five regional offices. The central office comprises the director and his/her staff and four operational divisions. The operational divisions are Correctional Programs, Administration, Medical Services and Industries, Education and Vocational Training. In addition, at the central office, there is an Office of General Counsel and Office of Inspections. The five regional headquarters are located in Atlanta, Dallas, Philadelphia, Dublin (near San Francisco) and Kansas City. Each is headed by a regional director.

There are approximately 115 federal confinement facilities with approximately 100,000 inmates. All federal prisoners who are physically able are required to complete regular daily work assignments. The prisoners have the opportunity to participate in educational training, vocational training, work, religious, and counseling programs.

The federal classification system is based on the concept that prisoners should be placed in the least-restrictive institution possible that is nearest to their homes. Approximately one-third of the federal prisoners are classified as Security Level 1. This is the lowest level and permits inmates to be retained in open institutions, such as prison camps.

The federal prison system uses Federal Prison Industries, Inc. to sell its products and services to other federal agencies. The Federal Prison Industries, Inc. goes by the corporate name of UNICOR. It is wholly owned by the federal government with the mission to support the Federal Bureau of Prisons through the gainful employment of inmates in work programs. Federal inmates may obtain gainful employ-

THE FORD PINTO CASE

On September 13, 1978, Ford Motor Company was indicted by a grand jury in Elkhart, Indiana on three counts of reckless homicide based on the deaths of three teenagers who were killed in the fiery crash of a Ford Pinto. The victims died of burns suffered when the Pinto burst into flames after being rear-ended. The Pinto was developed by Ford to sell for about $2,000. The design was completed on a rush schedule. For design reasons, the gas tank was placed behind, rather than over, the rear axle. This placement made it more probable that the car would explode and burn in a rear-end collision than similar-sized compact automobiles. Evidence was presented that Ford was aware of the problem and that the car could have been modified for a cost of $15.30 per car, but that the executives at Ford decided to go ahead with the project to save money. The Ford Motor Company was acquitted on March 13, 1980. Had Ford been found guilty, the company could have been fined $175,000. A $175,000 fine for Ford would be comparable to the average wage-earner paying a fine of $3.25. It is estimated that approximately 500 people died because of this design.

No individuals were ever punished for their decisions. Compare this lack of punishment with the fact that individuals who kill store clerks in robberies are routinely given the death penalty.

ment with UNICOR to earn money and obtain valuable on-the-job training, vocational education, and apprenticeship programs.

The federal system has implemented a mandatory literacy program for federal inmates who read below certain grade levels. Eventually, the federal system plans to require mandatory literacy training for inmates who read below the twelfth grade level. All promotions in UNICOR and work assignments are contingent upon an inmate's achievment of the desired level of literacy.

The federal system also has an adult basic education program that provides the inmates with the opportunity to obtain GED high-school equivalency certificates and college courses. English as a Second Language is also provided for those inmates who need it. Most of these programs are funded in part by UNICOR.

The federal system operates four co-correctional facilities and one all-female institution. There are approximately 7,000 female inmates in the federal system.

Driver's License Revocation Is Not a Punishment

The Supreme Court of Colorado held that the initiation of separate criminal proceedings after the resolution of an administrative license revocation hearing did not violate the double jeopardy clause of the U.S. Constitution.

Henry John Deutschendorf was charged with driving under the influence and other offenses. The state department of revenue notified him that is was suspending his license. At the administrative hearing, the hearing officer determined that the blood test was not properly administered to him and did not suspend his license. Next, his attorney moved to dismiss criminal charges against him on the basis that proceeding both administratively and criminally was double jeopardy. On July 1, 1996, the Colorado Supreme Court denied his writ and stated that administrative driver's license revocation was not punishment.

Article

Golden Years Behind Bars: Special Programs and Facilities for Elderly Inmates[14]

Most researchers and policy makers deem the crimes of youthful offenders to be more serious and dangerous for society than the crimes committed by older people. However, in recent years, crime and the elderly has emerged as an issue of increasing importance. While we are more accustomed to seeing the elderly as victims, attention has begun to shift to how the elderly are increasingly the perpetrators of crime. A common portrayal of the elderly offender has been the "victimless" felon writing bad checks or the senior citizen who shoplifts in order to survive or attract attention. The elderly are not only committing more crimes, their offenses are also more serious, offenses which at one time were reserved exclusively for the young. As a result, elderly offenders are presenting complex challenges to our nation's prison systems.

Approximately 381,000 persons ages 50 and older are arrested annually in the United States (*Uniform Crime Reports, 1990*). Of these, 15 percent are arrested for serious felonies such as murder, forcible rape, robbery, aggravated assault, burglary, larceny, motor vehicle theft, and arson. As more of the older population commits violent offenses, the likelihood that they will become incarcerated becomes apparent. *The Corrections Yearbook* reported in 1992 that 709,587 inmates were confined to state prisons nationwide including the District of Columbia. Of these prisoners, 35,032 were over the age of 50, representing a 50 percent increase in four years. This age group comprises approximately five percent of the total inmate population.

The Corrections Yearbook further reported that the Federal Bureau of Prisons housed 66,472 prisoners, of which 6,554, or about 10 percent, were 50 years of age or older. By the year 2005, this over-50 prison population is expected to increase to 16 percent. Of course, as our state prison systems expand, so will our federal prisons. The number of inmates will continue to increase and will exceed 100,000 by 1995. By the year 2000, a projected 137,000 inmates will be in the federal system.

It appears that the population of older prisoners will continue to increase well into the 21st century. For example, Virginia currently has 15,000 prisoners in the general population, and 2,500 of these have special needs. This sector of the prison's population includes over 800 elderly inmates. By the year 2000, the prison population is expected to total 32,000, with 8,532 exhibiting special needs. Again, it is projected that approximately one-third of those in the special needs category will be classified as geriatric. Numerous other states also face similar increases.

Chaneles has estimated that by the year 2000, if present trends continue, the number of long-term prisoners over 50 will be approximately 125,000, with 40,000 to 50,000 over 65 years of age. This projection is based on new admissions and the fact that there are currently 13,937 natural lifers (life without parole), 52,054 lifers (parole possibilities), and 125,996 inmates serving 20 years or more. In addition, another 2,214 prisoners are currently serving time on death row. These groups comprise 22 percent of all inmates in state and federal prisons.

Research Rationale

While the number of older prisoners is now manageable in most states, the trend toward an aged inmate population is raising questions that will significantly affect correction programs in the coming decades. Older offenders pose unique and costly problems for corrections departments already struggling to cope with outdated and overcrowded facilities. Many states are faced with an increased number of aging prisoners who are in need of acute or chronic medical care. It is estimated that the average elderly prisoner suffers from three chronic illnesses. Many older offenders need corrective aids and prosthetic devices including eyeglasses, dentures, hearing aids, ambulatory equipment, and special shoes. Correctional systems are faced with making necessary adjustments to accommodate the special needs of aging inmates. Issues, such as providing special diets and round-the-clock nursing care, building new facilities or altering old ones, and restructuring institutional activities, are becoming more frequent topics of discussion.

Older prisoners differ from younger inmates not only in their need for medical care, but also in their psychosocial needs. Walsh found that older male inmates expressed a greater need for privacy and for access to preventive health care and legal assistance than younger men. Older inmates are often unable to cope with the fast pace and noise of a regular facility. Studies have also found that older inmates reported feeling unsafe and vulnerable to attack by younger inmates and expressed a preference for rooming with people their own age. Vega and Silverman also reported that abrasive relations with other inmates were the most disturbing incidents elderly prisoners had to cope with while incarcerated. Fifty-five percent of their respondents indicated that abrasive situations occurred daily. These factors, among others, often result in increasing stress for older inmates.

The physical condition and structure of institutions also create significant problems for elderly inmates. Prison systems are primarily designed to house young, active inmates. Older, frail offenders often find the prison environment cold and damp, and the stairs and distance to the cafeteria difficult to cope with. Inmates with limited mobility may find many prisons' physical designs too stressful to negotiate, and they simply withdraw into an isolated state.

The purpose of this research is to provide a comprehensive description of the special policies, programs, and facilities for geriatric inmates in United States prisons. Another goal is to determine the most pressing concerns correctional systems face in responding to the special needs of elderly prisoners. Other research questions focus on developing future programs and policies and identifying research topics useful for correctional officials in responding better to the needs of aging inmates. Implications for policy and practice are also addressed.

During the first half of 1990, a nationwide survey was conducted soliciting information from the 50 states and the District of Columbia. An open-ended questionnaire and comprehensive prison program checklist was mailed directly to the administrator of health services for each state correctional system. Those corrections officials who failed to respond to the mailed survey were interviewed by telephone. A follow-up phone inquiry was conducted in June 1992 to allow each correctional unit to report any recent changes in program or facility development. The results reported here are based on a 100 percent response rate.

Survey Results

Policies and Programs

A shortcoming of the studies of older prisoners is the failure of both researchers and correctional officials to agree on what constitutes "elderly." Some authors define "elderly" as 65 years of age and older, some suggest 60 years, while others have reported 55 years, and many use 50 years of age or older. Likewise, states reporting special programs for aging inmates use a variety of ages to indicate special need. However, 50 years of age and older is the most common definition found in this study. Several correctional officials suggested that the typical inmate in his 50s has a physical appearance of at least 10 years older. In addition, the declining health of many inmates contributes to them being "elderly" before their time.

From responses to this survey, it is evident that most states do not have any specific written policies which address aged or infirm inmates. In practice, however, the needs of older inmates are addressed, to the extent possible, in the course of the classification process. Typically, all inmates including the elderly are screened in the admission process. Generally, housing and work assignments are made with regard to the inmate's health, security level, and location of family. In this regard, older inmates who possess numerous chronic health problems are granted special treatment based on their inferior health status.

For example, in Washington state, inmates with infirmities related to old age are likely to be transferred to the state penitentiary, where a number of cells in one unit have been designated for use by such inmates. Older inmates, who require long-term inpatient care, would be considered for transfer to the state reformatory, which has the largest inpatient unit in the system. Those who require special services, other than inpatient care, are transferred to the Special Needs Unit at Washington Correction Center.

A few states, such as Texas, Alaska, Mississippi, and South Carolina, make some policy decisions based solely on age. In Texas, the inmate is medically classified according to medical history, general health, physical findings, and age. Inmates 50 to 55 years of age receive a classification requiring lighter, slower duties. Inmates 55 and over are provided a classification that restricts the inmate from harder, heavier work and may allow for reduced work hours. Alaska reports occasionally providing a modification in sentencing for disease onset in the elderly. In Mississippi, inmates over 50 years of age are housed in geriatric units if their security classification permits. In South Carolina, inmates may retire from work at age 65. Numerous states also provide physicals annually for inmates over the age of 50, rather than every other year as they do for the general prison population.

Although most states do not have a policy based strictly on age, they do provide compassionate leave for those inmates who are terminally ill or not capable of physically functioning in the correctional system. Generally, the prognosis is six months or less to live, and specific criteria with regard to custody classification and medical requirements must be fulfilled. In some states, nursing home placement is a practical alternative. However, nursing home administrators may not be favorable to the notion of accepting ex-prisoners who have life histories of crime and violence, even if they are ill.

When compassionate leave is impossible due to the nature of the crime, correctional policy, or lack of available alternatives, prisons are developing policies and programs to better serve the terminally ill. For example, McCain Correctional Hospital in North Carolina has incorporated the hospice concept into its geriatric/infirm facility. Family members are permitted to spend extended periods of time with the dying inmate, and hospice supervisors work closely with the inmate and his family.

Geriatric Facilities

An increasing number of states do routinely house older inmates apart from the general population and offer them unique programming or services. In specific states (including Alabama, Georgia, Illinois, Kansas, Kentucky, Maryland, Michigan, Minnesota, Mississippi, North Carolina, New Jersey, Ohio, South Carolina, Tennessee, Texas, Virginia, West Virginia, and Wisconsin) elderly inmates are housed in special units often described as "aged/infirm," "medical/geriatric," "disabled," or simply "geriatric." Most of these units frequently mix older inmates with younger disabled ones. Whenever possible, same-aged inmates are grouped together in dormitory style cells. Generally, those states reporting some form of special housing have one or two facilities within their prison systems where older inmates are grouped.

Special considerations are usually given to accommodate safely the handicapped and less physically able. Stairs are minimal, and distances from various facilities in the institution (e.g., canteen, recreation room) are reduced. Educational, vocational, recreational, and rehabilitative programs have been expanded to accommodate the elderly. A few facilities now employ psychologists and counselors with professional training in geriatrics, so there is a greater awareness of the unique social, psychological, and emotional needs of these inmates.

One of the first and more comprehensive facilities to accommodate elderly inmates was developed in South Carolina. In 1970, prison officials began providing special facilities for the elderly. The state, renowned for its harsh sentencing practices, has always had a large number of long-termers growing old behind bars. Due to the need for more space, the state's prison for the elderly moved into a former tuberculosis hospital at State Park in 1983. The majority of minimum custody inmates are housed at the State Park Correctional Center, which has 100 male beds and 11 female beds for handicapped elderly. South Carolina is the only state that reported housing its older female prisoners in a special geriatric facility.

Twenty-four-hour medical coverage is available at State Park. Thirteen nurses are on duty around the clock. A doctor is assigned to the facility full-time and writes an average of 925 prescriptions a month. In addition to providing two daily sick calls, pill line, and emergency and routine treatment, the medical staff provides educational programs geared to the needs of the residents. Those inmates on dialysis and chemotherapy are bused daily to a nearby hospital.

Some states are developing "nursing-home-like settings" within the prison environment, which provide a greater degree of shelter. For example, Mississippi has a geriatric unit that houses 85 offenders. In 1987, the old hospital was remodeled and specifically designed as a nursing home in a correctional setting. In this type of unit, 24-hour nursing care is provided and sick call is available weekly. A physician checks with the unit daily. In addition to the nursing staff, a psychiatric assistant provides recreational activities, and a case manager is also assigned to the unit.

Special Concerns

Rising medical costs in conjunction with health care mandates are having a tremendous impact on a significant number of states. Thirty percent of the states listed rising costs as the most pressing concern. An important issue for 26 percent of the state units is meeting the special needs of older inmates who are "aging in place" with numerous chronic health problems and limited Activities of Daily Living (ADL) functions. As one correctional health official stated, "a significant number of prisoners 50 years and over have a number of chronic illnesses that require long-term care. Another problem is lack of previous dental care requiring the provision of dental prosthesis and long-term dental care." Other problems listed by some states included a lack of community support and appropriate programming for the older inmates, in addition to the victimization of frail, aged inmates.

Planning for the Future

Numerous states indicate that they have future plans to implement special programming and/or facilities for the geriatric and handicapped prison population. Responses to the survey question ranged from immediate plans to establish new facilities, to ongoing discussions or research, to long-range plans to build or remodel facilities, to no plans whatsoever. For example, Maine, Maryland, Kentucky, and Montana currently have building plans in place or are converting current structures for their elderly and infirm inmates. Other states such as Arkansas, Nevada, New Jersey, Ohio, South Carolina, and Wyoming have long-range plans to build nursing-home-like facilities. Delaware, Georgia, Iowa, Michigan, and Washington have recently undergone major feasibility studies to determine better the needs of the ever-increasing number of older prisoners. Arizona, Tennessee, Texas, and Virginia have recently opened new geriatric/special needs units. Pennsylvania reported the development of new geriatric services and support systems, as well as special training for correctional staff. Finally, Texas is in the process of developing appropriate programming for its new geriatric unit.

Research Needs

As older prisoners become the focus of concern for many prison systems for the next generation, state prison officials do not have adequate research outcomes to help them solve the problem. Prison officials surveyed in this study stressed that indicators are needed to help identify more clearly "model programs" that are adequately meeting the special needs of the elderly inmate. For example, while this survey discovered a variety of programs and facilities instituted in certain states, a need still exists to provide a systematic program evaluation of these efforts. Important questions remain regarding the effectiveness of such programs in meeting the needs of aging prisoners. Research, in this case, would emphasize the (1) living environment or custodial care, (2) humanitarian care, and (3) therapeutic care. An evaluation research design would focus on how effectively these programs currently meet the physical, medical, social, and mental needs of the aging prisoner.

Other research information desired by correctional officials includes: (1) What are the general health care needs of this special population? (2) What is the average annual medical cost for aged offenders? (3) What incarceration alternatives are available for frail, elderly inmates and what is the post-release success of elderly prisoners? (4) What is the nature of family relationships for those growing old in prison? (5) How will states determine who gets costly health care services and who does not? (6) What projections can be made utilizing data from states with life without parole concerning the size and cost of their older prison populations in the coming decades? (7) What are the typical coping strategies for those who enter prison later in life? Finally, correctional officials also pressed an interest in additional research information concerning sentencing and parole policies for the elderly.

Policy Implications

In many ways, geriatric programming in the prison setting is in a developmental stage. While it is obvious that correctional officials are becoming more sensitive to the special needs of aging inmates, barriers continue to exist that interfere with the ability of states to respond more effectively. For example, most states are faced with the rising costs of medical care and general overcrowding. In the past decade, the war on drugs and tough mandatory sentencing laws have doubled the number of inmates. Overcrowding, AIDS and other issues have hindered many states from implementing special programming for the aging inmate. Currently, the prison system is demanding 1,100 new beds every week.

Although studies have found that older inmates prefer to be housed with people their own age, some correctional officials find no need for or responsibility to provide special consecration to older offenders. Others feel older inmates provide a sense of stability to the general prison population and should not be housed separately. From this perspective, older inmates should be given housing and work assignments based on their health and the type of custody they require. Other placement considerations should be work skills and family status. Placing an inmate in a special unit for the elderly, hundreds of miles away from family could be detrimental to the inmate.

Older offenders may also have a difficult time being assigned to facilities providing special needs because slots are limited. In particular, those states converting a small wing for older inmates may have a long waiting list. Also, there is still disagreement regarding the ethical obligation to provide inmates with such acute care as heart bypass surgery or kidney transplants when others in society may not have access to or the money for the same level of care. Thus, due to lack of space, philosophy, or costs, some elderly inmates may not benefit from socialized programming. Of course, health access and care may vary from state to state.

A major problem in meeting the special needs of older inmates is that, in many states, there are still few aging inmates. For example, in Vermont, North Dakota, South Dakota, Hawaii, and Maine, where there are few elderly inmates, separate facilities or programs cannot be justified. In such states, correctional units have little choice but to mainstream elderly inmates in the general prison system. This is particularly true for aging female inmates, as they typically make up a small portion of the total female population.

Another barrier to responding fully to the special needs of aging inmates is the lack of adequately trained prison staff. As one prison official confessed, "I know how to run prisons, not old-age homes." Moreover, not everyone who works in a correctional environment may have the aptitude or the essential skills needed to manage elderly people. Careful selection for sensitivity to the unique requirements of geriatric inmates should be an important consideration. Training, involving administrative personnel, line security staff, and health providers, should include an increased knowledge of growing old and how this knowledge specifically affects the elderly in a prison environment. Prison staff need to be specifically trained to understand more fully the social and emotional needs of the elderly, the dynamics of death and dying, procedures for identifying depression, and a system for referring older inmates to experts in the community.

While states are responding by providing special units for older inmates, programming for elderly inmates has not kept pace. Although older inmates may be grouped together in a special needs facility, they often have nothing to do to pass the time. Physical activities popular with younger inmates may not be well-suited to many elderly inmates. Vocational training programs, a primary activity for much of the prison population, serve no purpose for long-term older offenders who are unlikely to return to the workforce. In most prisons, counseling is geared to rehabilitating younger inmates rather than coping with issues such as chronic illness or death. Instead of preparing the inmate for reentry as a productive member of society, wellness programs that aim to keep the individual alert and active are needed. Walking, gardening, woodworking, ceramics, low-impact exercises, prison support groups, and other more passive recreational activities can prove successful among older inmates.

The diversity of the growing number of older offenders should also be recognized and incorporated into rehabilitative programs. For example, the elderly first offender should be integrated into prison life differently than the repeat offender. The first offender is likely to be more anxious, fearful, depressed, and suicidal than the chronic offender. Aging inmates coming into an institutional setting late in life with the realization that prison may be their final home may experience a tremendous shock to their system. Williams (1989) found that new offenders were more withdrawn and passed their time sleeping, watching television, or performing some other solitary activity. Other inmates, imprisoned for long periods of their lives may fear returning to the free world.

In other situations, locating family members who may accept an aging inmate as well as provide necessary care-giving tasks may be difficult. Some family members also may be aged and in poor health. The nature of the crime may have created a conflict among family members, resulting in a break in kinship ties. Such inmates may have few or no visits from close friends or relatives on the outside. The lack of a supportive social network may adversely affect the incarcerated elderly, because significant others are key factors that serve to buffer the negative effects of incarceration.

In order to transfer elderly offenders back to the community, housing and financial assistance must usually be secured for inmates who have been imprisoned for long terms and who have lost all contacts in the community. Parole decisions should be handled on a case-by-case basis. Prison staff should maintain good relationships with a variety of social service agencies, such as social security officials and nursing home personnel. Older offenders will need assistance in getting their social security reinstated and in determining if they are eligible for Medicaid. Intervals for parole review of older inmates should be more frequent, especially in cases where terminal illnesses have been diagnosed.

Correctional officials are just beginning to grapple with the large number of elderly prisoners. The increased probability of longer sentences due to the increased use of habitual offender statutes with life without parole and mandatory minimum sentencing will pose unique and costly problems for corrections departments in the future. Additional research is needed to assist correctional officials in their decision-making processes and in the implementation of quality programs and facilities. Prisons, like other social institutions in society, must be prepared for the "graying of America."

{End of Article}

SUMMARY

One of the characteristics of prison populations that concerns us is the increasing absolute numbers and the increases per 100,000 in the rate of incarceration. Included within the prison population are various groups of individuals who need special care and treatment. The term "career criminals" is used to identify those persons who make, or attempt to make, a living committing crime. Generally, career criminals are property offenders. They begin their criminal career early in their juvenile years. Most view crime as a safe and enjoyable way to obtain a good life. They expect to return to a life of crime after they are released from confinement. The average career criminal is normally in and out of prison or jail all of his or her life. Most career criminals live, however, at or below the poverty level when not confined in prison.

Under current law, prison authorities must keep juveniles out of the "sight and sound" of adult inmates. The definition of juveniles varies by age according to the states' definitions. In addition, they must keep juveniles who have committed crimes in the usual sense in institutions different from those that youths charged with status offenses such as truancy, failure to go to school, and incorrigibility.

The professional criminal or white-collar criminal refers to a person of respectability and high social status who commit crime in the course of his or her occupation. Examples of white-collar crimes include embezzlement by bankers, overcharging by doctors in billing under Medicare Programs, and price-fixing in government contracts. It is estimated that white-collar crimes cost our society about $100 billion a year. Many white-collar criminals have extensive financial resources to employ when combating law enforcement efforts to control their activities.

Violent crime is normally committed by the young. Accordingly, we tend to think of prisoners as being young. All indications are, however, that the number of elderly prisoners will grow. Elderly prisoners need a variety of special care and treatment considerations. Elderly inmates suffer from illnesses such as diabetes, pulmonary diseases, circulatory problems, arthritis, and Alzheimer's disease. By far the greatest number of arrests for the elderly are larceny-thefts, mainly shoplifting. In addition, recent studies indicate the increasing problems of deviant behavior facing the elderly may be leading to or associated with criminal activity. For example, alcoholism and alcohol-related offenses, such as drunkenness, make up a large portion of the arrests of older people.

Statistics indicate that the incarceration rate of female inmates has exceeded that for males. For example, the male population in prisons increased by 112 percent in the 1980s, and the female population increased by 202 percent during the same time. Similar growth has been noted for the 1990s. The increases in arrest rates of females for index crimes over the past 20 years exceeds the increases in male arrest rates. Despite the increasing numbers of female offenders, women are still arrested for only about one in five index crimes. Three-fourths of the female arrests for index crimes are theft-related offenses. Women are also arrested for prostitution. However, the arrest rates for prostitution have decreased in the past 20 years. The most frequent non-index crime for which women are arrested are driving under the influence, minor assaults, drug abuse violations, fraud, and disorderly conduct.

While one in every four people arrested in the United States is female, only one woman out of every 25 is eventually sent to prison. Approximately 70 percent of the women are given probation when convicted. About 10 females out of every 25 arrested serve some time in jails. The typical female offender is African-American, between the ages of 25 to 34, never married, unemployed at the time of her arrest and generally a high-school dropout with a history of previous involvement in the criminal justice system as a juvenile. In addition, the inmate is in prison for a nonviolent crime.

DISCUSSION QUESTIONS

1. Describe the career criminal's life-style.

2. Explain the problems caused by the aging of the prison population.

3. What special problems do female prisoners cause?

4. What types of individuals are considered "white-collar" criminals?

5. Is the criminal justice system gender-biased?

ENDNOTES TO CHAPTER 3

1. Ruth Masters and Cliff Roberson, *Inside Criminology* (Englewood, NJ: Prentice-Hall, 1989), p. 366.

2. Peter W. Greenwood and Allan Abraham, *Selective Incapacitation*, prepared for the National Institute of Justice (Santa Monica, Ca.: Rand Corp., 1981) and Jan Chaiken et al. *Doing Crime* (Santa Monica, Ca.: Rand Corp., 1982).

3. Richard C. McCorkle, Terance D. Miethe, and Kriss A. Drass, "The Roots of Prison Violence: A Test of the Deprivation, Management," and "Not-So-Total Institution Models," *Crime & Delinquency*, Vol. 41, No. 3, July 1995, pp. 317-331.

4. Donna Martin Hamparian, *The Young Criminal Years of the Violent Few* (Washington, D.C.: U.S. Department of Justice, 1985).

5. Edwin H. Sutherland, *White Collar Crime* (New York: Holt, Rinehart and Winston, 1959).

6. Sue Titus Reid, *Crime and Criminology*, 6th ed. (New York: Harcourt Brace Jovanovich, 1991), p. 70.

7. Edith Flown, "The Special Problems of the Female Offender," in L.E. Ohlin, ed. *We Hold These Truths* (Richmond, Va. Virginia Division of Justice and Crime Prevention, 1972).

8. Lawrence Greenfield and Stephanie Minor-Harper, *Women in Prison, 1990* (Washington, D.C.: Department of Justice, 1991).

9. William Sessions, *Uniform Crime Reports: 1994* (Washington, D.C.: Federal Bureau of Investigation, 1995).

10. National Advisory Commission on Criminal Justice Standards and Goals, *Corrections* (Washington, D.C.: U.S. Department of Justice, 1976), p.377-378.

11. ABA Standards, *Legal Status of Prisoners*, Standard 23-5.7.

12. *The Gender Bias Task Force of Texas Final Report* (Austin, Tx: State Bar of Texas, Department of Research and Analysis, 1994)

13. *Committee on Gender Bias in the Courts, Final Report*, National Coalition of Free Men (1991).

14. Ronald H. Aday, PH.D. Gerontology Program Director, Middle Tennessee State University. Reprin. ed with permission of Dr. Aday. This article was originally printed in *Federal Probation*, June 1994, Vol. 58, No. 2. Footnotes and charts are omitted.

This teary-eyed young man is very glad to be graduating from boot camp.

CHAPTER 4

ALTERNATIVES TO INCARCERATION

KEY TERMS

Boot camp programs

Community service programs

Diversion

Recidivism

Restitution

Shock incarceration

CHAPTER OBJECTIVES

After reading this chapter, the reader will be able to:

☐ Explain why the processing of prisoners is often called "risk management."

☐ Explain why diversion is considered as the "front door" program.

☐ Identify the concepts involved with "shock incarceration."

☐ Explain the three psychological principles involved in rehabilitative programs.

☐ List the advantages of using community service instead of prison as a sanction.

☐ Explain the dual focus involved in selecting people for community service.

☐ Analyze the organizational issues involved in community service.

☐ Explain the issues involved in the supervision of community service.

This chapter will explore many of the alternatives to incarceration. The primary alternative being used in the United States today is probation. While probation is considered the backbone of our present corrections (see Chapter 5), innovative programs and controls schemes have been developed as alternatives to incarceration and probation. Often these sanctions are referred to as *intermediate sanctions*. Processing of offenders in the criminal justice system has been referred to as *risk management*. Prior to the 1970s, most offenders were either confined to prison or placed on probation, with the majority of offenders being placed on probation. As explained in Chapter 1, probation is not as popular as it once was. Accordingly, to reduce the prison population, alternative sanctions were developed. Two of the most popular sanctions used are diversion and shock incarceration, each of which is discussed in this chapter.

DIVERSION

Diversion is designed to funnel offenders away from the criminal justice system and into community programs, which should be more beneficial for the offender and the community than incarceration. Diversion is frequently used to refer to release of the accused pending trial. In the late 1960s and 1970s, it was a popular concept. Diversion is based on the assumption that the diverted individual will participate in some treatment program in return for the removal from the criminal justice system process before trial. Diversion is commonly referred to as the "front door" program because it limits the number of people entering jail or prison facilities.

Typical targets for diversion are individuals with drug and alcohol problems. Many researchers contend that diversion actually widens the criminal justice system's net, in that people who would not have been processed through the criminal court system are processed with the intention of referring them out to diversion programs. A major rationale for diversion is that less intervention by the criminal justice system will make it more likely that the individual will be rehabilitated.

The National Advisory Commission on Criminal Justice Standards and Goals, in its report, "Courts," suggested the following guidelines for using diversion:

> In appropriate cases, offenders should be diverted into noncriminal programs before formal trial or conviction. Such diversion is appropriate where there is a substantial likelihood that conviction could be obtained and the benefits to society from channeling an offender into an available noncriminal diversion program outweigh any harm done to society by abandoning the criminal prosecution.[1]

Diversion programs have been used extensively to divert juveniles out of the juvenile justice system. The diversion programs for juveniles include remedial education, foster homes, group homes, and local counseling facilities and centers.

SHOCK INCARCERATION

Since their inception in 1983, shock incarceration/probation programs, also known as *boot camps*, have enjoyed considerable popular
support.[2] Like other intermediate sanctions, the programs are intended
to alleviate institution overcrowding and to reduce recidivism. In addition, because they are perceived as being "tough" on crime (in contrast
to some other intermediate sentences like probation), they have been
enthusiastically embraced as a viable correctional option for delinquent
youths. In addition, the presumed combination of cost savings and punitiveness has proven irresistible to politicians.

There has been a remarkable growth of boot camp prisons nationwide. In January 1984, there were only two states, Georgia and
Oklahoma, who had boot camp programs. By 1992, 25 states and the
Federal Bureau of Prisons were operating a total of 41 programs. Two
years later, 1994, five more states had either opened boot camp programs or were in the planning process to open them. In 1984, Georgia's
program capacity was 250 beds, by 1994, the capacity had expanded to
over 3,000 beds. These figures pertain only to those programs developed statewide and do not include the programs developed at the county
level.

Characteristics of Shock Incarceration

As the name suggests, boot camp programs are modeled after
military boot camp training. Participation in military drill and ceremony,
physical training, and hard labor is mandatory. Inmates begin their day
before dawn and are involved in structured activities until "lights out,"
approximately 16 hours later.

The military style training is generally supplemented with rehabilitative programming such as drug treatment/education or academic
education. The emphasis placed on such programs varies. New York,
for example, has structured the program as a therapeutic community.
Rehabilitative programming, therefore, plays a central role in the program. In other states, rehabilitative programming is peripheral to the
military boot camp experience.

As the boot camp programs have developed, rehabilitative programming has come to play a more prominent role in the day-to-day routine. The earliest boot camp models devoted little time to such programs. Many of those pioneering programs have since been enhanced with additional therapeutic services. Programs developed in recent years have placed a greater emphasis on rehabilitative programing from the start.

The boot camp programs are designed for young, male offenders convicted of nonviolent offenses. Eligibility and suitability criteria were developed to restrict participation to this type of offender. For example, a March 1992 survey of shock incarceration programs revealed that the majority of programs (61.5 percent) then in operation limited participation to individuals convicted of nonviolent offenses. Fifty percent of the programs further restricted participation to individuals serving their first felony sentence. Most programs have minimum and maximum age limits. The minimum age limit was generally 16 years of age and the maximum 23 years of age. Female offenders are permitted to participate in about 50 percent of the programs. The number of beds available to females, however, has been limited. Several state courts have ruled that failure to include female offenders in the programs was a gender discrimination violation.

Evaluation of Boot Camp Programs

As noted earlier, a major goal of the programs was to reduce recidivism by means of rehabilitation and deterrence. Specific rehabilitative strategies included teaching accountability or responsibility, developing self-worth or self-esteem, or providing education or substance abuse education or treatment. In addition, the shock incarceration programs are designed to serve as specific deterrents.

It is hoped that the difficult nature of the military-style training or the harsh reality of prison life would deter participants from future offending and thus reduce recidivism. An examination of a core element, military-style training, which includes military drill and ceremony, physical training, strict discipline, and physical labor, is necessary to determine if there is any value to the regimented military routine.

Research on specific deterrence has not been promising. Researchers have previously reported limited or no deterrent effect as the result of incarceration in a training school.[3] In addition, similar research on the Scared Straight program has failed to find evidence of a deterrent effect.[4] Realistically, it is unlikely that the boot camp experience will lead to increased perceptions of either the certainty or severity of punishment. In terms of general deterrence, there is no reason to believe that individuals on the street will be deterred by the threat of serving time in a boot camp prison. In fact, camp participants interviewed revealed that prior to arriving at the boot camp, they did not believe that they would have trouble meeting program requirements.

Aside from deterrence, however, the experience of day-to-day routine may have some beneficial by-products. Political support for these programs seems, in part, to be based on the idea that the regimented life-style and discipline of the boot camp will be transferred to life on the outside. Completing the highly structured and demanding program is further expected to inspire a sense of accomplishment that may generalize to other activities. This sense of accomplishment is reinforced in many programs by graduation ceremonies that are attended by family and friends.

Former shock incarceration participants reported that the program helped them to "get free" of drugs and to become physically fit. Other advantages mentioned by offenders included learning to get up in the morning and being active all day. Thus, the military-type regimen appeared to promote physical health by ensuring a drug-free environment, balanced diet, and sufficient exercise.

Contrary to popular opinion, however, it is unlikely that the long hours of hard labor characteristic of shock incarceration will improve work skills or habits. The labor that is often required of shock incarceration participants is largely menial, consisting of picking up trash along highways, cleaning the facility, or maintaining grounds. Researchers have noted that for work programs to be successful, i.e., promote rehabilitation, they must "enhance practical skills, develop interpersonal skills, minimize prisonization, and ensure that work is not punishment alone."[5] Considering the type of work generally required of inmates, it appears unlikely that it will be of much value in and of itself.

In short, the basic shock incarceration model may have some merit independent of rehabilitative programming. To summarize, positive by-products attributed to the core elements of shock incarceration alone may include physical fitness, drug-free existence, the experience of a structured life-style, and a sense of accomplishment.

Catalyst for Change

The basic shock incarceration experience is designed to induce stress. Incarceration, too, by its very nature, produces stress. Stress levels peak early during a period of incarceration and gradually taper off.[6] Research has revealed that prison inmates were most receptive to personal changes (e.g., self-improvement classes, education, or training) during this period of high emotional stress. Within a period of several months, as stress levels tapered off, however, desire to change did also. Inmates who, for example, had enrolled in self-improvement classes dropped out in favor of institutional jobs. In one study, the researchers concluded that the desire for change was related to the emotional distress experienced at the onset of the prison term. They argued further that treatment programs should begin as early in the prison term as possible to take advantage of the motivation to change.[7]

These research findings may be relevant to shock incarceration. Not only are inmates incarcerated, but they are forced to participate in a physically demanding and stressful program. At the same time, most programs require participation in rehabilitative programming ranging from academic education, to drug treatment, to individual counseling. Generalizing from the findings then, the basic shock incarceration experience may make participants particularly receptive to the rehabilitative programing that is required of them. The program experience may initiate a period of self-evaluation and change.

The implications of this approach are twofold. First, the basic program may function predominantly as a catalyst for change. Therefore, shock incarceration programs that do not also offer rehabilitative programming will have no effect other than those previously discussed. Secondly, if shock incarceration programs, by definition, function primarily as catalysts due simply to the stress-inducing nature of the program, attention then must shift to the adequacy of rehabilitative programming.

Rehabilitative Programming

Over 20 years have passed since a researcher, referring to correctional treatment, suggested that "nothing appears to work."[8] In response, prominent researchers in the field of corrections reviewed the extant literature on the effectiveness of treatment programs and concluded, on the contrary, that effective treatment existed and that, on average, appropriate treatment reduced recidivism by 50 percent.[9] The key, of course, was the word "appropriate."

Appropriate treatment was defined as treatment guided by three psychological principles:

1) Intensive treatment should be matched with high-risk offenders.

2) Treatment should address "criminogenic needs."

3) Treatment should follow general strategies of effective treatment (e.g., anticriminal modeling, warm and supportive interpersonal relations) and match the type of treatment (e.g., cognitive or behavioral) to individual characteristics.[10]

On the other hand, intervention strategies that have generally been found to be ineffective are those that are nondirective (use strategies that lack definite guidelines and are loosely organized), use behavior modification techniques that focus on incorrect targets (techniques that focus on the wrong problems or attaining the wrong goals), and emphasize punishment.[11]

The first principle suggests that more intensive treatment should be reserved for offenders who are considered higher risk. This is because high-risk offenders respond more positively to intensive treatment than do lower-risk cases who perform just as well or better in less intensive treatment. Examination of the types of offenders targeted by this study's multi-site programs reveals that participants tended to be young, male, first-felony offenders. Many of these offenders were drug-involved as well. Therefore, by virtue of age and gender, as well as the fact that many shock incarceration participants are drug-involved and would otherwise serve prison time, they appear to be relatively high-risk offenders.

The second principle requires that treatment programs target the criminogenic needs of offenders. Criminogenic needs are dynamic needs of offenders that, when addressed, reduce the likelihood of recidivism. Criminogenic needs may vary from individual to individual. Important criminogenic needs include substance abuse treatment, prosocial skill development, interpersonal problem-solving skills, and prosocial sentiment.

By and large, shock incarceration programs attempt to address criminogenic needs. Seven states incorporated substance abuse education/treatment; six states provided vocational training; six states included academic education; four states taught problem-solving or decision-making skills. Three states also provided intensive supervision upon release, which extended treatment/education to the community and sometimes provided job training and opportunities.

There are, however, additional program characteristics that may influence the effectiveness of programming. The length of the program itself is one. Four of the programs in the multi-site study were 90 days long. Others ranged from 90 to 180 days. It would appear that six months of substance abuse treatment and/or education is more likely to have a positive outcome than three months. In fact, researchers have reported that the length of drug treatment is related to successful outcome. This may be true of other program components as well. Programs that provide intensive supervision upon release as treatment opportunities may more effectively address criminogenic needs.

Another important component that may influence programming is the voluntary nature of the program. In some programs participation was completely voluntary. Offenders must have volunteered to participate and could drop out of the program at any time. In others, participation was mandatory. Offenders were forced to participate and were not permitted to drop out voluntarily. It has been hypothesized that offenders who volunteer to participate in shock incarceration possess a greater sense of control than those for whom participation is mandatory. A sense of control may consequently lead to higher levels of commitment to the program.

The third principle, responsivity, outlines styles or modes of effective treatment that are components of effective treatment programs. Effective styles of treatment use firm but fair approaches to discipline, anti-criminal modeling, and concrete problem solving. Workers in these programs "relate to offenders in interpersonally warm, flexible, and enthusiastic ways, while also being clearly supportive of anti-criminal, attitudinal and behavioral patterns. Furthermore, effective programs must be cognizant of the fact that individual characteristics may interact with treatment style or mode of delivery. For example, highly anxious individuals are not as likely to benefit from stressful, interpersonal confrontation as would less anxious individuals.

What is most evident from the media reports and visits to boot camp prisons, though, is confrontation (e.g., drill sergeants screaming at inmates). Although staff and inmates directly involved in the programs say the discipline and staff authority is firm and relatively fair, outsiders who view the program, and some program dropouts, accuse the staff of domination and abusive behavior. Program staff generally attempt to act as anti-criminal models, reinforcing anti-criminal styles of thinking, feeling, and acting. However, few programs hire psychologists or others experienced in behavior modification techniques who are intimately involved in the training of staff.

Shock incarceration programs provide a combination of punitive and rehabilitative program elements that are expected (in many programs) both to deter and to rehabilitate. The basic program model contains the more punitive elements including hard work, physical training, and military drill and ceremony. These elements may have some positive value. For example, they may promote physical health, a drug-free environment, and a sense of accomplishment. However, it is unlikely that any of the individual programs' components will lead to increased discipline, accountability, or improved work habits as frequently hypothesized. Based on previous research on deterrence, it is also unlikely that they will have a deterrent effect.

Rehabilitative programming in shock incarceration programs has received increased emphasis over the years. If the basic military model is viewed primarily as a catalyst for personal change, rehabilitative programming is of great importance because the other benefits of the program are minimal and, most importantly, are not related to recidivism.

Examination of the three guiding principles of effective treatment, however, reveals that shock incarceration programs probably do not maximize their treatment potential. Although rehabilitative programming attempts to target criminogenic needs, the effects of such programming is mediated by the responsivity principle, which stipulates that treatment is most effective when counselors relate to offenders in a warm and supportive manner and provide anti-criminal modeling and problem solving. Thus, although staff may try to provide anti-criminal modeling, the authoritarian atmosphere may not be conducive to effective treatment. The following sections discuss the effectiveness of boot camp programs in changing inmate attitudes, recidivism, and positive activities in the community upon release.

Attitude Change

A frequent assumption made regarding incarceration is that the pains of imprisonment will be accompanied by the harms of imprisonment. That is, the pains of imprisonment lead to negative attitudes toward prison, staff, and programs (i.e., prisonization), thus prison will have a detrimental impact on offenders.

Inmates are hypothesized to form a "society of captives" characterized by anti-staff attitudes. As a consequence, offenders just reject constructive aspects of the prison such as treatment or education programs that may give them the skills needed to succeed when they return to the community.

An equally destructive influence of incarceration may be the development (or exacerbation) of general antisocial attitudes. Reviews of the evaluation literature indicate a positive association between antisocial attitudes and criminal activities. Most theories of crime also recognize the significance of criminal cognitions or attitudes.

The impact of shock incarceration on inmate attitudes has not yet been fully explored. It has been hypothesized that the boot camp environment, with its strict rules, discipline, and regimentation, may increase the pains of imprisonment and as a result promote the development of increased anti-staff, anti-program, and antisocial attitudes. According to this view, the regimental routine may have a negative impact on participants. Offenders may leave the boot camp prison angry, disillusioned, and more negative that they would have been had they served time in a traditional prison.

On the other hand, the negative effect of the regimented routine may be offset or mediated by the rehabilitative programming required of inmates. As discussed earlier, though, the amount of daily routine varied among programs in this study. In New York's boot camp program, with its emphasis on rehabilitation, inmates may have developed more antisocial or anti-program/staff attitudes. Changes in inmate attitudes, then, may vary as a function of the type of program. Offenders graduating from more treatment-oriented programs may not change at all or may change in a positive direction, while offenders graduating from programs that emphasize work and physical training may develop more negative attitudes over time.

The impact of boot camp prisons on inmate attitudes during incarceration (attitudes toward the program/staff and antisocial attitudes) was assessed in this phase of the evaluation. The attitudes of offenders serving time in the shock incarceration programs were compared with the attitudes of demographically similar offenders serving time in traditional prisons. Attitudes toward the shock incarceration program (or prison) and antisocial attitudes were assessed once after the offenders arrived at the boot camp (or prison) and again three to six months later, depending upon the length of the shock incarceration program. Programs differed in critical dimensions, such as the emphasis placed on rehabilitation, the voluntary nature of the program, and program difficulty-dimensions that might be expected to influence attitudinal change.

The researchers opined that boot camp entrants became more positive about the boot camp experience over the course of the programs. In contrast, prison inmates either did not change or developed more negative attitudes toward their prison experience. In addition, there was no evidence that attitudinal change varied as a function of the type of boot camp.

When the antisocial attitudes were measured, there were no differences between boot camp inmates and prison inmates. Both types of inmates became less antisocial during their time in confinement.

Changes in attitudes may also be related to the characteristics of the program, such as the amount of time devoted to rehabilitation versus work and physical training, the number of offenders dismissed from the program, and the voluntary nature of the program. Neither time devoted to rehabilitation nor voluntary exit was significantly related to program attitude. However, time devoted to rehabilitation, program rigor, and voluntariness appeared to lead to greater reductions in antisocial attitudes.

Despite differences among the programs in content and implementation, the results of this study were surprisingly consistent. Boot camp inmates became more positive about the program over time, while offenders serving prison time did not develop more positive attitudes. Both groups reflected less antisocial attitudes over time. This was true of enhanced boot camp programs that emphasized treatment as well as programs that emphasized military training, hard labor, and discipline.

The finding of the study that boot camp inmates and prison inmates become less antisocial during incarceration supports some current research indicating that prison may have some positive influence on some inmates. However, it is important to remember that these offenders were different from the general prison population. By and large, they were young and had been convicted of relatively minor offenses.

Recidivism

One of the first questions asked about boot camp programs is, "Are they successful?" By successful, many people mean, "Do they reduce the criminal activity of offenders subsequent to release?" The researchers concluded that the impact of boot camp programs on offender recidivism is at best negligible. The results suggest that offenders who are released from shock incarceration programs appear to perform just as well as those who serve longer prison terms. Accordingly, longer prison terms do not serve as an additional deterrent.

Shock incarceration programs are still experimental. The researchers concluded that it would be irresponsible to continue placing offenders (particularly juveniles) in such programs without more carefully monitoring their effects at both the individual- and system-levels. If success is measured in terms of recidivism alone, there is little evidence that the in-prison phase of boot camp programs have been successful.

Are boot camp programs successful in achieving their objectives? Programs that clearly defined their major objectives, such as those that had two major objectives—reducing prison crowding and changing offenders were the most effective. These programs were most effective in reducing prison crowding. The results examining the effectiveness of the programs in changing offenders are less positive. There is evidence that some positive things happened during the in-prison phase of the programs. There is little evidence, however, that the programs have had the desired effect of reducing recidivism and improving the positive activities of offenders who successfully completed the program.

Article

COMMUNITY SERVICE: A REVIEW OF THE BASIC ISSUES[12]

Introduction

It is clear that the use of community service as a sentencing alternative is a major judicial and correctional trend in the United States. In part driven by tax-limiting initiatives such as propositions 13 in California and 2.5 in Massachusetts, community service seemingly has high potential in the continued search for more effective and less costly methods of dealing with offenders. The trend toward community service is driven by economic considerations brought about by the efforts to balance the federal budget. These efforts forecast that there will be a reduction in federal funds available to states, counties, and municipalities that will impact the criminal justice systems generally and correctional systems specifically.

In addition to these economic influences, the prospects for community service were significantly bolstered by enactment of the Federal Comprehensive Crime Control Act of 1984, effective November 1, 1987, which states:

If sentenced to probation, the defendant must also be ordered to pay a fine, make restitution, and/or work in community service.

Changes and directions in the federal correctional system—probation, parole, and institutions—have often established trends for corrections at state and local levels.

The definition of *community service* varies in the professional literature, but for purposes of this commentary, it is a court order that an offender perform a specified number of hours of uncompensated work or service within a given time period for a nonprofit community organization or tax-supported agency. It clearly is distinguished from monetary restitution to the victim or payment of a fine to a political jurisdiction: restitution and fine, as in the federal legislation noted above, also may be part of a court order. In a generic sense, community service has been labeled as "restitution"—a sanction imposed by an official of the criminal justice system requiring an offender to make a payment of money or service to either the direct or a substitute crime victim. Community service has had other labels, among them court referral, reparation, volunteer work, symbolic restitution, service restitution, and, for those individuals who perform community service without an adjudication of guilt, pretrial diversion and pretrial intervention.

More pragmatically, however, the specific use of community sanctions is of recent origin, emerging conceptually in England in the late 1960s and operationally in 1972, with Parliament granting the courts authority to order convicted offenders to perform community service. Within just a few years, the program was expanded in England and introduced into the United States and Canada.

Considerable literature on this sentencing and correctional alternative has been generated since that time, and at least two major bibliographies are now available which reflect that growing interest.

There are several issues that should be carefully reviewed prior to the decision to begin community service as a sentencing alternative or enhancement. The purpose of this article is to review the more significant issues and the options available to the judicial and correctional decision makers as each issue is examined. The issues include, but are not limited to, offender eligibly, criteria for selection, organizational models for community service, community service investigations, sentencing considerations, assignments to community service programs, supervision, and evaluation.

Judicial and Correctional Philosophy

Community service, as with any other sanction, should support the overall philosophical orientation of the criminal justice system and its judicial and correctional decision makers specifically. That philosophical orientation—whether it be rehabilitation, restitution, deterrence, retribution, punishment, or something else, singly or in combination—should be translated into community service program goals, objectives and orientation. Simply stated, operational decisions should be developed from some shared understandings about community service as a sentencing alternative—an alternative to confinement, fines, restitution, and/or other traditional penalties, with special attention focused upon the offender and the community. Operationally, a community service program may be developed to increase the penalty to an appropriate level of deterrence (just desert). Such programs may marginally repay the community for criminal damages by helping the community meet its needs for unpaid workers (e.g., highway cleanup, school maintenance, etc.).

It is not our purpose to argue here what the purposes for community service should be, but it is important to emphasize the need for decision makers to specify why community service would be a useful sentencing alternative for them. If they state the goals that they seek, they can design programs to achieve these goals.

Offender Eligibility

Community service has been utilized mostly by the lower courts for individuals convicted of offenses considered less serious, especially misdemeanors, including traffic violations. An option to be considered is the use of community service for more serious offenders. Within the federal system, even apart from the Comprehensive Crime Control Act requirements, community service has been ordered for white-collar and corporate offenders, and even for corporations. The inclusion of felons, in addition to misdemeanants, appears a rational expansion of community service, providing that the threat to community safety is always considered and minimized. The issue of dangerousness clearly is a critical correctional issue.

Concerns about dangerousness may be reflected in mandated exceptions to the utilization of community service for people (1) committing certain types of offenses, (2) exhibiting particular traits or characteristics in their background, such as drug addiction, or (3) committing offenses with weapons or violence. Indeed, as the question of offender eligibility is considered, it may be appropriate to consider whether there is any reason why individuals entering into, or being processed through, the criminal justice system, who otherwise are deemed appropriate for a judicial or correctional release to the community, should be barred from community service. This would include adults and juveniles, felons, misdemeanants, probationers, parolees, individuals, corporations, those convicted of offenses and those diverted from the justice system.

Selection for Community Service

Selection for community service requires a dual focus: on the offender and on the community. In considering individuals, explicit and objective criteria are necessary to prevent in community service the sentencing disparities that have been so well-documented nationwide in other sentencing options. It has been noted that "the lack of standards or guidelines means that similar offenders can receive very different community service sentences for the same offense from a given judge, from two judges in the same jurisdiction, or from judges in different jurisdictions."

Allegations that community service sentences are applied in an unfair or discriminatory fashion also flow from a lack of criteria. The question of equity assuredly will surface if the community service sanction is applied only to the poor and the minorities or, contrastingly, only to middle- or upper-income offenders.

In determining selection criteria, assigning an offender to community service requires attention to community safety, to the offender's attitude and special skills or talents, to the seriousness of the offense, to the availability of a suitable community service placement, and to the wisdom of selecting other sentencing alternatives. As the community is examined, several other important issues emerge, including the public's attitude toward specific offenses and offenders, as well as the impact of community service on perceptions of the justice system by the citizenry. It is important that the public see community service as both a benefit to the community and a reasonable judicial disposition of the offender.

The process by which the criteria are established may be as important as the criteria themselves. It has been suggested that a "core group of advocates" consisting perhaps of members of the judiciary, corrections, and the community, join together to establish the standards for selection to community service.

Organizational Issue

A community service program of any size requires some administrative structure. The two most common administrative entities are the probation agency and a volunteer bureau. There may also be a combined effort in which the probation agency has some oversight of those functions that are uniquely offender-connected within the volunteer bureau. In this case, the probation office and the private organization have mutually supportive and compatible roles. A third type of administrative entity is the private organization created solely for the purpose of overseeing community service activities. An example of this third type is the Foundation for People, a nonprofit corporation established in Los Angeles under the aegis of the Probation Office of the U.S. District Court for the Central District of California. One of its several activities is to work with the federal courts to arrange community service for white-collar offenders and assist in the vocational training, counseling, and job-placement of blue-collar offenders.

There are several important distinctions that enter into the issue of the probation agency, volunteer bureau, or other entity providing the organizational structure for community service. The probation agency and the volunteer bureau are established in the community and have important connections with other organizations that already play a role in community-based corrections, which could serve as the foundation for the community service function. Probation, as an established part of the criminal justice system, can provide a legitimacy and stability to a community service program and affect both judicial and community acceptance. Volunteer bureaus long have been involved in identifying and matching community needs with individuals able to offer a variety of services.

Regardless of the agency charged with the community service function, it is assumed in this writing that the order to community service is usually a condition of probation. However, it may be appropriate for community service to be ordered by the court without probation, particularly for less serious offenses, and in those smaller jurisdictions in which the court has continuous firsthand contact with the agency providing the community service function. The organization with the administrative responsibility must be able to provide some form of community service investigation, discussed below, as well as to supervise community service. Therefore, it must have the authority to insure compliance with the court order.

In making an organizational decision, there is a need to focus on two basic functions: developing a plan to join offenders with community service and supervising these offenders in that service obligation.

These functions parallel the traditional investigation and supervision functions of probation, but this similarity is not to be interpreted as a preference for the probation agency option. Let us examine these functions separately.

The Community Service Investigation

The community service investigation is similar to a presentencing investigation and report. This investigation determines the appropriateness of community service as a sanction. A number of important issues surface in a community service investigation and report, especially in the development of a plan for community service. Some of the issues are:

- What constitutes an appropriate community service investigation?

- What is an appropriate format for a community service report?

- Should there be an investigation and report on all individuals eligible to receive a community service sentence or only on specific individuals? If the latter, is it at the direction of the court, the discretion of the probation agency or volunteer bureau, or upon request by the prosecutor, the defendant, or the defense attorney?

- Should a community service investigation and report be separate from, an adjunct to, or part of the formal presentence investigation and report? Indeed, for some minor offenses, would a community service investigation and report be an appropriate substitute for a presentence investigation and report? How much (additional) time should be allowed for the investigation, the preparation of a report, and the development of an appropriate plan?

- Does the community service investigation and report require a "specialist," familiar with the community and its needs, who is able to connect offender and community?

- Should the community service investigation and report be conducted before or after the imposition of a community service requirement?

- Should the agency responsible for the investigation and report also be charged with supervision of the community service?

- From an administrative perspective, how many community service investigations and reports are the equivalent of a presentence investigation and report?

Some Sentencing Considerations

The addition of community service as a sentencing alternative creates several unique issues for the court. Obviously, traditional considerations relating to the imposition of sentence remain, such as the concern for justice, equity, protection of the community, and rehabilitation. If there is an order of community service in lieu of confinement in a local custodial facility, a question of equivalence arises. How many hours of community service are the equivalent of a day in custody? Is it a day-for-a-day, two for one, three for one, or some other ratio? If it is a day-for-a-day, then is the equivalent of a 30-day jail sentence 30 eight-hour days of community service, or 90 eight-hour days? In the interest of fairness and equity, these ratios need to be established.

If on the other hand, the court wishes to impose community service instead of a fine—perhaps because the offender simply will be unable to pay a fine—what is the dollar equivalent of an hour of community service work? Is it minimum wage, the prevailing wage in the community, or is it equal to the offender's normal hourly rate—perhaps $4 an hour for one offender and $25 an hour for another? Is it more equitable to have a uniform "equivalency" or to have equivalency individualized? If the latter, one of these offenders could work off a $1,000 community service obligation with 250 hours of service; the other could accomplish the same in 100 hours.

Community service can be thought of as providing some of the equity that is credited to the day-fine principle pioneered in Scandinavia and now found in several other nations, including Austria and Germany. Under this principle, an offender is sentenced to a fine of his or her earnings for a given number of days, so that the amount of money involved varies with the size of the earnings. As administered in Sweden, the fine is collected by that country's equivalent of our Internal Revenue Service, which collects all taxes or other money owed to the government. This agency determines the amount of the fine from its records of the offender's past taxable earnings, deducts an amount for necessities and dependents, but imposes some fine-per-day of the penalty, even on those whose only income is from welfare. They collect almost every fine without jailing by allowing installment payments with interest for those who cannot pay immediately, but attaching salaries and even seizing possessions if there is a persistent failure to pay. Our courts, by imposing a penalty of a specified number of days of community service, are getting the same amount of service from each offender punished in this way, regardless of contrasts in the price that the services of different persons command per day when compensated in the free market.

It seems essential that the court fix both the precise number of hours of community service to be performed and the period of time during which the obligation is to be completed. Regardless of whether the number of hours was determined by the nature of the offense or the background of the offender, some other "arithmetic" needs to be completed. That arithmetic must focus on the balance between the number of hours to be performed and the length of time given for completion of community service. An order for 400 hours of community service approximately equals one day, or perhaps two evenings, of service per week for a year. Is that a reasonable assessment when examining all of the factors the offense, the offender, the offender's family and employment obligations, the community's needs for the service to be performed, and the feeling that "justice was done"? Or would 400 hours of community service over two years be more appropriate, considering all of the variables?

One last numeric item: there seemingly should be both a minimum and maximum number of hours that can be ordered. It is assumed that there is some number of hours below which the administrative burden to the agencies involved in the delivery of community services would be inefficient and ineffective, and a number above which the offender could not hope to comply with the order. While we do not intend to be prescriptive here, the courts need to establish a meaningful range; perhaps from a 30-hour minimum, equivalent to one day a week for one month for a minor offense or offender, to as much as 400 hours per year for five years, a total of 2,000 hours of service, for the most serious offense or offender that still would permit imposition of a community-based correctional alternative.

Community Service Assignments

Following an investigation and report, and an order by the court for community service, there is a requirement to assign the offender to a specific community activity. As noted, this assignment may be made through a probation agency, volunteer bureau, or other organization designated to administer the community service effort. There are two basic perspectives about the assignment issue: the first argues for a matching offenders with community service based on the skills or talents of the offender and the documented needs of the community. An often-cited example is the assignment of a physician ordered to perform community service to a program in which medical skills may be utilized, such as a public health or "free" medical clinic of some sort. This kind of matching of abilities and needs may or may not seem as appropriate. A second type of matching attempts to connect the community service assignment to the offense committed. For example, the assignment of an offender without medical service skills convicted of driving under the influence to a hospital emergency room—where there is considerable opportunity to see the harm done by drinking drivers— may not provide much relevant service, but it may serve as a good deterrent.

An alternative to these two types of matching is the more or less random assignment of offenders to community activities as offenders become available through the system and community needs are identified. Simply put, if two or three projects are identified as valid community needs requiring the services of 25 individuals, one assigns to these projects the next 25 offenders ordered to community service by the court, regardless of the number of hours ordered or the special abilities of the offenders. Offenders may be allowed to request participation in one or another of the community services identified. This method has the advantage of simplicity, and perhaps some basic equity, although it is clear that the hypothetical physician mentioned above is not providing the most meaningful service to the community, particularly if the community service project at that time is clearing trash from the side of the road.

All approaches require basic data about the offense, offender, and the community service requirements, but the matching approach—in contrast to randomness—requires considerably more data about these matters. Personal data about skills and abilities are needed, as is related information about employment schedules, indicating hours of the day and days of the week available for service, and special clothing or other needed equipment. Indeed, systems involved in matching also require considerable specificity about the nature of the tasks to be accomplished and the skills required of the offender for their accomplishment. A large matching system most likely would be computer-based, whereas a smaller system might simply use 3x5-inch index cards.

A number of other related issues surface about the assignment phenomena: what agencies are eligible to receive community service? Agencies with a religious orientation or involvement might be ineligible because of perceived violations of the doctrine of separation of church and state, while assignments to political organizations, public interest or pressure groups, or controversial collectivities of citizens create other problems. Then, too, there are special problems associated with organized labor and with some citizen perceptions that community service deprives "honest citizens" of employment opportunities. Even apart from the issue of legitimacy of organizations to receive services, there are questions as to whether such community services should be provided to individuals as opposed to organizations. . . for example, to individual victims of crime.

Supervision of Community Service

The supervision function, whether performed by a probation agency, volunteer bureau, or other organization, also raises some significant issues. Among them are questions that focus on disclosure about the offender, the offense, and personal background to the community organization receiving the offender's service. Is there a reverse side of that coin that assures the offender at least a minimum right to privacy? And during the time that the offender is performing community service, does the community service sponsoring agency—the volunteer bureau, for example—have some degree of liability for the offender's behavior? If the offender is injured while performing community service, are there disability rights vested in that service? And should individuals sponsoring community service activities have personal insurance to protect them against a variety of potential legal actions that may grow from the connection to community service? While the charging of fees to offenders for probation services has been emerging nationwide, would it be appropriate for similar charges to be extended for community service investigations and supervision? Finally, would it be appropriate for the tax-supported agencies or the nonprofit community organizations receiving community services to pay the court for the services received?

Apart from these issues, there are more traditional questions about community service supervision, ranging from the identification of those who provide it, the frequency of contact with the offender and the community service supervisor or agency, the nature and schedule of reports, reassignment determinations, and the overall relationship between probation supervision and community service supervision, particularly if two separate agencies are involved.

Under some circumstances, there may be important questions raised about compliance with the community service court order. What constitutes a violation: would it be a failure to complete all of the assigned hours in the prescribed time or, in the shorter time frame, a failure to appear to perform service on one or more occasions? Would a belligerent or disruptive attitude warrant cessation of a community service order? Probation and parole supervision long have had explicit conditions or standards of behavior. Is there a need for a parallel series of community service guidelines for those involved in both the supervision and performance of community service?

Evaluation of Community Service

At a minimum, two areas of community service need assessment: the first centers on measures of offender success and failure; the second upon some determination of cost-benefits. The cost-benefit analyses must consider both the criminal justice system and the community. In short, effectiveness and efficiency are required targets for analysis.

Definitions of success and failure for offenders involved in the many varieties of community corrections long have been troublesome.

Although we do not address that conflicted arena here, we note that community service does not make those assessments simpler, but rather more complex. An overall evaluation should go beyond that which could be generated by data as to whether or not the offender completed the required number of hours of community service within the court-ordered period of time.

Several examples may illustrate the complexity. The first focuses on the definition of success and failure by asking how the two are related in probation and community service. Consider an offender who successfully completes a court-ordered community service obligation but is declared in violation of probation for behavior that is not related to the community service. How is the offender's overall performance to be assessed?

If costs are the focus of evaluation, two different sets of cost data may be examined. The first may be the value of services provided the community, calculated at some arbitrary hourly or daily rate such as the national minimum wage or an average local wage. The overall dollar value of the services provided are the number of hours of service multiplied by the value of those hours for a given period of time. A second set of data may be derived from the "savings" obtained by having offenders provide community service instead of being in local custody. This may be calculated as the daily custodial rate multiplied by the number of confinement days not served minus the cost of community service. It is probable that estimates of monies saved by the justice system from the non-incarceration of offenders who are performing community service may be markedly different from estimates of the value of the community service developed from hourly or daily wage comparisons, and that the two might be added. This difference would grow if calculated to include welfare assistance given to families of confined offenders. If community service serves as an alternative to the capital costs of constructing a custodial facility, the savings, even when prorated in some fashion, become enormous. If these community services generate activities and projects which otherwise might not have been accomplished—that is, things which the community could not have done without these court ordered services—perhaps some other dollar equivalents would be justified.

Finally, improvements in community feelings about "justice" generally and the criminal justice system specifically on one hand, or the improvement of the offender's personal feelings of self worth which may be generated from performing a service to the community on the other, cannot be measured readily, but nevertheless need assessment.

Summary

Community service, as a sentencing option, has an operational history of about 15 years. There is every reason to believe that its utilization in America and elsewhere will expand significantly during the next decade. Because it has evolved and grown so rapidly, there has not yet been adequate time or attention given to identifying the issues that surround its use or to develop standards for that use. Indeed, there is some evidence of a failure to understand that the many issues that have been or yet may be identified are completely interrelated.

The authors have not been prescriptive, but would argue that there is a mandate to examine carefully a number of issues about community service. Some of these have been identified—judicial and correctional philosophies, offender eligibility and selection criteria, organizational arrangements, community service investigations and supervision, sentencing considerations, community service assignments, and evaluation. If community service is to become a truly viable sentencing option, these areas need thoughtful consideration by those academicians, administrators, practitioners, and researchers concerned with criminal justice.

{End of Article}

SUMMARY

Diversion is designed to funnel the offender away from the criminal justice system and into community programs that should be more beneficial than incarceration. Diversion is frequently used to refer to the release of the accused pending trial. In the late 1960s and 1970s, it was a popular concept. Diversion is based on the assumption that the individual diverted will participate in some treatment program in return for the removal from the criminal justice system process before trial. Diversion is commonly referred to as the "front door" program, because it limits the number of people entering jail or prison facilities.

Since their inception in 1983, shock incarceration/probation programs, also known as boot camps, have enjoyed considerable popular support. Like other intermediate sanctions, the programs are intended to alleviate institution overcrowding and to reduce recidivism. In addition, because they are perceived as being "tough" on crime, in contrast to some other intermediate sentences such as probation, they have been enthusiastically embraced as a viable correctional option for delinquent youths. In addition, the presumed combination of cost savings and punitiveness has proven irresistible to politicians.

As boot camp programs have developed, rehabilitative programming has come to play a more prominent role in the day-to-day routine. The earliest boot camp models devoted little time to such programs. Many of those pioneering programs have since been enhanced with additional therapeutic services. Programs developed in recent years seemed to place a greater emphasis on rehabilitative programing from the start.

It is clear that the use of community service as a sentencing alternative is a major judicial and correctional trend in the United States. In part, driven by tax-limiting initiatives such as propositions 13 in California and 2.5 in Massachusetts, community service seemingly has high potential in the continued search for more effective and less costly methods of dealing with offenders. The trend toward community service also is driven by economic considerations brought about by efforts to balance the federal budget. These efforts forecast that there will be a reduction in federal funds available to states, counties, and municipalities that will impact the criminal justice systems generally and correctional systems specifically.

DISCUSSION QUESTIONS

1. Explain the concept behind shock incarceration.

2. How does shock incarceration differ from prison?

3. Explain the concept behind diversion.

4. What are the advantages of diversion for the defendant? Disadvantages?

5. How successful have shock incarceration programs been?

6. What are the three psychological principles considered in determining the appropriate treatment of an offender?

ENDNOTES FOR CHAPTER 4

1. National Advisory Commission on Criminal Justice Standards and Goals, *Courts* (Washington, D.C.: Government Printing Office, 1973).

2. "Multisite Evaluation of Shock Incarceration: Evaluation Report," *National Institute of Justice Research Report*, November, 1994.
Note: this section is an abridgement of the report and the conclusions noted are those of the researchers.

3. R. Lot, R. Regal, and R. Raymond, "Delinquency and Special Deterrence, " *Criminology*, Vol. 15, Part 4, pp. 539-547 (1978).

4. J.O. Fickenauer, *Scared Straight! And the Panacea Phenomenon* (Englewood Cliffs, NJ: Prentice-Hall, 1992.)

5. P. Gendreau and R.R. Ross, "Revivication of Rehabilitation: Evidence From the 1980s," *Justice Quarterly*, Vol. 4, pp. 349-408 (1987).

6. E. Zamble and F. Porporino, "Coping, Imprisonment, and Rehabilitation: Some Data and Their Implications," *Criminal Justice Behavior*, Vol. 17, No. 1, pp. 53-70 (1990).

7. Ibid.

8. R. Martinson, "What Works? Questions and Answers About Prison Reform," *Public Interest*, Vol. 35, pp 22-54 (1974).

9. D. A. Andrews, I. Zinger, R. D. Hoge, J. Bonta, P. Gendreau and F. T. Cullen, "Does Correctional Treatment Work? A Clinically Relevant and Psychologically Informed Meta-Analysis," *Criminology*, Vol. 28, No. 3, pp. 369-404 (1990).

10. D. A. Andrews, J. Bonta, and R. D. Hoge, "Classification for Effective Rehabilitative: Rediscovering Psychology," *Criminal Justice and Behavior*, Vol. 17, No. 1, pp. 19-52 (1990).

11. F. Cullen and P. Gendreau, "The Effectiveness of Correctional Rehabilitation: Reconsidering the 'Nothing Works' Debate," in L. Goodstein and D. L. Mackenzie (eds.), *The American Prison: Issues in Research and Policy* (New York: Plenum Press, 1989.)

12. Robert M. Carter, Jack Cocks, and Daniel Glaser, "Community Service: A Review of the Basic Issues," *Federal Probation*, March, 1987, pp. 4-10. Reprinted with permission (notes omitted).

Checking in with your probation officer is a must.

PROBATION

Intensive supervision
  probation

Jail therapy

Probation

Regular probation

Revocation of probation

Shock probation

Split sentencing

Technical probation

CHAPTER OBJECTIIVES

After studying this chapter, the reader will be able to:

☐ Explain why probation is the most often used sanction for felony offenders.

☐ Identify what is involved with the granting of probation.

☐ List the four categories of probation.

☐ Explain the contributions of John Augustus to probation.

☐ Explain the philosophy involved in probation.

☐ Decribe the criteria for granting probation.

☐ List the usual condtions placed on defendants when they are placed on probation.

☐ Analyze the issues involved in determining what constitutional rights individuals on probation retain.

☐ Explain the two questions involved in revoking probation based on new criminal activity.

☐ Explain the functions of probation.

☐ Identify the popular philosophies in contemporary probation.

Probation refers to a conditional release of a defendant. Probation can have several different meanings within our present criminal justice system. *Probation* can be used to describe a sentence that has been given to a defendant in which the defendant is placed and maintained in the community under the supervision of an agent of the court.

1. Probation refers to a status or class (i.e., he or she is on probation and thus subject to certain rules and conditions that must be followed in order to avoid being institutionalized).

2. Probation also refers to an organization (i.e., the county probation department).

Once a defendant is found guilty, the most frequently used method of court disposition is probation. It is clear that not every defendant should be institutionalized. Nationwide, over 70 percent of all felony defendants who are convicted receive probation.

Probation is a disposition, which involves no confinement, or, at most, only a short period of confinement, under specific conditions. Under probation, the court retains authority over the case to supervise, modify the conditions, and resentence the defendant if the terms of probation are violated. Probation is a legal status created by the court. While the classic definition of probation as set forth above indicates that it does not involve commitment, it is being increasingly linked to a short period of commitment at a training school, boot camp, or other local custody facility.

Probation permits the defendant to remain in his or her community under the supervision of a probation officer. Probation usually involves:

1) A judicial finding that the defendant is guilty

2) The imposition of conditions upon the defendant's continued freedom

3) The provisions of means of helping him or her meet these conditions and for determining the degree to which he or she needs them

Probation is more than giving the defendant another chance. Its central thrust is to give him or her positive assistance in adjustment in the free community.[1]

Probation may generally be classified in four different categories:

1. Regular probation

2. Intensive probation

3. Deferred adjudication probation

4. Pretrial diversion probation[2]

Deferred adjudication and pretrial diversion were discussed in Chapter 1. *Regular probation* is defined as the release of a convicted offender under conditions imposed by the courts for a specified period of time. *Intensive supervision probation* is for offenders who are too antisocial for the relative freedom afforded by regular probation yet not so seriously criminal to require incarceration. Approximately 40 states have some form of intensive supervision probation.[3]

HISTORY OF PROBATION

John Augustus of Boston is considered the originator of the concept of probation. As early as 1841, Augustus, a private citizen, requested that Boston judges release young defendants under his supervision. It is estimated that over an 18-year period, he supervised about 2,000 individuals on probation. Most of these were youths age 16 to 19. He helped them get jobs and reestablish them in the community. Only a few of the individuals under his supervision became involved in subsequent criminal behavior.

John Augustus was born in Burlington, Massachusetts in 1785. He moved to Lexington about 1806 and established a shoe factory in his home. About 1820, he established a shoe factory in Boston. Apparently in 1829, he moved from Lexington to Boston. His Boston shop at 5 Franklin Street was near the police court. It was at this shop, according to him, that he received frequent calls for individuals seeking his help.

It appears that it was the Washington temperance movement that first led Augustus to visit the police court and later the municipal court in Boston. The movement resulted in the formation of the Washington Total Abstinence Society in Boston in 1841. The society's members pledged not only to refrain from using intoxicating drinks but also to restore to temperance those who were addicted to alcohol. The members visited the police court and attempted to rescue the drunks.

Augustus's first probation experience was in August 1841. Set forth below is his description of the experience:

> In the month of August 1841, I was in court one morning, when the door communicating with the lock-room was opened and an officer entered, followed by a ragged and wretched looking man. . . I imagined from the man's appearance that his offence was that of yielding to his appetite

for intoxicating drinks. . . the man was charged with being a common drunkard. The case was clearly made out, but before sentence had been passed, I conversed with him a few moments, and found that he was not yet past all hope and reformation, although his appearance and his looks precluded a belief in the mind of others that he would ever become a man again. . . I bailed him, by permission of the Court. He was ordered to appear for sentence in three weeks from that time. He signed a pledge and became a sober man; at the expiration of this period of probation, I accompanied him into the court room; his whole appearance was changed and no one, not even the scrutinizing officers, could have believed that he was the same person who less than a month before, had stood trembling on the prisoner's stand. The Judge expressed himself much pleased with the account we gave of the man, and instead of the usual penalty, imprisonment in the House of Corrections, he fined him one cent and costs.[4]

Augustus continued to appear in court to receive on probation alcoholics who appeared likely prospects for rehabilitation. From 1841 until his death in 1859, his ! ome became a refuge for people he had bailed until more permanent places could be made for them.

Augustus's work inspired the Massachusetts legislature to authorize the hiring of a paid probation officer for Boston. By 1880, probation was extended to other jurisdictions within the state. Missouri and Vermont soon copied the Massachusetts procedures. The federal government established a probation system in 1925. By that date, most other states had also adopted similar systems.

STATUS OF PROBATION

Probation is based on the philosophy that the average defendant is not a violent dangerous criminal, but one that needs additional guidance in order to conform to society's demands. Probation generally involves the replacing of the defendant's commitment to a secure facility with a conditional release. Probation is essentially a contract between the defendant and the court. If the defendant complies with certain orders of the court (conditions of probation), the court will not require the defendant to be committed to a correctional facility. If the defendant later violates the terms of the contract, the court is no longer restricted by the contract and may commit the defendant to a correctional facility.

In some states, at the time the defendant is placed on probation, he or she is informed as to the terms of the commitment being probated. For example, the defendant may be committed to a state for 10 years with the commitment probated for five years. If the defendant stays out of trouble for five years, then the commitment is never served. If the defendant's probation is revoked, then the defendant is committed to serve his or her 10-year term.

In most states, the defendant is placed on probation for a certain period of time. If the probation is revoked, then the defendant receives a commitment the length of which is determined at a disposition hearing after the probation is revoked.

In some states, juries may recommend probation. However, even in those states where the juries may decide the punishment (e.g., Texas) only the judge may grant probation. Most states have restrictions on the granting of probation for certain serious or violent crimes. In addition, it appears that the death penalty may not be probated. This is based on the fact that the death penalty is limited to those cases in which the defendant is beyond rehabilitation and to probate the penalty would indicate that there is hope the defendant will be rehabilitated.

The length of the probation period may vary. A five-year period appears to be a common one for adult felony cases. In fact, the Federal Criminal Code recommends that federal probation periods last for five years. In juvenile cases, the period of probation is usually until the juvenile reaches the age of majority or 21 years of age.

In many adult cases, the judge grants probation only if the defendant agrees to serve a period of local time (jail). For example, one judge, as a matter of policy, will not grant probation in felony cases unless the accused does at least 30 days in the local jail. This practice is known as *split sentencing*.

Shock probation is frequently used in the case of first-time young offenders. In these cases, the judge grants probation only after the accused has sampled prison life. Shock probation is designed to give defendants a "taste of the bars" before placing them on probation. Evaluations of shock probation have indicated that shock probation's rate of effectiveness may be as high as 78 percent. Critics of shock probation claim that even a brief period of incarceration can reduce the effectiveness of probation, which is designed to provide the offender with non-stigmatized community-based treatment. The boot camp form of shock probation is discussed later in this text.

EXTENT OF PROBATION

There are approximately 1,900 probation agencies in the United States. About half are associated with a state-level agency and the remaining with county or city governments. Approximately 30 states have combined probation and parole agencies. While prison populations have been increasing at a rapid rate in the past 20 years, it appears that the number of people on probation has been increasing at an even faster rate. On any given day, there are approximately 1.8 million individuals in the United States on probation. Over 50 percent of those are under the age of 18. One of the reasons for the popularity of probation is its low cost. It costs less than $5.00 per day to maintain a defendant on probation.

CRITERIA FOR GRANTING PROBATION

Listed below is the recommended criteria for granting probation developed by the American Law Institute's Model Penal Code. The criteria is also used in many juvenile cases:

1. The court shall deal with a person who has been convicted of a crime without imposing sentence of imprisonment unless, having regard to the nature and circumstances of the crime and the history, character and condition of the defendant, it is of the opinion that his or her imprisonment is necessary for protection of the public because:

    a. There is undue risk that during the period of a suspended sentence or probation the defendant will commit another crime.

b. The defendant is in need of correctional treatment that can be provided most effectively by his or her commitment to an institution.

c. A lesser sentence will depreciate the seriousness of the defendant's crime.

2. The following grounds, while not controlling the direction of the court, shall be accorded weight in favor of withholding sentence of imprisonment:

a. The defendant's criminal conduct neither caused nor threatened serious harm.

b. The defendant did not contemplate that his or her criminal conduct would cause or threaten serious harm.

c. The defendant acted under a strong provocation.

d. There were substantial grounds tending to excuse or justify the defendant's criminal conduct, though failing to establish a defense.

e. The victim of the defendant's criminal conduct induced or facilitated its commission.

f. The defendant has compensated or will compensate the victim of his criminal conduct for the damage or injury that he sustained.

g. The defendant has no history of prior delinquency or criminal activity or has led a law-abiding life for a substantial period of time before the commission of the present crime.

h. The defendant's criminal conduct was the result of circumstances unlikely to recur.

i. The character and attitudes of the defendant indicate that he or she is unlikely to commit another crime.

j. The defendant is particularly likely to respond affirmatively to probationary treatment.

k. The imprisonment of the defendant would entail excessive hardship to the defendant or his or her dependents.

3. When a person has been convicted of a crime and is not sentenced to imprisonment, the court shall place him or her on probation if he or she is in need of the supervision, guidance, assistance or direction that the probation service can provide.

CONDITIONS OF PROBATION

A probated disposition is an act of clemency on the part of the court. Accordingly, in most states, the court may place conditions that restrict an individual's constitutional rights. For example, a judge may require the defendant to voluntarily submit to searches and/or drug testing when requested by the probation officer. Generally, there are two sets of conditions that are imposed on a probationer: standard conditions that are imposed on every probationer, and special conditions designed for a particular defendant. Set forth on the following page are the standard rules or conditions of probation used in the state of Texas. These are similar to those used in other states.

PROBATIONERS' RIGHTS

The courts have ruled that probationers (those on probation) have fewer constitutional rights than other citizens. The theory is that probation is an act of mercy by the courts, therefore certain conditions can be placed on individuals accepting probation.

The three major issues in probationers' rights are:

1) Search and seizure

2) Right of confidentiality

3) Revocation of rights

Search of Probationers

Courts have traditionally held that defendants on probation may be searched by their probation officers without the need for a warrant

Texas Code of Criminal Procedure, Article 42.12

1. Commit no offense against the laws of the state of Texas or of any other state or of the United States.
2. Avoid injurious or vicious habits.
3. Avoid persons or places of disreputable or harmful character.
4. Report to the probation officer as directed.
5. Permit the probation officer to visit him at his home.
6. Regularly attend school or work faithfully at suitable employment as far as possible.
7. Remain within the county unless travel outside the county is approved by probation officer.
8. Pay any fines imposed and make restitution or reparation in any sum that the Court deems proper.
9. Support your dependents.
10. Participate in any community-based program as directed by the court or probation officer.
11. Reimburse the county for any compensation paid to appointed defense counsel.
12. Compensate the victim for any property damage or medical expense sustained by the victim as a direct result of the commission of the offense.

or probable cause. The basis of the search is that the defendant, by accepting the conditions of probation, has consented to waive his or her rights against unreasonable searches and seizures as a condition of being granted probation. Some states, however, limit the right to search without warrant or probable cause to only probation officers and not to other law enforcement members. The courts have also held that probationers' homes may be searched without a warrant. The courts have also indicated that probationers may be required to consent to future searches as a condition of probation.

The courts have held that the probation officer-client relationship is not a confidential relationship and therefore, the probation officer may testify as to matters related to him or her in confidence by the probationer.

Revocation of Probation

Probation may be revoked by the court if the individual commits either a new crime or violates a technical condition of the probation. Technical violations are those violations that do not involve criminal misconduct. For example, failure to report to the probation officer as required is considered a technical violation of the probation contract. As a general rule, the courts will seldom revoke probation for technical violations unless the violations are frequent or constitute a threat to society.

Probation officers are also given alternatives to handle technical violations without referral to the court. In many cases, a warning to the probationer by the probation officer is sufficient to correct the problem. A more controversial alternative is that of *jail therapy*. Jail therapy is the act of placing the probationer in jail, then without holding a hearing, releasing the probationer after a short stay.

In most states, the probation officer may modify or recommend the modification of the conditions of probation if it appears that the conditions are impossible to meet, unreasonable, or inappropriate. For example, federal policy places a duty on the probation officer to request modification of the probation conditions when necessary to reduce risk or to assist the probationer's rehabilitation.[5]

Technical violations for which probation has been revoked include:

- Failure to pay off civil judgment for fraud
- Failure to make child support payments when probationer was able to do so
- Failure to report
- Associating with persons known not to be "law-abiding"

Even when the probationer commits a new crime, probation is not automatic. Generally probation officers are required to report to the court when the officer has knowledge that a probationer has committed a crime. In addition, in most cases the probation officer is required to make a recommendation regarding the issuance of a warrant and initiation of revocation proceedings. Federal policy provides:

A violation of any federal, state, or local law that is punishable by any term of imprisonment must be reported immediately to the court or Parole Commission. In making a recommendation regarding issuance of a warrant, the officer must consider the risk posed by the new offense behavior. If it appears that the violation represents a significant threat to community safety or signals a risk of flight, the officer should recommend the issuance of a warrant.[6]

Two questions are apparent when considering revocation of probation based on new criminal activity. If the revocation of probation is based solely on the commission of a new crime, should the court await the disposition of the new charge before revoking probation? If the probationer is acquitted or the criminal proceedings on the new charge are terminated prior to the government obtaining a conviction, can the conduct still be the sole basis to revoke the probation? Both the ABA *Standards Relating to Probation* and the National Advisory Commission Standards indicate that revocation of probation based solely on the commission of another crime should not occur until after the disposition of those charges. In most states, however, there are no statutory restrictions that require courts to delay revocation until the new charges are disposed of.

Disposition includes the court accepting a plea of guilty or *nolo contendere* and the finding by the court or jury of guilt. Disposition does not extend to final disposition because the appellate process can be quite lengthy. Both standards provide, however, that the court should have discretion to detain the probationer without bail while awaiting trial on the new charge involving a violent crime.

Revocation does not require the probationer to be found guilty in order to vacate the probation for criminal misconduct. In cases where the probationer is not convicted on the new charges, generally there are no constitutional or statutory grounds that prohibit the court from using the incident to vacate probation. In most cases, if the court or jury finds the probationer not guilty on the new charge or charges, the courts do not revoke probation solely on that misconduct. There are exceptions to this general rule, which are usually determined on a case-by-case basis. If the charges are dropped for other reasons, usually a case-by-case review is also used to determine if probation should be revoked.

Revocation of probation is possible after the term of probation has expired under certain circumstances. If a revocation warrant is issued prior to the expiration of the period of probation, the court may proceed within a reasonable time to revoke the probation. In addition, if the probationer has fled from supervision before the completion of the term of probation, when located, he or she generally is subject to revocation of probation. In many states, the statutes governing probation provide that the term of probation is tolled (ceases to expire) if the probationer is charged with new criminal misconduct, cannot be found, or flees the jurisdiction. In most states, the initiation of revocation proceedings also tolls the time period.

Before probation may be revoked, the probationer has certain procedural due process rights. Generally, when the probation officer makes the decision to revoke probation, the offender is notified and a formal hearing is scheduled. The rules for revoking probation and parole are generally the same. There are three major U.S. Supreme Court decisions in this area that pertain to adult probation, but would presumably apply also to juvenile probationers.

Mempa v. Rhay, decided by the court in 1967, held that a probationer was constitutionally entitled to counsel in a revocation of probation hearing in which the imposition of the sentence had been suspended. Most lower courts interpreted this case to apply only in those situations that involved deferred sentencing and not in those cases in which the probationer was sentenced at the time of trial. Accordingly, some jurisdictions provide counsel at revocation hearings and other jurisdictions do not. While this case involved an adult criminal case, it appears to be applicable also to juvenile probation revocations.

The Supreme Court in *Morrissey v. Brewer* required an informal hearing to determine if there is probable cause to believe that an individual on parole had violated the terms of his parole. If the informal hearing establishes probable cause of a parole violation, then a formal hearing needs to be held to determine if parole should be revoked. At

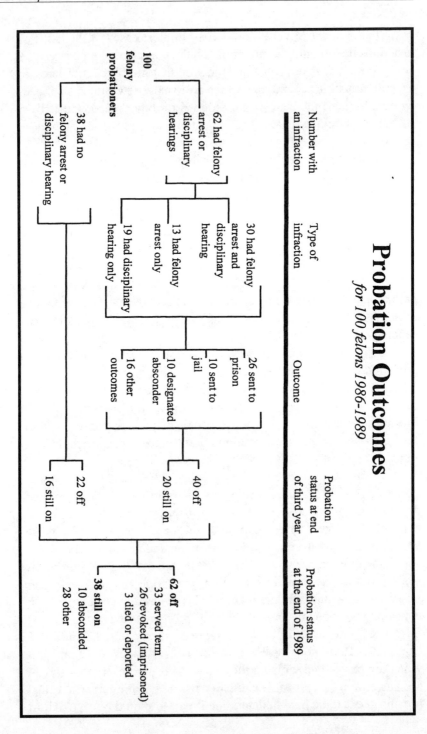

Probation Outcomes
for 100 felons 1986-1989

Number with
an infraction

Type of
infraction

Outcome

Probation
status at end
of third year

Probation status
at the end of 1989

**100
felony
probationers**

62 had felony
arrest or
disciplinary
hearings

38 had no
felony arrest or
disciplinary hearing

30 had felony
arrest and
disciplinary
hearing

13 had felony
arrest only

19 had disciplinary
hearing only

26 sent to
prison

10 sent to
jail

10 designated
absconder

16 other
outcomes

40 off

20 still on

22 off

16 still on

62 off
33 served term
26 revoked (imprisoned)
3 died or deported

38 still on
10 absconded
28 other

the formal hearing, the parolee has procedural due process rights. The lower courts have applied the *Brewer* case to probation revocations. [The *Morrissey v. Brewer* case is reprinted in Chapter 7.]

In *Gagnon v. Scarpelli*, the Supreme Court held that both probationers and parolees have a constitutionally limited right to counsel in revocation proceedings.[7] In many states, probationers and parolees have a right to counsel by state statute or court decision. For example, a California court announced as a judicially declared rule of criminal process that a probationer is entitled to representation of retained or appointed counsel at formal proceedings for the revocation of probation.[8] The rule set forth in *Gagnon* is that a case-by-case determination of the need for counsel is the sound discretion of the state authority responsible for administrating the probation and parole system. If the probationers or parolees dispute the key issues, and the issues can only be fairly presented by trained counsel, the appointment of counsel for indigent probationers or parolees should be made. The court also noted that participation by counsel will probably be most undesirable and unnecessary in most revocation hearings.

The state must prove an accused is guilty beyond a reasonable doubt in a criminal trial. Proof beyond a reasonable doubt requires that the jury or judge be fully satisfied, entirely convinced, or satisfied to a moral certainty. The standard of proof in a revocation hearing, however, is a preponderance of evidence. This is the same standard used in civil cases. A *preponderance of evidence* is defined as evidence that is of greater weight or more convincing than the evidence offered in opposition to it. This standard is much lower than required in a criminal trial.

FUNCTIONS OF PROBATION

As noted earlier, a probation department's primary goal is to provide services designed to help defendants overcome their problems and their environments. For probation to be successful, the reasons why the defendant came into contact with the justice system must be resolved, and the defendant must be reintegrated into the community. Probation is preferred over other forms of disposition for the following reasons:

- It allows the defendant to remain in the community and function at a fairly normal level while providing protection for the community against further law violations.

- It helps the defendant avoid the negative effects of institutionalization.

- Probation decreases the stigma of the labeling process, because the description of the crime is usually worded in a less severe manner than in those cases involving other dispositions.

- The rehabilitation program is facilitated by keeping the defendant in the community and living at home.

- Probation is much less expensive than institutionalization.

FUTURE OF PROBATION

Many individuals have voiced concerns regarding the placing of criminals on probation. Despite this, it appears that probation will continue as the most popular form of alternative sentencing available to judges. Part of the appeal of probation is based on its low cost and flexibility. There appears to be a trend to use probation in conjunction with community treatment programs.

PROBATION OFFICES

Generally there is a probation office for each court. In large urban areas, the probation offices of several courts may be merged into one office. The individual in charge of a probation office is normally called the "chief probation officer" (CPO). It is the duty of the CPO to carry out policy and to supervise the probation officers.

The probation officer's analysis of the defendant's personality and the development of a personality profile of the defendant occurs during the diagnosis functions. Diagnosis also involves the formulation of the treatment necessary to rehabilitate the juvenile (i.e., the PO diagnoses that the defendant has a drinking problem). The treatment supervision refers to the duties of the PO after the defendant has been placed on probation. During the treatment supervision phase, the PO should evaluate the effectiveness of the treatment programs ordered by the court.

GUIDING PHILOSOPHIES FOR PROBATION IN THE 21ST CENTURY[9]

Opinion polls conducted over the past several decades have consistently shown that while crime is viewed as an important public concern, it has not been ranked by the majority of Americans as the most pressing problem facing the country. Other concerns, including the economy and unemployment, have traditionally eclipsed citizens' anxieties about crime. Yet in January 1994, the public, for the first time in nearly 60 years of opinion polling, ranked crime as the nation's most important problem.

Public anxieties about crime and violence have been fueled by media attention and political rhetoric. In the process, enormous attention has been focused on responding to the problem by proposing measures that include hiring thousands of additional police officers, banning assault weapons, imposing strict sanctions for repeat offenders, and expanding prison capacity.

Despite all the attention paid to the justice system's response to crime, there has been little public discourse about the role the probation system is to play in the process. On one hand, the failure to consider the future of probation is understandable since researchers, policy makers, and the public have tended to ignore this vital component of the justice system. Conversely, however, the failure to plan for the future of probation seems a crucial oversight since about two-thirds of all offenders under correctional supervision are on probation. As the nation augments its police forces, sanctions more offenders, and prisons experience increased overcrowding, many authorities have suggested that even more offenders will be channeled into the probation system. There is already evidence of this trend, between 1984 and 1990, probation caseloads rose from 1.74 million people to 2.67 million people—a 53.4 percent increase. Hence, some scholars have proposed that "probation crowding" presents more of an immediate threat to both the criminal justice process and to community protection than does prison crowding.

Given these developments, there is a pressing need to consider thoughtfully the role that probation will play in managing crime and criminal offenders. More than anything else, there is a need to identify the philosophies that will guide probation as we prepare for the next millennium. The purpose of this article is to explore the direction that probation might take in the near future. To accomplish this, we have drawn from the probation literature and have identified apparent trends for the probation profession.

The Need for Articulating a Coherent Mission and Philosophy for Probation

If there has been a recurrent theme in the probation literature over the past few decades, it has been the compelling need for the profession to articulate a distinct mission and for agencies to define their responsibilities in accomplishing that mission. Scores of critics have noted that in the absence of developing an overriding philosophy, probation's very survival is in jeopardy. Identifying the mission of probation represents a crucial, threshold issue. Both theoretically and practically, everything that an agency seeks to accomplish flows from its mission. Succinctly stated, organizational mission statements, philosophies, and goals imbue agencies with a source of legitimacy, provide employees with a sense of direction and a source of motivation, enable agencies to set goals and form guidelines, and provide the foundation on which to establish performance criteria. On a more practical level, Clear and Latessa's work suggests that organizational philosophies and priorities are important forces in shaping the actual work strategies employed by officers.[10]

Despite the need to develop a clear-cut mission for probation, there has been considerable disagreement about the role that probation should, or can, play in the criminal justice process. At the risk of oversimplification, authorities have proposed probation models that range from control to case management to offender rehabilitation. Yet despite all that has been written, probation continues to be plagued by an uncertain mixture of goals and philosophies that incorporate, to varying degrees, all of these elements. To understand where probation appears to be headed in the future, it is instructive to review briefly its historical evolution, identify predominant philosophies that seem to be guiding probation today, and then to note some of the calls that have been made for reform.

The Evolution of Probation Philosophies

From its inception, and until at least the mid-1960s, probation was guided by a casework-type philosophical ideology. Under this mandate, the purpose of probation was to identify causal factors of the offender's behavior and to intervene so that the offender could reform his or her conduct and avoid further contact with the legal system. In effect, the control of crime was to be attained through treatment.

Beginning in the 1960s, questions were raised about the efficacy of the rehabilitative model in corrections. The publication of Lipton, Martinson, and Wilks celebrated study suggesting that "nothing works" all but sounded the death knell for the rehabilitative ideal in corrections.[11] In the wake of this now-famous study, authorities sought to identify other workable models for probation. Some, for example, suggested that probation officers should function as "resource brokers" for offenders under supervision. Under this mandate, probation officers were to assess offenders' needs and then channel them to social service agencies that could address those needs. Although mentioned infrequently in the literature, the brokerage approach seems to enjoy considerable support among probation officers today. Importantly, at the same time that probation was attempting to devise an appropriate alternative model, public support began to erode, skepticism about the ability of probation to control and rehabilitate offenders increased, and fiscal resources diminished.

Through the 1980s, a combination of factors contributed to an overcrowding crisis in prisons and jails across the nation. With the "war" on drugs, campaigns to crack down on drunk drivers, the enactment of harsher sentencing statutes, and efforts to constrict judicial discretion in sentencing, the per capita rate of offenders under correctional supervision rose to levels never encountered before in the history of the United States. As prison and jail populations swelled in response to the "get tough" approach on crime, even more offenders were subjected to probation supervision. Concurrently, highly publicized studies questioned whether probation was a viable sanction for felony offenders. In their study, for example, Petersilia et al. found that nearly two-thirds of those on felony probation were re-arrested.[12] In response, probation began to devise strategies to comport with prevailing public and political sentiments that suggested the need to protect society by closely monitoring and controlling probationers.

Popular Philosophies in Contemporary Probation

Although it would be impossible to identify any one philosophy that dominates probation today, it is possible to examine indicators of operant philosophies in contemporary probation. At perhaps the broadest level, one indicator of correctional philosophies may be found in those portions of each of the 50 states' legal codes that specify the approaches to be employed by departments when handling offenders. In their study of states' legal codes, Burton, Dunaway, and Kopache found that "by far, the major legislated correctional goal is rehabilitation." Burton and his colleagues qualified their findings in two ways, however. First, although rehabilitation is the most commonly prescribed correctional goal, recently enacted statutes tended to incorporate punitive goals. Second, Burton et al. noted that a majority of the states prescribed multiple goals—including reintegration, punishment, custody, public protection, and deterrence—for their correctional departments. In sum, Burton et al.'s research suggests that while state codes endorsed rehabilitation as their primary goal, most also included some form of goals oriented toward offender punishment and control.[13]

Another indicator of probation philosophies is reflected in a collection of studies that have asked probation officers what they perceive their primary responsibilities to be. If anything can be concluded from this body of research, it is that probation officers endorse dual goals. More specifically, although probation officers continue to endorse offender rehabilitation, they also express substantial support for offender control.

A final important indicator of contemporary probation philosophies is found in the variety of probation programs implemented across the country in the past decade. A number of intermediate sanctions have been introduced to the probation system. These programs include intensive supervised probation, house arrest, shock incarceration, boot camps, community service, restitution, and day fines. Of these, the program that has perhaps attracted the greatest amount of attention has been intensive supervision probation (ISP). Petersilia and her colleagues predicted, for instance, that "ISP will be one of the most significant criminal justice experiments in the next decade."[14] Although ISP has taken several forms, virtually all ISP programs emphasize the strict control of offenders through restricting liberty, mandatory treatment programs, and the establishment of employment requirements. In essence, ISP programs are engineered to control offenders through strict supervision. Today, every state, plus the federal probation system, has some form of ISP program.

Despite the popularity of ISP, questions remain about its use. First, and foremost, questions have been raised about the uncertainty of goals for ISP programs. Most ISP programs endorse formal goals that include reducing jail and prison overcrowding, employing cost-effective alternatives to imprisonment, preventing criminal behavior by probationers, and using appropriate intermediate punishments that are based in the community. Other than the last of these goals, others have questioned whether ISP programs, in general, are accomplishing their stated mission. Many ISP programs, because of rigorous eligibility requirements, have actually widened the net by subjecting less serious offenders to more restrictive probation conditions. Because of the close offender supervision provided by ISP, offenders are much more likely to be revoked from probation and sentenced to jail or prison time. Thus, there are indications that ISP may actually contribute to prison and jail overcrowding instead of reducing it. Doubts have also been raised about the claimed cost savings of ISP and whether ISP programs prevent crime and reduce recidivism.

Tonry has raised a valid question: If ISP has failed to accomplish its stated goals, then why does it continue to be endorsed as a viable correctional approach?[15] First, ISP strategies are in line with popular sentiments that offenders should be held accountable for their crimes. In essence, the strict supervision characteristic of ISP has provided probation with enhanced credibility. Second, ISP has provided probation employees with "more visibility, acknowledgment, and respect." Finally, ISP is in line with prevailing political ideologies that endorse punishment and fiscal responsibility. As Clear and Hardyman concluded, the public relations success of ISP has been phenomenal:

While most observers had given probation up for dead only a few years ago, in its "new, improved" version it appears to have returned stronger than ever. Legislators are virtually falling over each other trying to sponsor legislation funding for intensive supervision alternatives to incarceration. The intensive supervision movement of the 1980s has helped revitalize probation, establishing it once again as a powerful cog in the machinery of justice.[16]

In summarizing the above information, it can be said that there are mixed goals operating in contemporary probation. State statutory provisions and probation officers themselves generally support dual goals revolving around offender rehabilitation and control. Yet at the same time, the focus on various forms of intermediate sanctions reveals an orientation toward sanctioning and controlling offenders. Taking all these factors into account, what is the mission of probation likely to be in the future?

Philosophies That Will Guide Probation in the 21st Century

Although varying in degree and prominence, probation has always been characterized by a dual emphasis on reform and control, and this will inevitably remain the case as we approach the 21st century. At the same time, however, there are many good reasons to suspect that future probation goals will contain strong themes of offender rehabilitation. Although states have embarked upon massive prison building projects during the past decade, there are questions whether they will be able to operate these facilities in the coming years, meaning that probation will become even more of a mainstay sanction in the future. Consider the remarks of Friel:

States that recently initiated capital expansion programs are beginning to realize that while they may be able to build capacity, they may not be able to afford to operate these new facilities. Sure, construction is expensive, but if you issue 20- or 30-year bonds to cover the cost, the bill will not come due for a generation, even though the interest paid will double or triple the cost. But operational costs must come from appropriated funds. . . The fiscal crisis for the states in the future will be operating their new prisons, not building the. . . [In the future] We will put the worst of the worst in prison for a long time. The second tier of offenders will go to prison as well, but will serve shorter sentences, and the rest will be supervised in the community by whatever means possible.[17]

In effect, Friel's predictions suggest that the economic strains of punitive sanctions will force the public to reassess justice policies, which, in turn, we believe, will lead to greater use of reform-oriented strategies.

A second reason why offender rehabilitation will supplant control ideologies is implicitly suggested in a recent study that questions conventional wisdom about the threat felony probationers present to community safety. In the past, research has suggested that a significant proportion of those placed on probation continue to commit crime. In perhaps the most often cited study on the topic, Petersilia and her colleagues reported that about two-thirds of offenders released on felony probation in California were rearrested during a 40-month follow-up. Other studies have found recidivism rates for probationers that range from about 20 percent to more than 50 percent. Yet in their study of arrestees in New Orleans from 1974 to 1986, Geerken and Hayes found that only eight percent of all adults arrested in that city for burglary or armed robbery involved offenders on probation. Based on their findings, Geerken and Hayes concluded that, "any restriction in probation and parole policy short of elimination, therefore, can only have a very minimal effect on the crime rate."[18] Suggestions, for example, that alternatives to incarceration be reserved for less violent, property offenders. . . or that probationers be supervised more intensively. . . can therefore also have little effect." Based on the evidence from this limited study, the implementation of additional "get tough" approaches like ISP would seem to contribute little to community protection.

A third reason to suspect that rehabilitation will become a guiding correctional philosophy lies in public attitudes. On one level, even recent popular publications have begun to question whether punitive measures are a rational approach to the country's crime problem. Perhaps most important, research questions the notion that the public has

rejected offender rehabilitation in favor of offender control and surveillance. In their study of public attitudes, Cullen, Cullen, and Wozniak
found that the public was reluctant to accept the idea that offenders
should simply be warehoused.[19] Based on their findings, Cullen and
his colleagues concluded:

> Although citizens clearly believe that the state has the
> legitimate right to sanction offenders on the basis of just
> deserts, they also believe that criminal penalties should serve
> utilitarian goals. Further, the evidence indicates that among
> the utilitarian goals, rehabilitation is supported as much as
> and usually more than either deterrence or incapacitation.
> It thus appears that the rehabilitative ideal has withstood
> the many attempts to discredit it and remains firmly anchored
> in the American value structure.

Another study by the Edna McConnell Clark Foundation revealed
that when the public was informed about various sentencing options
and their costs, they supported non-incarcerative options. More specifically, subjects in the study expressed support for sentencing options that stressed rehabilitation for a range of serious but nonviolent
offenders.

Evidence of growing support for reformation ideologies is also
evident in the academic criminal justice literature. Much of what has
been written stems from dissatisfaction with the ability of the present
system to respond effectively to the nation's crime problem. A sam-
pling of conclusions in recent articles on the topic suggests that many
criminal justice professionals cited the potential for intermediate sanctions for involving offenders in rehabilitative programs. With the corrections system overwhelmed by large numbers of drug-addicted offenders, many of whom are repeat offenders, and with the evergrowing
inmate population outstripping even the most ambitious prison construction plans, a renewed and widespread interest in rehabilitation is
emerging, even among many prosecutors.

The findings reported. . . suggest that it is time to reconsider the
respective roles of rehabilitation and surveillance in [ISP] programs. . .
Up to this point, our attention has been focused on evaluating the effectiveness of increased surveillance in community settings. It is now
time to evaluate the effectiveness of increased offender treatment (e.g.,

substance abuse, employment, and family problems) in these same community settings, both alone and in combination with closer surveillance.

ISP programs may be important not for the surveillance and control afforded offenders, but for the relationships that develop as a result of closer contact. In our rush to embrace this new wave of intermediate sanctions, we have not adequately considered the implications of this basic change in the officer-offender relationship for subsequent offender recidivism. If Braswell is correct, closer contacts that lead to a strong relationship between offenders and probation officers have a greater deterrent effect than an equal number of surveillance contacts that do not involve such close interaction.

An analysis of the rehabilitative ideal and the ensuing policies indicates that, in spite of the fact that currently this orientation is on the decline, it has not vanished completely. This orientation has deep historical and traditional roots in Western, especially American, culture; and the fact that the alternative penal and control approaches do not show much better results in social control contributes to the tenacity of this penal idea and policy, not only among social scientists, but in the public opinion as well.

Using various alternative sanctions, correctional systems have been "turning up the heat" on probationers. But our study of these new sanctions found: no discernible improvement in the delivery of "better justice"; a doubling of the cost compared with regular probation; a reduction in public safety; an increase in the prison overcrowding problem; no effect on offender recidivism; and a belated rediscovery that only the inclusion of treatment services will have any positive effect on reducing recidivism. As to the so-called rediscovery of treatment services, it has been shown once again that ideology has little respect for evidence. From the late 1970s to 1990, about a dozen reviews have appeared in the literature indicating that treatment services can reduce offender recidivism and that punishment and sanctions cannot.

The above comments are consistent with recent research by Petersilia and Turner. In their study of 14 intensive supervision programs around the country, they found that offenders in ISP programs who received treatment had significantly lower recidivism rates when compared with those who did not, even when controlling for offender background characteristics.

The Emergence of Reform-Based Probation Ideology Tempered by Offender Control

We suggest that future probation goals are likely to have a strong emphasis on offender rehabilitation. This is not to say that concerns about controlling and punishing offenders will simply disappear. On the contrary, programs like ISP will continue to thrive, but there will be a more coherent "system" of punishments in the future. In their seminal work on the topic, Morris and Tonry proposed the creation of a graduated system of penalties. These authors noted the need to devise an orderly mix of alternative sanctions, suggesting that judges could select from predetermined possible sentences to meet the needs of individual offenders. It seems inevitable that such a system will slowly become realized in probation; the philosophy driving this system will be premised upon reforming the offender, rather than simply controlling, punishing, or monitoring law breakers.

In order for such a system to work, several modifications must be made to the existing system. First, sentences must be arrayed and ranked according to their severity. Byrne, for instance, has suggested a ranked system of alternative penalties, ranging from least to most severe, that include: (1) restitution, (2) day fine with restitution, (3) community service, (4) active probation, (5) intensive probation, (6) house arrest, (7) residential community corrections, (8) split sentences, (9) jail, and (10) prison. Second, the correctional and legal systems must come to a new understanding about the use of a graduated system of alternative sanctions. In the past, alternative sanctions have functioned as a net-widening device where offenders were subjected to stricter controls than would have been the case without an array of available intermediate punishments. For the future, there is a pressing need to begin to match punishments with various types of offenders and offenses. Some scholars have suggested the need for articulating "exchange rates," to identify the number of days under various forms of community supervision that would be equal to a single day of incarceration in a traditional correctional facility. For example, authorities would need to determine that number of days of house arrest are equal to one day of incarceration, or that one year in prison is equal to "x" number of years on ISP. It is worth noting that the idea of using exchange rates is compatible with offender reformation: both ideologies are premised on a notion of individualized justice, in which sentences are meted out on the basis of the nature of the offense and the needs of individual offenders.

It is unclear how the idea of using "exchange rates" might be translated into practice so as to avoid grave sentencing disparities. Morris and Tonry have suggested that mandatory sentencing guidelines be created that govern judges' use of intermediate sanctions. Under this approach, exchange rates would be calculated for various offenses; judges would select from among the available alternative sanctions to fit the needs of the individual offender. Yet there are serious concerns about tying the use of intermediate sanctions to mandatory sentencing guidelines. In their study of criminal justice professionals' opinions about intermediate sanctions, DeJong and Franzeen found "a widespread disliking among criminal justice officials for mandatory sentencing of any kind, not only among judges, but among most probation officials and even several prosecutors as well."[20] The opposition to mandatory intermediate sanction guidelines is no doubt the product of professionals' experiences with the approach at both federal and state levels. DeJong and Franzeen found that criminal justice professionals attributed much of the present prison overcrowding problem to determinate sentencing; officials expressed concerns that mandatory guidelines would have the same effect by overloading any system devised for imposing intermediate sanctions.

One likely alternative to mandatory guidelines would be the development of voluntary or model guidelines to guide the imposition of intermediate sanctions. To be effective, this approach would necessitate informing and educating the judiciary, correctional officials, and the public. This would obviously be a massive undertaking, but there are clear indications that when properly informed, the public is supportive of alternative sanctions. While a voluntary system would invariably result in sentence disparities, it is difficult to imagine that the disparities would be any greater, and would most likely be less, than they are under the present system.

Implementing a graduated penalty system could have other benefits as well. Under such an approach, offenders could also be "educated" about the consequences of continued criminality. As it stands today, there is evidence that at least some offenders perceive sentences to ISP as harsher than sentences to prison. In one RAND study, offenders sentenced to prison were given the option of participating in ISP or going to prison. In the first year, one-third of those who had originally chosen the probation option changed their minds and asked to be sent to prison. A subsequent study in Texas found that "a preference for prison is more likely among offenders who are African-American, older, unmarried, and widely exposed to crime and institutional corrections, and who share beliefs that probation has grown stricter and that other offenders now prefer prison to probation." Implicitly, these findings suggest that at least some offenders perceive current punishment structures as inverted. Under a graduated system of penalties to which judges adhere, this phenomenon would likely disappear.

Summary and Conclusion

We acknowledge that our proposal suggesting reform-based philosophies will emerge to guide probation in the coming years is at odds with others who have written about the future of probation in America. On the fringes, writers have suggested ideas ranging from abolishing the terms "probation" and "treatment" to reorganizing probation work so that officers would provide the court with investigative services but would no longer supervise offenders.

Despite suggestions to the contrary, we believe that concerns with offender reform will command greater attention in the next decade. This prediction does not simply reflect hopeful speculation on our part but, we believe, is anchored in recurring themes in the literature. First, there are indications that, more and more, the public has begun to question current crime control strategies. Importantly, much of the criticism is based upon economic concerns. Despite pouring billions of dollars into prison construction and incarcerating a growing proportion of the population, citizen fear has continued to rise. Friel has noted that 80 percent of the cost of corrections is consumed by prisons. Ironically, this component of the correctional system only handles about 25 percent of the offender population. The remainder is managed by probation, parole, and other community-based programs. Doubts have been raised about whether the public will be willing to continue to allocate a significant proportion of their tax dollars to institutional corrections. In the future, the public will not abandon the crime problem. Instead, it is likely that renewed interest will be generated in examining cost-effective programs that promise not only community protection but also hope for reforming those who have come into contact with the justice system.

Although important, economic considerations are not the only factors that support our predictions that reform-based ideologies will guide probation in the future. Research suggests that there continues to be strong public support for the idea that corrections should seek to rehabilitate offenders. Studies also suggest the emergence of a renewed and widespread interest in offender treatment among criminal justice professionals. In addition, states' statutory provisions, although articulating multiple goals, continue to endorse offender rehabilitation as a guiding correctional philosophy.

It is somewhat ironic to note that much of the interest generated for community corrections in the past decade is attributable to control-oriented programs, such as intensive supervision probation, house arrest, and electronic monitoring. Community corrections, including probation, have capitalized upon this exposure by emphasizing such issues as offender accountability, reduced correctional costs, and the promise to alleviate institutional overcrowding. In the process, probation has generated renewed public and political support. With this support, probation is poised, perhaps more powerfully so than was ever the case in the past, to harvest a larger share of the resources available to the justice system. The irony of the situation lies in the fact that research questions the efficacy of intermediate sanctions premised solely on the control of offenders. Evaluations, for example, of traditional ISP programs suggest that they may increase probation costs, exacerbate prison overcrowding, and do little to enhance community protection. At the same time, however, research suggests that when ISP is coupled with treatment programs, recidivism rates can be substantially reduced. Thus, policymakers and probation leaders are faced with a dilemma that is as old as the probation profession itself. On one hand, members of the profession must continue to attend diligently to the control aspects of their work. Control themes have been, and will continue to be, an important part of probation work. On the other hand, offender reform strategies will emerge as a guiding force for probation during the next decade. Although ISP and related programs will continue to grow in the coming years, we suggest that most, if not all, will incorporate treatment programs.

What do these predictions mean for those who work in probation? The simplest answer is that probation will both change and remain the same. There will be change in the sense that, as departments incorporate mission statements that emphasize offender reformation, agency goals, programs, and objectives will be modified to comport with this redirected orientation. Research suggests that despite past programmatic shifts, probation workers continue to support reform-based ideologies. Thus, in many ways, much about the probation profession and those who work in it will remain the same. Hopefully, those workers who support offender reform will be funneled into treatment-based programs. Because there will be a greater diversity of intermediate sanctions, those workers who are oriented toward offender control will likewise find a number of positions in the probation system that mesh with their interests.

Case

STATE V. FULLER
(Montana Supreme Court, No. 95-343, decided 4/16/96)

Question: May a state condition probation for a sex offender upon participation in a treatment program that requires total honesty and then prosecute the defendant on the basis of what he admits in treatment?

Facts: In suspending the defendant's 10-year prison term in favor of probation, the sentencing court ordered him to "follow all policies" of the treatment program on which his probation hinged. One of the policies was that participants reveal every sex crime they ever committed. The defendant compiled, his revelations were relayed to the police, and new charges were brought.

Holding: No. The state may not condition probation upon participation in a treatment program that requires total honesty and then prosecute the defendant for any crimes that he admits in treatment.

In *Minnesota v. Murphy,* 465 U.S. 420 (1984), the U.S. Supreme Court held that the defendant needs to invoke his privilege against self-incrimination for it to apply. The ultimate result in *Murphy* was contrary to the result here, but the Montana Court explained that the cases are factually distinguishable. The difference, the court said while quoting *Murphy,* is that in *Murphy* the defendant was merely required to refrain from lying to a state agent, whereas this defendant was faced with a "required choice" between making incriminating statements and jeopardizing his conditional liberty by remaining silent.

It did not matter that, under the court's ruling in *State v. Imlay,* 813 P.2d 979 (1991), the lower court actually lacked power to revoke the defendant's probation for failure to admit to a criminal act. The defendant was faced with a credible threat, and he should not be required to have known that the threat was empty, the majority said.

Justice Trieweiller, joined by Justice Gray, concurred in the majority opinion and accused the dissent of crediting the defendant with more knowledge of his rights than can be reasonably expected.

Justice Nelson, dissenting and joined by Chief Justice Turnage and Justice Erdmann, argued that the principle established in *Imlay* freed the defendant from the "classic penalty situation." The dissenters also said that this case cannot be distinguished from *Murphy.*

The Defendant Matthew C. Fuller appeals the denial of his motion to dismiss rape and sexual assault charges, to which he entered conditional guilty pleas. The events leading to the charges began in 1992, when Fuller was convicted of three counts of attempted sexual assault. The district court sentenced him to 10 years imprisonment, but suspended the sentence and imposed probation. One condition of the probation was that Fuller "obtain and/or continue his enrollment and participation in [an] outpatient Sex Offender Treatment Program" and "follow all policies of that program." This court later reversed the attempt convictions.

In the meantime, however, Fuller was accepted into a treatment program. Patients are not admitted into the program if they are in denial or do not honestly disclose their offense history. Further, patients will be terminated from the program for exhibiting dishonesty or denial during the treatment. The employees of the treatment center are required to report to the authorities any evidence they possess about past or present offenses committed by individuals in the program.

During treatment, Fuller disclosed several past offenses, including the three at issue here. Until these disclosures, there had been no investigation of the offenses.

Fuller never asserted his Fifth Amendment privilege or refused to answer. Instead, he fully and honestly answered the questions put to him by the treatment program, in accordance with the district court's order. However, failure to invoke the privilege does not preclude the benefit if the defendant is placed in a situation in which he is not "free to admit, deny, or refuse to answer." *Minnesota v. Murphy*, 465 U.S. 420, 429 (1994) [citing *Garner v. U.S.*, 424 U.S. 648, 657 (1976)]. In such cases, the privilege is said to be "self-executing." The U.S. Supreme Court has applied this exception to different types of cases, including those in which the government prevents a voluntary invocation of the Fifth Amendment in by threatening to penalize the individual should he or she invoke it. This foreclosure of access to the Fifth Amendment is termed a "classic penalty situation."

Fuller claimed the state placed him in a classic penalty situation. Consequently, he says, his failure to invoke the Fifth Amendment should be excused, and the state is prohibited from using any disclosure made in treatment in a subsequent prosecution.

The district court ordered Fuller to enter and comply with the program. If he failed to comply, his probation would be revoked and he would be sent to prison. It is therefore undisputed that the state compelled Fuller to divulge past activities that it knew would be criminal. It is further undisputed that the information divulged by Fuller was self-incriminatory and was the sole trigger of his conviction of three additional crimes.

The state insists these circumstances did not rise to the level of a classic penalty situation because the district court never threatened to punish Fuller for exercising his Fifth Amendment privilege. At any time Fuller could have invoked his privilege against self-incrimination and the district court could not have lawfully punished him for its invocation and his consequent refusal to speak.

This decision is supported by the U.S. Supreme Court's interpretation of the Fifth Amendment as articulated in *Murphy*, even though it reached the opposite conclusion in that case. In *Murphy* the defendant's probation required that he participate in a sex offender treatment program, that he report periodically to his probation officer, and that he "be truthful with the probation officer in all matters." 465 U.S. at 422.

After Murphy left the treatment program, a counselor informed his probation officer that, while in treatment, Murphy had confessed to a rape and murder. When the probation officer confronted Murphy, he again confessed. This information was the basis for Murphy's conviction of murder, The Supreme Court found that Murphy was not placed in a classic penalty situation because the Minnesota probation revocation statute did not impermissibly foreclose a free choice to be silent. It therefore concluded that Murphy's Fifth Amendment privilege was not self-executing and, since he had not invoked it, that it was properly deemed to have been waived.

{End of Case}

SUMMARY

Probation refers to the conditional release of a defendant. Probation can have several different meanings within our present criminal justice system. Probation can be used to describe a sentence that has been given to a defendant in which the defendant is placed and maintained in the community under the supervision of an agent of the court. Probation refers to a status or class (i.e., he or she is on probation and thus subject to certain rules and conditions that must be followed in order to avoid being institutionalized). Probation also refers to an organization (i.e., the county probation department). It is a disposition that does not involve confinement, or at most involves only a short period of confinement, that imposes conditions. Under probation, the court retains authority over the case to supervise, modify the conditions, and resentence the defendant if the terms of probation are violated. Probation is a legal status created by the court. Although the classic definition of probation as set forth above indicates that it does not involve commitment, it is being increasingly linked to a short period of commitment at a training school, boot camp, or other local custody facility.

John Augustus of Boston is considered the originator of the concept of probation. As early as 1841, Augustus, a private citizen, requested that Boston judges release young defendants under his supervision. It is estimated that over an 18-year period he supervised about 2,000 individuals on probation. Most of these were youths age 16 to 19. He helped them get jobs and reestablish themselves in the community. Only a few of the individuals under his supervision became involved in subsequent criminal behavior.

Probation is based on the philosophy that the average defendant is not a violent dangerous criminal, but one that needs additional guidance in order to conform to society's demands. Probation generally involves the replacing of the defendant's commitment to a secure facility with a conditional release. Probation is essentially a contract between the defendant and the court.

DISCUSSION QUESTIONS

1. Describe the conditions that lead to the development of the concept of probation.

2. What are your opinions regarding the place that probation should take in the future of corrections?

3. Briefly summarize the rights of probationers.

4. Explain the differences between technical violations and substantive violations of the terms of probation.

5. Why is probation so popular with judges? prosecutors? defense counsel?

6. Explain the significance of the court's hold in *State v. Fuller.*

ENDNOTES FOR CHAPTER 5

1. President's Commission on Law Enforcement and Administration of Justice, *Task Force Report: Corrections* (Washington, D.C.: GPO, 1967) p.130.

2. Rolando del Carmen, Betsy Witt, Thomas Caywood, and Sally Layland, *Probation Law and Practice in Texas* (Huntsville, TX: Criminal Justice Center, Sam Houston State University, 1989).

3. Paul F. Cromwell and George G. Killinger, *Community-Based Corrections*, 3d ed. (St. Paul: West, 1994).

4. John Augustus, *First Probation Officer,* reprint of *Report of the Labors of John Augustus, for the Last Ten Years, in Aid of the Unfortunate* (Boston: Wright & Hasty, 1852), New York: National Probation Association, 1939, p. 4.

5. *Supervision of Federal Offenders*, Monograph No. 109 (Washington, D.C.: GPO, 1991).

6. Ibid.

7. *Gagnon v. Scarpelli*, 411 U.S. 778 (1973).

8. *People v. Vickers,* 25 Cal. App. 3d 1080 (1972).

9. Richard D. Sluder, Ph.D., Allen D. Sapp, Ph.D., and Denny C. Langston, Ph.D. The authors are all with the Criminal Justice Department at Central Missouri State University. Dr. Sluder is assistant professor, Dr. Sapp is professor, and Dr. Langston is associate professor. The article in based on a paper presented at the March 1994 annual meeting of the Academy of Criminal Justice Sciences, Chicago, Illinois. The article is reprinted with permission from *Federal Probation*, June, 1994. Note: many of the footnotes are omitted.

10. T.R. Clear and E.J. Latessa, "Probation Officers' Roles in Intensive Supervision: Surveillance Versus Treatment," *Justice Quarterly* (1993) Vol. 10, No. 3, pp. 440-462.

11. R. Martinson, "What Works? Questions and Answers About Prison Reform," *The Public Interest*, 1974, Vol 42., pp. 22-54.

12. Joan Petersilia, "Community Supervision: Trends and Critical Issues," *Crime and Delinquency*, 1985, Vol. 31, pp. 339-347.

13. V.S. Burton, Jr., R.G. Dunaway, and R. Kopache, "To Punish or Rehabiliate? A Research Note Assessing the Purposes of State Correctional Departments as Defined by State Codes," *Journal of Crime and Justice*, 1993, Vol. 16, No. 1, pp. 177-188.

14. J. Petersilia, S. Turner, J. Kahan and J. Peterson, *Granting Felons Probation: Public Risks and Alternatives* (Santa Monica, CA: Rand Corp., 1985).

15. M. Tonry, "Stated and Latent Functions of ISP," *Crime and Delinquency*, 1990, Vol. 36, No. 1, pp. 174-191.

16. T. R. Clear and P.L. Hardyman, "The New Intensive Supervision Movement," *Crime and Delinquency*, 1990, Vol. 36, No. 1, pp. 42-60.

17. C.M. Friel, "Crime, Justice, and the Paradigm Shifts of the 1990s," Presentation to the Southeast Region Summit on Violent Crime, July 8, 1992, Charlotte, NC.

18. M. R. Geerken and H.D. Hayes, "Probation and Parole: Public Risk and the Future of Incarceration Alternatives," *Criminology*, 1993, Vol. 31, No. 4, pp. 549-564.

19. F. T. Cullen, J. B. Cullen, and J. F. Wozniak, "Is Rehabilitation Dead? The Myth of the Punitive Public," *Journal of Criminal Justice,* 1993, Vol. 16, pp. 303-317.

20. W. DeJong and S. Franzeen, "On The Role of Intermediate Sanctions in Correctional Reform: The Views of Criminal Justice Professionals," *Journal of Crime and Justice*, 1993, Vol. 16, No. 1, pp. 47-73.

CHAPTER 6

JAILS AND MISDEMEANANTS

Booking

Classification process

Court liaison

Jails

Lockups

Orientation

State jail felony

CHAPTER OBJECTIVES

After studying this chapter, the reader will be able to:

☐ Identify the two features of the early English jails that are common with our present jails.

☐ Explain the early history of jails.

☐ Explain the functions of jail standards and list the organizations that have developed jail standards.

☐ Analyze the present functions of our jails.

☐ Explain the "revolving door" concept involving our jails.

☐ Describe common jail procedures.

☐ Explain the many problems involved with the operation of our jails.

JAILS

The word *jail* comes from the Latin root of the term *cavea* meaning cavity, cage, or coop. It is also an alternate form of the word *gaol,* which is pronounced like the word *jail* and has a Norman-French origin. Jails were originally considered as "public cages or coops." Jails existed in ancient Egypt, Greece, and Rome. The early jails were nothing but unscalable pits, dungeons, suspended cages, and sturdy trees to which prisoners were chained while awaiting trial.

During the Anglo-Saxon feudal period in England, the country-side was divided into units of government originally known as "shires." Each shire had a shire-reeve (sheriff) as its chief law enforcement officer. The shire-reeve was appointed by the crown and was charged with the responsibility of maintaining a jail. Each shire-reeve was required to establish a place to secure offenders until the next meeting of the king's court in that area. It appears that cities and municipalities also operated detention facilities. Two features of the early English jails are common elements in present-day United States facilities: jails were the responsibility of the local government, and they were operated by the shire-reeve.

Prior to the 20th century, jails were often places of filth and disease. Jail fever, a form of typhus, was a common result of the unsanitary conditions of the jails. Generally, jails were poorly supported by local government. Many jailers were appointed for life and earned their living from the fee system, which provided payments to the jailer by jail residents or their families to maintain the facility. In some cases, individuals were required to pay an additional fee to be released. Items such as food, clothing and toiletries were sold to the inmates by the jailers. In addition, it was a common practice for jailers to hire out jail inmates for manual work in the communities.

Such deplorable conditions helped bring about the establishment of certain basic rights that later appeared in the U.S. Constitution. The rights included:

- The 1628 Petition of Right, which assured the right to freedom before trial.

- The 1679 Habeas Corpus Act, which provided a remedy for illegal incarceration.

- The 1689 English Bill of Rights, which outlawed the imposition of excessive bail.

Jail Standards

Although correctional standards existed for many years, it was not until the 1970s that guidelines for jails became important. In addition, during the 1970s most states established jail standards commissions or boards. Presently, jail standards have been established by the American Correctional Association, the American Bar Association, the National Sheriff's Association, the American Psychological Association, the American Public Health Association, and even the United Nations.

The standards vary by state. In many jurisdictions, the courts have become the chief enforcers of jail standards. Areas of concern to the courts are overcrowding, medical services, library services, available recreation, and the safety of inmates.

New York City Challenges Jail Standards

In May, 1996, the City of New York filed a federal suit to strike down a 1978 agreement that forced the city to improve living conditions for prisoners.[1] The agreement resulted in the establishment of standards that still regulate almost every aspect of the city's 20,000 inmates, covering everything from how often the jailhouse windows should be washed (four times a year) to how many prisoners should be held in a dormitory room. Similar suits are pending in federal courts in South Carolina and Iowa.

The city contends that enforcing the standards costs too much and that the city, not the courts, should decide how the jails are run. The city also argues that the Prison Litigation Reform Act, passed by the U.S. Congress in April 1996, has placed restrictions on what courts could require prison systems to do. Prisoners' rights advocates contend that without the court decree, prisoners would have fewer rights and jail conditions would sharply deteriorate.

The present decree covers over 90 orders, stipulations, and work plans. It designates how much time inmates may spend in the law library and the hours they are to be locked in their cells. It regulates the prices in the jail barber shop, inmate access to telephones, and the minimum amount of borax to be used in cleaning the floors.

Uniformed male inmates fill a crowded recreation room in the San Diego County Jail while watching television.

Role of Jails

There are approxiamtely 3,500 jails operating in the United States. They represent the most widely used type of confinement in the United States. Jail populations change daily as people are admitted and released. It appears that jails will remain basically temporary local detention units that have only minimal concern for the identification and mediation of inmate problems. The major distinction between jails and prisons continues to be that jails are locally controlled and its residents have a shorter length of stay.

Generally, jails are used for two types of prisoners: those convicted of minor crimes and sentenced to short terms of confinement, and detainees who are awaiting trial and who either do not qualify for bail or cannot afford bail set in their cases. Some have estimated that at least four times as many people pass through our jails annually than the number that are incarcerated in state and federal institutions.

Generally, jails are operated by local governments, such as counties or cities. Jails differ from prisons in that prisons are administered, operated, and funded by the state or the federal government. Jails are used to punish persons convicted of minor offenses and who are sentenced to confinement for a year or less. Prisons are used to punish persons convicted of major crimes (felonies) and in most cases sentenced to one year or more. Jails differ from "lockups" in that lockups are generally operated by the police and are located in police stations or headquarters. A *lockup* is a temporary holding facility. Arrestees are usually held in a lockup for no more than 48 hours (excluding weekends and holidays). Lockups are also used to hold juveniles until their parents can be summoned or another placement can be arranged. Although there has been extensive research on jails, there has been little on lockups, despite the fact that there are over 15,000 being used in the United States.

The Revolving Door

The *revolving door concept* refers to defendants who are arrested, remain in jail only long enough to dry out, then return to the streets, drink more, and then land back in jail. This concept is especially evident in cases involving the "common drunk." Several studies have indicated that over 50 percent of the misdemeanor arrests are for drunkenness or offenses directly related to drinking. The police make over two million arrests per year for public drunkenness. A high percentage of all misdemeanor convictions are for alcohol-related offenses. The typical sentence is time in jail. It is estimated that approximately 50 percent of the individuals serving jail time as the result of a misdemeanor conviction would be treated in other types of facilities, i.e., hospitals, drug treatment centers, etc., if such facilities were available.

Most researchers will agree that alcoholism is a major problem and the alcoholic is neither deterred nor cured by frequent trips to jail. The sheer number of cases involving drunks makes it necessary to establish alternatives to automatic jailing.

Jail Facts

According to the National Coalition for Jail Reform's pamphlet, *Look at Your Jail*, there are approximately 6,500,000 commitments to jail each year in the United States. Approximately 40 percent of those in jail are awaiting trial. About 600,000 mentally ill people go through our jails each year. The suicide rate for adults in jails is 16 times greater than for the general public. Approximately 70 percent of the jail inmates are incarcerated for nonviolent offenses. Approximately 35 percent of our jails are more than 50 years old. Jails are expensive: it costs an average of $18,000 to keep one person in jail for a year. It costs about $75,000 per bed to build a new jail.

Female Jail Inmates

Approximately nine percent of jail inmates are female. Approximately 75 percent of female jail inmates have dependent children. Although some of the larger urban jails have adequate facilities for females, most jails are small and lack sufficient space to separate female residents. In addition, because of their limited number, special services and programs for female residents are limited or nonexistent in most jails. For the most part, the needs of female residents in our jails have been ignored.

A group of female inmates clad in orange uniforms cleans a cell while on a work detail.

JAIL PROCEDURES

Because jails vary greatly in size, organization, and facilities, it is impossible to make definitive statements regarding jail procedures. The basic operating procedures of jails can generally be divided into five categories: intake, classification, orientation, court liaison, and release.

Intake

Intake or booking is the point of entry in jails. The intake process involves the transfer of responsibility for the arrestee from the law enforcement officer to the jail. The individual is booked and logged into jail records. *Booking* consists of a series of steps including verification of the arrest warrant, assignment of jail number, property check, fingerprinting, photography, and other preliminary identification processes. Normally at this stage in the process, the arrestee is permitted to make his or her traditional one telephone call. The intake process may vary according to the time of day of the arrival. Frequently, the arrestee is agitated and uncooperative. In addition, often the arrestee is under the influence of drugs or alcohol. The intake process is a high-stress period for many arrestees and special precautions should be taken to prevent suicides.

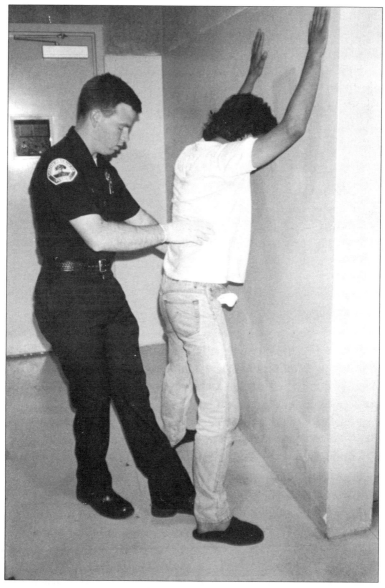

A thorough jail search, from top to bottom.

Classification

The *classification process* is concerned with the identification, categorization, and assignment of the inmate to various levels of security, programs, and work. The initial classification is concerned with housing and any special needs. Factors that need to be considered in the classification decision include age, sex, type of offense charged, prior criminal history, special medical needs, and available jail space.

Some of the larger urban jails have temporary holding areas, single cells, multiple cells, dormitory type cells, sobering or detoxification units, observation cells, segregation cells, hospital wards, and individual rooms. In these large jails, it is easier to provide the proper classification and housing for residents. Most jails, however, are much smaller and many have only one type of cell for residents.

A frequent problem is the lack of verifiable information available on the arrestee. Often the jail staff must rely on their own records and the data provided by law enforcement personnel and the information obtained from the arrestee. Of particular concern is the ability of the jail staff to recognize arrestees who need special medical or mental health treatment.

Orientation

Because confinement in jail places a person in a dependant status, proper orientation is needed for individuals who have not been previously confined. The orientation process should inform the residents of jail rules and procedures. In addition, any special programs or other assistance that is available should be explained to the new residents. An effective orientation process can help relieve the stress and conflict present with new arrestees. Most jails provide standard informational handouts for new arrivals that explain the rules, etc. Many arrestees have only limited reading ability and, thus, need special assistance in understanding the rules and facilities.

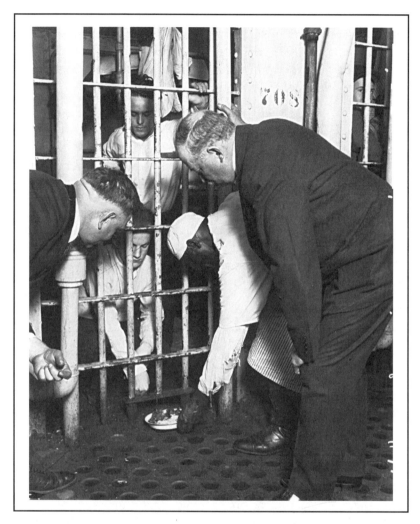

An aide slides a dinner plate under the iron bar door of a Cook County Jail cell as the two cell prisoners, sheriff and another official watch.

Court Liaison

The *court liaison* or *court appearance process* is critical to jail operations because jail residents make frequent and repeated court appearances. For example, most residents will make a court appearance within 24 hours of being arrested with subsequent appearances to follow. The safe and timely delivery of jail residents to court requires detailed planning and a significant number of staff to supervise the process. Generally, jails are located in close proximity of the courthouse because of the required close working relationship. In some jurisdictions, judges hold initial hearings in the jail.

Release

The *release process* must consider whether the release is on bail, completion of sentence, dismissal of charges, transfer to another institution, or some other form of release. It is also important that the proper resident is released. Accordingly, it is crucial to make positive identification of the releasee. In addition, any personal property that was taken from the arrestee is required to be returned to him or her.

STATE JAIL FELONY

Several states have created a new punishment category, the state jail felony. In 1994, for example, Texas designated 55 offenses as state jail felonies.[2] A *state jail felony* is more serious than a misdemeanor and less serious than a felony. The punishment range for a state jail felony is from 180 days to two years in a state-controlled jail. Generally people sentenced to confinement under a state jail felony are subject to mandatory community supervision on completion of confinement. There is no parole, no credit for good time, or special enhancement provisions. State jails are intended to be secure facilities built especially for the confinement of convicted state jail felons and would be less expensive to build and operate than current prisons.

Deferred adjudication may still be used with state jail felons. After a state jail felon is released from confinement, the judge must set a period of supervision that may generally range from two to five years. The judge may extend the period of supervision at any time up to one year after the period of community supervision has expired. Generally, a judge may impose any reasonable condition of community supervision on a state jail felon.

Smoking in Jail

In 1996, New York City banned smoking in its 16 jails. The ban is part of a national trend sweeping the nation's jails and prisons. Prior to the ban, the city's jail commissaries were selling 8,000 packs of cigarettes a day. Cigarettes were not only used for smoking, but as a form of currency in a system which required inmates to wait as long as two weeks to be allowed commissary privileges. Cigarettes were also used to buy drugs and razors (the jails' weapon of choice). Inmates will not have access to any other nicotine products. In addition, gum is not allowed, because it could be used to jam locking devices.

Several prisoners' rights organizations have protested the ban. According to them, a cigarette really helps to calm things down, especially for the addicted smoker. They also claim that tensions and hostilities will increase. The jail administrators contend that the ban is necessary for health and safety reasons and is also motivated by a growing concern over lawsuits regarding secondhand smoke.

At least 68 jurisdictions with 619 jails and prisons have instituted total or partial bans on smoking. Those jurisdictions include Los Angeles County jails and prisons in the states of Texas, North Carolina, West Virginia, Georgia, Indiana, and Nebraska. Since the ban, cigarettes have become a valued contraband. The going price in Los Angeles County jails in 1996 was $5 a cigarette. In Vermont, the contraband became such a problem that the officials rescinded the ban.[3]

Case

Paul PATZIG, Administrator
c. t. a. of Estate of Annette M. Patzig, Deceased, Appellant,
V.
Joseph O'NEIL, Commissioner
of Police of the City of Philadelphia, (and others)
and City of Philadelphia. (D.C. Civil Action No. 76-1287)

United States Court of Appeals, Third Circuit. (577 F.2d 841)

Parents of individuals who apparently committed suicide after being arrested brought action against city and city police employees, alleging violations of Civil Rights Act as well as independent state law claims. The United States District Court for the Eastern District of Pennsylvania, Charles R. Weiner, J., granted defendants' motion for directed verdict at end of plaintiffs' case, and plaintiffs appealed. The Court of Appeals, Garth, Circuit Judge, held that: (1) arrest for drunken driving at 4:30 a.m. on Saturday followed by confinement for five hours pending arraignment before magistrate did not, without more information, constitute deprivation of due process rights; (2) it was not unreasonable for city police to hold arrested individual for arraignment; (3) plaintiffs failed to establish violation of their daughter's Eighth Amendment rights; (4) evidence concerning whether arresting officer had probable cause to make warrantless arrest presented jury question; (5) where arresting officer was never served, he could not be held liable for false arrest, and (6) case would be remanded to district court for its consideration concerning exercise of pendent jurisdiction with regard to state law claims against city.

Affirmed in part, reversed in part, and remanded.
OPINION OF THE COURT
GARTH, Circuit Judge.

This appeal involves various civil rights claims and pendent state law claims arising out of the arrest, custody and subsequent suicide of Annette Patzig. The district court granted the defendants' motion for a directed verdict at the end of the plaintiffs' case. We affirm as to all defendants except the City of Philadelphia. As to the City, we reverse, limiting our reversal solely to the Patzigs' false arrest claims.

On February 21, 1975, the decedent Annette Patzig, accompanied by two friends (Christine Conan and Cynthia Slough), visited a private night club in Philadelphia, arriving at 11:30 p.m. Patzig, according to Conan's testimony, had two drinks. Conan drank heavily and became intoxicated.

Patzig's other friend, Slough, was injured during the course of the evening and was rushed to a hospital. Patzig and Conan, upon learning this fact, left the club in Patzig's automobile in search of Slough. Patzig was driving the car. At trial, Conan testified that the decedent was sober at the time she left the club, and was able to drive.

Because the two girls did not know to which hospital Slough had been taken, they drove to several center city hospitals. At each one Patzig went into the emergency room to inquire about Slough. Again, according to Conan, Patzig was able to walk and talk normally. It should be noted, however, that during this time, Conan remained in the back seat of the car, lapsing in and out of consciousness.

At 4:30 a.m. Patzig, while driving the wrong way on a one-way street, was arrested by Officer McMullen of the Philadelphia Police Department on a charge of drunken driving. Conan testified that Patzig did not appear intoxicated at the time of her arrest. Patzig and Conan were taken to the local police station, and later, at 5:55 a.m., were transported to the Police Administration Building. At 6:07 a.m. Patzig was given a Breathalyzer test, the results of which were not conclusive. The test showed a blood alcohol level of 0.06%. A police surgeon administered a medical examination shortly thereafter (at 6:15 a.m.), and found that Patzig was sober and able to operate a motor vehicle as of the time of the examination. There was other testimony that Patzig did not appear to be intoxicated while in police custody.

Patzig was nevertheless detained in a cell with two other women pending arraignment before a magistrate. The cell had only one metal rack which could be used as a bed or bench. Because her two cellmates were using the rack, Patzig was required to sleep on the tile floor.

During the early part of her confinement, decedent manifested disturbance at her arrest, but exhibited no unusual behavior. During several cell checks by police matrons she was seen either standing or sleeping on the floor. Sometime between 9:00 a.m. and 9:40 a.m. (there is conflicting evidence as to this), Patzig was allowed to make a telephone call. After her call, she refused to return to her original cell. Patzig was then taken by a matron and a police officer to a cell near the end of the cell corridor. The cell to which she was taken was situated between vacant cells. Patzig was the sole occupant in this cell. There was testimony that she was isolated in this manner because she was creating a disturbance.

Patzig then began to act hysterically, shouting, flushing the toilet, and banging the bars of the cell. A police matron attempted to quiet her, failed, and left her alone. Patzig continued to act in this manner for approximately 30 minutes. She then became quiet. At 10:00 a.m., a matron found Patzig hanging by her belt. She was later pronounced dead.

The autopsy revealed a blood alcohol level of 0.0% at the time of death. Extrapolating from this datum and the result of the Breathalyzer, a medical expert concluded that Patzig's blood alcohol level at the time of arrest was 0.085% to 0.09%. The autopsy also indicated the presence of barbiturates in her blood. There was testimony that the decedent was in the habit of taking large doses of barbiturates, which can cause the same clinical symptoms as alcohol intoxication.

Patzig's parents instituted the present lawsuit, alleging violations of the Civil Rights Act, as well as pendent state law claims. The defendants included the Philadelphia Police Commissioner, as well as various police supervisors, police officers and police matrons (some of whom were identified by name and others of whom were listed as John Doe's). Additionally, the plaintiffs joined the City of Philadelphia, alleging jurisdiction under 28 U.S.C. 1331 and asserting an implied cause of action under the Fourteenth Amendment.

The constitutional violations alleged by the plaintiffs can be distilled into three essential claims:

First, that Patzig was arrested without probable cause in violation of her right against unreasonable search and seizure; second, that the delay in taking Patzig before a magistrate abridged due process; third, that the treatment Patzig received while in custody constituted cruel and unusual punishment. . .

After the plaintiffs had presented their evidence, the district court granted the defendants' motion for a directed verdict under Fed.R.Civ.P. 50(a), and entered judgment against the plaintiffs This appeal followed. . .

Because this is an appeal from a directed verdict for the defendant, we must examine the record in a light most favorable to the plaintiff, and review the specific evidence in the record and all inferences reasonably capable of being drawn therefrom. We must determine whether, as a matter of law, the record is critically deficient of that minimum quantum of evidence from which a jury might reasonably afford relief....[I]f the evidence is of such character that reasonable men, in the impartial exercise of their judgment may reach different conclusions, the case should be submitted to the jury.

The plaintiffs' second (due process) and third (cruel and unusual punishment) constitutional claims are clearly without merit. The district court did not err by directing a verdict as to these claims. . .

An arrest for drunken driving at 4:30 a.m. on a Saturday, followed by confinement for five hours pending arraignment before a magistrate does not, without more issues, constitute a deprivation of due process rights. . . Many times arraignments are not until the next morning and are nonetheless held sufficiently prompt. . . Delay between arrest and arraignment from 4:30 p.m. to 10:30 p.m., during which time the defendants held plaintiff in custody and allegedly interrogated her. . . is not considered per se a violation of her civil rights.

. . . .Given this positive Breathalyzer test, it was not unreasonable for the Philadelphia police to hold Patzig for arraignment. Moreover, during the period after her arrest, the police were processing her, and were administering tests, the results of which might have been exculpatory. Given the necessity for the time of arrest and processing and testing Patzig, there was no unnecessary delay in bringing her before a magistrate.

Insofar as plaintiffs allege that Patzig was subjected to "cruel and unusual punishment," we note that "[i1 t is questionable whether the Eighth Amendment's prohibition. . . is applicable to a pretrial detainee, the most accepted view being that the amendment's proscription applies only after conviction. The due process clause, however, protects pretrial detainees from abusive treatment. . . In order to establish a constitutional violation under the Eighth Amendment, it is necessary that there be a deliberate indifference to the prisoner's needs. . .

A reading of the evidence before the district court reveals that police personnel may have acted negligently, perhaps even callously, but such actions do not amount to the "intentional conduct characteriz-

ing a constitutional infringement." More is needed than a naked aver-
ment that a tort was committed under color of state law.

.... The judgment of the district court will be affirmed insofar as
it grants a directed verdict in favor of the defendants as to the due
process and "cruel and unusual punishment" claims. [Note: Regulations called for two women per cell, if possible. Cell checks were required every 15 minutes. The matrons made checks only every 30 minutes. The belt had never been taken from her as required by regulations.]

What do you think?

1. Should the city be held responsible for her suicide?

2. If plaintiffs could establish that, had the matrons
followed regulations, then Annette could not have
committed suicide, should the estate receive damages?

3. Do the jail administrators have a duty to prevent
jail suicides?

{End of Case}

Jail Suicides

Inmates confined in jails have among the highest rates of suicide in the United States. Over 400
jail inmates commit suicide each year.[4] The typical
jail suicide victim is a young, single male arrested
for a crime involving alcohol or is presently under
the influence of alcohol. Generally, the victim takes
his life within three hours of incarceration.

The new Sacramento County Jail was built downtown and designed to fit in with the highrise/business look of the city.

SUMMARY

Prior to the twentieth century, jails were often places of filth and disease. Jail fever, a form of typhus, was common in the jails. The causes of jail fever were attributed to the unsanitary conditions of the jails. Generally jails were poorly supported by local government. Many jailers were appointed for life and earned their livings from the fee system. The deplorable conditions helped bring about the establishment of certain basic rights that later appeared in the U.S. Constitution.

Presently, there are jail standards established by the American Correctional Association, the American Bar Association, the National Sheriff's Association, the American Psychological Association, the American Public Health Association, and even the United Nations. The standards vary by state. In many jurisdictions, the courts have become the chief enforcers of jail standards. Areas of concern to the courts are overcrowding, medical services, library services, available recreation, and the safety of inmates.

There are approximately 3,500 jails in operation in the United States. They represent the most widely-used type of confinement in the United States. Jail populations change daily as people are admitted and released. It appears that jails will remain basically temporary local detention units that have only minimal concern for the identification and mediation of inmate problems. The major distinctions between jails and prisons continue to be that jails are locally controlled and their residents have a shorter length of stay.

Generally, jails are used for two types of prisoners: those convicted of minor crimes and sentenced to short terms of confinement, and detainees who are awaiting trial and who either do not qualify for bail or can not afford the amount of bail set in their cases. It is estimated that at least four times as many people pass through our jails annually than the number that are incarcerated in state and federal institutions.

Most jails are operated by local governments, such as counties or cities. Jails differ from prisons in that prisons are administered, operated, and funded by state or federal governments. Jails are used to punish people convicted of minor offenses and who are sentenced to confinement for a year or less.

DISCUSSION QUESTIONS

1. Discuss the role and purpose of jails in our present system.

2. How do jails differ from prisons?

3. Jail standards have caused some local jurisdictions to spend a significant percentage of their budget upgrading jails. Should communities be required to take money from other needed areas to upgrade their jails?

4. What duties should a jail administrator have concerning the safety and well being of jail inmates?

ENDNOTES FOR CHAPTER 6

1. New York Times, May 31, 1996, Page B3.

2. Ken Anderson and John Bradley, *Texas Sentencing*, (Bulverde, Texas: Omni Publishing, 1996).

3. New York Times, July 7, 1996, A17.

4.Lindsay M. Hays and Joseph R. Rowan, *National Study of Jail Suicides: Seven Years Later*, (Alexander, Va: National Center on Institutions and Alternatives, 1988).

Cell searches become a way of life.

CHAPTER 7

DOING TIME

KEY TERMS

Cleared count

Commisaries

Gang associates

Institutionalized personality

Lock down

Prizonization

Put down

Script

Train

CHAPTER OBJECTIVES

After studying this chapter, the reader will be able to:

☐ Explain the concept of prizonization.

☐ Explain the inmate social system.

☐ Describe the role inmate gangs play in prisons.

☐ Define the term "prison argot" and explain the role it plays in prison.

☐ Outline the inmate code.

☐ Describe the methods used to control inmate movements.

☐ Explain the importance of classification.

This chapter is designed to provide the reader with some understanding of what a prisoner experiences in "doing time day for day." Much of the material for this chapter was obtained from personal interviews with prisoners in California and Texas prisons. When an offender is confined, the major deprivations he or she experiences include loss of liberty, loss of outside links, moral rejection, deprivation of material amenities, sexual frustration, and loss of identity.[1] And as Dostoevski noted, the prisoner learns patience.

Most offenders will admit that they committed the crime for which they were incarcerated for, and most will admit that they made a mistake. This does not mean, however, that they feel they should be in confinement. When discussing confinement as a correctional tool almost all offenders will point out the injustices in the system. They will cite examples of people who committed more serious crimes but were not confined because of special treatment or special status. Most prisoners have the "Why me?" attitude when discussing their situation.

> *Every man who gets whipped for a sin claims that other men have done more, and been whipped less.*
>
> E.W. Howe, 1911

PRISONIZATION

Prisonization is the term used to indicate the taking on of the folkways, mores, customs, and general culture of prison life. It is the process of assimilation into prison life. During the process of prisonization, inmates become socialized as prisoners. Every person who enters prison undergoes prisonization to some degree.[2] Prisonization begins almost immediately upon arrival at the first institution or reception center. The first step in the prisonization process is the integrative step where a person leaves his or her individualism and becomes an anonymous figure in a subordinate group. An inmate number replaces the name. The prisoner no longer chooses what clothes he or she wears, but wears the clothes of a subordinate group. The prisoner soon learns that the warden and "rank" is all-powerful. The prisoner begins to use prison slang or argot. He or she learns to eat in haste. Many, for the first time in their lives, experience abnormal sexual behavior.

The offender going through prisonization, forms an *institutionalized personality*. This personality type is characterized by moving like a robot in a routine patterns, losing any initiative, living on a day-to-day basis, forgetting the past, and avoiding the future. The offender begins to look forward to simple diversions from the dullness of prison life such as the next meal, a TV program, or the next movie that will be allowed to be viewed. Often, when these small diversions are withheld from the offender, a violent reaction will occur. Once when interviewing an inmate who assaulted a guard, the inmate justified the assault because the guard would not allow him to have a piece of cake as dessert after the evening meal. Apparently the guard felt that the offender had already received his dessert and was attempting to obtain a second one. The inmate stated that he had waited all day for a piece of cake. The inmate, a three time loser, was convicted of assaulting the guard and received an additional 50 year prison sentence for the assault. Note: In almost all jurisdictions, it is required by statute that prisoners who are convicted for criminal offenses committed in prison will have their new sentence "stacked" or "tacked on the end" of their present term (i.e., served consecutively, and not concurrently).

During the prisonization process, the offender learns to speak prison argot. *Prison argot* is a language that is unique to prison. The offender learns prison argot much the same way as a person who moves to a foreign land learns to speak the local language. Listed below are some of the more common terms or slang used by prisoners. The prison language, however, differs among institutions much the same way as dialect among various regions differs in some countries.

Prison Slang

Croaker—Doctor

Screws—Guards

Right guys—Inmates who obey the inmate code and oppose staff

Square johns or straights—Inmates who obey prison regulations and do not adhere to inmate code

Merchants—Inmates who yield power by selling scarce goods and contraband

Outlaws—Inmates who are aggressive and rely on force

Squealers—Inmates who are informants

Wolves—Homosexuals who are prone to prey on others

Fangs—Inmates who passively accept homosexual advances

Fish—New inmates

Hard time—Doing your time day for day without hope of early parole

Script—Items used as a substitute for money in prison

Shank—Knife or blade

Bos—What inmates call staff [spelled backwards is sob (son of a bitch)]

Chill out—Calm down

Hack—Correctional officer

Dr. Feelgood—The psychologist

Waste—To kill someone

Roll-over—To become an informant

Phone off the hook—A correctional officer is within hearing distance

Clicking—When several inmates physically assault or manipulate a weaker inmate

Hogging—When one inmate is forced to fight another inmate until one of the two succumbs

To take off the count—To kill

Crew—The gang

New boot—An inmate new to prison.

Steel—Knife

Run—A cell block

Touch—To beat another inmate

Punk—Weak inmate who is the property of a stronger inmate

Ride with an inmate—A new or weaker inmate who pays protection

Hochecking—A number of inmates who approach another inmate ordering him to provide money or sex for protection

Inmates are issued I.D. cards at the reception center. It is a rule infraction for an inmate not to have his or her I.D. card on them at all times. Offenders are not allowed to have money in their possession. Offenders who have money with them when they are committed are required to surrender their money at the reception center. They may exchange their money for items at the commissary or have it deposited in their inmate trust fund. In most cases, the inmate's prison number is his or her trust account number. Family members or other persons who want to send money to a prisoner must send the money to the institution to be deposited in the inmate's trust fund. In some states, the inmates are allowed to establish bank accounts but may not have any blank checks in their possession. Since they are not allowed to possess money, inmates find other items to use in lieu of money. For example, a popular item that is used by many inmates are bags of coffee. Prior to their banning, cigarettes were popular as "script."

Commissaries are stores within the prison where items not furnished by the institution may be purchased. The inmate uses his or her I.D. card to make commissary purchases. Those charges are then deducted from the inmate's trust fund. Access to the commissaries are often restricted to inmates for rules violations. Generally there are two types of purchases that may be made at the commissaries—regular and special. *Regular purchases* are those that happen again and again, such as buying candy and soft drinks. Regular purchases are generally limited to about $60.00 per month in most states. Special purchases are items that are generally bought once such as radios, fans, and clothing. *Special purchases* must be approved by a staff member. While it is a rule violation for inmates to purchase items for other inmates or to trade items purchased at the commissary, inmates regularly trade items in an active underground economy.

All states have some type of personal cleanliness and grooming standards. For example, Texas requires inmates to shower one time each day, brush their teeth daily, male inmates must be clean shaven. Male inmates are issued one disposable razor each week. No beards, mustaches or hair under their lips is allowed. Hair must be kept trimmed up to the back of their necks and heads and neatly cut with no block style, Afro, natural or shag haircuts allowed. Female inmates cannot have extreme haircuts and no mohawk nor "tailed" haircuts.

Each inmate is assigned a bunk in a cell or dormitory. They can not change bunks without permission. Each inmate is also assigned a locker. Inmates may not use lockers or bunks not assigned to them. They are prohibited from hanging towels, blankets, clothing, etc. in their living area in a manner that blocks an officer's view of any area.

Joe Acosta arrived at the Federal Correctional Institute, Bastrop, Texas one May morning to begin serving a sentence for possession and transfer of a controlled substance. Joe, a seasoned veteran of prison life, immediately looked around for old friends with whom he had served with before. He found several. They discussed old times and compared this "country club" to some of the state prisons that they had served in. To the observer, it was an experience very similar to those encountered by the soldier or marine being transferred to a new base and looking for old friends he had served with before on other military bases. The defendant in one the leading U.S. Supreme Court decisions involving constitutional rights was named Acosta. When Joe was asked if he was the defendant in that case, he stated that no, it was his uncle.

In the early 1980s, the author taught a criminology class for college credit to offenders in a federal correctional institution. As the class discussed the various theories on why individuals committed crimes, the prisoners responses were very similar to those of regular students in university criminology classes. Taking the discussions one step further after an offender had explained his favorite criminological theory, I asked the offender if that was why he committed his crime. Invariably, the student would respond with comments that while he agreed with a certain crime causation theory, it did not apply to him because. . . and he would then attempt to neutralize or rationalize his conduct.

INMATE SOCIAL SYSTEM

Prisoners in a prison setting develop inmate leaders and followers. From numerous interviews regarding the informal chain of command in prisons, it appears that like any large group there are inmates who are leaders and inmates who are followers. Generally the social

The Hole

If the shoe fits...

Pelican Bay Prison was opened by the state of California in 1990. It is considered by many as the most modern and secure penal facility in the United States. It was built to isolate and punish the state's most troublesome prisoners. Inmates are locked in windowless eight-by-ten cells for all but 90 minutes a day. Whenever they are allowed out of their cells, offenders are required to be in waist restraints and handcuffs with a double escort and under the gun, except when showering or exercising alone in a tiny courtyard. They eat in their cells on food trays passed through narrow openings. The offenders are not allowed to take education classes, work, nor do they get time off for good behavior. There are few visitors.

background of the leaders are not much different from those of the followers. The inmate leaders, however, have usually served more time in prison and are more frequently in prison for violent crimes than the followers. It was rare that a first-timer, nonviolent inmate was labeled as a leader. As noted later, in today's prisons, often the inmate leaders are gang leaders.

The concept of a separate inmate social system was first discussed by Sykes and Messinger in 1960.[4] They suggest that prisoners have a pervasive value system and that this value system takes the form of an explicit code of behavior. In recent interviews with prisoners in Texas and California prisons, it appears that almost 40 years later, prisoners still assert the maxims with great vehemence. Often the violation of the code will result in retaliatory action by fellow prisoners. In some cases, it appears that while the prisoners assert these maxims vocally, but they violate them when it is to their advantage and the chances that other prisoners will know of their violations are minimum. As Sykes and Messinger noted, the actual behavior of the inmates range from full adherence to the maxims to deviance of various types. The maxims are listed below:

1. *Don't interfere with inmate interests.*

   This is accomplished by not "ratting" on a con, not being nosey, not talking too much, keeping off a man's back, and not putting an inmate on the spot. The value involved in this maxim is that of being loyal to your class- inmates (group).

2. *Minimize emotions.*

   Don't lose your head. Play it cool. Emotional friction should be minimized and ignore the minor irritants of confinement.

3. *Don't exploit your fellow inmate.*

   One inmate should not take advantage of another inmate. This is accomplished by not selling favors, not welshing on debts, and not being a racketeer.

4. *Be tough; be a man.*

   Inmates should be able to take it. When confronted with aggressive behavior, stand tall. Don't start fights, but don't run from one that someone else started.

5. *Don't trust the screws.*

   Guards and other correctional officers are not to be trusted. In conflicts between a correctional officer and an inmate, the correctional officers are always wrong. Don't be a sucker and work with the hypocrites.

Standing Tall

Arthur Glenn was serving a ten year sentence in a Texas correctional institution in Houston County, Texas. While serving time, he was indicted and convicted of assaulting another offender with a dangerous weapon. For this offense, his third felony conviction, he received the minimum sentence of 25 years. Arthur insisted that he hit the other offender in self-defense. It appears that Arthur came up to the victim from behind and hit him in the head with a lock swinging from the end of a rope. To Arthur, this was self defense. The victim had stolen some items from Arthur and had bragged about it. Arthur told the jury that he had no alternative but to take protective action against the victim. According to him to fail to take the action would have left him a marked person and everybody would take what they wanted from him.

Most studies on inmate subcultures consider prisons as contained and isolated institutions. They tend to place focus on prisoners being subject to numerous restrictions within a very coercive environment, cut off from the outside world.[5] Later studies have challenged these assumptions and have pointed out that preprison and extraprison influences have a significant impact on the prison social culture. Later studies have criticized both sets of assumptions and consider them as unrealistic and no longer applicable to today's prison conditions.[6] According to the latest studies, if an inmate social code does exist, it is unlikely that black and white inmates would be equally committed to the same values. Prison populations contain a variety of racial and ethnic groups and are not homogeneous. These groups display a range in solidarity and function. Accordingly, the inmate code of conduct is different for each racial and ethnic group. Jacobs conducted a study on the social structure and concluded that the groups or cliques have a wide range of solidarity and function. According to him, the cliques range from a group of offenders who shared common interests to tightly knit organizations in which the members cooperate in rackets, thefts, and violence. Often the cliques share leisure hours together and protect each other from attacks.[7]

Put Down

The slang term "put down" eloquently describes the emotional effect of being put in prison. It is hard to realize just how humiliating ("put-down") prison life can be even in well-run institutions. Accordingly, sooner or later, the prisoner must lose his spirit, or he must rebel.[12]

GANGS

Have prison gangs replaced the inmate social system? Prior to the 1960s, the inmate social system was dominated by a few powerful inmates. These leaders, primarily white, used their power to stabilize the inmate social system. They were allowed to rule by the prison staffs in return for stability and control. In several states, like Texas the inmate rulers became all powerful under a builder tender system, until a federal court ruled in *Ruiz v. Estelle*[8] that the state could not allow inmates to supervise other inmates. In *Ruiz*, Justice Wayne Justice ruled that the use of building tenders (inmates) who worked for the staff and maintained order through fear and intimidation was unconstitutional. There were some strong opinions regarding the removal of building tenders (B.T.s). Some examples are as follows:

"Getting rid of B.T.s, turnkeys, and countboys was a good thing because in the old days it was a simple matter for them to "cross out" (lie about the inmate to a staff member) somebody they didn't like."

"In a way, they were a good thing. They kept the noise down and the blacks in line."

"It was bad when the B.T.s were here because they stole your property and they also ran protection scams. The "greys" [guards] never did nothin' about it neither."

According to Paige Ralph, the traditional accommodations between inmate leaders and prison staff were disrupted and replaced by gangs. Ralph concludes that the prison gangs of today are highly organized enterprises with a deadly profit motive.[9] He also points out that the civil rights movement of the 1960s allowed inmates to become more assertive to the point where they seemed almost militant in their manner of seeking redress from the courts. That judicial intervention, like removal of building tenders, intended to make prisons safer and more humane, but actually created a vacuum that allowed gangs to develop. According to Ralph, the presence of gangs in prison provides protection, a way to "beat the man," and access to illicit goods and services. In addition, the gang offers solidarity and brotherhood, thereby providing social and psychological support for its members. As one gang member stated: "As long as a man's a brother, you ain't gonna let nothing happen to him. If he has problem, then you have a problem. If you have a problem, then he has a problem."

While gang members represent only 2.5 percent of California's total offender population, they were responsible for over 200 homicides and thousands of stabbings during a recent eight year period. In addition, approximately seven percent of the California total offender population are "gang associates." *Associates* are "wannabe" gang members and others who actively support gang activity. According to the latest estimates, associate gang members, not being gang members, are not locked down and thereby account for 70 percent of the criminal activity of the prison gangs in California prisons. Texas recently estimated that 92 percent of the homicides and 80 percent of the prison assaults are gang related.[10]

Accordingly many studies believe gang members and associate members adhere more enthusiastically to the gang's code of conduct than to those of the institution. The most common punishment for breaking a gang rule is death. The leading prison gangs include the Black Guerrilla Family, Texas Syndicate, Mexican Mafia, and the Aryan Brotherhood. There are also street gangs like the Bloods, Crips, Vice Lords, Hells Angels, Skinheads, and Latin Kings who have infiltrated prisons. A 1992 survey by the American Correctional Association identified 1,153 different prison gangs in the United States.[11]

Before accepting a person as a gang member, sponsorship is mandatory. Every member must meet certain requirements and generally a period of internship is necessary. The Aryan Brotherhood, for example, requires that the recruit go through a six-month indoctrination during which he learns the rules and conduct code. During that period he is tested by the members in certain situations to see how he reacts. At first, he will not be allowed to attend gang meetings. If successful, after the indoctrination, the individual is accepted as a full-fledge gang member. Only after the member has been accepted can the inmate identify himself with a tattoo or patch. Most institutions have an administrator whose duties include the monitoring of gang activity. These individuals screen inmate mail and look for other signs of gang membership in order to identify those prisoners with gang affiliation.

PRISON ROUTINE

Classification

The degree of freedom that an offender has in prison and the privileges that he or she gets are based largely on his or her security classification. The purposes of classification include:

- To systematically identify inmates as to their needs regarding training programs, security needs, and/or treatment needs

- To assign offenders to minimum, medium, or maximum security institutions or supervision levels on the basis of their predicted likelihood of recidivism, escape, or disciplinary infractions

- To assign offenders to appropriate treatment approaches on the basis of psychological, developmental, and/or personality characteristics

- To identify and prioritize offender needs

The courts have held that any classification criteria used by the correctional institutions must be rational and reasonable. In most jurisdictions, classifications are accomplished by classification boards appointed by the warden. The classification criteria cannot be arbitrary or capricious. The courts have also held that prisoners cannot be reclassified in retaliation for the exercise of a constitutional right such as filing lawsuits and grievances. While a state has no duty to protect individuals who are not in state custody, they have a duty to protect from harm inmates taken into custody and held against their will. Accordingly, one aspect of classification procedures should be to protect the prisoner from himself or herself and from others.

Recently, the courts have held that the institutions may segregate HIV-positive inmates from the general population. Other court cases have held that the failure to segregate HIV-positive inmates also does not violate the Eighth Amendment rights of the noninfected offenders. Accordingly, it appears that the state may or may not segregate HIV-positive inmates from the general population.

Shakedowns

All prisoners are subjected to *shakedowns* or cell searches. Prisoners have no Fourth Amendment rights regarding "a reasonable expectation of privacy." Accordingly, prisoners' possessions are subjected to being searched without the necessity for a warrant or probable cause. The officers must, however, respect the inmate's property and cannot recklessly destroy property in the search process. For example, in one search conducted in an Illinois prison, the officer doing the search destroyed a magazine belonging to the prisoner. The prisoner successfully sued in court to be reimbursed for the cost of the magazine ($3.00). The court also awarded the lawyer who handled the case for the prisoner $5,000 in legal fees.

Searches may not be used to single out and harass any particular person. Since inmates have proven to be ingenious at finding unsuspected hiding places, the searches may be very detailed. Body searches can range from frisk (an external pat-down of the body) to internal body-cavity searches. Generally there are three types of searches:

- Routinely at predetermined, but unannounced, times

- Randomly at undetermined and unannounced times

- Based on information or reasonable suspicion

Sexual Activity

A 1968 study of American prisons stated that virtually every slightly-built young man admitted to prison is approached within a day or two of his admission. Many are overwhelmed and are repeatedly gang raped. Others enter into a housekeeping arrangement with an individual who, in exchange for being his woman, is protected by the tormentor. According to the study, only the toughest and more hardened young men escape penetration of their bodies. Correctional insti-

In 1997, Shannon Ratliff, an inmate, was prosecuted for assaulting a correctional officer. She was convicted and sentenced to serve an additional prison term. In an interview with Shannon, she expressed regret for her actions, but stated that she had to prevent the correctional officer from coming into the cubicle. She is twenty-three years old and attractive looking. Shannon stated that she was "holding jiggers." According to her, the term "holding jiggers" means that you are the lookout while two other female inmates are having sex. Shannon now has two felony convictions. Her next felony conviction will classify her as an habitual criminal.

tutions are designed to deprive the offenders of sexual activities. For the most part, prisons are a single sex environment filled with young offenders with active sex drives. Accordingly, homosexuality exists.

Inmates and Guards

What is the relationship between inmates and guards? While maxim five noted earlier states not to trust the screws, many observers have commented on the relationships between guards and inmates. Victor Hassine, an inmate in a Pennsylvania correctional institution noted that he was surprised to discover that there was no open hostility between guards and inmates. He also noted that often many guards and inmates went out of their way to establish relationships with each other. That inmates often befriended guards in hopes of obtaining extra privileges such as special shower time or the overlooking of some minor infraction. He noted that, in many cases, there were unwritten agreements between the two whereby the inmates get what they want by being friendly and non aggressive, while the guards ensure their own safety by not strictly enforcing the rules. He concluded that most guards who are assaulted are assaulted for attempting to enforce some petty rule. Hassine noted that for the most part, inmates exploited the guards' desire for safety, and the guards exploited the inmates' needs for autonomy.[13] Subsequent interviews with prisoners in both California and Texas prisons support the above conclusions by Hassine.

Controlled Movement

In addition to being isolated from the outside world, segregation is used within institutions to isolate offenders from each other. The justification for segregation is based on the premise that segregating offenders from each other minimizes the offenders opportunity for disruptive behavior. In addition, it restricts their opportunity to plan escapes and deal in contraband. One aspect of segregation is the controlled movement of offenders. The degree of movement allowed within the institution depends largely on the institution's security classification. Two methods to control movement frequently used are very similar to those used in many of our schools—individual passes and group movement.

Probably the most controlled movement institution in the United States is the U.S. Penitentiary at Marion, IL.[14] At Marion, if an offender refuses to move as directed, a five-man unit in riot helmets and flack jackets approaches him. Each man on the team is assigned a body part—an arm, a leg, etc. They take him down, chain him and carry him to the desired location. Most offenders are locked in their cells for 22 hours each day. Until 1990, the inmates' food came in cellophane wrappers. The cellophane wrappers were banned because the offenders were melting the cellophane and fashioning it into crude blades.

External movement of offenders from one institution to another is normally accomplished by the use of prescheduled movements. For example in Texas, the state uses a "train" to move prisoners from one location to another. The "train" is a nickname for the bus network used whereby prisoners being moved from one institution to another are required to ride the scheduled bus to a central location and are then placed on another bus to the new location. The "train" operates similarly to the United Parcel Service or Federal Express except that buses are used and the cargo is humans.

Counts

A significant portion of each day in prison is taken up by the mandatory counts. A *count* is the determination by physical sighting of the precise location of all offenders in an institution. When count is "cleared" this means that all offenders have been physically accounted for. In maximum security institutions, count is taken about every two hours. In other institutions it is taken at least three times each day. Anytime a count does not match the number of offenders on the official roster, a "lock down" is instituted until a satisfactory recount is made or it is determined that an offender is missing. A "lock down" is a situation where all offender movement is stopped, and no one is allowed to enter or leave the institution until the lock down is lifted. If an inmate is missing or a discrepancy still exists after a recount, emergency search procedures are instituted.

An Escape

Paul Tollar, a long-term offender, was a trustee and was on an outside working detail. Across from the prison grounds was a local bar. He walked off from the work detail and went into the bar. He ordered a cold beer and a pack of cigarettes. He had two problems—he had no money and the bar being adjacent to the prison was a local hangout for off-duty correctional officers. One of his unit correctional officers was in the bar. Paul was arrested before he got his beer and smoke. He was tried and convicted of escape. He received ten additional years for the escape.

SUMMARY

When an offender is confined, the major deprivations he or she experiences include loss of liberty, loss of outside links, moral rejection, deprivation of material amenities, sexual frustration, and loss of identity. Prisonization is the term used to indicate the taking on of the folkways, mores, customs, and general culture of prison life. It is the process of assimilation into prison life. During the process of prisonization, inmates become socialized as prisoners. Every person who enters prison undergoes prisonization to some degree. During the Prisonization process, the offender learns to speak prison argot. Prison argot is a language that is unique to a prison. The offender learns prison argot much the same way as a person who moves to a foreign land and learns to speak the local language.

All states have some type of personal cleanliness and grooming standards. Generally, no beards, mustaches or hair under their lip is allowed. Hair must be keep trim up to the back of their neck and head and neatly cut with no block style, Afro, natural or shag haircuts allowed. Female inmates cannot have extreme haircuts and no mohawk or "tailed" haircuts. Each inmate is assigned a bunk in a cell or dormitory. Inmates cannot change bunks without permission. Each inmate is also assigned a locker and may not use lockers or bunks which are not assigned to them.

The concept of a separate inmate social system was first discussed by Sykes and Messinger in 1960. They suggest that prisoners have a pervasive value system and that this value system takes the form of an explicit code of behavior. Often the violation of the code will result in retaliatory action by fellow prisoners. In some cases, it appears that while the prisoners assert these maxims vocally, they violate them when it is to their advantage, and the chances that other prisoners will know of their violations are minimum.

Prior to the 1960s, the inmate social system was dominated by a few powerful inmates. These leaders, primarily white, used their power to stabilize the inmate social system. They were allowed to rule by the prison staffs in return for stability and control. The traditional accommodations between the inmate leaders and prison staffs were disrupted and replaced by gangs. The prison gangs of today are highly organized enterprises with a deadly profit motive. The civil rights movement of the 1960s allowed inmates to become more assertive to the point where they seemed almost militant in their manner of seeking redress from the courts. That judicial intervention intended to make prisons safer and more humane, but actually created a vacuum that allowed gangs to develop. The gangs offer solidarity and brotherhood, thereby providing social and psychological support for its members.

Correctional institutions are designed to deprive the offenders of sexual activities. For the most part, prisons are a single sex environment filled with young offenders with active sex drives. Accordingly, homosexuality exists.

In addition to the separation from the outside world, segregation is used within institutions to isolate offenders from each other. The justification for segregation is based on the premise that segregating offenders from each other minimizes the offenders opportunity for disruptive behavior. In addition, it restricts their opportunity to plan escapes and deal in contraband. One aspect of segregation is the controlled movement of offenders.

A significant portion of each day in prison is taken up by the mandatory counts. A count is the determination by physical sighting of the precise location of all offenders in an institution. When count is "cleared," this means that all offenders have been physically accounted for. In maximum security institutions, count is taken about every two hours. In other institutions it is taken at least three times each day.

DISCUSSION QUESTIONS

1. Explain the concept of prisonization.

2. How is life in prison different from life in the "free world"?

3. Analyze the relationships between inmates and guards.

4. Explain the purpose of "counts."

5. Why are inmates "movements" controlled?

6. Explain the concepts behind the inmate social system.

7. Why did gangs develop in prison?

8. What can be done to reduce the gang problem in prisons?

ENDNOTES FOR CHAPTER 7

1. Leon Radzinowicz and Marvin Wolfgang, *The Criminal in Confinement* (New York: Basic Books, 1971). While this reference is over 25 years old, it appears that modern offenders face the same deprivations.

2. Donald Clemmer, *The Prison Community* (New York: Holt, Rinehart and Winston, 1968).

3. Kevin Leary, "A Prisoner's Nightmare," *San Francisco Chronicle*, July 5, 1991, p. 41.

4. Gresham M. Sykes and Sheldon L. Messinger, "The Inmate Social System," *Theoretical Studies in the Social Organization of the Prison*, (New York: Social Science Research Council Pamphlet No. 15, 1960).

5. Richard W. Snarr, *Corrections*, 3rd ed. (Madison: Brown & Benchmark, 1996).

6. Neal Stover and Werner Einstadter, *Analyzing American Corrections*, (Belmont, CA.: Wadsworth, 1988).

7. James B. Jacobs, *New Perspectives on Prisons and Imprisonment*, (Ithaca, NY: Cornell University Press, 1983).

8 503 F. Supp. 1265 (S.D. Texas, 1980).

9. Paige H. Ralph, "From Self-Preservation to Organized Crime: The Evolution of Inmate Gangs," *Correctional Contexts: Contemporary and Classical Readings* (Los Angeles: Roxbury, 1997).

10. Salvador Buentello, "Combatting Gangs in Texas", *Corrections Today*, Vol. 54. No.5 (July, 1992) p. 58.

11. G. Camp and C. Camp, *Prison Gangs: Their Extent, Nature and Impact on Prisons.* (Washington: U.S. Dept. of Justice, 1985).

12. Paul W. Keve, *Prison Life and Human Worth* (Minneapolis: University of Minnesota Press, 1974) pp. 41-42.

13. Victor Hassine, *Life Without Parole* (Los Angeles: Roxbury, 1996).

14. Christopher Dickey, "A New Home for Noriega?" *Newsweek*, January 15, 1990, pp. 66-69.

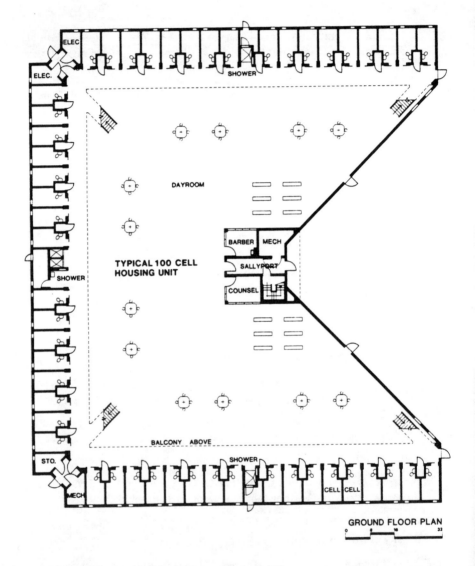

ELEC

ELEC.

SHOWER

DAYROOM

TYPICAL 100 CELL
HOUSING UNIT

BARBER MECH

SALLYPORT

COUNSEL

SHOWER

BALCONY ABOVE

SHOWER

STO.

MECH

CELL CELL

GROUND FLOOR PLAN

0   8   16   32

A typical housing unit with single occupancy cells.

CHAPTER 8

INSTITUTIONAL PROCEDURES

KEY TERMS

Aftercare

Custody designation

Diagnostic centers

Flat time

Mandatory supervision

Orientation process

Parole

Segregative classifications

CHAPTER OBJECTIVES

After studying this chapter, the reader will be able to:

☐ Explain the inmate orientation process.

☐ Identify the various classifications used for offenders in prison.

☐ Describe the discipline system for state institutions.

☐ Explain the grievance system for offenders.

☐ Analyze the requirements for "rules of conduct."

☐ List the types of release from state penal institutions.

☐ Analyze the factors involved that attribute to prison building costs.

☐ Describe the history of parole.

☐ Compare and contrast the differences between adult and juvenile parole.

☐ Explain the "due process" rights involved in parole revocation.

☐ List and define the methods that are used to discharge an offender from parole.

WHY PRISONS?

The following questions should be examined regarding prisons.

• What purpose do prisons serve?

• What purpose should prisons serve?

• Under what conditions should prisoners be held?

• What rights and privileges should prisoners forfeit?

• What should prisoners be obliged to do?[1]

The prisons of the 1830s were organized on the principles of order and regularity. Each prisoner was isolated in a cell and the rule of total silence was strictly enforced. By the 1900s, the institutions tended to model themselves on the outside community and afforded the inmates the opportunity to mix with other prisoners and to work in groups. It was also during the early 1900s that prisons began to specialize.

Assaults on Prison Guards Increase

In 1990, there was one assault on a prison guard for every 321 inmates. In 1996, there was one assault for every 171 inmates. Some prison officials believe the demise of early release and curtailment of parole causes inmates to believe that they have nothing to lose by being belligerent. Other officials believe that the increase is due to the fact that prisoners, many of them repeat offenders, have become more hardened.[2]

Diagnostic Process

Defendants convicted of felonies are often ordered to diagnostic facilities within the state department of corrections for diagnostic and treatment services. In many states, defendants may be retained in the diagnostic facilities for a period not to exceed 90 days. During that stay, defendants are examined and a report of the diagnoses and recommendations are submitted to the court. Time spent in confinement at a diagnostic facility is generally credited to the defendants as part of their confinement term.

Inmate Orientation Process

Inmates of state prisons/correctional institutions are generally first sent to a diagnostic unit or a reception center. The main function of these reception and *diagnostic centers* is to receive and process inmates. Inmates who do not speak English or only limited English are identified in order to receive the necessary type of language assistance while in the orientation process and later when assigned to a regular prison unit.

Inmates' money and property are taken from them. A receipt will be made for each inmate's money and property. Inmates are given a physical examination by the medical staff. The medical staff will inquire about the inmates' medical histories. Any special medical needs of the inmates will be noted in the inmates' records. Urgent medical care is given and inmates are housed according to security needs. Each inmate is generally given psychological testing. Inmates indicating psychological problems are generally referred for further testing. Additionally, inmates are tested to determined their educational needs.

Railing lines a narrow walkway which runs before the prison cells on level four of San Quentin Federal Penitentiary in California.

Inmates are given sociological interviews. During these interviews, the inmates are asked questions about their criminal history, social history, institutional history, educational history, employment history, family history, military history, drug and/or alcohol histories, and any other pertinent information. The interviews should verify information in their records. Inmates are advised that they may be subject to disciplinary actions for giving untruthful information during the interview process. A summary of all information collected on each inmate will be used to help classify him or her.

The orientation process includes providing inmates with information regarding the department's policies, programs, educational services, rules, classification procedures, disciplinary procedures, and other inmate activities and programs. They are generally fingerprinted and the prints are sent to the state department of public safety and the FBI.

Most states use classification committees to determine the first unit to which an inmate will be assigned. Inmates do not have a right to choose their unit assignment. The committees make their decisions based on all information collected, the inmate's safety needs, the inmate's security needs, and the inmate's treatment needs. In most states, the committees also recommend the inmate's custody level, good-time earning category, housing assignment, and job assignment.

Inmates undergo classification before they are assigned to a unit. Classification means putting inmates who are alike together. Generally states use segregative classifications and custody levels. Segregative classifications are assigned to inmates based on age and previous incarceration. A typical segregative class system is as follows:

I—first offender, age 17-21 years of age

IA—first offender, age 22-25 years of age

IB—first offender, 26 years of age or older

II—second offender, 17-21 years of age

IIA—second offender, 22-25 years of age

IIB—second offender, 26 years of age or older

IIC—multiple offender

Custody Levels

After the inmates spend a couple of weeks going through the diagnostic process, the inmates are assigned custody levels. A custody designation does two things. It tells how much supervision the inmate needs and with whom and where he will live. The inmate's custody depends on how he or she behaves. If the inmate does not follow rules, the inmate will be given a custody and watched closely. If the inmate behaves, he or she will be given a less restrictive custody. There are five custody groups:

1. **Maximum.** Also referred to as administrative segregation. It is used on inmates who must be separated from the general population because they are dangerous, either to other inmates or staff, or they are in danger from other inmates. These inmates leave their cells, for the most part only for showers and limited recreation.

2. **Close**. This level is used for inmates who have serious and/or long disciplinary records. Close custody inmates generally live in cells. They can not work outside the security area without armed supervision.

3. **Medium.** This level is used for inmates who live in cells and may work outside the security fence with armed supervision. In some states, especially with female inmates, medium custody inmates live in dormitories.

4. **Minimum (in).** This level refers to inmates who can live in dormitories or cells inside the security fence. They can work outside the fence under direct armed supervision.

5. **Minimum (out).** This level allows inmates to live in dorms outside the security fence. They may also work outside the security fence with little supervision.

Discipline

Inmates confined to institutions are required to obey a lengthy list of policies. When an institution employee observes an inmate commit an infraction, the employee is generally required to submit a disciplinary report. The inmate receives notice of the report with written notification of the charge and a hearing date. At the hearing, the hearing officer receives the evidence that is presented by the institutional division and any that is present by the inmate. The formal rules of evidence do not apply to these hearings. At the hearing, the hearing officer decides whether or not the inmate committed the infraction. Possible punishments include loss of time credited for good conduct or participation credit, solitary confinement, extra work, loss of certain privileges for stated periods of time (recreation, commissary, television, access to personal property, or contact visits), and reprimands. Generally, the inmate may appeal the hearing officer's finding and/or punishment to the unit warden.

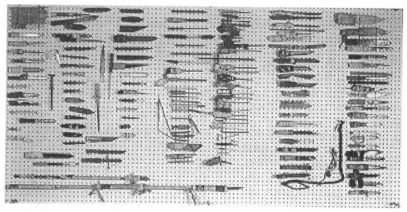

Typical weapons confiscated from maximum security prisoners.

Disciplinary Hearing Procedures

American Bar Association's Standard 23-3.2 Relating to the Legal Status of Prisoners provides:

(a) At a hearing where a minor sanction is imposed, the prisoner should be entitled to:

(1) Written notice of the charge, in a language the prisoner understands, within 72 hours of the time he or she is suspected of having committed an offense; within another 24 hours the prisoner should be given copies of any further written information the hearing officer may consider.

(2) A hearing within three working days of the time the written notice of the charge was received.

(3) Be present and speak on his or her own behalf.

(4) A written decision based upon a preponderance of the evidence, with specified reasons for the decision. The decision should be rendered promptly and in all cases within five days after conclusion of the hearing.

(5) Appeal, within five days, to the chief executive officer of the institution, and the right to a written decision by that officer within 30 days, based upon a written summary of the hearing, any documentary evidence considered at the hearing, and the prisoner's written reason for appealing. The chief executive officer should either affirm or reverse the determination of misconduct and decrease or approve the punishment imposed. Execution of punishment should be suspended during the appeal unless individual safety or individual security will be adversely affected thereby.

(b) At a hearing where a major sanction is imposed, in addition to the requirements of paragraph (a), the prisoner should be entitled to have in attendance any person within the local institution community who has relevant information, and to examine or cross-examine such witnesses except when the hearing officer(s):

(1) Exclude testimony as unduly cumulative; or

(2) Receive testimony outside the presence of the prisoner pursuant to a finding that the physical safety of a person would be endangered by the presence of a particular witness or disclosure of his or her identity.

(c) Disciplinary hearings should be conducted by one or more impartial persons.

(d) Unless the prisoner is found guilty, no record relating to the charge should be retained in the prisoner's file or used against the prisoner in any way.

The Supreme Court has approved a distinction between disciplinary proceedings that may result in the imposition of major punishments such as loss of good time and solitary confinement and minor punishments which affects only privileges.[3] Regarding the requirement that the person or persons conducting the hearing be impartial, the courts have held that no hearing officer should have been involved in the circumstances or investigation of the alleged violation.

When the misconduct involves the violation of a prison rule and criminal misconduct, there is no formal bar to disciplinary action and referral of the matter to criminal courts. The drafters of the standards contend that it is preferable administrative policy to refrain from pursuing both actions concurrently. Many states, like Texas, as a matter of routine pursue both avenues. In one recent Texas case, a prisoner lost three years worth of good-time credit at a disciplinary hearing for assaulting a correctional officer and was then prosecuted in the local district court for assault on a peace officer.

Grievances

Most state prisons and local jails have grievance procedures for inmates who feel that they have been mistreated or have not received proper credit. Generally the inmate must file a written claim on an approved form. In most states, if the grievance is denied and the inmate has exhausted his or her administrative remedies, the inmate may file a petition with a district or superior court.

The ABA Standards provide:

(a) Correctional authorities should authorize and encourage correctional employees to resolve prisoner grievances on an informal basis whenever possible.

(b) Every correctional institution should adopt a formal procedure to resolve specific prisoner grievances, including any complaint arising out of institutional policies, rules, practices, and procedures, or the action of any correctional employee or official.

Grievance procedures should not be used as a substitute appellate procedure for individual decisions reached by adjudicative bodies, for example, parole, classification, and disciplinary boards, although a complaint involving the procedures or general policies employed by any correctional adjudicative body should be subject to grievance procedures.

(c) Correctional authorities should make forms available so that a grievant may initiate review by describing briefly the nature of the grievance, the persons involved, and the remedy sought.

(d) The institution's grievance procedure should be designed to ensure the cooperation and confidence of prisoners and correctional officials and should include:

(1) Provisions for written responses to all grievances, including the reasons for the decision;

(2) Provision for response within a prescribed, reasonable time limit. A request that is not responded to or resolved within 30 working days should be deemed to have been denied;

(3) Special provision for responding to emergencies;

(4) Provision for advisory review of grievances;

(5) Provision for participation by staff and prisoners in the design of the grievance procedure;

(6) Provision for access by all prisoners, with guarantees against reprisal;

(7) Applicability over a broad range of issues; and

(8) Means for resolving questions of jurisdiction.

Courts have held that the right to petition for redress of grievances is a First Amendment right.[4] It appears that common sense would also indicate that as many disputes as possible between prisoners and administrators should be worked out informally. In addition, an effective grievance procedure should reduce number of cases filed in court involving inmate complaints. As a general rule, before filing a court action regarding the conditions of confinement, the prisoner must exhaust his or her administrative remedies. A formal grievance process is considered an administrative remedy that should be exhausted prior to the inmate filing judicial papers. By filing a grievance, the inmate provides the institution with an opportunity to correct any wrongs without resorting to court action.

RULES OF CONDUCT

The American Bar Association's (ABA) Joint Task Force on the Legal Status of Prisoners contains the below standard regarding rules of conduct:

(a) Correctional authorities should promulgate clear written rules for prisoner conduct. These rules and implementing criteria should include:

    (1) A specific definition of offenses, a statement that the least severe punishment appropriate to each offense should be imposed, and a schedule indicating the minimum and maximum possible punishments for each offense, proportionate to the offense; and

    (2) Specific criteria and procedures for prison discipline and classification decisions, including decisions involving security status and work and housing assignments.

(b) A personal copy of the rules should be provided to each prisoner upon entry to the institution. For the benefit of illiterate and foreign-language prisoners, a detailed oral explanation of the rules should be given. In addition, a written translation should be provided in any language spoken by a significant number of prisoners.[5]

The authors of the above standards feel that many prison rule books contain ambiguities and that correctional officers often believe that publications of this sort provide sufficient guides for ascertaining violations. According to the authors, prison regulations should be concise. The courts have held that due process requires a schedule of penalties for violation of penal rules and that the punishment must bear some proportionality to punishable misconduct, measured in some objective fashion. Disproportionate penalties will be struck down by the courts, both within and without prison walls.[6] When challenging a prison rule for a disproportionate penalty, however, the prisoner must "demonstrate disparities in punishment that are not reasonably related to legitimate state interests."[7]

RELEASE FROM CONFINEMENT

In most states, there are three ways in which an inmate may be released from confinement: parole, mandatory supervision, and discharge. *Parole* is the discretionary release of an inmate from prison when he or she completes a prescribed portion of his or her sentence and the parole board agrees that the release will not increase the likelihood of harm to the public. Parole is discussed in the next section. *Mandatory supervision* is the release of an inmate from prison when he or she completes a prescribed portion of his or her sentence. For example, an inmate could receive a sentence of confinement for two years with two years mandatory supervision when released. Mandatory supervision differs from parole in that the defendant is informed when sentenced as to the release date, whereas a parole date must be

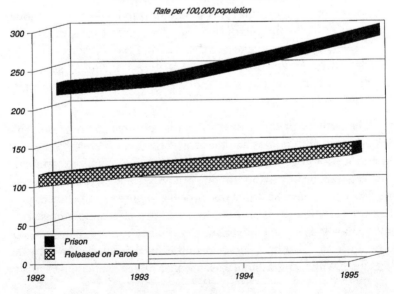

Prison and Parole Increases
Rate per 100,000 population

approved by a parole board. Not all states use the concept of mandatory supervision. Once released, the inmate is on mandatory supervision and under the close supervision of his or her parole officer as long as the inmate follows the conditions of his or her supervision. Should the inmate violate the conditions of supervision, the inmate may be returned to confinement. *Discharge* is the outright release of the inmate after he or she serves his or her entire sentence minus any partication or good-time credit given. An inmate who serves his or her time, often referred to as serving the sentence "flat time," is not subject to any form of supervision.

RELEASE ON PAROLE

Parole is the conditional release of a defendant from a correctional institution prior to the completion of his or her term of confinement. In theory, the defendant is released from the correctional institution at a time when he or she can best benefit from the release and continued supervision after release. Note: parole is a conditional release of the defendant to the community under supervision of a parole officer.

Parole is often used incorrectly to refer to the release of any defendant from custody. It differs from probation in that probation usually requires little or no confinement and probation is administered by the courts on a county-wide basis. Parole is generally administered by a statewide agency on a statewide basis. Normally parole is granted only after the defendant has served a significant portion of his or her confinement. Probation is considered a pre-institutional procedure. Parole, on the other hand, is considered a continuation of the correctional process. Unlike probation, a person on parole has already completed a portion of his or her term of confinement. Release is conditional and may be revoked if the terms of parole are violated.

In many states, the term "aftercare" is used in lieu of parole for juvenile cases. To many social service providers, the concept of juvenile aftercare is more acceptable than the use of the phrase juvenile parole. In this text, the two terms are used interchangeably. It appears that about half the states use "aftercare" and the other half use "parole."

The word *parole* is taken from the French. Its literal translation is "a word of honor given or pledged." It was first used by the military to release prisoners of war who promised to refrain from attempting to escape or to forbear from taking up arms against their captors. Presently, it generally means a conditional release on good behavior from a correctional institution.[8]

The parolee usually requires more supervision than a youth on probation. The parolee has been confined and must readjust to society. In addition, the parolee may be bitter toward society, remorseful, and resentful of his or her period of confinement.

A typical parole board meeting.

HISTORY OF PAROLE

Parole in America can be traced back to the houses of refuge that were established in the latter part of the nineteenth century. Parole is, however, more English and European than American. It was first used by the English to offer a conditional release from prison for those prisoners who agreed to work for a certain period of time to regain their freedom. Parole, unlike probation, was originally motivated by economic pressures rather than humanitarian concerns. Parole provided employers with cheap labor and relieved the British government from having to pay the expenses of imprisonment.

Alexander Maconochie and Sir Walter Crofton

The concept of parole is often credited to England's Alexander Maconochie and Ireland's Sir Walter Crofton.

Alexander Maconochie was born in Edinburgh, Scotland. After a distinguished career in the British navy, he was appointed the first Professor of Geography at University College in London. Later, he became involved in studying prison conditions at the Tasmania Island penal colony. In 1838-39, he published *Thoughts on Convict Management and Supplement to Thoughts on Convict Management.* He wrote that the proper object of prison discipline is to prepare men for discharge: to reform prisoners and prepare them to separate with advantage both to themselves and to society after their release. Maconochie devised five ideas to serve the rehabilitation purpose:

1. Sentences should not be imprisonment for a period of time, but for the performance of a determined and specified quantity of labor. Time sentences should be abolished and task sentences should be substituted.

2. The quantity of labor a prisoner must perform should be expressed in a number of marks that he must earn, by improvement in conduct, frugality of living, and habits of industry, before he can be released.

3. While in prison, a prisoner should earn everything he receives, all else should be added to his debt of marks.

4. When qualified by discipline to do so he should work in association with a small number of other prisoners, forming groups of six or seven, and the whole group should be answerable for the conduct and labor of each member of the group.

5. In the final stage of the prison term, the prisoner should be given a proprietary interest in his own labor and be subject to a less rigorous discipline.

Sir Walter Crofton used Maconochie's ideas in the Irish Prison System. Idea 5 (above) developed into the concept of conditional release, i.e., parole. The gradual approximation to freedom in every successive stage of discipline—from maximum security to trustee to conditional release or parole.

GOOD-TIME CREDIT

In colonial America, criminals were sentenced to prison for stated periods of time and were not released until the term had expired. Good-time credit was not used until 1817, when New York passed the first good-time law. The *good-time law* allowed for a reduction in the fixed term based on the prisoner's cooperative good conduct and behavior while in prison. Other states soon passed similar statutes that were firm and straightforward. Generally, the good-time laws permitted the prison term to be reduced by one-fourth for terms of five or less years. The prisoner would need to obtain a certificate of good behavior from the principal confinement keeper to obtain the credit. By 1916, all states had adopted some form of good-time statutes.

In recent years, there has been a trend by states to require that inmates serve a longer period of time before they are eligible for pa-

Women prisoners participate in a graduation ceremony after completing the STEP program on Riker's Island, New York City, New York.

role. Traditionally, inmates were eligible after serving 25 percent of their time. Several states now require inmates to serve at least 30 percent of their time before being eligible for parole. In some states an inmate is required to serve more time before being eligible for parole if the crime involved the use of a dangerous weapon. The federal government has abolished the use of parole. Presently, the federal government uses "supervised release" in lieu of parole.

SUPERVISED RELEASE

As noted above, the federal government now uses *supervised release* in lieu of parole. Under the Federal Sentencing Guidelines, the judge is required to order a term of supervised release to follow imprisonment when a sentence of imprisonment of more than one year is imposed. In addition, the judge may order a term of supervised release to follow imprisonment in any other case.[9] It appears that the judge may consider the need for a term of supervised release to facilitate the reintegration of the defendant into the community in those cases where the supervision is not mandatory. It can also be used to enforce a fine, restitution order, or other condition of release. If the defendant is convicted under a statute that requires a term of supervised release, the term shall be at least three years but not more than five years.

The terms of the supervised release shall include a condition that the defendant not commit another federal, state, or local crime. In addition, the defendant may not possess illegal controlled substances during the period of release. Other conditions that the court may impose include conditions that are related to the nature and circumstances of the offense and the history and characteristics of the defendant. The court may also impose conditions to afford adequate deterrence to criminal conduct, to protect the public from further crimes of the defendant, and to provide the defendant with needed educational or vocational training, medical care, or other correctional treatment in the most effective manner.

Supervised release may be revoked and the defendant returned to confinement. If the defendant commits a crime of violence, involving a controlled substance, firearm possession violation, or any federal or state felony offense, the court must, on a finding that the violation has occurred, revoke the defendant's supervised release. If the defendant commits a misdemeanor or violates other conditions of release, the court may revoke the defendant's release.

Another method used to gain freedom included petitions for pardons. Because some of the early laws mandated long sentences, juries would frequently petition the governor to grant pardons. In some cases, pardons were used to make more room in the overcrowded prisons. It is noted that prison overcrowding is an old and continuing problem with our correctional systems.

PAROLE TODAY

Most defendants, after release from institutions, return to the communities from which they came. Generally, defendants are released from confinement long before the expiration of their maximum period of commitment. In some states, the defendant must serve a minimum time before being released. In nine states, the judge who committed the defendant must agree to the release before the defendant may be released early. The problem with this latter practice or requirement is that often the committing judge is too busy with other cases and does not have sufficient time to review the case and make a viable recommendation as to the release decision. In addition, because no new presentencing reports are prepared, the judge may act on dated or incomplete information. For these reasons, judicial involvement in the early release decision has been eliminated in most states.

Most experts assign two goals to parole: first, protection of the society; second, the proper adjustment of the defendant. Presently, it appears that the most important goal is the protection of society. Many see the two goals as conflicting ones pitting society against the defendant. A better approach appears to be the concept of protecting society by rehabilitating the defendant.

Parole includes the objective of assisting the parolee in integration into the community. Therefore, the defendant must be assisted in coping with the problems faced upon release and to adjust to the status of being a parolee. To be a permanent benefit to society, parole agencies must assist in the development of the defendant's ability to make good decisions that are behaviorally acceptable to the community.

The functions of the institution include classifying the defendant's readiness for release and the risk factors upon release of the defendant. The duty of the parole officer is, among other things, to assist in the rehabilitation and reintegration of the defendant into the community and to reduce the likelihood of the defendant committing further criminal acts.

THE RELEASE DECISION

In most states, parole services are administrated by the state agency that is also responsible for the correctional institutions. There are, however, no clear-cut organizational patterns as to who makes the early release decision. In some states, the decision is made by the parole board, in others by an adult correctional agency, a lay board, or the correctional institution staff. In addition, in many states, the state officials have delegated the decisional authority to local agencies.

PAROLE SERVICES

Parole services consist of the various programs and components of the criminal justice system necessary to facilitate the goals and purposes of parole. Parole services include the classification tasks performed at the institution, counseling sessions, and the education classes provided by the institution. Prior to release, generally pre-parole investigations are conducted to obtain the necessary background information to devise parole plans for the defendants. Parole services continue until the defendants are released from parole.

The President's Commission on Corrections' Report called for a maximum active caseload of 50 probation cases per officer or counselor.[11] Although there is no empirical justification noted for the figure of 50, it does appear to be a reasonable number. Unfortunately, most parole officers have caseloads so large that routine contact is conducted only through the telephone. Many persons have advocated that reducing the caseload sizes would result in greater success in rehabilitating the defendants. Research indicates that the problems of rehabilitation are more complex, and reducing the caseload size alone is not sufficient to make the system more successful.

REVOCATION OF PAROLE

Generally it is the function of the paroling agency to revoke a defendant's parole. The U.S. Supreme Court in *Morrissey v. Brewer*,[12] involved two parolees in Iowa who were originally sentenced for forgery. About six months after being released on parole, their parole was revoked for violation of parole conditions. The two parolees appealed the revocation decision on the grounds that their paroles were revoked without a hearing and that the lack of a hearing deprived them of their due process rights. The Supreme Court held:

> The liberty of parole, although indeterminate, includes many of the core values of unqualified liberty and its termination inflicts a "grievous loss" on the parolee and often on others. It is hardly useful any longer to try to deal with this problem in terms of whether the parolee's liberty is a "right" or a "privilege." By whatever name, the liberty is valuable and must be seen as within the protection of the Fourteenth Amendment. Its termination calls for some orderly process, however informal.

The Court then stated that the "orderly process" included the below minimum standards of due process:

- Written notice of the claimed violations of parole

- Disclosure to the parolee of the evidence against him

- Opportunity to be heard in person and to present witnesses and documentary evidence

- A hearing before a neutral and detached hearing body

- A written statement by the fact finders as to the evidence relied on and the reasons for revoking parole

The Court also held that, before requiring a parolee to face a revocation hearing, there should be a preliminary hearing conducted to determine if there is probable cause or reasonable grounds to believe that the parolee has committed acts that would constitute a violation of parole conditions. Although *Morrissey v. Brewer* dealt with adult paroles, it appears that the requirements are also applicable to juveniles.

DISCHARGE FROM PAROLE

In many states, the defendant may be released or discharged from parole at any time after the defendant's release from the institution. Most states require defendants to be on parole for a minimum time, usually one year, before they may be discharged. To be effective, enough time is needed to work on the defendant's long-range needs and to help him or her achieve independence from the criminal justice system.

The release from parole may also be conditional. In some cases, the release is automatic after a certain period of time. After discharge, most juveniles are left to their own devices and are no longer supervised by the system. The decision to discharge the defendant from parole may have many pitfalls. For many defendants, survival in the community was possible only because of the assistance of their parole officer or counselor. Once this crutch is removed, the parolee may regress into the behavioral and attitude modes that were the underlying causes of the previous encounters with the law.

What due process rights should a parolee have when revocation of his or her parole is being considered? Does the following court decision provide adequate guidance in answering this question?

Case

Morrissey v. Brewer
U.S. Supreme Court
408 U.S. 471 Decided June 29, 1972

Two Iowa convicts whose paroles were revoked by the Iowa Board of Parole filed *habeas corpus* petitions in the United States District Court for the Southern District of Iowa, alleging that they were denied due process because their paroles were revoked without a hearing. The District Court denied the petitions on the ground that due process did not require a pre-revocation hearing, and the United States Court of Appeals for the Eighth Circuit affirmed...The United States Supreme Court reversed... In an opinion by BURGER,Ch. J., expressing the views of six members of the court, it was held that the minimum requirements of due process in revoking paroles include (a) written notice of the claimed parole violations; (b) disclosure to the parolee of evidence against him; (c) opportunity to be heard in person and to present witnesses and documentary evidence; (d) the right to confront and cross-examine adverse witnesses (**unless** the hearing officer specifically finds good cause for not allowing confrontation); (e) a neutral and detached hearing body such as a traditional parole board, members of which need not be judicial officers or lawyers; and (f) a written statement by the fact finders as to the evidence relied on and reasons for revoking parole.

The court further held that a preliminary hearing officer's determination that there is probable cause to hold a parolee for the parole board's final decision on parole revocation warrants the parolee's continued detention pending the final decision; but the court expressly permitted the question whether a parolee is entitled, in a parole revocation proceeding, to the assistance of retained counsel or to appointed counsel if he is indigent.

BRENNAN, J., joined by MARSHALL, J., concurred in the result on the ground that due process also requires that the parolee be allowed the assistance of retained counsel at his revocation hearings.

DOUGLAS, J., dissented on the grounds that a parolee who does not commit a new offense should not be arrested or jailed until his parole is revoked, and that a parolee is entitled to counsel in parole revocation proceedings.

Mr. Chief Justice BURGER, delivered the opinion of the Court.

We granted certiorari in this case to determine whether the Due Process Clause of the Fourteenth Amendment requires that a state afford an individual some opportunity to be heard prior to revoking his parole.

Petitioner Morrissey was convicted of false drawing or uttering of checks in 1967 pursuant to his guilty plea, and was sentenced to not more than seven years' confinement. He was paroled from the Iowa State Penitentiary in June 1968. Seven months later, at the direction of his parole officer, he was arrested in his home town as a parole violator and incarcerated in the county jail. One week later, after review of the parole officer's written report, the Iowa Board of Parole revoked Morrissey's parole, and he was returned to the penitentiary located about 100 miles from his home. Petitioner asserts he received no hearing prior to revocation of his parole.

The parole officer's report on which the Board of Parole acted shows that petitioner's parole was revoked on the basis of information that he had violated the conditions of parole by buying a car under an assumed name and operating it without permission, giving false statements to police concerning his address and insurance company after a minor accident, obtaining credit under an assumed name, and failing to report his place of residence to his parole officer. The report states that the officer interviewed Morrissey, and that he could not explain why he did not contact his parole officer despite his effort to excuse this on the ground that he had been sick. Further, the report asserts that Morrissey admitted buying the car and obtaining credit under an assumed name, and also admitted being involved in the accident. The parole officer recommended that his parole be revoked because of "his continual violation of his parole rules."

The situation as to petitioner Booher is much the same. Pursuant to his guilty plea, Booher was convicted of forgery in 1966 and sentenced to a maximum term of 10 years. He was paroled November 14, 1968. In August 1969, at his parole officer's direction, he was arrested in his home town for violation of his parole and confined in the county jail several miles away. On September 13, 1969, on the basis of a written report by his parole officer, the Iowa Board of Parole revoked Booher's parole and Booher was recommitted to the state penitentiary, located about 250 miles from his home, to complete service of his sentence. Petitioner asserts he received no hearing prior to revocation of his parole.

The parole officer's report, with respect to Booher, recommended that his parole be revoked because he had violated the territorial restrictions of his parole without consent, had obtained a driver's license under an assumed name, operated a motor vehicle without permission, and had violated the employment condition of his parole by failing to keep himself in gainful employment. The report stated that the officer had interviewed Booher and that he had acknowledged to the parole officer that he had left the specified territorial limits and had operated the car and had obtained a license under an assumed name "knowing that it was wrong." The report further noted that Booher had stated that he had not found employment because he could not find work that would pay him what he wanted. He stated he would not work for $2.25 to $2.75 per hour and that he had left the area to get work in another city.

After exhausting state remedies, both petitioners filed *habeas corpus* petitions in the United States District Court for the Southern District of Iowa alleging that they had been denied due process because their paroles had been revoked without a hearing. The State responded by arguing that no hearing was required. The District Court held on the basis of controlling authority that the state's failure to accord a hearing prior to parole revocation did not violate due process. On appeal, the two cases were consolidated.

The Court of Appeals, dividing 4 to 3, held that due process does not require a hearing. The majority recognized that the traditional view of parole as a privilege rather than a vested right is no longer dispositive as to whether due process is applicable; however, on a balancing of the competing interests involved, it concluded that no hearing is required. The court reasoned that parole is only "a correctional device authorizing service of sentence outside the penitentiary," the parolee is still "in custody." Accordingly, the Court of Appeals was of that view that prison officials must have large discretion in making revocation determinations, and that courts should retain their traditional reluctance to interfere with disciplinary matters properly under the control of state prison authorities. The majority expressed the view that "non-legal, non-adversary considerations" were often the determinative factors in making a parole revocation decision. It expressed concern that if adversary hearings were required for parole revocation, "the full panoply of rights accorded in criminal proceedings," the function of the parole board as "an administrative body acting in the role of *parens patriae* would be aborted," and the board would be more reluctant to grant parole in the first instance—an apprehension that would not be without some basis if the choice were between a full scale adversary proceeding or no hearing at all.

Additionally, the majority reasoned that the parolee has no statutory right to remain on parole. Iowa law provides that a parolee may be returned to the institution at any time.

In its brief in this Court, respondent asserts for the first time that petitioners were in fact granted hearings after they were returned to the penitentiary. More generally, respondent says that within two months after the Board revokes an individual's parole and orders him returned to the penitentiary, on the basis of the parole officer's written report it grants the individual a hearing before the Board. At that time, the Board goes over "each of the alleged parole violations with the returnee, and he is given an opportunity to orally present his side of the story to the Board." If the returnee denies the report, it is the practice of the Board to conduct a further investigation before making a final determination either affirming the initial revocation, modifying it, or reversing it."

The State asserts that Morrissey, whose parole was revoked on January 31, 1969, was granted a hearing before the Board on February 12, 1969. Booher's parole was revoked on September 13, 1969, and he was granted a hearing on October 14, 1969. At these hearings, the State tell us—in the briefs—both Morrissey and Booher admitted the violations alleged in the parole violation reports.

Nothing in the record supplied to this Court indicates that respondent claimed, either in the District Court or the Court of Appeals, that petitioners had received hearings promptly after their paroles were revoked, or that in such hearing they admitted the violations; that information comes to us only in the respondent's brief here. Further, even the assertions that the respondent makes here are not based on any public record but on interviews with two of the members of the parole board. In the interview relied on to show that petitioners admitted their violations, the board member did not assert he could remember that both Morrissey and Booher admitted the parole violations with which they were charged. He stated only that, according to his memory, in the previous several years all but three returnees had admitted commission of the parole infractions alleged and that neither of the petitioners was among the three who denied them.

We must therefore treat this case in the posture and on the record respondent elected to rely on in the District Court and the Court of Appeals. If the facts are otherwise, respondent may make a showing in the District Court that petitioners in fact have admitted the violations charged before a neutral officer.

Before reaching the issue of whether due process applies to the parole system, it is important to recall the function of parole in the correctional process. During the past 60 years, the practice of releasing prisoners on parole before the end of their sentences has become an integral part of the penological system. Rather than being an *ad hoc* exercise of clemency, parole is an established variation on imprisonment of convicted criminals. Its purpose is to help individuals reintegrate into society as constructive individuals as soon as they are able, without being confined for the full term of the sentence imposed. It also serves to alleviate the costs to society of keeping an individual in prison. The essence of parole is release from prison, before the completion of sentence, on the condition that the prisoner abide by certain rules during the balance of the sentence. Under some systems, parole is granted automatically after the service of a certain portion of a prison term. Under others, parole is granted by the discretionary action of a board, which evaluates an array of information about a prisoner and makes a prediction whether he is ready to reintegrate into society.

To accomplish the purpose of parole, those who are allowed to leave prison early are subjected to specified conditions for the duration of their terms. These conditions restrict their activities substantially beyond the ordinary restrictions imposed by law on an individual citizen. Typically, parolees are forbidden to use liquor or to have associations or correspondence with certain categories of undesirable persons. Typically, also they must seek permission from their parole officers before engaging in specified activities, such as changing employment or living quarters, marrying, acquiring or operating a motor vehicle, traveling outside the community, and incurring substantial indebtedness. Additionally, parolees must regularly report to the parole officer to whom they are assigned and sometimes they must make periodic written reports of their activities. The parole officers are part of the administrative system designed to assist parolees and to offer them guidance. The conditions of parole serve a dual purpose: they prohibit, either absolutely or conditionally, behavior that is deemed dangerous to the restoration of the individual into normal society. And through the requirement of reporting to the parole officer and seeking guidance and permission before doing many things, the officer is provided with information about the parolee and an opportunity to advise him. The combination puts the parole officer into the position in which he can try to guide the parolee into constructive development.

The enforcement leverage that supports the parole conditions derives from the authority to return the parolee to prison to serve out the balance of his sentence if he fails to abide by the rules. In practice, not every violation of parole conditions automatically leads to revocation. Typically, a parolee will be counseled to abide by the conditions of parole, and the parole officer ordinarily does not take steps to have parole revoked unless he thinks that the violations are serious and continuing so as to indicate that the parolee is not adjusting properly and cannot be counted on to avoid antisocial activity. The broad discretion accorded the parole officer is also inherent in some of the quite vague conditions, such as the typical requirement that the parolee avoid "undesirable" associations or correspondence. Yet revocation of parole is not an unusual phenomenon, affecting only a few parolees. It has been estimated that 35-45 percent of all parolees are subject to revocation and return to prison. Sometimes revocation occurs when the parolee is accused of another crime; it is often preferred to a new prosecution because of the procedural ease of recommitting the individual on the basis of a lesser showing by the State.

Implicit in the system's concern with parole violations is the notion that the parolee is entitled to retain his liberty as long as he substantially abides by the conditions of his parole. The first step in a revocation decision thus involves a wholly retrospective factual question: whether the parolee has in fact acted in violation of one or more conditions of his parole. Only if it is determined that the parolee did violate the conditions does the second question arise: should the parolee be recommitted to prison or should other steps be taken to protect society and improve chances of rehabilitation? The first step is relatively simple; the second is more complex. The second question involves the application of expertise by the parole authority in making a prediction as to the ability of the individual to live in society without committing antisocial acts. This part of the decision, too, depends on facts, and therefore it is important for the board to know not only that some violation was committed but also to know accurately how many and how serious the violations were. Yet this second step, deciding what to do about the violation once it is identified, is not purely factual but also predictive and discretionary.

If a parolee is returned to prison, he usually receives no credit for the time "served" on parole. Thus, the returnee may face a potential of substantial imprisonment. We begin with the proposition that the revocation of parole is not part of a criminal prosecution and thus the full panoply of rights due a defendant in such a proceeding does not apply to parole revocations. Parole arises after the end of the criminal prosecution, including imposition of sentence.

Supervision is not directly by the court but by an administrative agency, which is sometimes an arm of the court and sometimes of the executive. Revocation deprives an individual, not of the absolute liberty to which every citizen is entitled, but only of the conditional liberty properly dependent on observance of special parole restrictions. We turn, therefore, to the question whether the requirements of due process in general apply to parole revocations. As Mr. Justice Blackmun has written recently, "This Court now has rejected the concept that constitutional rights turn upon whether a governmental benefit is characterized as a 'right' or as a 'privilege.' " *Graham v. Richardson*, 403 U.S. 365. . . Whether any procedural protections are due depends on the extent to which an individual will be "condemned to suffer grievous loss." *Joint Anti-Fascist Refugee Committee v. McGrath*, 341 U.S. 123... The question is not merely the "weight" of the individual's interest, but whether the nature of the interest is one within the contemplation of the "liberty or property" language of the Fourteenth Amendment. *Fuentes v. Shevin*, 407 U.S. 67... Once it is determined that due process applies, the question remains what process is due. It has been said so often by this Court and others as not to require citation of authority that due process is flexible and calls for such procedural protections as the particular situation demands. "[C]onsideration of what procedures due process may require under any given set of circumstances must begin with a determination of the precise nature of the government function involved as well as of the private interest that has been affected by governmental action." *Cafeteria and Restaurant Workers Union v. McElroy*, 367 U.S. 886, 895. . . . To say that the concept of due process is flexible does not mean that judges are at large to apply it to any and all relationships. Its flexibility is in its scope once it has been determined that some process is due; it is a recognition that not all situations calling for procedural safeguards call for the same kind of procedure.

We turn to an examination of the nature of the interest of the parolee in his continued liberty. The liberty of a parolee enables him to do a wide range of things open to persons who have never been convicted of any crime. The parolee has been released from prison based on an evaluation that he shows reasonable promise of being able to return to society and function as a responsible, self-reliant person. Subject to the conditions of his parole, he can be gainfully employed and is free to be with family and friends and to form the other enduring attachments of normal life. Though the State properly subjects him to many restrictions not applicable to other citizens, his condition is very different from that of confinement in a prison. He may have been on parole for a number of years and may be living a relatively normal life at the time he is faced with revocation. The parolee has relied on at least an implicit promise that parole will be revoked only if he fails to live up to the parole conditions. In many cases, the parolee faces lengthy incarceration if his parole is revoked.

We see, therefore, that the liberty of a parolee, although indeterminate, includes many of the core values of unqualified liberty and its termination inflicts a "grievous loss" on the parolee and often on others. It is hardly useful any longer to try to deal with this problem in terms of whether the parolee's liberty is a "right" or a "privilege." By whatever name, the liberty is valuable and must be seen as within the protection of the Fourteenth Amendment. Its termination calls for some orderly process, however informal.

Turning to the question of what process is due, we find that the State's interests are several. The State has found the parolee guilty of a crime against the people. That finding justifies imposing extensive restrictions on the individual's liberty. Release of the parolee before the end of his prison sentence is made with the recognition that with many prisoners there is a risk that they will not be able to live in society without committing additional antisocial acts. Given the previous conviction and the proper imposition of conditions, the State has an overwhelming interest in being able to return the individual to imprisonment without the burden of a new adversary criminal trial if in fact he has failed to abide by the conditions of his parole.

Yet, the State has no interest in revoking parole without some informal procedural guarantees. Although the parolee is often formally described as being "in custody," the argument cannot even be made here that summary treatment is necessary as it may be with respect to controlling a large group of potentially disruptive prisoners in actual custody. Nor are we persuaded by the argument that revocation is so totally a discretionary matter that some form of hearing would be administratively intolerable. A simple factual hearing will not interfere with the exercise of discretion. Serious studies have suggested that fair treatment on parole revocation will not result in fewer grants of parole.

This discretionary aspect of the revocation decision need not be reached unless there is first an appropriate determination that the individual has in fact breached the conditions of parole. The parolee is not the only one who has a stake in his conditional liberty. Society has a stake in whatever may be the chance of restoring him to normal and useful life within the law. Society thus has an interest in not having parole revoked because of erroneous information or because of an erroneous evaluation of the need to revoke parole, given the breach of parole conditions. . . And society has a further interest in treating the parolee with basic fairness: fair treatment in parole revocations will enhance the chance of rehabilitation by avoiding reactions to arbitrariness. Given these factors, most States have recognized that there is no interest on the part of the State in revoking parole without any procedural guarantees and all that is needed is an informal hearing structured to assure that the finding of a parole violation will be based on verified facts and that the exercise of discretion will be informed by an accurate knowledge of the parolee's behavior.

We now turn to the nature of the process that is due, bearing in mind that the interest of both State and parolee will be furthered by an effective but informal hearing. In analyzing what is due, we see two important stages in the typical process of parole revocation.

(a) *Arrest of Parolee and Preliminary Hearing.* The first stage occurs when the parolee is arrested and detained, usually at the direction of his parole officer. The second occurs when parole is formally revoked. There is typically a substantial time lag between the arrest and the eventual determination by the parole board whether parole should be revoked. Additionally, it may be that the parolee is arrested at a place distant from the state institution, to which he may be returned before the final decision is made concerning revocation. Given these factors, due process would seem to require that some minimal inquiry be conducted at or reasonably near the place of the alleged parole violation or arrest and as promptly as convenient after arrest while information is fresh and sources are available...Such an inquiry should be seen as in the nature of a "preliminary hearing" to determine whether there is probable cause or reasonable ground to believe that the arrested parolee has committed acts that would constitute a violation of parole conditions...

In our view, due process requires that after the arrest, the determination that reasonable ground exists for revocation of parole should be made by someone not directly involved in the case. It would be unfair to assume that the supervising parole officer does not conduct an interview with the parolee to confront him with the reasons for revocation before he recommends an arrest. It would also be unfair to assume that the parole officer bears hostility against the parolee that destroys his neutrality; realistically the failure of the parolee is in a sense a failure for his supervising officer. However, we need make no assumptions one way or the other to conclude that there should be an uninvolved person to make this preliminary evaluation of the basis for believing the conditions of parole have been violated. The officer directly involved in making recommendations cannot always have complete objectivity in evaluating them. *Goldberg v. Kelly* found it unnecessary to impugn the motives of the caseworker to find a need for an independent decision maker to examine the initial decision.

This independent officer need not be a judicial officer. The granting and revocation of parole are matters traditionally handled by administrative officers. In *Goldberg,* the Court pointedly did not require that the hearing on termination of benefits be conducted by a judicial officer or even before the traditional "neutral and detached" officer; it required only that the hearing be conducted by some person *other* than one initially dealing with the case. It will be sufficient, therefore, in the parole revocation context, if an evaluation of whether reasonable cause exists to believe that conditions of parole have been violated is made by someone such as a parole officer other than the one who has made the report of parole violations or has recommended revocation. A State could certainly choose some other independent decision-maker to perform this preliminary function. With respect to the preliminary hearing before this officer, the parolee should be given notice that the hearing will take place and that its purpose is to determine whether there is probable cause to believe he has committed a parole violation. The notice should state what parole violations have been alleged. At the hearing the parolee may appear and speak in his own behalf; he may bring letters, documents, or individuals who can give relevant information to the hearing officer. On request of the parolee, persons who have given adverse information on which parole revocation is to be based are to be made available for questioning in his presence. However, if the hearing officer determines that the informant would be subjected to risk of harm if his identity were disclosed, he need not be subjected to confrontation and cross-examination.

The hearing officer shall have the duty of making a summary, or digest, of what occurs at the hearing in terms of the responses of the parolee and the substance of the documents or evidence given in support of parole revocation and of the parolee's position. Based on the information before him, the officer should determine whether there is probable cause to hold the parolee for the final decision of the parole board on revocation. Such a determination would be sufficient to warrant the parolee's continued detention and return to the state correctional institution pending the final decision. As in *Goldberg,* "the decision-maker should state the reasons for his determination and indicate the evidence he relied on . . ." but it should be remembered that this is not a final determination calling for "formal findings of fact and conclusions of law." 397 U.S. at 271; 25 L.Ed.2d at 300. No interest would be served by formalism in this process; informality will not lessen the utility of this inquiry in reducing the risk of error.

(b) *The Revocation Hearing.* There must also be an opportunity for a hearing, if it is desired by the parolee, prior to the final decision on revocation by the parole authority. This hearing must be the basis for more than determining probable cause; it must lead to a final evaluation of any contested relevant facts and consideration of whether the facts as determined warrant revocation. The parolee must have an opportunity to be heard and to show, if he can, that he did not violate the conditions, or, if he did, that circumstances in mitigation suggest that the violation does not warrant revocation. The revocation hearing must be tendered within a reasonable time after the parolee is taken into custody. A lapse of two months, as the State suggests occurs in some cases, would not appear to be unreasonable.

We cannot write a code of procedure; that is the responsibility of each State. Most States have done so by legislation, others by judicial decision usually on due process grounds. Our task is limited to deciding the minimum requirements of due process.

We have no thought to create an inflexible structure for parole revocation procedures. The few basic requirements set out above, which are applicable to future revocations of parole, should not impose a great burden on any State's parole system. Control over the required proceedings by the hearing officers can assure that delaying tactics and other abuses sometimes present in the traditional adversary trial situation do not occur. Obviously a parolee cannot relitigate issues determined against him in other forums, as in the situation presented when the revocation is based on conviction of another crime.

In the peculiar posture of this case, given the absence of an adequate record, we conclude the ends of justice will be best served by remanding the case to the Court of Appeals for its return of the two consolidated cases to the District Court with directions to make findings on the procedures actually followed by the Parole Board in these two revocations. If it is determined that petitioners admitted parole violations to the Parole Board, as Iowa contends, and if those violations are found to be reasonable grounds for revoking parole under state standards, that would end the matter. If the procedures followed by the Parole Board are found to meet the standards laid down in this opinion that, too, would dispose of the due process claims for these cases.

We reverse and remand to the Court of Appeals for further proceedings consistent with this opinion.

Reversed and remanded.

{End of Case}

COSTS OF PRISONS

Building and running prisons are very expensive. Prison construction costs are usually expressed as cost per prison bed and are attained by dividing total costs by the number of available beds. In 1996, the average cost per bed to build a maximum security prison was about $80,000. The cost to build medium security prisons was about $60,000 per bed and about $35,000 per bed to build a minimum security prison. There is a wide range in construction costs across the United States. This range is caused by the variation of construction costs in different regions of the nation: land costs vary, some systems use prison labor to help offset the costs, the amount of space allotted per prisoner in different prison designs varies, and accounting methods differ in each state. Regarding accounting methods, in some states architectural fees and insurance costs are included, where they are excluded in other states. In addition, construction costs usually do not include finance charges, which could triple the initial costs. In addition to the construction costs, the long-term operating costs are also staggering. It costs approximately $25,000 per year, per bed to keep prisoners confined. As you can see, prison bed space is expensive for taxpayers and takes up a considerable portion of the federal and state revenues.

A rectangular gray prison ship floats in New York Harbor.

■ From 1987 to 1995 state government expenditures on prisons increased by 30 percent, while spending on higher education fell by 18 percent, said the study by the Justice Policy Institute, a research and advocacy organization based in Washington D.C.

■ "These findings prove that in the funding battle between prisons and universities, prisons are constantly coming out on top," said Vincent Schiraldi, director of the Policy Institute.

■ From 1980 to 1994, the number of adults in prison nationwide tripled from 320,000 to 992,000, according to the Justice Department. This increase in the corrections population and the accompanying growth in prison construction occurred in an era marked by historically high crime rates. Over the same period, enrollment in institutions of higher education increased from 12 million to 14.7 milion people, marking a 22 percent increase overall, and a small but steady increase in the proportion of college-age population.

■ Taking construction spending as a measure of governmental priorities, the Justice Policy Institute study noted that California has built 21 prisons since 1984 and only one new university.

IS FURTHER PRISON EXPANSION WORTH THE COSTS?[13]

In recent decades a primary response to crime has been to expand prison populations, which in 1993 exceeded 4.5 times the figure 25 years ago. State and federal governments have established longer sentences and mandatory minimum sentences, assuming that such action would reduce crime by deterring and incapacitating criminals.

Perhaps the most important question in penology today is whether further prison expansion is worth the expense. Cost-benefit analysis of imprisonment has been tried in the past, but it is suspect due to the questionable assumptions used. Much new information is now available, however, permitting reasonably firm estimates.

This article first compares the direct and measurable costs and benefits. The latter are mainly savings to victims from crimes not committed because prison populations were expanded; these include the value of items that would have been stolen and the pain victims would have suffered from violent crime. The direct costs are the expenses of building and operating prisons. I also outline the potential costs and benefits that cannot be quantified or cannot be attributed to changes in prison populations and crime rates.

Direct Benefits

The first step in determining the direct benefits is to estimate how many crimes are avoided when prison populations expand. Lack of adequate data here has long been a major stumbling block to making cost-benefit calculations. This year, however, two major research efforts independently reached nearly the same conclusions with different research procedures. W. Spellman, a researcher who authored *Criminal Incapacitation*, using prisoners' accounts concerning the volume of crime they committed, concluded that increasing prison and jail populations by one percent reduces index crime by 0.12 percent to 0.20 percent, with a best estimate of 0.16 percent. Marvell and Moody, conducting econometric analysis of crime rates and prison populations, concluded that each 1 percent increase in state prison populations reduced crime by at least 0.16 percent in 1971 to 1989. The reduction reached 0.21 percent in the period after 1976. The Spellman estimates are a little lower probably because they pertain to prison plus jail inmates, whereas Marvell and Moody studied prison populations only. Spellman's estimate, in addition, is limited to the incapacitation effect, and Marvell and Moody include deterrence and other crime-reduction effects of imprisonment.

Marvell and Moody also studied the average impact per additional state prisoner, producing an estimate of nearly 21 crimes averted per year. When broken down by crime type, each additional inmate leads to, on average, 0.06 fewer rapes, 0.63 fewer robberies, 6.10 fewer burglaries, 12.65 fewer larcenies, and 1.11 fewer vehicle thefts. There is no discernible impact on homicides and assaults.

The most obvious and easily calculated benefit of crime reduction is avoiding economic loss to potential victims. The Department of Justice publishes two estimates of victims' losses, one from the National Crime Survey (NCS) and the other from the Uniform Crime Reports (UCR). The NCS includes the value of stolen property, medical expenses, and pay loss for worked missed. The NCS figures lead to an estimate of $13,000 saved per additional prisoner in 1994 dollars. The UCR figures produce a higher estimate, $21,000, because citizens tend to report crime more often when the loss is greater and because the NCS excludes commercial crimes, which involve greater property loss for robbery and burglary (but not larceny). As a rough estimate, I take the average of the two measures, or $17,000 direct costs to victims saved per additional prisoner for index crimes. In addition, I add $2,000 for fraud and forgery which are not index crimes, for a total of $19,000.

This is probably an underestimate, although not seriously so. The UCR measure includes only costs of items stolen. The NCS excludes costs incurred after the interview date (which took place sometime between the crime and six months later), and many victims probably did not know the cost of medical care paid directly by their insurers. Medical costs, however, are only a small portion of total costs even for violent crime. The estimates might be higher if I could include victimless crime, such as gambling and drug offenses, but the impact of prison expansion is probably small because many other people are available to provide the illegal services, taking the place of those imprisoned.

Also not included are costs associated with psychological injuries, such as pain and suffering, which are difficult to measure but which are important and should be included if possible. The civil courts routinely give monetary damages for psychological injuries, and recent studies have used data for damage awards to estimate the costs of psychological injury in crimes. The results are rough averages of $51,000 for each rape, $17,000 for each robbery, and $700 for each burglary. These translate into $3,000 avoided for rape for each additional prisoner on average (0.06 times $51,000), $11,000 for robbery, and $4,000 for burglary.

In all, the calculable direct benefits from crime reduction total to some $37,000 per additional prisoner, about half for monetary loss and half for psychological injury.

Direct Costs

The best estimate of prison operating and construction costs per prisoner is $22,920 to $26,245 per year in 1989 dollars. Taking the average and adjusting for inflation leads to a rounded estimate of $30,000 in 1994 dollars. If the inmates were not imprisoned, they would most likely be on probation, so I must subtract the cost of supervising a probationer, which Cavanagh and Kleinman in their book *A Cost Benefit Analysis of Prison Cell Construction and Alternative Sanctions* estimate to be $1,000 per year (again after converting into 1994 dollars and rounding). The net costs, therefore, are $29,000 per prisoner.

Additional Putative Benefits

There are several other possible benefits to the crime-reduction impact of expanding prisons, but they are not included here because they apparently have little or no causal connection with crime reduction or because one cannot estimate the cost savings.

An important potential gain is alleviating the financial burden of the criminal justice system. In 1990, federal and state justice system expenses totaled $74 billion, or nearly $2,000 per index crime and $40,000 for crimes avoided per additional prisoner. Nongovernment crime costs for insurance and private security are probably even greater. The potential indirect costs savings, therefore, approach $100,000 a year per additional prisoner. But this cannot legitimately be considered a crime-reduction gain for the simple reason that, to the best of my knowledge, there is no reason to believe that such costs undergo a net decline because prison expansion reduces crime (for example, P.A. Langan and Moody, in their research on prison population, concluded that crime rate changes have little effect on prison populations).

Crime entails losses other than loss to victims: suffering by victims' families, increased fear of crime by acquaintances, loss to the victims' employers for sick leave, and commercial declines in high-crime neighborhoods. The latter is not truly a cost of crime because it means that other areas receive commercial gains, and the remaining potential benefits from crime reduction are too nebulous to calculate.

Other Putative Costs

More imprisonment also entails "downstream" costs that some try to attribute to the imprisonment. A prisoner's loss of legitimate earnings, which has been estimated to average some $10,000 a year, is not properly a cost because the loss typically means a job opening for someone else.

Prisoners' dependents are often on welfare, which costs the government another $10,000 or so per prisoner. Most of this is not properly a cost of imprisonment because (a) the dependents may be on welfare even if the prisoner were on the street, and (b) to the extent that additions to welfare result from the prisoner's loss of legitimate employment, the imprisonment provides employment opportunities for some whose families would otherwise be on welfare. On the other hand, welfare costs that result from loss of illegal income are true costs of increasing imprisonment. That is, when crime reduction through more imprisonment reduces theft losses, it also reduces criminals' incomes and perhaps causes some dependents to go on welfare. I have no basis for estimating, however, how often this happens and what portion of the welfare expenses can be considered a cost of imprisonment.

There are several other indirect costs that cannot be measured with information currently available. These include suffering by prisoners and relatives resulting from the imprisonment, relatives' costs

Racially mixed groups of prison inmates wearing blue uniforms gather at tables outside a row of makeshift barracks with plastic sheets thrown over the roofs at San Quentin Federal Penitentiary in California.

for visiting and telephoning inmates, and the possible "crime-school" effect of imprisonment.

Conclusions

Prison populations appear to be near an equilibrium point from a cost-benefit viewpoint. The most readily measured benefit, reduced monetary loss to victims, is some $19,000 per additional prisoner per year. This is substantially less than the most readily measured cost, $29,000 for prison operation and construction, less probation supervision costs. But reduction in psychological costs to victims, estimated to be worth $18,000 per prisoner, raises the benefits to $37,000. For all practical purposes, given the uncertainties involved, especially for psychological costs, there is no indication that the direct calculable costs ($29,000) and benefits ($37,000) of imprisonment differ appreciably.

Additional costs and benefits that are not quantified, such as suffering by victims' and inmates' relatives also appear to be roughly balanced. Potentially the most important benefit, reduction in overall criminal justice expenses, and a major potential cost, inmates' loss of earnings, cannot be included because there is little to suggest that they are truly benefits and costs in practice.

This leads one to ask what might make the incarceration strategy more worthwhile. Criminals vary greatly in the amount of crime they commit, and there is growing evidence that many of the most active criminals remain on the streets, while prisons contain large numbers of criminals less adept at evading capture. Surveys of inmates suggest that the vast majority of crimes are committed by a small percent of criminals who tend to have much lower apprehension rates than others. Reducing crime by expanding prisons is unlikely to be very cost-effective unless accompanied by greater efforts to imprison the most active criminals. Lawmakers, therefore, should seek to improve police effectiveness as a way to make better use of prisons.

{End of Article}

SUMMARY

The prisons of the 1830s were organized based on the principles of order and regularity. Each prisoner was isolated in a cell and the rule of total silence was strictly enforced. By the 1900s, institutions tended to model themselves on the outside community and afforded the inmates the opportunity to mix with other prisoners and to work in groups. It was also during the early 1900s that the prisons began to specialize. Generally, a defendant who has been convicted of a felony may be ordered to a diagnostic facility within the state department of corrections for diagnostic and treatment services. The orientation process includes providing inmates with information regarding the department's policies, programs, educational services, rules, classification procedures, disciplinary procedures, and other inmate activities and programs.

Most states use classification committees to determine the first unit to which an inmate will be assigned. Inmates do not have a right to choose their unit assignment. The committees make their decisions based on all information collected: the inmate's safety needs, the inmate's security needs, and the inmate's treatment needs. After the inmates spend a couple of weeks going through the diagnostic process, the inmates are assigned custody levels. A custody designation does two things: it tells how much supervision the inmate needs and with whom and where he will live.

Inmates confined in institutions are required to obey a lengthy list of policies. When an institution employee observes an inmate commit an infraction. The employee is generally required to submit a disciplinary report.

In most states, there are three ways in which an inmate may be released from confinement: parole, mandatory supervision, and discharge. Parole is the discretionary release of an inmate from prison when he or she completes a prescribed portion of his or her sentence and the parole board agrees that the release will not increase the likelihood of harm to the public.

Parole is often used imprecisely and incorrectly to refer to the release of any defendant from custody. It differs from probation in that probation usually requires little or no confinement and probation is administered by the courts on a county-wide basis. Parole is generally administered by a statewide agency on a statewide basis. Normally parole is granted only after the defendant has served a significant portion of his or her confinement. Probation is considered a preinstitutional procedure. Parole on the other hand is considered a continuation of the correctional process.

Parole in America can be traced back to the houses of refuge that were established in the latter part of the nineteenth century. Parole is, however, more English and European than American. It was first used by the English to offer a conditional release from prison for those prisoners who agreed to work for a certain period of time to regain their freedom. Parole, unlike probation, was originally motivated by economic pressures rather than humanitarian concerns. Parole provided employers with cheap labor and relieved the British government from having to pay the expenses of their imprisonment.

In recent years, there has been a trend by states to require that inmates serve a longer period of time before they are eligible for parole. Traditionally inmates were eligible after serving 25 percent of their time. Several states now require inmates to serve at least 30 percent of their time before being eligible for parole.

DISCUSSION QUESTIONS

1. Differentiate between probation and parole.

2. How does the historical development of parole differ from that of probation?

3. What are the major goals and objectives of parole?

4. What factors should be considered in releasing the youth in society?

5. Explain the significance of the *Morrissey v. Brewer* case.

ENDNOTES FOR CHAPTER 8

1. Norval Morris and David J. Rothman, *The Oxford History of the Prison: The Practice of Punishment in Western Society*, NY: Oxford, 1995, p.ix.

2. Victoria Advocate, June 22, 1996, p.5A.

3. Hughes v. Rowe, 449 U.S. 5 (1980).

4. *Nickens v. White*, 622 F.2d 967 (8th Cir. 1973).

5. ABA Standards for Criminal Justice, Legal Status of Prisoners, Standard 23-3.1.

6. *Weems v. United States*, 217 U.S. 349 (1910).

7. *Rhodes v. Robinson*, 612 F.2d 766 (3d Cir. 1972).

8. Robert M. Carter and Leslie T. Wilkins eds., *Probation, Parole, and Community Corrections* (New York: John Wiley, 1976).

9. United States Sentencing Commission, *Guidelines Manual*, Section 5D1.1 (Nov. 1994).

10. Most researchers in the area contend that the reverse situation may be more correct. In general, females mature faster than males.

11. President's Commission on Law Enforcement and Administration of Justice, *Task Force Report: Corrections*, (Washington, D.C.; GPO, 1976) p. 60.

12. 408 U.S. 471 (1972).

13. By Thomas B. Marvell, Director Justice Research, Williamsburg, Virginia, *Federal Probation*, December, 1994, Vol. 58, No. 4. Footnotes and references omitted.

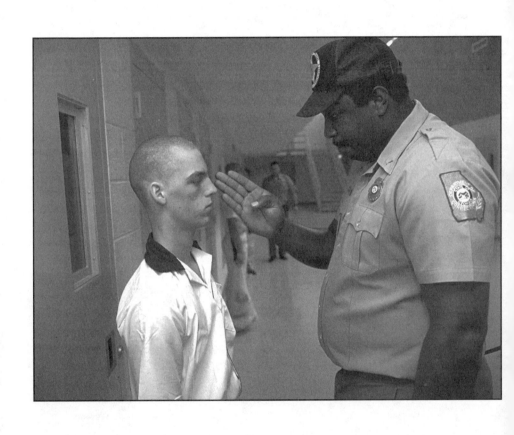

CHAPTER 9

JUVENILE CORRECTIONS

KEY TERMS

Child saving movement

Halfway houses

Juvenile detention centers

Shelters

Parens patriae

CHAPTER OBJECTIVES

After reading this chapter, the reder will be able to:

☐ Explain the development of juvenile corrections.

☐ Trace the development of juvenile court.

☐ Analyze the impact of the *Gault* decision on juvenile justice.

☐ Analyze the present role of juvenile justice.

☐ Identify the critical steps in the waiver of juvenile court jurisdiction.

☐ List the criteria for juvenile diversion programs.

☐ Differentiate between juvenile trials and adult criminal trials.

☐ Explain the juvenile's right to treatment.

☐ List the types of trials handled by juvenile court.

☐ List the problems involved in juvenile corrections.

☐ Explain the conditions of confinement in juvenile institutions.

☐ Describe the steps involved in the release decision in juvenile institutions.

☐ Analyze the effectiveness of group homes.

The primary issues in juvenile justice that are hotly debated today include:

• Whether the juvenile's needs or rights are paramount to society's needs for security.

• What is the proper scope of authority for juvenile justice?

- What processes should be used to adjudicate and make disposition of juvenile offenders?

- What reforms are necessary to improve juvenile justice?

HISTORY OF JUVENILE JUSTICE

At common law, children over 14 years of age were treated as if they were adults. Children under the age of seven were considered incapable of committing crimes. Children between the ages of seven and 14, were "presumed" incapable of committing crimes. However, the state could, by establishing the maturity of the child in question, hold him or her accountable as an adult. Even when formally treated as adults, however, children were rarely punished as harshly as adults by the criminal courts.

In early English history the doctrine of *parens patriae* was developed. According to this doctrine, the king could intervene in family life to protect the child's estate from dishonest parents or guardians. *Parens patriae* can be roughly be defined as the duty of the state to act as a parent in the interest of the child. This principal expanded and now includes the right of the state to intervene to protect child welfare against parental neglect, incompetency and abuse.[1]

The Reform Movement of the nineteenth century also developed a concern for children in general. A "child saving" movement, which was directed at children in need or trouble, grew out of this general concern. The *child savers* attempted to save children by using houses of refuge and reform schools. These institutions were based on the contemporary idea that children's environment made them bad and that removing the youths from poor homes and unhealthy associations and placing them in special homes, houses of refuge, or schools would cause the children to give up their bad and evil habits and would in fact reform the children.[2]

ESTABLISHMENT OF THE JUVENILE COURT

The influence of the child savers prompted the development of the first juvenile court in Cook County, Illinois, in 1899. The Illinois

Juvenile Court Act set up an independent court to handle criminal law violations by children under 16 years of age. The court was also given responsibility for supervising care of neglected, dependent, and wayward youths. The Juvenile Court Act also set up a probation department to monitor youths in the community, and it directed juvenile court judges to place serious offenders in secured training schools for boys and industrial schools for girls. The purpose of the act was to separate juveniles from adult offenders and to provide a legal framework in which juveniles could get proper care and custody.

By 1940, every state in the United States had established a juvenile justice system. The juvenile justice systems were normally created as divisions of family court. As the juvenile court movement spread throughout the United States, it provided for the use of a quasi-legal type of justice. The main concern of the juvenile courts was the best interest of the child. Accordingly, the courts did not adhere strictly to legal doctrine, protect constitutional rights, or conduct their proceedings according to due process requirements. The general theory was that these were not criminal courts, the youths did not have rights as if they were being tried in an adult criminal court.

For many years, the stated goals of the juvenile justice system were to prevent juvenile crime and to rehabilitate juvenile offenders. In the 1980s, an additional goal was imposed on the juvenile courts to protect society.

Our early reform schools were generally punitive in nature and were based on the concept that rehabilitation could only be achieved through hard work. In the 1950s, the influence of therapists, like Carl Rogers, promoted the introduction of psychological treatment in juvenile corrections. By 1960, group counseling techniques were standard procedure in the vast majority of juvenile institutions.

Just as the due process revolution affected prisoners' rights and defendants' rights, the U.S. Supreme Court also drastically altered the juvenile justice system. In a series of cases, it established that juvenile delinquents are protected under the due process clause of the U.S. Constitution and therefore have constitutional rights in juvenile proceedings.

As a result of the influence of constitutional requirements in juvenile proceedings, the distinction between adult and criminal juvenile justice systems is much less now than it was 40 years ago.

IN RE GAULT

FACTS. Jerry Gault, a 15-year-old boy, was taken into custody by the sheriff of Gila County, Arizona. He was arrested based on a complaint of a woman who said that Jerry and another boy had made an obscene telephone call to her. At the time, Gault was on a six-month probation, having previously been declared a delinquent for stealing a wallet.

Based on the verbal complaint, Gault was taken from his home. His parents were not informed that he was taken into custody. When his mother appeared in the evening, she was told by the superintendent that a hearing would be held in juvenile court the following day.

The next day, the police officer who had taken Gault into custody filed a petition alleging Gault's delinquency. Gault, his mother, and the police officer appeared at a judicial hearing before a judge in his chambers. Mrs. Cook, the complaining witness, was not at the hearing. Gault was questioned about the telephone calls and was sent back to the detention home. He was released a few days later.

On the day of Gault's release, his mother received a letter indicating that a hearing would be held on his delinquency status a few days later. When the hearing was held, the complainant, Mrs. Cook, was still not present. There was no transcript or a recording of the proceedings. At the hearing, the juvenile officer stated that Gault had admitted making the lewd telephone calls. Neither the boy nor his parents were advised of any of his rights including the right to be silent, the right to be represented by counsel, or the right to a due process hearing. At the conclusion of the hearing, the juvenile court committed Jerry as a juvenile delinquent to the state's industrial school in Arizona for the period of his minority, i.e. six years.[3]

This, in effect, meant that Gault got six years for making an obscene phone call. Had he been an adult and convicted of the same crime, the maximum punishment would have been no more than a $50.00 fine and/or 60 days in jail.

Attorneys on behalf of Gault filed a writ of *habeas corpus* with the Superior Court for the State of Arizona. The request for the writ was denied. The decision was appealed to the Arizona Supreme Court and that was denied. The denial by the Arizona Supreme Court was then appealed to the U.S. Supreme Court. The U.S. Supreme Court in a far-reaching decision, agreed that Gault's constitutional rights were violated. The Supreme Court indicated that at the very minimum, notice of charges is an essential right of the due process of law, as is the right to confront witnesses and to cross-examine them, the right to counsel, and the privilege against self-incrimination.

Several items not answered by the court in reversing the Arizona's determination of delinquency were whether Gault had a right to a transcript, or whether there was a right to an appellant review.

The significance of the Gault case is that it established that a child in a delinquency adjudication proceedings has procedural due process constitutional rights as set forth in the Constitution. Note: this case was confined to rulings at the adjudication stage of the judicial process.

PRESENT ROLE OF JUVENILE JUSTICE

Our juvenile justice system is independent from, yet interrelated with, the adult criminal justice system. The juvenile court system developed on the concept of *parens patriae*. Starting in the 1960s, the concept was modified to one of procedural due process and in the 1980s to one of controlling chronically delinquent youths. It appears that the juvenile system will continue to evolve as we hunt for a more efficient system.

What is the present role of our juvenile justice system?

1. To provide a social welfare program designed to assist and act as the wise parent

2. To protect the constitutional rights of children

3. To rehabilitate delinquents

4. To protect society from violent youths

JUVENILE DIVERSION

The most common screening out of juveniles after they have been processed into the court system is through the use of diversion. *Diversion* is very popular in the juvenile justice system since it was recommended by the President's Commission on Crime in 1967. There are several reasons for the growing popularity of diversion: it helps to reduce the increasing caseload; it provides more flexibility than the juvenile justice treatment programs currently in existence; it costs less per capita than the use of institutionalization of juveniles.

WAIVER OF JUVENILE COURT JURISDICTION

Prior to the first juvenile court established in Illinois in 1899, juveniles were tried for violations of law in adult criminal court. Today, most statutes provide that juvenile court shall have primary jurisdiction over children under the age of 17. There are provisions in all

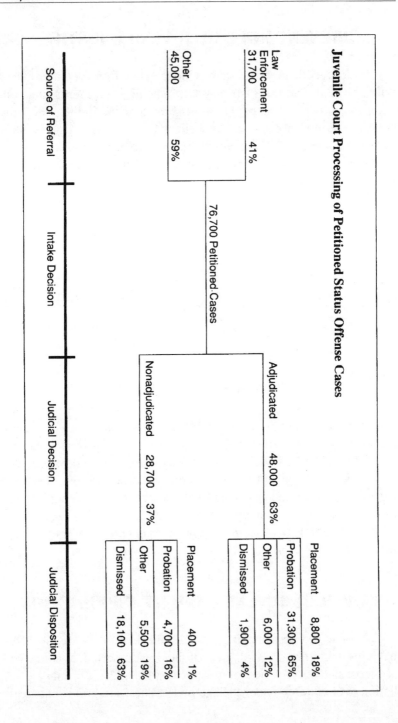

Juvenile Court Processing of Petitioned Status Offense Cases

state statutes, however, in which juvenile court can waive jurisdiction and allow the juvenile to be tried in adult criminal court in cases involving serious crimes. The transfer of juveniles to criminal court is often based on statutory criteria. The two major criteria for waivers are the age of the child and the type of the offense alleged in the petition. For example, many jurisdictions require the child to be at least 15 before he/she may be tried as an adult.

The nature and effect of the waiver is significant to the juvenile. Accordingly, the United States Supreme Court has imposed several procedural protections for juveniles in the waiver process. The first major court decision in this area was that of *Kent v. United States*.[4] This case challenged the provisions of the District Court of Columbia, which stated that juvenile court could waive jurisdiction after a full investigation. The Supreme Court held that the waiver proceeding is a critically important stage in the juvenile process, and therefore, the juveniles must be afforded minimum requirements of due process of law.

Consistent with the minimal requirements, the following conditions are considered necessary before a valid waiver may occur:

1. A hearing must be held on the motion to waiver.

2. The child is entitled to be represented by counsel at the hearing.

3. The attorney representing the juvenile must be given access to all records and reports considered by the court in reaching a waiver decision.

4. The court must provide a written statement of the reasons for the waiver decision.

Prior to 1975, the procedure in most states was that if a juvenile was charged with a serious offense, there would be an adjudication hearing to determine whether the juvenile had committed the offense. If the court found that the juvenile committed the offense, there would be a hearing to determine whether a waiver of juvenile court jurisdiction should be entered and the juvenile tried in adult criminal court. In 1975, however, the case of *Breed v. Jones* held that jeopardy attaches when the juvenile court begins to hear evidence as to whether the juvenile committed the offense. Therefore, if an adjudication hearing is

ARREST RATES FOR JUVENILE OFFENDERS

per 100,000 population

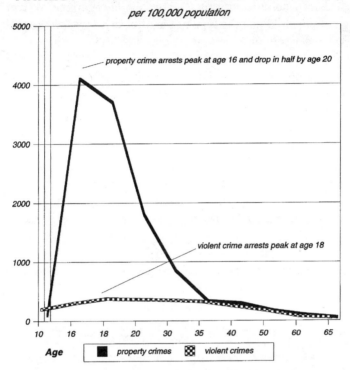

property crime arrests peak at age 16 and drop in half by age 20

violent crime arrests peak at age 18

Age ▪ property crimes ▨ violent crimes

held prior to the waiver hearing, the juvenile cannot be waived to adult criminal court because that would constitute double jeopardy.[5] After the *Breed v. Jones* case, the courts of all the states were modified to establish a waiver hearing first. Then if it was determined that the juvenile should be retained in the juvenile court system, a hearing on the adjudication phase would take place.

JUVENILE TRIALS

Juvenile courts dispose of about 1.5 million delinquency cases each year. The trial process in juvenile court is referred to as the *adju-*

dicatory hearing. It is in this hearing that the court determines whether or not the juvenile committed the offenses alleged in the petition. During the adjudication process, the juvenile has the constitutional right to a fair notice of the charges, the right to be represented by counsel, the right to be confronted by and cross-examine witnesses, and the privilege against self-incrimination. In addition, the juvenile court in adjudicating the juvenile a delinquent, must use the standard of proof beyond a reasonable doubt.

At the conclusion of the adjudicatory hearing, the court is required to enter a judgment either sustaining the petition (i.e., finding that the accused committed the crimes alleged in the petition) or dismissing the petition. Once the juvenile has been adjudicated a delinquent, the court must make a determination as to the disposition of the child

DISPOSITION

At the separate disposition hearing, the juvenile court should look at the record of the delinquent, the family background, the needs of the accused, and the safety of the public. A juvenile court judge has broad discretion in determining the disposition of the juvenile. Some of the standard dispositions are dismissal of the petition, suspended judgment, probation, placement in a community treatment program, or commitment to a state agency that is responsible for juvenile institutional care. This latter disposition is basically a commitment to a reformatory or other state institution for juveniles. In addition, the court has the power to place the child with parents or relatives under extensive or moderate supervision. It can make dispositional arrangements with private youth-serving agencies, or it can have the child committed to a mental institution.

As in adult criminal court, probation is the most commonly used formal sentence for juvenile offenders. In fact, many states require that before a youth may be sent to an institution, the youth must have failed on probation unless the juvenile has been charged with a serious felony.

Probation may include placing the child under the supervision of the juvenile probation department for the purposes of community treatment. The conditions of probations are normally spelled out in the state court's order. There are general conditions that all delinquents are re-

quired to obey, such as to obey the law, to stay away from other delinquents, to attend school, etc. There are also special conditions of probation that may require the child to participate in certain training, treatment, or education programs.

Source of Referral of Delinquency Cases by Offense

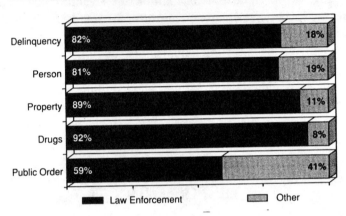

Delinquency Case Rates by Age at Referral

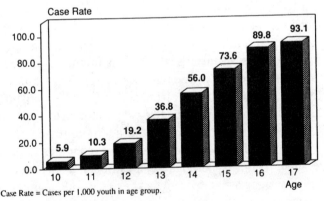

Case Rate = Cases per 1,000 youth in age group.

Source: U. S. Dept. of Justice

INSTITUTIONALIZATION

The most severe disposition that a judge may make at a juvenile
court hearing is the institutionalization of the juvenile. In most states,
this means that the child can be committed until he or she is 21 years of

age. Note that the disposition of commitment to an institution is an indeterminate sentence unlike that of most adult courts.

Many professionals involved in delinquency and juvenile law have questioned the practice of committing juveniles to institutions. Deinstitutionalization of juveniles has been attempted by using small residential facilities, operated by juvenile care agencies, to replace the larger state schools. The success of deinstitutionalization of juveniles is still being debated by scholars and professionals.

THE RIGHT TO TREATMENT

Although it has not directly stated that juveniles have a right to treatment while incarcerated, it appears that the Supreme Court is leaning in that direction. The Court of Appeals for the 7th Circuit indicates that *Nelson v. Heyne* upheld the constitutional right to treatment for institutionalized juveniles under the Fourteenth Amendment; and recent decisions by the U. S. Supreme Court seem to indicate that juveniles do have a right to receive treatment if committed to a juvenile institution.[6]

TYPES OF CASES HANDLED BY THE JUVENILE COURTS

Violent Youths

Violent youth crimes represent only about seven percent of juvenile court caseloads. However, they account for 11 percent of the detentions, 12 percent of the out-of-home placements, and 27 percent of the transfers to adult criminal courts.[7] The courts are more likely to file petitions in cases involving violent offenses than in any other types of cases.

Property Cases

Property offenses are a major part of the juvenile crime problem. Approximately 30 percent of all juvenile arrests are based on property offenses. Shoplifting was the most common offense for youths under 15 years of age. Burglary was the most common property offense for older youths. Female offenders are more likely to be involved in shoplifting. Males were more likely to be involved in burglary.[8]

Approximately 25 percent of the youths arrested for property offenses are detained. Juveniles involved with motor vehicle thefts were the ones most likely to be detained awaiting disposition of the case.

TYPES OF INSTITUTIONS

Currently, juveniles who have been adjudicated as delinquent and committed may be held in one of six types of facilities. The six types are:

- Detention centers

- Shelters

- Reception/diagnostic centers

- Training schools

- Ranches or camps

- Halfway houses or group homes

Detention centers are short-term, secure facilities that hold juveniles awaiting adjudication, disposition, or placement in an institution. *Shelters* are also short-term facilities that are operated like detention centers, but are non-secure with a physically unrestricted environment. *Reception/diagnostic centers* are also short-term facilities that are used to screen youths for assignments to appropriate levels of custody and institutions.

Training schools are generally long-term secure facilities that are used only for adjudicated delinquents. *Ranches, forestry camps,* and *farms* are long-term, non-secure facilities used for adjudicated juveniles. *Halfway houses* or *group homes* are non-secure facilities that are used to help integrate youths back into the community. They may be either long- or short-term facilities.

As you may have discerned from the above, there are two levels of security: secure and non-secure. *Secure facilities* are characterized by their locks, bars, and fences. Movement is typically restricted in a secure facility. *Non-secure facilities* are characterized by their lack of bars, locks, and fences. In addition, non-secure facilities permit a greater freedom of movement for youths within and around the facility.

CONDITIONS OF CONFINEMENT IN JUVENILE FACILITIES

In a recent study of conditions of confinement in U.S. juvenile detention and correctional facilities, conducted by ABT Associates for the Office of Juvenile Justice and Delinquency Prevention (OJJDP), institutional crowding was found to be pervasive.[9] Thousands of juvenile offenders, more than 75 percent of the confined population, were housed in facilities that violated one or more standards related to living space (facility design capacity, sleeping areas, and living unit size). Between 1987 and 1991, the percentage of confined juveniles living in facilities in which the daily population exceeded design capacity increased from 36 percent to 47 percent. Crowding was found to be associated with higher rates of institutional violence, suicidal behavior, and greater reliance on the use of short-term isolation.

The study, required by Congress in its 1988 amendments to the Juvenile Justice and Delinquency Prevention Act, is the first such nationwide investigation of conditions in secure juvenile detention and correctional facilities. Using nationally recognized correctional standards as a gauge, researchers assessed how juvenile offenders' basic needs were met, how institutional security and resident safety were maintained, what treatment programming was provided, and how juveniles' rights were protected.

The study included surveys mailed in 1991 to all 984 public and private juvenile detention centers, reception and diagnostic facilities, training schools, and ranches in the United States. In addition, experienced juvenile correctional practitioners conducted two-day site visits to a representative sample of nearly 100 facilities in the fall of 1991. These facilities held about 65,000 juveniles on the date of the 1991 Children in Custody census, or about 69 percent of the juveniles con-

A police officer plays chess in a non-secure facility with a teenaged boy.

fined on that date in the United States. During 1990, these facilities received nearly 690,000 admissions, including readmissions and transfers of juveniles from other facilities.

Based on standards conformance and related outcome measures, researchers concluded that serious and widespread problems existed in the areas of living space, health care, institutional security and safety, and control of suicidal behavior. In important areas of treatment, rehabilitation, and education, the evaluation demonstrated the need for more rigorous assessment of how facilities are meeting juveniles' needs in these areas.

The study found several areas in which conditions of confinement appeared to be generally adequate: basic needs such as food, clothing, hygiene, recreation, and accommodations. An important overall finding was that, generally, conformance to existing standards does not guarantee adequate conditions for juveniles in custody. For example, although more than 90 percent of juvenile detention facilities conformed to the fire inspection requirement, more than half of the 30 detention centers visited had at least one unmarked fire exit in a sleeping area. Two-thirds did not have fire escape routes posted. In some, fire exits were blocked.

In many cases the standards only require the existence of policies, procedures, or programs, without stipulating performance measures or desired outcomes. Thus, interpretation of standards conformance is problematic. Over the 12 months prior to the mail survey, researchers estimated that:

- Juveniles injured 6,900 staff and 24,200 other juveniles.

- 11,000 juveniles committed 17,600 acts of suicidal behavior, with 10 suicides in 1990.

- More than 18,600 incidents required emergency medical care.

- More than 435,800 juveniles were held in short-term isolation (one to 24 hours) and almost 84,000 were isolated for more than 24 hours.

- 9,700 juveniles escaped from custody.

In March 1993, OJJDP officials, ABT researchers, juvenile correctional experts, and youth advocates from across the country assembled in Washington, D.C., to react to the findings. While there was general concurrence about the findings, some experts speculated that facility conditions have deteriorated since 1991, citing substantial state and local budget cuts, resulting in staff reductions, staff turnover, and strain on facility program and maintenance budgets.

Compounding these pressures are demographic shifts that already show a steady growth in the juvenile population at risk. Concern was voiced that problems of crowding and related conditions will not only persist, but will increase, to the serious detriment of juveniles for whom rehabilitation is still a hope. They were especially concerned about the impact on minority youth. Between 1987 and 1991, the minority populations in detention and correctional facilities grew from 53 percent to 63 percent of the confined population.

In announcing the study's release, Attorney General Janet Reno declared, "This study puts an exclamation point on the obvious conclusion that America must not only take better care of its children before they get into trouble, but also not abandon them once they are in trouble."

GROUP HOME PROGRAMS

As noted earlier, one type of institution used in juvenile corrections is the group home. A group home has been defined as a long-term juvenile facility in which residents are allowed extensive contact with the community, such as attending school or holding a job.[10] The below report discusses the problems that the group home treatment programs are experiencing.[11]

The study noted that significant changes have occurred in the juvenile justice system in the last several decades. Due to recent emphasis on rehabilitation, reform, and above all, concern for the welfare of young offenders, the juvenile justice system has employed a wide variety of options in treating young offenders. Optimism about rehabilitation and dissatisfaction with the traditional "lockup" in detention homes has caused many to consider residential treatment and the rehabilitation of juveniles in family-type centers rather than conventional incarceration. The popular trend, therefore, has been deinstitutionalization. Due to this dominant philosophy, group home treatment programs, one of oldest options in treating young offenders, gained a special momentum during the 1960s and 1970s. The availability of federal dollars, the rising concern of numerous child-care institutions, and above all, the dissatisfaction with detaining juveniles have caused group homes to proliferate as a viable alternative and supplement to juvenile institutions.[12]

Unlike many alternatives for juveniles, group homes have been recognized for providing a family-type atmosphere where the youths and house parents (counselors and case workers) often establish the same warm and intense ties that one would hope to find in healthy families. Stewart and Associates, by tracing 906 juvenile offenders in a three-year period, recorded that such family-type atmosphere has a significant impact on the recidivism rate of juvenile offenders. Group home treatment programs, as they found, are particularly effective when first-time offenders are referred to such programs. Similarly, Gaier and Sarnacki suggested that group home treatment is an effective approach in interrupting delinquent behavior, because it is designed to alter the delinquent's environment and provide a meaningful family-type setting. According to Murray and Dox, institutions have a greater "suppression" rate on subsequent arrests than do group home treatment programs.

Group home treatment programs are also recognized for their cost efficiency in providing a workable alternative for unruly and delinquent children. At the time that most local governments are pressed with budgetary concerns, group home treatment programs are viewed as a promising alternative. One recent investigation by the Department of Justice regarded group home treatment programs as a viable option in saving the juvenile justice system from budgetary problems. The investigation further revealed that group home treatment programs have been appealing to juvenile court judges due to both their effectiveness in treating young offenders and their cost efficiency.

The Treatment

The group home treatment program in this study was established in the mid-1970s by a local juvenile probation officer due to his dissatisfaction with the local juvenile court's referral of the majority of unruly and delinquent children to state facilities. The program began by housing a few unruly, disturbed, and runaway children in the 1970s, later accepting juveniles with various problems and backgrounds in the 1980s. The program started with a few hundred dollars donated by local businesses and grew to have an operational budget of over $350,000 in the late 1980s. Despite the rapid growth in a short period, the program solely functions on donations and charitable contributions by citizens and local businesses without relying on local or state funds.

The treatment program rests on providing a therapeutic community, elevating childrens' self-esteem, reducing stress, and providing group orientation. The program offers community service projects (helping senior citizens, beautifying the community, etc.), assists in obtaining employment, organizes athletic activities, and helps residents with educational and vocational programs. Overall, the program focuses on building a positive attitude and respect for others. In particular, being in a position to provide service to others enables the juvenile to help rather than hinder.

Two male juvenile sex offenders play roles during a therapy session at the Texas State School.

Conclusions

Treatment of juveniles in the community and rehabilitation of young offenders in a group home setting has become a hotly debated subject. The recent "get-tough-on-crime" policy, coupled with the national concern regarding the drug problem, has motivated many decision makers to re-evaluate the juvenile justice process. During the last few years, a number of states have moved toward more stringent and punitive measures to deal with young offenders. Motivated by the increasing number of serious offenses committed by juveniles and the ineffectiveness of community treatment programs in reducing recidivism, proponents of stiffer sentencing have proposed the departure from the rehabilitative efforts and the re-implementation of punitive measures. In such debates, group home treatment programs have been attacked frequently for their leniency and their inability to punish and change young offenders.

Some believe that the entire juvenile justice system is becoming tougher. A few states have already revised their juvenile justice system, reflecting more concern for retribution and deterrence than for rehabilitation and reform. In Washington, for instance, the entire juvenile justice code has been revised to include detention and determinate sentencing. By dropping the family court's jurisdiction over status offenders, the Washington legislatures have explicitly noted that the aim of the new legislation is primarily the protection of citizens and community through tougher sentencing rather than the welfare of juvenile offenders. Other states have followed the same path. California, Colorado, Delaware, Florida, and New Mexico have adopted legislation that focuses more on retribution and deterrence than concern for juveniles. It is believed that the remaining states will adopt more punitive measures in dealing with young offenders, especially the violent and recurring offenders, before the turn of this decade.

Many believe that this recent development will undermine the entire rehabilitative effort. Recent concern for punishment will ultimately jeopardize the existence of community treatment programs, and in particular, group home program facilities. Proponents of stiffer punishment, however, believe that nothing will be lost. A high recidivism rate, in their view, is an indication that group home programs have failed to live up to their intent.

The current findings, however, suggest a different outlook. The analysis of sample cases revealed that the productivity or success of group homes could be maximized if certain factors are taken into consideration. First, it was found that group home programs would be highly effective in the rehabilitation and reform of young offenders if such an option is considered in the early stages of delinquent behavior. Precisely, group home programs are most effective (77 to 80 percent) if juveniles are dispositioned to such treatment programs immediately following the first or second delinquency act. Conversely, they are least effective (33 to 15 percent) when group home facilities were considered after five or more delinquent acts.

Secondly, the "get tough" approach against young offenders may not reduce the number of repeated offenses committed by this group. Records indicate that group home programs are the least effective when the child has served a period of time in state detention facilities prior to his or her referral to a group home program. In comparison, those previously placed on probation had a higher rate of success in group home programs. These findings lead to arguments that suggest that the reimplementation of determinate sentencing and the application of punitive measures by confining juveniles to detention facilities may result in a higher rate of recidivism and ultimately the elevation of offenses committed by juveniles. Hence, in the long run, we can conclude that such an approach will cause a dramatic increase in the population of adult felons, because the juvenile justice system will have failed to serve its clientele properly. On face value, the "get tough" approach may appear promising, it may also cause unexpected results.

Finally, to depart from a productive alternative that has proven to be effective in reforming young offenders while reducing the costs of the juvenile justice system is premature. In light of the recent war on drugs and the substantial cuts to juvenile justice system budgets in favor of efforts to combat drug kingpins, it does not seem logical to revoke an alternative that has proven to be cost effective. Group home treatment programs could become productive if they are used properly. To maximize their success and reduce the rate of repeated offenses by juveniles, this option must be made a priority rather than considered an option after dissatisfaction with other alternatives in the juvenile justice system.

JUVENILE RELEASE DECISIONS

Unlike the adult parole process, most juveniles' release times are not determined at the post-sentencing hearing. Generally, the juvenile's length of commitment is determined by the youth's progress toward rehabilitation. In some jurisdictions, progress is measured by a token system that awards a specific number of points for various actions. This is similar to the "task sentences" referred to by Maconochie.

Although there is a general agreement that youths should be released as soon as they are ready, there are no valid measures to determine if a juvenile has been successfully rehabilitated or has undergone a real change of attitude. The criterion used to determine if the juvenile has been successfully rehabilitated and thus should be released is generally whether or not the juvenile conforms to institution rules or causes problems. Thus, by appearing to have been reformed, the youth receives the earliest release date. Accordingly, the youth's conduct and behavior in the institution may be based solely on the desire to please his supervisors to obtain release.

The question of when to release the youth depends on predictions of the youth's future behavior. The policy considerations that are required to be evaluated before the youth is released include:

- Has the youth been reformed?

- Is it unlikely that the youth will commit another serious offense?

- Was the youth's behavior acceptable during his or her confinement?

- Does the youth have a home or other place, such as a group home, to live?

- Will suitable employment, training, or treatment be available for the youth on release?

- What is the youth's own perception of his or her ability to handle reintegration into the community?

- Are the seriousness of the youth's past offenses and the circumstances in which they were committed sufficiently severe so as to preclude release?

PAROLE

Most juveniles, after release from institutions, return to the communities from which they came. Generally, juveniles are released from confinement long before the expiration of their maximum period of commitment. In some states, juveniles must serve a minimum time before being released. In nine states, the judge who committed the juvenile must agree to the release before he/she may be released early. The problem with this latter practice or requirement is that often the committing judge is too busy with other cases and does not have sufficient time to review the case and make a viable recommendation as to the release decision. In addition, because no new presentencing reports are prepared, the judge may act on dated or incomplete information. For these reasons, judicial involvement in the early release decision has been eliminated in most states.

Most experts assign two goals to parole: protection of the society and proper adjustment of the youth. Presently, it appears that the most important goal is the protection of society. Many see the two goals as conflicting ones involving society versus the youth. A better approach appears to be the concept of protecting society by rehabilitating the youth.

Parole includes the objective of assisting the parolee in integration into the community. Therefore, the youth must be assisted in coping with the problems faced upon release and to adjust to the status of being a parolee. In order for the parolee to be a permanent benefit to society, parole agencies must assist in the development of the youth's ability to make good decisions that are behaviorally acceptable to the community.

SUMMARY

At common law, children over 14 years of age were treated as if they were adults. Children under the age of seven were considered incapable of committing crimes. For children between the ages of seven and 14, it was presumed that they were incapable of committing crimes, however the state could, by establishing the maturity of the child, hold him or her accountable as an adult. Even when formally treated as adults, children were rarely punished as harshly as adults were punished by the criminal courts.

In early English history the doctrine of *parens patriae* was developed. According to this doctrine, the king could intervene in family life to protect the child's estate from dishonest parents or guardians. *Parens patriae* can be roughly defined as the duty of the state to act as a parent in the interest of the child. This principal expanded and now includes the right of the state to intervene to protect child welfare against parental neglect, incompetency and abuse.

Our juvenile justice system is independent yet interrelated with the adult criminal justice system. The juvenile court system developed based on the concept of *parens patriae*. Starting in the 1960s, the concept was modified to one of procedural due process and, in the 1980s, to one of controlling chronically delinquent youths. It appears that the juvenile system will continue to evolve as we search for a more efficient system.

The transfer of juveniles to criminal court is often based on statutory criteria, and the two major criteria for waivers are the age of the child and the type of the offense alleged in the petition. As in adult criminal court, probation is the most commonly used formal sentence for juvenile offenders. In fact, many states require that before a youth may be sent to an institution, the youth must have failed on probation unless the juvenile has been charged with a serious felony.

Juveniles who are adjudicated as delinquent may be sent to one of six types of facilities. These include: detention centers, shelters, reception/diagnostic centers, training schools, ranches and camps, halfway houses and group homes. The juvenile's length of commitment to any of these facilties is generally determined by the youth's progress toward rehabilitation. The criterion used to determine if a juvenile has been successfully rehabilitated is typically whether the juvenile conformed to the rules and regulations of the institution while confined.

Parole may include placing the child under the supervision of the juvenile department for the purposes of community treatment. The conditions of the parole are normally spelled out in the state court's order. There are general conditions that all delinquents are required to obey, such as to obey the law, to stay away from other delinquents, to attend school, etc. In addition, there may be special conditions of probation that require individuals to participate in certain training, treatment or education programs.

DISCUSSION QUESTIONS

1. Explain the differences between juvenile corrections and adult corrections.

2. Summarize the history of juvenile justice.

3. What reforms are necessary to improve juvenile justice?

4. When should a juvenile be tried as an adult? Why?

5. How do juvenile trials differ from adult trials?

ENDNOTES TO CHAPTER 9

1. Ralph Weisheit and Diane Alexander, "Juvenile Justice Philosophy and Demise of Parens Patriae," *Federal Probation,* December 1988, p. 56.

2. Anthony Platt, *The Child Savers* (Chicago: University of Chicago Press, 1969).

3. *In re Gault,* 387 U.S. 1, (1967).

4. 383 U.S. 541 (1966).

5. 421 U.S. 519 (1975).

6. 491 F.2d 1430 (7th Cir., 1974).

7. Jeffery Butts and D.J. Connors-Beatty, "Juvenile Court's Response to Violent Offenders," *U.S. Department of Justice, Office of Juvenile Justice and Delinquency Prevention, Special Report,* April 1993.

8. Ellen H. Nimick, "Juvenile Court Property Cases," *U.S. Department of Justice, Office of Juvenile Justice and Delinquency Prevention, Special Report*, November 1990.

9. Barbara Allen-Hagen, "Conditions of Confinement in Juvenile Detention and Correctional Facilities," *Office of Juvenile Justice and Delinquency Prevention, Fact Sheet #1*, April 1993.

10. John N. Ferdico, *Criminal Law and Justice Dictionary,* (St. Paul: West, 1992.)

11. Bahram Haghighi and Alma Lopez, "Success/Failure of Group Home Treatment Programs for Juveniles," *Federal Probation*, September 1993.

12. Citations and references have been omitted.

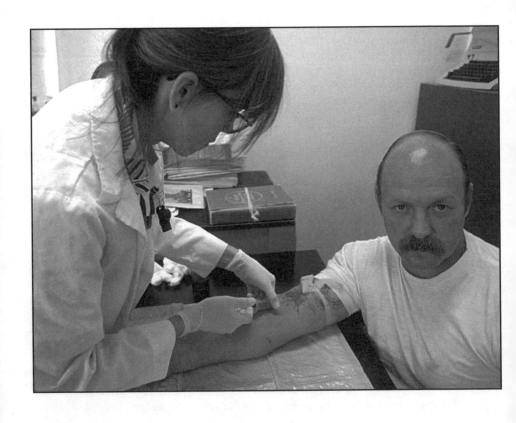

CHAPTER 10

SPECIAL APPLICATIONS OF DETENTION AND CORRECTIONS

KEY TERMS

Coeducational institutions

Group counseling

Megan's Law

Privatization

Restorative justice

CHAPTER OBJECTIVES

After studying this chapter, the reader will be able to:

☐ Explain the concepts behind Megan's Law.

☐ Analyze the use of chemical castration in dealing with sex offenders.

☐ List the objectives of coeducational institutions.

☐ Analyze the concept of prison privatization.

☐ List the four forms that privatization may take.

☐ List the problems involved in treating and correcting sex offenders.

☐ Explain the problems involved in confining offenders who have AIDS.

☐ Explain the concepts involved in restorative justice.

This chapter discusses the special applications of detention, such as medical problems, coeducational institutions, the sex offender industry, and electrified fences.

HEALTH PROBLEMS

AIDS

Any discussion of contagious diseases starts with AIDS [HIV (Human Immunodeficiency Virus)]. AIDS is a fairly recent disease, first discovered in 1981. It is caused by a virus that damages the body's immune system destroying the body's ability to fight off germs and leaving the body susceptible to certain diseases that generally do not occur in individuals with healthy immune systems. The diseases, such as PCP pneumonia and certain cancers, are usually fatal. In recent months, more has been discovered regarding the virus, and effective treatment or cure may be discovered soon.

Not all persons who test positive for HIV have full-blown AIDS. If the individual tests positive for HIV, then a series of blood tests must be taken to determine if the person has HIV/AIDS infection. It appears that HIV individuals without AIDS symptoms can spread the infection even if they never develop full-blown AIDS. It appears that for HIV to spread, infected blood must enter the bloodstream of another person. Casual contact does not transmit HIV. Generally, the spread occurs through heterosexual or homosexual activity and blood-to-blood contact, such as drug needle sharing.

Execution Isn't the No. 1 Killer in Prisons[1]

During the fiscal year 1993-94, 138 prisoners died of AIDS and 19 were executed in Texas prisons. According to the latest figures, the disease is taking more than twice as many lives in Texas prisons than either heart disease (64 for the same year) or cancer (61 for the same year), the second- and third- highest causes of death behind bars. It is estimated that at least two percent of all prisoners are HIV-positive. During the fiscal year '93-'94, the state of Texas earmarked about $427 million for inmates' health care, including mental health and drug abuse treatment. About $255 million was spent directly on medical treatment. The medical treatment is provided by the University of Texas Medical Branch (UTMB). The prison system pays UTMB $159 per month, per prisoner in the system for medical treatment. UTMB provides a health maintenance organization (HMO) type of medical service for all prisoners. Probably the main difference between regular HMOs and the UTMB one for the prisoners is that the prisoners do not have to make any "co-payments."

A young man clad in a long blonde wig applies purple lipstick.

There are three major concerns in dealing with prisoners who test positive for HIV: preventing the spread of the virus to others, protecting employees who deal with infected prisoners, and the legal rights of infected prisoners. Offenders with AIDS need special treatment and medical needs. Offenders who test positive for HIV, but present no symptoms also create a special problem because they may spread the virus. Those offenders, however, have privacy rights claims regarding who may be notified regarding their condition. One issue that administrators must face is whether HIV/AIDs individuals should be segregated from the general institution population. Another issue is whether all prisoners should be subjected to mandatory HIV testing. Most states currently test inmates on their request or upon clinical indication of need. Approximately 16 states test all incoming prisoners. Five states test all prisoners being released from an institution.

Mental Health Problems

One major problem facing correctional institution directors is handling the mentally disordered offender. While there are conflicting opinions regarding the relationship between mentally disordered persons and involvement in criminal behavior, research indicates that a large segment of the population in correctional institutions have serious mental problems. One study concluded that about 10 percent of prisoners have severe or significant psychiatric disabilities. To handle the most seriously mentally disabled offender, most states have at least one prison that has special treatment programs and facilities for the mentally disordered offender.

Other correctional institutions have either a full-time or part-time psychological service team that works with offenders. Many institutions and parole authorities require a psychological profile of offenders under their care. Accordingly, a good portion of the psychological resources are used to administer and interpret standardized psychological tests.

Mental health professionals in correctional institutions generally provide counseling and crisis intervention services. Counseling approaches use either individual or group counseling. *Individual counseling* is one-on-one counseling and is generally part of a larger treatment program and requires a large number of visits. The high ratio of offenders to counseling personnel makes it difficult in most situations to conduct any extensive individual counseling programs.

Group counseling is a planned activity with three or more clients present for the purpose of solving personal and social problems. While most professionals would prefer to do individual counseling, group counseling allows the mental health teams to provide more service to more offenders. Group counseling is also practical because there is an availability of offenders with similar types of problems. Group counseling, in most institutions, focuses on personal and social needs. It is different from group therapy which is generally concerned with deep-seated psychological problems and needs to be directed by highly-trained mental health professionals.

SEX-OFFENDERS

Registration Laws

Most states have some form of sex-offender registration law that requires convicted sex offenders to register when they move into a community. Sex offender registration laws are often called "Megan's laws", after Megan Kanka, who was raped and strangled by a known sex offender.

In 1994, Jesse K. Timmendequas confessed to strangling and raping Kanka when she was seven years old. She had just finished the first grade. Timmendequas lived across the street. He was a slight man with dirty blond hair and a nervous preoccupation with himself. He had pleaded guilty twice before to sexually assaulting small children. In 1981, a judge had labeled him a "compulsive, repetitive sexual offender." After he had served more than seven years for the 1981 crime, he was released. He and two other convicted child molesters had quietly moved into a neighborhood made up of split-level homes, where people tend to mind their children well. Before the killing, he appeared to the neighbors as pleasant and had helped an elderly man move furniture. His classmates in high school considered him "one of those quiet kids." A therapist stated that: "He would pout and then go hide. He spent a lot of time in bed."

The cases against him stemming from the assaults in 1979 and 1981 were handled routinely in the legal system. He benefitted from plea bargains in both cases. One prosecutor justified the plea bargain on the fact that, because child victims make poor witnesses, he was reluctant to take the case to trial.

His first known case occurred in 1979. He was 18 years old and his victim was five years old. He told police that he just wanted to look at her vagina. But the little girl stated that he smelled her and touched her. For that offense he pleaded guilty to attempted aggravated sexual assault. The judge in that case concluded that, "While he certainly has mental or psychiatric problems, these seem to be of the type which can be dealt with best in an outpatient setting." He was given a suspended sentence on the condition that he go for counseling. Later cited for violating the terms of his suspended sentence, he served nine months in the Middlesex County Adult Correctional Center.

His second known case occurred in 1981, only months after he was released from the correctional center. The victim, who was seven years old at the time, was found unconscious in the woods near her neighborhood home. Examination revealed that sexual contact had occurred. There were blue marks on her neck where she had been choked and her stomach had black and blue marks on it. He was charged with five felonies and attempted murder. As the result of his plea bargain, all charges except the attempt was dropped. The judge imposed the maximum 10-year sentence and stated that he "constituted a danger to the public at large and to young children in particular." At that time, a 10-year sentence in New Jersey really meant six years and eight months with credit for good behavior. He was sent to Avenel, New Jersey's center for sexual offenders. Avenel's therapeutic approach to sexual offenders has been criticized for years by officials who claim that they "coddle" offenders. Supporters contend that therapy helps some child molesters and rapists, who are destined to return to the streets, gain enough insight to control themselves. Both sides admit that sex-offender treatment programs are particularly frustrated by the many offenders who do not open up for treatment. Individuals who were at Avenel at the time say that Timmendequas never seemed engaged in therapy.

Megan's death has since become a part of the national psyche. Many states have passed laws named for her requiring that communities be notified when sex offenders move in. On May 17, 1996, President Clinton signed a federal "Megan's Law." The Random House Webster's College Dictionary added *Megan's Law* as a new term in the language. Megan's mother speaks often around the country, lobbying for the law and warning parents to take care of their children.

Public records in New Jersey and interviews with people who knew Timmedequas and with psychologists, detectives, lawyers, a judge and other professionals who dealt with him picture him as the type of sex offender who defies efforts at rehabilitation.[2] One of his earlier victims, who was attacked in 1981, described the turmoil she felt 15 years later. When she heard he was accused of killing Megan, she said she "wanted to kill him herself" and "that they didn't stop him the first time."

Under Megan's Law, when an the individual is released from prison, the warden has a duty to notify him or her of this requirement. If the individual moves or intends to reside in a new location for a period of time (normally about seven days) he or she must register with the local law enforcement agency. In most states, at the time that he or she registers, the individual must submit a photograph and fingerprints. Except for certain identifying data on the registration form, the information is available to the public.

One of the issues involved in Megan's Law is whether it may be applied to people already convicted before the state act was passed. A sex offender who had completed his sentence before the enactment of the statute argued that it was a violation of his constitutional rights to require him to comply with the statute. The U.S. Court of Appeals for the Third Circuit held that the purpose of the statutes was not to punish the plaintiff, but to safeguard the public. Accordingly, the registration requirement can be explained only in terms of helping law enforcement agencies keep tabs on certain offenders and that the impact of the registration was not significant enough to brand it punishment.[3]

The New Jersey statute in question is typical of notification statutes. Under it, all people who complete sentences for certain crimes involving sexual assault must register with local law enforcement agencies. The registrant must provide certain identifying information to the local agency in the municipality in which he or she lives. He or she must confirm the address every 90 days and notify the agency if he or she moves. In addition, when the offender moves, he or she must notify the law enforcement agency in his or her new municipality. The prosecutor in the county in which the offender lives must determine whether the registrant poses a low, moderate, or high risk of re-offense. Under Tier I (low risk), notification is the only requirement. Under Tier II (moderate risk), the prosecutor must ensure that schools, licensed day care centers, summer camps, scout organizations, etc. are notified. Notification is not shared with the public under Tier II. Under Tier III (high risk), the law enforcement agencies are required to notify members of the public who are likely to encounter the registrant. Notification of individuals and organizations under Tiers II and III include the registrant's name, a recent photograph, his physical description, offense, address, place of employment or schooling, and a description and license number of his or her automobile.

Treating Sex Offenders: An Industry?

In 1995, state prisons held about 93,000 convicted sex offenders. The number of convicted sex offenders has increased about 46 percent in the past five years. It is estimated that for every sex offender in prison, there are two out in the communities on parole or probation. Therapy for sex offenders is the popular, though controversial, solution. There is, however, substantial evidence that therapy does not work. For example, a 1993 Canadian study by R. Karl Hanson of the Solicitor General's Office found that approximately 42 percent of imprisoned child molesters are later reconvicted for violent or sexual crimes. The study also concluded therapy did not change the reconviction rate, despite the fact that therapy programs generally accept only those persons considered "treatable."

In 1996, the United States had more than 2,000 known sex-offender treatment programs, more than triple the approximate 640 in 1986. Some of the treatment programs are based in prisons. In the communities, solo practitioners, private clinics and nonprofit agencies run programs. Even the Salvation Army offers limited therapy services at some of its facilities. The "sex-offender treatment" industry now has its own associations, holds conferences, publishes books and a professional journal. Some therapists even advertise their services on the Internet. The Association of Treatment of Sexual Abusers, headquartered in Beaverton, OR, has seen its membership grow from 25 in 1986 to over 1,000 current members. Safer Society, a major publisher on this subject matter, has annual sales of textbooks, workbooks, and videotapes of about $500,000 a year.

One of the problems in sex-offender treatment programs is the lack of definite certification guidelines. As of May 1996, only one state (Washington) required sex-offender treatment providers to pass a certification test to practice in the field. Texas maintains a registry of treatment providers. Elsewhere, just about anyone can "hang out a shingle."

The sex-offender treatment programs generally differ sharply from traditional psychotherapy. Therapists often do not guarantee confidentiality to clients to help parole and probation officers determine if the offender has violated the terms of his release. Often parole and probation officers steer offenders to programs that cooperate with law enforcement. Jerome Miller, of the National Center on Institutions and Alternatives in Washington, D.C., claims that this high level of cooperation makes therapists a "part of the crime-control industry." [4]

The methods used by many therapists are considered controversial. The most controversial is the drama therapy method. Under this therapy, sexual crimes are acted out with the sex offenders acting as victims of the crimes. Profanity and physical reenactments of past traumas are standard in drama therapy. Another popular treatment program is to encourage offenders to confront each other about their crimes in group counseling sessions. Some therapists encourage the offenders to write letters of apology to victims or pretend to deliver a eulogy at the victim's mock funeral. These latter programs are designed to help offenders develop "victim empathy."

Chemical Castration

In 1996, California passed a statute that permits the chemical castration of repeat child molesters. The statute is controversial and has raised a group of ethical and constitutional issues. In addition, some doctors contend that using the testosterone-lowering hormone poses medical problems and may not be effective.

An injectable form of Provera is used for the castration. The injectable form is widely known as "Depo Provera." Provera is a widely used female contraceptive, but has not been widely tested on males. The known side effects include increased blood pressure and a higher risk of blood clots.

Under the new law, offenders convicted of repeatedly molesting children will be given weekly injections of the drug as a parole condition. Critics state that although the drug appears to be effective when used with other forms of therapy, they question its effectiveness when used alone. There is no requirement under the law that individuals be evaluated medically or psychiatrically to see it they have a condition that would respond to the treatment. Under the present law, even a female child molester must undergo such treatments as a condition of parole.

The concept of chemical castration can be traced to the research started by John Money, a prominent John Hopkins professor, in the mid-1960s. In a 1991 John Hopkins' study, fewer than 10 percent of 626 chemically castrated had committed new sexual offenses within five years of their treatment. The researchers noted, however, that although the drug lowers sex drive, it does not prevent a man from having erections or fathering children. It was also noted that when an individual finishes his parole and stops taking the drug, his sexual drive returns.

The California law requires that Provera, or a similar drug, be administered one week before release to inmates serving a second prison term for molesting a child under the age of 13. The law also permits the judge to order treatments for first-time child molesters. The new law, which became effective January 1, 1997, is likely to be challenged in court. Similar legislative proposals are pending in Texas, Florida, and Wisconsin.

In 1983, in one of the first cases involving this issue, a Michigan judge sentenced the great-grandson of the founder of Upjohn Co. to be chemically castrated. The defendant had been found guilty of having sexual intercourse with his 14-year-old stepdaughter. He never received the injections because a Michigan appeals court overturned the sentence and he served a prison term.

The California Department of Corrections states that between 1993 and 1995, there were 687 sexual offenders paroled for the types of crimes described in the law. The department also estimates that the program will cost the state of California about $1.6 million per year to operate.[5]

COEDUCATIONAL CORRECTIONS

Juvenile coeducational institutions have existed for many years in some states. The first adult coeducational prisons in the United States were opened in 1971 by the Federal Bureau of Prisons. Since then, many other coed adult state and federal facilities have opened. In 1996, there were almost 100 facilities in the United States for adults and many more for juveniles.

Research has indicated that single-sex experience and long-term deprivation of heterosexual contact causes the same kinds of problems in both male and female institutions. The concept of coeducational institutions may seem extreme to many, but the major purpose of co-educational institutions is to provide both females and males daily opportunities for interaction which appears to reduce levels of tension and violent homosexual predations among the inmates in single sex prisons. Inmates tend to have a more positive feeling about serving their time, feel they are safer from violence, and benefit from the generally less controlled atmosphere.

One research study listed 12 objectives of co-corrections.[6] The 12 are listed below:

1. To reduce the dehumanizing and destructive aspects of confinement by allowing continuity or resumption of heterosexual relationships.

A small group study at a table in a literacy workshop at a coeducational institution.

2. To reduce the institutional control problem through the weakening of disruptive homosexual systems, reduction of predatory homosexual activity, lessening of assaultive behavior, and the diversion of inmate interests and activities.

3. To protect inmates likely to be involved in "trouble" were they in a same-sex-institution.

4. To provide an additional tool for creating a more normal, less institutionalized atmosphere.

5. To cushion the shock of adjustment for releasees, by reducing the number and intensity of adjustments to be made.

6. To realize economies of scale in terms of more efficient utilization of available space, staff, and programs.

7. To provide relief of immediate or anticipated overcrowding, sometimes of emergency proportions.

8. To reduce the need for civilian labor, by provision of both light and heavy inmate work force.

9. To increase diversification and flexibility of program offerings, and equal access for males and females.

10. To expand treatment potentials for working with inmates having "sexual problems," and development of positive heterosexual relationships and coping skills.

11. To provide relief of immediate or anticipated legal pressures to provide equal access to programs and services for both sexes.

12. To expand career opportunities for women, previously often "boxed into" the single state women's institution, as co-correctional staff.

ELECTRIFIED FENCES

With the rapid increase of inmate populations, we need to find additional cost-effective ways of building and operating prisons.
Kevin Carruth, Deputy Director, California
Department of Corrections

In November 1993, the California Department of Corrections moved to replace continuously staffed guard towers with lethal electrified perimeter fences at the Calipatria State Prison in Imperial County. By 1996, 23 electrified fences had been installed in other state prisons. With the use of electrified fences, as many as 10 towers, or 48 staff positions, can be deactivated. The electrified fences are installed between two parallel chain-link security fences. They consist of 15 to 18 stainless-steel stranded wires, horizontally oriented and installed on insulators attached to metal fence posts. The wires are spaced as various intervals. They are closer together at the lower portion of the fence (about 8 inches apart) and gradually increase in spacing toward the upper portion of the fence (about 13 inches). The top wire is one foot higher than the two perimeter security fences. At the bottom of the fence is a concrete-grade beam that elevates the bottom wire to approximately 13 inches above the ground.

Circular detection rings are attached to the lower fence wires. These rings trigger an alarm if the wires are spread vertically and come in contact with an adjacent ring or wire. The wires are charged with more than 5,000 volts and very low amperage many times the dosage considered lethal. The electrified fences are typically divided into four-to-six separate zones for location monitoring and emergency response. The safety features for the electrified fences include:

- At least 10 feet of space between the electrified fence and the exterior perimeter security fence

- Security glazing panels to eliminate accidental contact at sally port where the electrified fence terminates

- Interlocking panels that de-energize power, ground the high-voltage fence wires, and verify that the fence has been deactivated before maintenance or emergency response crews go between perimeter fences

- High-voltage test meters used for maintenance or emergency response personnel to provide an additional independent check that the fence has been deactivated prior to staff entry between perimeter fences

- Graphic warning signs on the inner and outer perimeter security fences in English and Spanish

- Annual safety and operations training for security and maintenance personnel

The stated primary objectives in developing the statewide electrified fence project included:

- Provide a physical and psychological deterrent

- Reduce staffing costs by providing alternative perimeter security

- Maintain the same level of perimeter security as provided by 24-hour staffing of guard towers to prevent inmate escapes and protect public safety

- Maintain a cost-efficient system of perimeter security, both in terms of construction and life-cycle costs

- Prevent accidental contact by staff, inmates, and the public based on the location, design, construction and operation of the electrified fences

- Avoid, to the extent possible, accidental and unintentional electrocution of wildlife

- Standardize the electrified fence for new facilities based on a prototypical design, site adapted as needed to meet existing conditions

It is estimated that California's electrified fence project saves the state an average of $1.5 million a year.[7]

PRIVATE CORRECTIONS

To reduce the growing costs of prisons, at least 20 states have used *privatization* as one answer to the problem. Privatization is the delivery of correctional services by a private organization, usually a for-profit corporation. Privatization can take four forms: (1) use of contract services to take care of vital correctional services (e.g., medical services or food services); (2) private sector financing of prison construction; (3) operation of prison industries by private enterprise, e.g., using chain gangs to work farms owned by non-governmental entities; and (4) contracting out the total management and operation of correctional institutions to private enterprise. The privatization of adult institutional corrections has been used to some extent in the states of Texas, New Jersey, and Tennessee as well as in the federal prison system.

Correctional officers who work for state and local correctional organizations have qualified immunity from prisoners' lawsuits under 42 USC 1983. [Section 1983 lawsuits are discussed in Chapter 10.] Should correctional officers who work for private corporations that have contracts with the state to run prisons also have qualified immunity? The U.S. Court of Appeals for the Sixth Circuit held that they were not entitled to the same immunity as publicly employed correctional officers.[8] The Court stated that "because private corporations are not principally concerned with enhancing the public good, the appropriate balance between the vindication of constitutional guarantees

Private institutions tend to be newer facilities and incorporate modern designs. The photo above depicts a modern cell wing command center. All doors, lights, windows, entries and exits are controlled and monitored from this location using closed circuit television.

and the furtherance of the public interest cannot be struck by a liability rule which assumes as its starting point a public employee acting primarily for the benefit of the public."

The following article deals with "restorative justice" which views crime as a violation of one person by another, rather than as a violation against the state. The first goal of restorative justice is to restore the victim to his or her original position and then take corrective action against the offender.

Article

RESTORATIVE JUSTICE: IMPLICATIONS FOR ORGANIZATIONAL CHANGE[9]

Moving a corrections system to embrace a new paradigm of justice is no easy task. It requires creative leadership and vision. It also requires a highly disciplined, long-term commitment to implementing a new approach through a collaborative process involving all staff members. This article reports on the journey toward restorative justice through systemic change in the Dakota County Community Corrections Department in Minnesota.

Correctional systems are offender-driven, with little attention given to the needs of individual victims or the victimized community. Even in those jurisdictions attempting to respond more effectively to victims' needs, the emphasis tends to be upon the importance of offenders paying restitution to victims, often in the context of restitution payment being therapeutic for the offender. Rarely are victims given the opportunity to play a more active role in the justice process.

The criminal justice system is focused on the state as the victim, with the actual victim being placed in a very passive role with little input. In the criminal justice system, adversarial relationships and processes are normative, as is the imposition of severe punishment in order to deter or prevent future crime. The fact that criminal behavior represents interpersonal conflict is ignored. The manner in which the criminal justice system frequently deals with victims and offenders often heightens the conflict.

There is an increasing national interest, however, in embracing the principles of a different paradigm of justice. *Restorative justice* views crime as a violation of one person by another, rather than as a violation against the state. Dialogue and negotiation are typical, with a focus upon problem-solving for the future rather than establishing blame for past behavior.

Severely punishing offenders is less important than providing opportunities to empower victims in their search for closure through gaining a better understanding of what happened and being able to move on with their lives, to impress upon offenders the real human impact of their behavior, and to promote restitution to victims. Zehr (1990) notes that, instead of ignoring victims and placing both victims and offenders in passive roles, restorative justice principles place both the victim and the offender in active and interpersonal problem-solving roles.

These principles of restorative justice are now being seen in a growing number of communities through North America and Europe. In the past, advocates of restorative justice tended to focus on specific program initiatives in local communities. Today, restorative justice is more frequently being advocated in the context of broad systemic change in entire correctional systems. The Balanced and Restorative Justice (BARJ) project, supported by the Office of Juvenile Justice and Delinquency Prevention of the U.S. Department of Justice, is the clearest example of such systemic- change advocacy. The BARJ project is working intensively with five juvenile corrections systems in various parts of the country in an effort to initiate fundamental change in the manner in which those justice systems operate.

Restorative justice has tapped into a stream of energy and excitement within corrections departments nationwide. For many, this energy has remained inert for years under the pressures of changing public expectations, legislative mandates, public safety demands and escalating probation caseloads. Probation departments are rediscovering the personal and professional motivations behind their staffs' entry into the corrections field. Typically, those motivations are to promote offender change, to assist crime victims toward wholeness, and to make individual communities safer. For too long, the emphasis has been on surveillance and monitoring, instead of those tenets brought forth by restorative justice principles, such as competency development of the offender, victim participation services, offender accountability, and community involvement and responsibility. Discovering this energy is a promising beginning for productive changes in corrections, but it is not enough. Planning for systemic changes in a bureaucratic organization is not easy even in the most fertile environments. Multiple barriers exist, ranging from workloads to politics.

Dakota County is part of the Minneapolis/St.Paul metropolitan area, located just south of Minneapolis. With a population of 310,000, it is one of the fastest growing counties in the state. The Dakota County Community Corrections Department was selected as one of five jurisdictions nationwide to receive technical assistance through the BARJ project. Consultation services and training were provided for the purpose of helping the department learn about, and adopt, policies and programs consistent with restorative justice principles.

Dakota County is now one year into its planning process and is about to implement a number of practical restorative justice recommendations. The purpose of this article is to illustrate some of the planning activities needed to prepare the department for fundamental changes in the approach to, and delivery of, restorative services. This is not to suggest that there is only one way. Each agency has different resources, assets, deficits, priorities, motivations, and systemic environments that require varying approaches to planning changes. The authors hope this article will help flesh out some of the issues that agencies should think through and the activities they should undertake in a restorative justice planning process.

Preparing for Change

Perhaps the biggest mistake many organizations make when attempting to adopt restorative justice principles is miscalculating what a restorative justice agency is. "Too often, restorative justice is viewed as a program, such as victim-offender mediation or community-work service, or seen as a politically correct way of naming the activities already in place in probation departments. As a result, real changes don't take place. A new program is developed or an existing program is renamed and yet the desired outcomes are only achieved superficially, if at all.

Restorative justice is a way of thinking. It is a fundamentally different framework for understanding and responding to crime and victimization in communities. Correctional systems adopting a restorative justice approach are no longer driven by offender concerns only. Instead, they acknowledge the need for a three-dimensional response involving victims, offenders, and the community. Once correctional agencies clearly understand restorative justice, their activities will naturally follow it. However, agencies can't plunk down the latest restorative justice program and think that they are now performing restorative corrections. The transition is easier if agencies have staff members who "think restorative justice." If they develop policies that have a clear purpose, that brings about wholeness in victims, offenders, and communities.

An illustration might be helpful. A supervisor of a probation intake unit has hired a new probation officer who will be writing presentence investigation reports. Often in such a situation, the tendency is to train the officer by explaining what the headings are in the report, when the report is due, and the various do's and don'ts. When we do this, we are describing the activities that we want accomplished. We also do this when explaining probation contact standards. The probation officer is told how often each offender is required to be seen for the corresponding risk level. Rarely do we discuss what is the purpose of the investigative report or the offender contact. What is the outcome we are looking for? How does the desired outcome respond to the needs of individual victims and the victimized community? If we simply describe the activities we expect the new officer to complete, we are not encouraging the new officer to think independently. Therefore, every time a new circumstance arises, the officer needs to consult with the supervisor in order to determine what the supervisor expects in that circumstance. We free up our personnel when we allow them to understand and work toward the restorative justice outcome and not simply perform a set of tasks.

Staff members in correctional agencies will not behave the way we want them to until we stop telling them how to act and instead tell them who they are and what outcomes we are looking for in their work. When we tell the probation officer that he or she is a restoration officer who is responsible for bringing about repair to the victim, competency development in the offender, and safety to the community, we have defined who the officer is and what outcomes we expect. That individual then is freed up to do his or her job and is less preoccupied with the specific activities that may or may not bring the department closer to meeting restorative justice goals. Despite the volatile nature of crime, there are very few circumstances in which the restorative justice "roadmap" won't allow the officer to determine the best course of action.

Restorative justice is a way of thinking, a way of behaving, and a way of measuring. Until we change the way we think about why probation exists, we can't change our behavior. We can't measure the changes until our behavior changes.

One of the first steps in preparing for a restorative justice planning process is making sure that the agency leadership understands what restorative justice is. On the surface, the concept seems simple enough. In practice, it is much more difficult. Often, people grasp the concept but are not sure how the concept is put into practice. As with so many conceptual frameworks, one can justify most activities depending on one's understanding and emphasis on parts of the framework. Understanding a new conceptual framework requires careful study and discussion through readings, conferences, and intra-staff dialogue. It is often the skeptics of the organization who can be most helpful in the preparation stage. The skeptic might be the one to ask, "Why are we doing this? What is not working properly that needs to be fixed? How is this really different from what we are doing now?" These questions test the leadership's knowledge of the concept and help identify the concerns agency staff might have.

It is useful for agency leadership to examine the existing organizational readiness for change. Is the agency ripe for positive change? What are the risks that might result in triggering momentum toward negative change? How motivated is the staff for change of any kind? What pressures exist that might make the timing for the planning process good or bad? Janssen (1987) speaks of organizational change in the context of a "Four-Room Apartment." These apartments, or stages, are: (1) contentment, (2) renewal, (3) denial, and (4) confusion. The collective staff attitude about the agency mission and direction, and the staff understanding of the need for change are usually predominantly in one of these stages. When organizational change occurs, it tends to move in a motion from the upper left to the bottom right (i.e., from contentment to denial to confusion to renewal and back to contentment again). Naturally, the organization is most motivated for change in the confusion and renewal stages. Restorative justice provides a compelling reason for an organization to move into the renewal stage, which is often characterized by vibrancy, excitement, energy, and creativity. The actual organizational approach to restorative justice, however, should differ depending on the current stage of the organization. For example, if the agency is in the denial stage, the organization will need a great deal of time to discuss what isn't working well and the reasons to initiate change.

Agency workload can be a major barrier to an open discussion of the merits of a restorative justice planning process. When staff members are burdened by ever-increasing workloads, it can be extremely difficult even to initiate the discussion. Staff members tend to view it as yet another meeting added to their workday, which prevents them from getting their job done. On the other hand, workload can be a motivating factor. Many probation officers have begun to realize that caseload pressures have taken away job satisfaction and overall probation effectiveness. Given tight budgets and limited resources, relief from the burgeoning workload is not likely to be provided soon. These circumstances can be a major motivating factor, making an organization ready for change. Agency circumstances must be considered before initiating a planning process. The question of how the time invested in restorative justice planning will benefit the department, the clients served, and individual staff work must be answered before a planning process may successfully be launched.

The Trial Balloon

After agency leaders make an organizational assessment of readiness, they must introduce the restorative justice concept to the agency staff through a variety of presentations and smaller discussion groups. Because such a planning effort will affect every staff position represented both horizontally and vertically across the department, all staff members need to be exposed to an overview of the restorative justice framework, preferably simultaneously. It is helpful to answer the question "why" at this point. Why would the department undergo a large-scale planning process and invest up to hundreds of hours of staff time for what appears to be an abstract concept? Possible questions for management to expect include: What needs to be changed? How would this improve services? How would this help me with my workload? Am I going to be expected to increase services to victims when I can't deliver sufficient services to offenders? If the community is supposed to be more involved, who is going to take the responsibility to foster that involvement? Are my day-to-day job responsibilities going to change? Is this planning process voluntary on my part?

These questions should not imply that the workforce will view restorative justice in a negative light. More often, probation staffs respond with enthusiasm and hope. It makes sense to them, especially as it becomes obvious that the social problems are becoming more complex and the criminal justice system can't be expected to be the sole response to the problem. Nonetheless, the agency director should expect a number of practical questions that seek to bridge the intellectual gap between the abstract concept, which delivers well on promise, and the detailed answers to "how does it affect me?"

At this introduction stage, the agency may be most vulnerable to adopting quick fixes. The staff members most excited by the restorative justice framework will want to channel their energy into work products. Those intrigued by the concept but overwhelmed by current day-to-day activities will seek short-term solutions, such as replicating a successful program started in another jurisdiction. Managers will be attracted to quick responses to avoid protracted planning processes that consume inordinate amounts of time. However, this is the time to exercise maximum discipline and self-restraint. The agency director can recognize staff time constraints by offering a longer planning time frame. Many staff members will welcome a longer time frame so that they can study the matter further and be involved in the planning process if they are offered the opportunity. Because restorative justice is a new way of thinking and of organizing agency activities, it requires a lengthy period of time to understand and implement. It takes time to anticipate and plan for the fallout of major changes. Quick changes will result in problematic chain reactions, which can jeopardize the positive environment. The challenge to the agency director is to keep the excitement vibrant while holding back any "quick fixes."

Setting the Stage

Changing the way we think as individuals is not easy. We have a patterned way of conceptualizing and responding to events. It is no different with an agency and can be exacerbated by the diversity of the staff. Each organization has a culture of its own, a milieu that tends to perpetuate certain behaviors and attitudes and discourage others. To alter this culture takes time and forethought. There are three "cultural shift rules of thumb" which can help in the planning process.

1. Involve all the staff members and support them.

Agency leadership cannot sustain a long-term cultural shift by fiat. It is the staff members who deliver the core services. They will either agree with, and act on, restorative justice, or they won't. An internally motivated individual is nearly always better at delivering the product than one externally motivated. Ownership of an agency mission and its outcome is best accomplished when the "stakeholders" in that agency have been a part of defining that mission and outcome.

It's not enough to encourage staff members to participate. Often, barriers exist that prevent full participation. They may be large workloads or inconveniently scheduled meeting times. Staff members may require management reassurance that input is genuinely sought, even if the staff members' ideas are contrary to those of the administration. Most of us as employees seek both formal and informal permission to get involved and express opinions openly without fear of retaliation or labeling. Staff members need to know that the agency is interested in improving services, that staff members are in the best position to offer ideas that work given their direct experience, and that management is willing to reduce barriers that might prohibit them from participating. It is not necessary for all staff members to be involved in the planning process, but involvement of a large portion of the agency is helpful. These staff members will later become the ground swell of support and initiative.

There will always be, however, a small percentage of employees who will not offer input and who will disparage attempts to improve services. It is important to give these employees a chance to express their views and to attempt to accommodate any legitimate concerns, but not to allow unproductive criticism to lead to an erosion of the planning process.

2. Take time.

There are no shortcuts to good planning, especially when it involves a foundational change (or enhancement) of corrective philosophy or principles. Restorative justice threatens existing thinking patterns, and staff members need time to reflect on its principles, challenge its assumptions, and test its application.

For some, concepts must come from different sources in order to be credible. The technical assistance provided to Dakota County through the BARJ project was invaluable. Consultants from other jurisdictions presented information and demonstrated that restorative justice principles can be put into practice with positive results. Newspaper accounts, quotes from non-correctional personnel, and other sources all helped convey the message that restorative justice is not a whimsical fancy but a concept that has captured the curiosity, and often the support, of professionals of many disciplines.

3. Communicate, communicate, and communicate.

There can be no substitute for consistent and thorough communication. When workload increases, often the communication flow gets clogged and ineffective. Probation staff may be unaware of administrative planning activities and the time devoted to them. Assumptions are made about what is, or is not, happening. The administration makes assumptions about what is important to the staff. Constant communication is the only sure way to know how restorative justice is being received by personnel. This communication includes giving information, keeping the staff aware of planning efforts, and listening to staff observations, concerns, and ideas.

It is helpful to set up both formal and informal avenues for discussions on restorative justice. Staff members can be encouraged to attend outside training on the subject. Brown bag luncheons can be organized. Also, spontaneous discussions about restorative justice can often lead to excellent innovative thoughts. As one staff member noted, even "bad ideas are better than no ideas at all."

The Wind Test

The planners who are exploring the ideas and implications of restorative justice for the department will become the internal experts. They will understand the concept and begin to imagine how it can be implemented. A collective vision will begin to emerge. As the staff planners spend more time on the subject, the tendency will be to lose touch with those staff members who choose not to participate in the planning process. Periodic "wind tests" are helpful to assess whether the planners are getting too far ahead of the staff body.

Such tests might include sending out a memo describing the status of the planning project and inviting staff members either to sit in on a planning meeting or to express thoughts in writing or verbally. The agency might want to send out a survey (with a quick checklist format, along with an open-ended section for those who want to elaborate) to gauge how well staff members understand the restorative justice concept, whether they agree with it, and whether they have any other thoughts that would be useful to the planners. This reality check helps the planning group determine whether additional information is needed or if certain barriers or opportunities exist that need to be attended to. Some examples of Dakota County staff comments on such a survey early in the planning process included:

- In my opinion, restorative justice not only aids the victim, community, and the offender, but would help unify this department.

It would give us all a clearer mission and therefore a more consistent response from us.

- I think it is a way of thinking about correctional practice that is respectful toward offenders and victims.
- We shouldn't do the victim services piece.
- I agree with the general concepts, but still question how this will be put into practice.
- Restorative justice tends to be simplistic. A cure-all answer/ replacement to direct supervision, punitive consequences, and to supervising or monitoring increasingly large numbers of clients with insufficient staff.
- I am encouraged that the department is headed in this direction.
- Victims should have as many services as possible. I hope we will have a unit to deal specifically with restitution and additional informational services to be provided for them.
- Thanks for the opportunity to speak out as a department and wanting our input.

Communicating the results of the staff feedback is helpful. Staff members may or may not know how the rest of their colleagues are viewing the planning direction. It is useful to let them know that they are not alone in their concerns or to make them aware that there is a great deal of excitement about the potential benefits to the department.

The longer an agency studies restorative justice and considers possible recommendations, the more some staff members will want someone to come out and announce the changes that are to take place. Most of us do not like working in an environment in which there is an awareness that "something" is about to take place, but what that something is, and when it will happen, is unclear. Such an atmosphere produces anxiety. Management must resist this pressure to make quick decisions, to "decide and move on," or it can undermine the grassroots ownership process of the planning efforts. However, staff members must be reassured that the planning process will not be prolonged beyond a reasonable time frame and that they will receive opportunities to have their input considered before any final recommendations are implemented. Failure to provide some of these reassurances will create department-wide anxiety, which could grow into paranoia.

The Big Kick-Off

Perhaps what contributed most to the Dakota County BARJ Project success was the use of all-day "kickoffs," or training sessions, with national consultants who were credible, who were knowledgeable about corrections, and who had implemented restorative justice principles in programs and policies within their agencies. The BARJ model emphasizes the need for greater balance in corrections by focusing on the objectives of offender competency development, offender accountability, and community safety while concurrently focusing on the emotional and material needs of individual victims and victimized communities. Dakota County scheduled two all-day sessions (about nine weeks apart), one with the director of the Deschutes County, Oregon, Community Corrections Department on competency development, and one with the chief probation officer in Quincy, Massachusetts, on accountability and community safety.

The consultants provided an overview of what restorative justice means to a corrections agency. These overviews helped reiterate the basic tenets of the framework, which need to be repeated in order to ensure more comprehensive learning. Both consultants provided practical examples of how restorative justice was implemented in their regions in order to promote one of the three objectives. It was useful to use two consultants, as both had different approaches to the concepts and different presentation styles, which meant that both reached a different segment of the attending staff.

The all day sessions were divided into a presentation of how restorative justice can promote specific objectives within the BARJ approach, and a staff brainstorming process on how Dakota County might implement policy and program changes. The brainstorming served the following purposes:

1. It actively involved all members of the staff.

2. It required staff members to think about how restorative justice could help the agency in practical ways.

3. It gave staff members power over the department's future.

4. It tested the staff's understanding of restorative justice.

5. It provided the base from which to start action groups.

At the end of the second all-day consultation, the department staff had a more complete understanding of restorative justice and was beginning to envision how the department might deliver services differently if restorative justice provided the philosophical underpinnings of the agency's activities. At this time, staff members were solicited to volunteer for one of three action groups focusing on either competency development, accountability, or community safety. Approximately 50 percent of the department staff volunteered to serve on one of the action groups.

Nuts and Bolts

One way to organize the staff planning effort is to divide the assignment into smaller, more focused work groups, such as groups on community safety, competency development, and accountability. Dakota County staff members volunteered for a specific action group depending on which topic they thought they could contribute the most. Each group was to take the list of brain-stormed ideas from the two all-day training sessions, debate the merits of them, and refine or reject them. The groups were to expand upon the recommendations that they believed had merit and submit them to management. The groups described each proposed action step in more detail, gave a means to reach the objective, and provided a time line by which the action was to be completed and assigned to an individual department staff member who would be given the authority and responsibility to implement it.

The management provided each action group with a booklet that summarized the ideas generated and a list of guidelines designed to assist group members in staying on task and completing assignments. As few rules, as possible were given in order to maximize the creativity of the staff groups. Some rules were necessary. For example, many ideas were expressed that may have benefited the department but were not linked to restorative justice. To keep the tasks focused, the groups understood that each recommendation was to somehow bring the department closer to a restorative justice corrections system. If an idea could not be articulated in that context, the idea was set aside for further consideration outside of the BARJ project.

Of particular importance was that resource constraints were removed. Creativity can be stifled when lack of resources is mentioned each time an idea is expressed. A well-designed concept that appears, on the surface, to necessitate a large infusion of time or money can often be implemented with few additional resources. This can be done by carrying out the idea in stages or shifting the existing resource allocation priorities. Removing the resource consideration freed up the staff to concentrate on restorative recommendations.

Given the breadth of the staff planning effort, Dakota County set up a Restorative Justice Steering Committee made up of two action group representatives from each of the three groups and administrative staff. The steering committee solicited thoughts, concerns, and ideas from the staff, explored common themes, and served as troubleshooters to address potential problems. When confusion arose, the steering committee discussed the issue and clarified the matter through the action group representative. In addition, it was discovered that some restorative justice action steps did not fit neatly into any of the three action groups established. For example, the proposals for determining outcome measures and promoting community involvement required discussion outside of the action groups. Therefore, the steering committee took on the roles of consultant to the action groups, addressing potential problems and devising department-wide recommendations that were greater in scope.

Creating a Vision

Once the restorative justice recommendations are developed enough to explain their practicality to all staff, the groundwork for the next stage was laid. In Dakota County, a vision of where the department wanted to be five years later was needed. It was not enough to understand restorative justice and to have a series of recommended action steps to implement. The department needed a compelling vision of what the staff activities and outcomes should look like further ahead. This vision would help carry the agency toward its goal. Rather than just a potpourri of restorative justice recommendations, the staff needed to visualize what services would actually be like if the staff pushed ahead as planned.

All staff members involved in the action groups were invited to a "vision assembly." It was an all-day event at which staff members were to create a vision using the ideas proposed by the three action groups. The invitees were given this task:

Imagine that the Dakota County Community Corrections Department no longer exists. All of you have mysteriously evaporated. There are no units. All of the equipment remains, but the staff is gone. There is no history. There is only the future. You have been asked to create a community corrections department that is restorative in design. All other parts of the criminal justice system remain the same, the same judges, attorneys, social services, etc. The "system" practices remain the same, but how you might respond to those practices may change. You can keep the same organizational structure or alter it altogether. Whatever your model looks like, the only requirement is that it must fit a restorative justice framework.

The staff was divided into three groups, with each group assigned the same task. Staff members divided themselves into groups depending on how they classified their current views on what the department should look like in five years. The three groups were: the Tinkerers (those who ascribed to the opinion that the agency only needed to tinker with existing services, organizational structure, and policies), the Radicals (those who wanted to diverge sharply from existing practice), and the Moderates (those in between the two extremes). Each group then documented its vision.

Surprisingly, the similarities in how the three groups viewed the vision were far more common than the differences. More amazing was the fact that the Tinkerers were more apt to change the department sharply than the Radicals were. A collective vision began to emerge with the group as items of agreement were pulled together. This consensus became the foundation for the proposed vision and ultimately the final action plan. The vision was given to the steering committee to finalize the details before presenting it to the full staff.

Preparing for the Unveiling

The final stage of the change process included a session with one of the national consultants who had undergone similar planning efforts and a presentation to all of the staff for feedback and further refinement. By now in the process, there should have been no surprises. Management had communicated with staff members all through the process. Opportunities for input and feedback had been provided. The staff had been anticipating the final recommendations for some time. The time was right.

It is at this stage that things can unravel. Up to this point, no staff member has been immediately threatened with a change in his or her day-to-day work activities. No manager has been asked to change the way he or she manages the unit or supervises the unit staff. It is not uncommon for many of us to delay consideration of, or ignore altogether, those events that may never come to pass until they actually happen. At this stage it will be increasingly apparent that a staff member might be asked to do something that he or she has not done before or is not immediately competent to do without training and additional experience. For example, the probation officer may be requested to provide to the client competency development instruction instead of the traditional monitoring of the client's activities. This shift in emphasis means that the probation officer must learn a new set of skills. For many, this will represent an exciting change for the betterment of staff, client, and public. For others, it will cause anxiety and possibly fear.

Management should take into account these real concerns when it proposes the recommendations. It may appear as if the process has to start over, but such action won't be necessary. It does mean that some staff will once again need some time to think through the implications that change will have for them. Patience and reassurance is helpful to get staff and supervisors through this stage. Piloting a significant change with a subset of the staff can be a way of working through both the potential pitfalls and anxieties that come with any change.

What About the Rest of the System?

This article was written for the corrections administrator or planner who is seeking to initiate a planning effort in his or her corrections agency. Beginning a planning process for an entire criminal justice system would be a good subject for a different article. It would, however, be useful to comment here on the importance of including all the agencies in the criminal justice system when planning for restorative justice. Corrections is part of an interdependent system. Change in one part of the system affects other agencies in that system. Attempts to accomplish objectives can be thwarted or enhanced depending on the level of understanding and cooperation between each of the agencies.

Judicial commitment to restoration, for example, can be a key factor in how well a corrections agency meets its restorative objectives. For example, if a corrections agency develops a victim/offender mediation program that is not supported by the judiciary, the program can fail quickly. On the other hand, if the court supports restorative concepts, a type of synergy can occur, resulting in system-wide application of restorative principles.

Any thorough planning effort should include efforts at educating system representatives on restorative justice and provide opportunities for their input. These efforts should not be limited to the criminal justice system. A key tenet in restorative justice is that the community become more involved in correctional matters at all stages. The community contains the primary players who can prevent crime. And, when crime does occur, the community can intercede in 1) providing the victim assistance, support, and security, and 2) providing for offender accountability and opportunities for productive change.

In fact, restorative justice planning without significant involvement of community leaders and neighborhood activists falls short of comprehensive restoration. Communities are more motivated to get involved in crime matters today than perhaps ever before in modern history. As do corrections professionals, citizens need a framework in which to think about crime, its causes, and effective interventions. Although citizens are an important resource for corrections, they have not been tapped to a significant extent until recently.

Concluding Remarks

Restorative justice provides a helpful framework for understanding crime and its consequences in a far more balanced perspective. Instead of being offender-driven, it leads to policies and interventions that also address the needs of individual victims and community members in the justice process.

Moving a corrections department to adopt restorative justice as its mission requires creative leadership, vision, and maximum involvement of all agency staff through continual two-way communication. The journey toward a more balanced and restorative justice system also requires a deep commitment to long-term systemic change that is grounded in a spirit of collaboration, renewal, and hope.

{End of Article}

SUMMARY

There are three major concerns in dealing with prisoners who test positive for HIV: preventing the spread of the virus to others, protecting employees who deal with infected prisoners, and the legal rights of infected prisoners. Offenders with AIDS need special treatment and medical needs. Offenders who test positive for HIV, but present no symptoms, also create a special problem because they may spread the virus. Those offenders, however, have privacy rights regarding who may be notified about their condition. One issue that administrators must face is whether HIV/AIDs individuals should be segregated from the general institution population. Another issue is whether all prisoners should be subjected to mandatory HIV testing. Most states currently test inmates on their request or upon clinical indication of need.

In 1996, the United States had more than 2,000 known sex-offender treatment programs, more than triple the approximately 640 in 1986. Some of the treatment programs are based in prisons. In the communities, solo practitioners, private clinics and nonprofit agencies run programs. Even the Salvation Army offers limited therapy services at some of its facilities. The "sex-offender treatment" industry now has its own associations, holds conferences, publishes books and a professional journal. One of the problems in sex-offender treatment programs is the lack of definite certification guidelines.

In 1996, California passed a statute that permits the chemical castration of repeat child molesters. The statute is controversial and has raised ethical and constitutional issues. In addition, some doctors contend that using the testosterone-lowering hormone poses medical problems and may not be effective. An injectable form of Provera, widely known as "Depo Provera," is used for the castration. Provera is a frequently used female contraceptive, but has not been widely tested on males.

Juvenile coeducational institutions have existed for many years in some states. The first adult coeducational prisons in the United States were opened in 1971 by the Federal Bureau of Prisons. Since then, many other coed adult state and federal facilities have opened. In 1996, there were almost 100 facilities in the United States for adults and many more for juveniles.

Research has indicated that single-sex experience and long-term deprivation of heterosexual outlets causes the same kinds of problems in both male and female institutions. The concept of coeducational institutions may seem extreme to many. But, the major purpose of coeducational institutions is to provide both females and males daily opportunities for interaction, which appears to reduce levels of tension and violent homosexual predations among inmates in single-sex prisons. Inmates tend to have more positive feelings about serving their time, feel they are safer from violence, and benefit from the generally less-controlled atmosphere.

In November, 1993, the California Department of Corrections moved to replace continuously staffed guard towers with lethal electrified perimeter fences at the Calipatria State Prison in Imperial County. By 1996, 23 electrified fences had been installed in other state prisons. With the use of electrified fences, as many as 10 towers, or 48 staff positions, can be deactivated.

Moving a corrections system to embrace a new paradigm of justice is no easy task. It requires creative leadership and vision. It also requires a highly disciplined, long-term commitment to implementing a new approach through a collaborative process involving all staff members.

DISCUSSION QUESTIONS

1. Explain the problems caused by AIDS in the prison system.
2. Identify the problems involved in using chemical castration on sex offenders.
3. List the advantages and disadvantages of using coeducational corrections institutions.
4. What are the ramifications associated with using lethal electrified perimeter fences?

5. Explain the basic concepts behind restorative justice and how it is different from the usual practices.

6. As noted in Chapter One, crime was originally seen as only a violation against the victim, later it became a violation against the peace and dignity of the state. How has restorative justice fostered the return to the concept that crime is a violation against only the victim?

ENDNOTES FOR CHAPTER 10

1. "State News & Features," *Houston Chronicle,* August 18, 1996.

2. *New York Times*, May 26, 1996, page B6, Col. 1.

3. *Artway v. Attorney General of New Jersey*, CA3, decided April 12, 1996.

4. *Wall Street Journal*, May 24, 1996, p.1.

5. *Wall Street Journal*, September 19, 1996, p. B1.

6. J. Ross, et al, *Assessment of Coeducational Corrections* (Washington, D.C.: U.S. Government Printing Office, 1978) pp. 1-2.

7. Stan W. Czerniak and James R. Upchurch, "In Search of Security," *Corrections Today,* July 1996, pp. 62-67.

8. *McKnight v. Rees*, CA6, No. 95-5398, decided July 10, 1996.

9. Mark S. Umbreit, PH.D., and Mark Carey, *Federal Probation*, Vol. 59, No.1, March, 1995. Dr. Umbreit is director, Center for Restorative Justice and Mediation, School of Social Work, University of Minnesota. Mr. Carey is director, Dakota County Community Corrections, Hasting, Minnesota.

Electric chairs, such as this, are used along with lethal injection, gas chambers and firing squads to execute prisoners.

CHAPTER 11

CAPITAL PUNISHMENT

Aggravating circumstances

Capital cases

Mitigating circumstances

Proportionality of punishment

CHAPTER OBJECTIVES

After studying this chapter, the reader will be able to:

☐ Analyze the problems involved with the use of the death penalty.

☐ List the situations for which the death penalty may be imposed.

☐ Explain the procedural requirements for imposing the death penalty.

☐ Explain the history of the death penalty.

☐ List the arguments for and against the use of the death penalty.

☐ Analyze the characteristics of death row inmates.

☐ List the recent statutory changes in death penalty procedural requirements.

☐ Explain the methods of execution that have been used in the United States.

☐ Analyze the Eighth Amendment restrictions when considering the constitutionality of the death penalty.

☐ Explain the criminal history of inmates on death row.

CAPITAL CASES

Capital trials are expensive to try and they are sensational to the press. As former Supreme Court Justice Felix Frank furter stated: "When life is at hazard in a trial, it sensationalizes the whole thing almost unwittingly." Former Supreme Court Justice Robert H. Jackson, noting the problems with reviewing capital cases, stated that "appellate courts in capital cases, are tempted to strain the evidence and even, in close cases, the law, in order to give a doubt-fully condemned man another chance." He also noted that the fear of mistake produces excruciating delays in executions. He concludes that the punishment is not only slow, it usually never comes. The President's Crime Commission in 1968 noted that the emotion surrounding a capital case "destroys the fact-finding process."

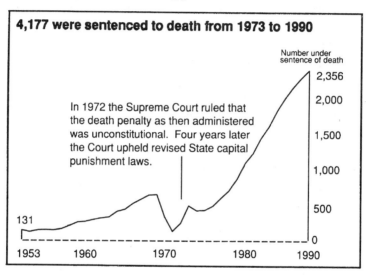

4,177 were sentenced to death from 1973 to 1990

Number under
sentence of death

In 1972 the Supreme Court ruled that the death penalty as then administered was unconstitutional. Four years later the Court upheld revised State capital punishment laws.

2,356
2,000
1,500
1,000
500
0

131

1953   1960   1970   1980   1990

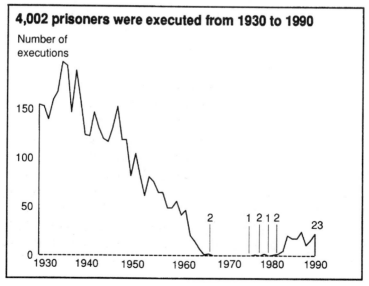

4,002 prisoners were executed from 1930 to 1990

Number of
executions

150
100
50
0

2   1 2 1 2   23

1930   1940   1950   1960   1970   1980   1990

Source: U.S. Dept. of Justice

The death penalty was the most common form of punishment in the seventeenth and eighteenth centuries. In England during that period, there were over 200 crimes for which it could be imposed. In one famous case, a six-year-old boy and his dog were hanged for the murder of an infant. Presently, in the United States capital punishment has been authorized only for aggravated criminal homicide.

The last public execution took place in Owensboro, Kentucky, on August 14, 1936. Approximately 20,000 people gathered in that small Kentucky town to witness it. The holiday atmosphere that surrounded the event was normal in those days. Reform groups upset that such solemn occasions were being transferred into circus-type events pressured the states to require that executions take place behind prison walls and in private. Since that date, executions have been conducted behind closed doors with only selected people allowed to observe.

Today, some people advocate the return to public executions. According to their arguments, if capital punishment deters crime, then why shouldn't all executions be seen by the largest possible audiences. In 1984, Texas inmate James David Autry petitioned the Texas Department of Criminal Justice to allow his execution to be televised. Twelve of the 44 television stations in Texas indicated that they would televise the execution if permitted. Twenty-six refused, and the others were either undecided or refused to state their position.[1]

As of 1995, approximately 77 percent of the people in the United States supported the use of the death penalty. The Death Information Penalty Center, however, contends that when the public is provided with alternative sentences such as life imprisonment without any possibility of parole that only a minority of people support the death penalty. The center contends that one reason the majority of the public supports the death penalty is the erroneous belief that criminals sentenced to life in prison are released after several years. According to the center, 33 states can impose life sentences without parole. In all other states, those who are sentenced to life are required to serve at least 20 years. It appears that the strongest argument used by people opposed to the death penalty is the prospect that innocent people may be executed. Other objections to the use of the death penalty include moral reasons, the argument that the death penalty is used arbitrarily, and that it is imposed in a racially discriminatory manner.

Michael Owen Perry

Michael Owen Perry is on death row in the state of Louisiana. He will probably never be executed. Perry was convicted of killing five members of his family on July 17, 1983. Apparently Perry went to his grandmother's house and calmly blew the heads off of his two sleeping cousins. He then walked across the backyard to his parents' house, where he killed his mother and two other people. He was found guilty of capital murder and sentenced to death. At his trial, the issue of his sanity was never raised.

While on death row, he was determined to be insane. The U.S. Supreme Court ruled that the state could not execute him until he regained his sanity and could therefore understand the nature and gravity of his punishment. In addition, the Louisiana Supreme Court ruled that the state could not forcibly medicate him in order to assist him in regaining his sanity for the purposes of executing him.

- Should it be cruel and unusual and thus a constitutional violation to execute a person who does not understand the nature and gravity of his punishment?

- Does it make sense to wait until an individual is sane before we kill him?

- What difference does it make if he understands the nature and gravity of the punishment if he is going to die immediately?

> On January 14, 1994, in one of his last acts as governor, Virginia Governor Douglas Wilder commuted to life with the possibility of parole the death sentence of Earl Washington, Jr.
>
> Washington had been convicted of murder committed during the course of a rape. Deoxyribonucleic (DNA) testing later established that he could not have been the rapist.[2]

Those who contend that the death penalty is unconstitutional typically base their legal argument on the cruel and unusual punishment clause of the Eighth Amendment to the U.S. Constitution. Those who support the death penalty point out:

Due Process—The due process clauses of the Fifth and Fourteenth amendments state that ". . .no person shall be deprived of life . . .without due process of law. Thus, the two amendments imply that the Constitution does not forbid the death penalty.

Incapacitation—Supporters of the death penalty contend that the potential for recidivism is serious enough to require the ultimate incapacitation.

Deterrent—Supporters argue that the death penalty serves as a strong deterrent to keep individuals from committing serious crimes. (*Note:* Opponents argue that the death penalty is not a deterrent, because murder is not a crime normally committed by rational people.)

Proportional—Punishing criminals with the death penalty conforms to the requirement that the penalty be proportional to the crime.

Public Opinion—Supporters contend that the majority of the public supports the death penalty.

Those who argue against the death penalty use the following arguments to support their views:

Possibility of Error—There is a possibility of error and an innocent person will be executed.

Cruel and Unusual—The death penalty is a barbaric punishment and there is no place for it in modern society.

Discriminatory—The death penalty is most often used against minorities.

No Deterrent—The opponents argue that the death penalty does not deter others from committing serious criminal acts.

Rehabilitation—There is always the chance that a person might be rehabilitated.

THE DEATH PENALTY AND THE COURTS

The U.S. Supreme Court has had a tortured experiment in the constitutional regulation of the death penalty. Prior to 1972, the Supreme Court placed virtually no constitutional restrictions on the imposition of the death penalty. Most state legislatures had rejected the automatic death penalty statutes. The juries were generally instructed that if they found the defendant guilty of a capital crime, they must then decide between death and life imprisonment. Juries had virtually unguided discretion. In most cases, little information regarding the defendant's character, background, and previous criminal record was presented.

In 1972, the U.S. Supreme Court decided *Furman v. Georgia.* This case held by a 5-4 decision that the capital punishment statute in Georgia was unconstitutional. All nine justices wrote separate opinions. Each of the opinions concluded that juries should not be given unguided discretion in imposing the death penalty. The decision, while providing no guidance regarding the use of the death penalty, clearly established that all states' death penalty statutes were unconstitutional.

In 1976, the majority members of the Supreme Court concluded in *Greg v. Georgia,* that the authors of the cruel and unusual punishment clause did not intend to forbid capital punishment. They only intended to prohibit punishments not officially authorized by statute or not lying within the sentencing court's jurisdiction and any torture or brutal, gratuitously painful methods of execution.

As the result of the death penalty cases decided by the Court during the 1970s, the following guidelines or actions are considered necessary before a sentence involving the death penalty will be approved by the Court:

- The trial must be tried in separate phases. First, the question of the defendant's guilt must be established.

- At the same time guilt is established, the jury is also required to determine the existence of any special circumstances necessary for the imposition of the death penalty (e.g., murder for hire, murder committed to prevent arrest, prior conviction of murder, and murder committed by a prisoner serving a life sentence).

- If the defendant is found guilty of murder and one or more of the required special circumstances are determined to be present, further proceedings are held on the question of the penalty to be imposed.

Generally, special proceedings determine whether the defendant shall be sentenced to death or life imprisonment. After hearing the evidence at the special proceedings, the jury must weigh the evidence and determine if the mitigating circumstances outweigh the aggravating circumstances. If so, life imprisonment rather than the death penalty shall be imposed. In most states with the death penalty, the decision by the jury must be unanimous. If the jury fails to reach a decision, then life imprisonment is given. *Mitigating circumstances* are those circumstances that tend to reduce the severity of the crime (i.e., cooperation with the investigating authority, surrender, good character), whereas *aggravating circumstances* are those circumstances that tend to make the crime more serious (i.e., use of a deadly weapon, committing an offense against a law enforcement officer, taking advantage of a position of trust to commit an offense, etc.).

STATUS OF CAPITAL CASES

A review of the status of capital punishment for the year 1994 (the last year for which complete statistics are available) provides an overview of the numbers and demographics of those sentenced to death.[3] During 1994, 31 men were executed. Of these, 20 were white and 11 were black. The 31 people were under sentence of death an average of 10 years and two months. At the end of 1994, 34 states and the federal prison system held 2,890 prisoners under sentence of death, 5.9 percent more than the end of 1993. All had committed murder. Of persons under sentence of death, 1,645 were white, 1,197 were black, 23 were Native American, 17 were Asian American and eight were classified as "other race." The 224 Hispanic inmates under sentence of death accounted for 8.4 percent of inmates with a known ethnicity. Forty-one women were under a sentence of death. About two in five inmates sentenced to death were on parole or probation or in some other criminal justice status when they committed their capital offense.

Prisoners Under Death Sentence
by state

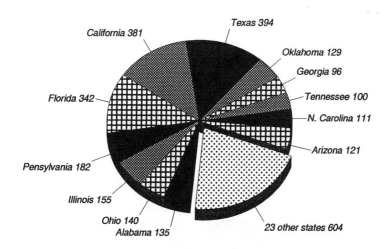

California 381
Texas 394
Oklahoma 129
Georgia 96
Florida 342
Tennessee 100
N. Carolina 111
Arizona 121
Pensylvania 182
Illinois 155
Ohio 140
Alabama 135
23 other states 604

Among inmates under sentence of death and with available criminal histories, two in three had a prior felony conviction; nearly one in
10 had a prior homicide conviction. During 1994, 304 prisoners under
a sentence of death were received by State prison systems from the
courts.

State death penalty executions in 1996

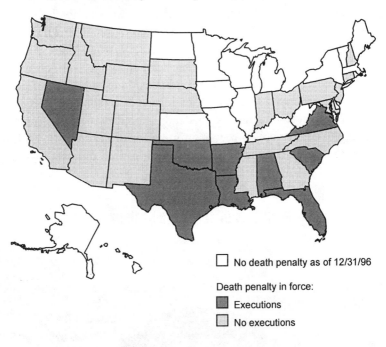

☐ No death penalty as of 12/31/96

Death penalty in force:

■ Executions

☐ No executions

Source: U.S.Dept. of Justice

Thirteen states executed 31 prisoners during 1994. The number
of people executed was seven fewer than in 1993. The prisoners executed during 1994 had been under sentence of death an average of 10
years and two months, about nine months more than the average for
inmates executed the previous year.

Texas held the largest number of death row inmates (394) on
December 31, 1994, followed by California (381), Florida (342), and
Pennsylvania (182). Six prisoners were in federal custody under a death

sentence. Between January 1 and December 31, 1994, 26 state prison systems received 304 prisoners under sentence of death. All were men. Eighteen of the executed prisoners were non-Hispanic whites; 10 were non-Hispanic blacks; one white Hispanic; one white with unknown Hispanic origin; and one black with unknown Hispanic origin. Twenty-three of the executions were carried out by lethal injection, six by electrocution, one by lethal gas, and one by hanging.

From January 1, 1977, to December 31, 1994, a total of 4,557 persons entered state and federal prisons under sentences of death, among whom 51 percent were white, 40 percent were black, seven percent were Hispanic, and two percent were of other races. During this 18-year period, a total of 257 executions took place in 24 states. Of the inmates executed, 140 were white, 98 were black, 17 were Hispanic, and two were Native American. Also during 1977-1994, 1,790 prisoners were removed from a death sentence as a result of dispositions other than execution (resentencing, retrial, commutation, or death while awaiting execution). Of all people removed from under a death sentence, 53 percent were white, 41 percent were black, 0.9 percent were Native American, 0.4 percent were Asian American, and 5 percent were Hispanic.

STATUTORY CHANGES

Most states have revised their capital punishment statutes in the past five years. Most of the changes involved additional aggravating circumstances, additional categories of victims permitting the application of the death penalty, and broadening of the law to allow a defendant to choose between two methods of execution. Examples of the changes include:

Alabama—Added to its list of capital offenses the use of any weapon from outside a dwelling or car to kill a person in that dwelling or car and use of a weapon from within a car to kill a person.

Colorado—Added to its penal code as aggravating factors the murder of two or more persons during the same criminal episode, and the intentional killing of a child under age 12.

Delaware—Added to its penal code as aggravating factors the murder of a child age 14 or younger by a person at least four years older than the victim, the killing of a nongovernmental informant in retaliation for providing information concerning criminal activity to an investigative agency, and premeditated murder resulting from "substantial planning" for the commission of that murder itself.

Florida—Added new sections to, and revised an act relating to, death sentences. In specifying conditions of a sentence to life in prison without the possibility of release, the revision eliminates a previous stipulation of release if the offense was a capital felony. The stipulation was that the offender could be released after 25 years. Florida lawmakers also amended a statute making confidential any information which, if released, would identify the executioner.

Idaho—Amended its penal code to remove the requirement that the court determine whether the sentence of death is disproportionate to the penalty imposed in similar cases.

Illinois—Added to its penal code the aggravating factors of intentional killing ordered or committed by the leader of a drug trafficking organization and intentional murder involving the infliction of torture.

Indiana—Added murder by intentionally discharging a firearm into an inhabited dwelling or from a vehicle and murder during criminal gang activity.

New Jersey—Added as an aggravating factor the murder of a person younger than 14 years of age.

North Carolina—Amended its code of criminal procedure to allow, only by order of a judge, the admission of a defendant's juvenile record as evidence in either the guilt phase or to prove an aggravating factor at sentencing.

METHODS OF EXECUTION

History

In pre-industrial societies, the death penalty was carried out by banishing the criminal to the wilderness where death was relatively certain. The effectiveness of banishment diminished as human skills and culture advanced and the chances of an individual surviving banishment greatly increased. Some of the ancient methods of execution included burning, hanging, stoning, boiling in oil, beheading, disemboweling, being buried alive, thrown to wild beasts, crucifying, drowning, crushing, impaling, shooting, flaying alive, and being torn apart. The list, although long, is not exhaustive of the creative methods used to carry out death sentences. As noted in an earlier chapter, Socrates was forced to drink poison as his method of execution.

In Colonial America and in Early England, hanging was the most common form of execution. The use of a firing squad was the second most common. The preferred form in France and other European countries was by use of the *guillotine*, a device consisting of a heavy blade that falls freely between two perpendicular groved posts.[4] The use of the electric chair began in New York in 1980. The electric chair has been called "America's most innovative contribution to the method of execution."[5] On August 6, 1890, William Kemmler, a convicted murder from Buffalo, was the first person executed in an electric chair at the Auburn Penitentiary in New York. The electric chair was hailed as a more humanitarian way to execute people. Many, however, claimed it was merely a promotional device for the developer of a New York electrical company.

Kemmler was strapped in a chair with leather straps. A headpiece was placed on his head, which was connected with electric wires. When voltage was transmitted through the headpiece, Kemmler's shoulders shot up. It appeared as though every muscle in his body went rigid. His face turned an intense red, then an ashen pallor. His eyes were glazed, pupils dilated. His right hand was clenched so tight that the nail had dug into the flesh. Spots appeared on his face. The electricity was shut off. His body sagged like a limp rag. They began to unstrap him from the chair. Suddenly, foam bubbled out of his mouth and a gurgling sound came from his throat. Quickly they replaced the headpiece and turned on the current again. He then sat up in the chair taut and then slumped. A wisp of smoke came from the top of his head.

In an unusual case, a convicted murderer (Francis) was sentenced to die in the electric chair. He was strapped in the chair and the execution began. The electrical system malfunctioned, however, and he was not killed when the current passed through his body. He then contended that to subject him to the process a second time was cruel and unusual punishment and thus a violation of the Eighth Amendment to the U.S. Constitution. By a five-to-four decision, the Supreme Court ruled against him and he was finally executed.[6]

Many, including Thomas Edison, advocated that the use of the electric chair was cruel and inhumane. In a search to make execution more humane, the gas chamber originated. The first person to die in a gas chamber was Gee Jon, a Chinese immigrant worker convicted of murder. California executed him on February 8, 1924, using cyanide gas. Jon was fastened in a chair. As the gas was pumped into the chamber, his head suddenly sagged backward. He appeared to lose consciousness. His head continued to move, but weaker each time. His eyes remained open. Six minutes later he was pronounced dead.

As the results of Supreme Court cases in 1970s, states were required to enact new capital punishment statutes. Some states, in order to reduce the opposition to capital punishment and make the passage of new laws easier, looked for ways to make execution more humane. As a result, the use of lethal injection gained favor. The first person to be executed by lethal injection was Charles Books, on December 6, 1982, in Oklahoma. Brooks was strapped to a hospital gurney. His arms were strapped to boards that projected from each side of the gurney. A catheter needle was inserted into his left arm. The needle was attached to a clear plastic tube. First a saltwater solution flowed into his arm. Then sodium thieopental (a quick-acting barbituate) was used. Next Pavulon (a drug similar to the curare plant extract used by South Americans to dip their arrows into to paralyze their prey) was used. Finally, he was administered potassium chloride, which is often used by doctors to regulate the heart. Too much of it, however, will cause cardiac arrest. As the drugs began to take effect, Brooks moved his head and muttered something. He then yawned and wheezed. He opened and closed his hand several times. He was pronounced dead seven minutes later.

Present Day

Lethal injection is the predominant method of execution (27 states). Twelve states authorize electrocution; seven states, lethal gas; four states, hanging; and one state, a firing squad. Fourteen states authorize more than one method: lethal injection and an alternative method, generally at the election of the condemned prisoner. However, five of these 14 stipulated which method must be used, depending on the date of sentencing; one authorizes hanging only if lethal injection could not be given; and one authorized lethal gas if lethal injection can not be given; and one authorizes lethal gas if lethal injection is ever ruled unconstitutional.

The method of execution of federal prisoners is lethal injection. For offenses under the Violent Crime Control and Law Enforcement Act of 1994, the method is that of the state in which the conviction took place.

The Death Penalty and the Eighth Amendment

Is the ban against cruel and unusual punishment embodied in the Eighth Amendment violated when the death penalty is imposed?

This question has plagued the courts for many years. What constitutes cruel and unusual punishment? Justice Thurgood Marshall stated in *Furman v. Georgia*:

Perhaps the most important principle in analyzing "cruel and unusual" punishment questions is the one that is reiterated again and again in the prior opinions of the Supreme Court: i.e., the cruel and unusual language must draw its meaning from the evolving standards of decency that mark the progress of a maturing society. Thus, a penalty that was permissible at one time in our nation's history is not necessarily permissible today.[7]

AUTOMATIC REVIEW

Of the 37 states with capital punishment statutes, 36 provide for review of all death sentences regardless of the defendant's wishes. Arkansas had no specific provisions for automatic review. Federal death penalty procedures do not provide for automatic review after a sentence of death has been imposed. While most of the 36 states authorize an automatic review of both the conviction and sentence, Idaho, Indiana, Montana, Oklahoma, and Tennessee require review of the sentence only. In Idaho, review of the conviction has to be appealed or forfeited.

In Indiana, a defendant can waive review of the conviction. The review is usually conducted by the state's highest appellate court regardless of the defendant's wishes. (In Mississippi the question of whether a defendant can waive the right to automatic review of the sentence has not been addressed; in Wyoming, neither the statute nor case law clearly preclude a waiver of an appeal.) If either the conviction or the sentence is vacated, the case could be remanded to the trial court for additional proceedings or for retrial. As a result of retrial or resentencing, the death sentence could be reimposed.

MINIMUM AGE

Eight jurisdictions do not specify a minimum age for which the death penalty can be imposed. In some states, the minimum age is set forth in the statutory provisions that determine the age at which a juvenile may be transferred to criminal court for trial as an adult. Thirteen states and the federal prison system require a minimum age of 18. Sixteen states indicate an age of eligibility between 14 and 17.

CHARACTERISTICS OF PRISONERS UNDER SENTENCE OF DEATH

In January 1995, 34 states and the federal prison system held a total of 2,890 prisoners on death row, a gain of 161, or 5.9 percent more than at the end of 1993. The federal prison system count remained steady at six. Three states reported 39 percent of the nation's death row population: Texas (394), California (381), and Florida (342). Of the 38 jurisdictions with statutes authorizing the death penalty, New Hampshire and Wyoming had no one under a capital sentence, and Connecticut, South Dakota, New Mexico, and Colorado had four or fewer.

Among the 34 states with prisoners on death row, 20 had more inmates than a year earlier, six had fewer inmates, and eight had the same number. Texas had an increase of 28, followed by California (18), Florida (17), Alabama (15), Pennsylvania (14), North Carolina (12), and Ohio (11). Idaho had the largest decrease (2).

The number of blacks under sentence of death increased by 86. The number of whites increased by 68, and the number of persons of other races (Native Americans and Asians or Pacific Islanders) increased by seven. The number of Hispanics sentenced to death rose from 209 to 224 during 1994. Twenty-five Hispanics were received under sentence of death, eight were removed from death row, and one was executed. Three-fourths of the Hispanics were incarcerated in four states: Texas (63), California (55), Florida (32), and Arizona (20).

The number of women sentenced to be executed increased from 36 to 41. Five women were received under sentence of death, and none was removed from death row or executed. Women were under sentence of death in 14 states. Nearly half of all women on death row at the end of 1994 were in Alabama, California, Florida and Illinois.

The median level of education for death row inmates was the twelfth grade. Of inmates under a capital sentence and with reported marital status, nearly half had never married; somewhat more than a fourth were married when they were sentenced; nearly a fourth were divorced, separated, or widowed. Among all inmates under sentence of death, 44 percent were age 30 to 39 on December 31, 1994, and 73 percent were age 25 to 44. The median age was 35 years. Less than one percent were younger than 20 and three percent were age 55 or older. The youngest offender under sentence of death was age 17; the oldest was 79. More than half of all inmates under the death sentence were age 20 to 29 when they were arrested for their capital offense; 11 percent were age 19 or younger; and less than one percent were age 55 or older.

From 1977, the year after the Supreme Court upheld the constitutionality of revised state capital punishment laws, to 1994, a total of 4,557 people entered prison under sentence of death. During these 18 years, 257 people were executed, and 1,790 were removed from under a death sentence by appellate court decisions and reviews, commutations, or death. (An individual may have received and been removed from under a sentence of death more than once).

Among individuals who received a death sentence between 1977 and 1994, 2,336 (51 percent) were white, 1,838 (40 percent) were black, 316 (7 percent) were Hispanic, and 67 (two percent) were of other races. The distribution by race of the 1,790 inmates who were removed from death row between 1977 and 1994 was as follows: 940 whites (53 percent), 735 blacks (41 percent), 90 Hispanics (five percent), and 25 persons of other races (one percent). Of the 257 who were executed, 140 (54 percent) were white, 98 (38 percent) were black, 17 (seven percent) were Hispanic, and 2 (one percent) were other races.

CRIMINAL HISTORY OF INMATES UNDER SENTENCE OF DEATH

Among inmates under a death sentence, for whom criminal history information is available, 67 percent had past felony convictions, including 9 percent with at least one previous homicide conviction. Among those for whom legal status at the time of the capital offense was reported, 42 percent had an active criminal justice status. Nearly half of these were on parole and a fourth were on probation. The others had charges pending, were in prison, had escaped from incarceration, or had some other criminal justice status. Since 1988, data have been collected on the number of death sentences imposed on entering inmates. Among the 1,976 individuals received under sentence of death during that time, about one in every seven entered with two or more death sentences.

Among prisoners executed between 1977 and 1994, the average time spent between the imposition of the most recent sentence received and execution was slightly more than eight years. White prisoners had spent an average of seven years and eight months, and black prisoners, 8 years and 10 months. The 31 prisoners executed in 1994 were under sentence of death an average of 10 years and two months. For the 257 prisoners executed between 1977 and 1994, the most common method of execution was lethal injection (131). Other methods were electrocution (114), lethal gas (nine), hanging (two), and firing squad (one). Among prisoners under sentence of death at year-end 1994, the average time spent in prison was six years and four months.

PRACTICUM

You are a probation officer in Broward County, Florida. You are assigned to develop a PSI (presentence report) on the defendant. He has been found guilty of capital murder. The only possible punishments are the death penalty or life in prison. How would you handle the below situations or answer the below questions? After you have answered the questions, read the following case. Does the case change your answers?

1. Should the requirements for PSIs be different in capital cases from non-capital cases?

2. Susan, a neighbor of defendant, states that he raped her, but she has never reported this offense to anyone. He stated that he or one of his brothers will kill her if she tells anyone. Susan requests that her statement and any mention of the rape be kept secret from the defendant. You decide that this information should be included in your PSI. What do you do? Does the defendant have the right to be confronted with this information?

GARDNER v. FLORIDA
430 U.S. 349, 97 S.Ct. 1197, 51 L.Ed.2d 393 (1977)

Justice Stephens announced the judgment of the Court and delivered an opinion, in which Justice Stewart and Justice Powell joined.

GARDNER was convicted of first-degree murder and sentenced to death. When the trial judge imposed the death sentence he stated that he was relying in part on information in a presentence investigation report. Portions of the report were not disclosed to counsel for the parties. Without reviewing the confidential portion of the presentence report, the Supreme Court of Florida, over the dissent of two justices, affirmed the death sentence. We conclude that this procedure does not satisfy the constitutional command that no person shall be deprived of life without due process of law.

On June 30, 1973, Gardner assaulted his wife with a blunt instrument, causing her death. On January 10, 1974, after a trial in the Circuit Court of Citrus County, Fla., a jury found him guilty of first-degree murder. The separate sentencing hearing required by Florida law in capital cases was held later on the same day. The state merely introduced two photographs of the decedent, otherwise relying on the trial testimony. That testimony, if credited, was sufficient to support a finding of one of the statutory aggravating circumstances, that the felony committed by Gardner "was especially heinous, atrocious, or cruel." In mitigation, Gardner testified that he had consumed a vast quantity of alcohol during a day-long drinking spree that preceded the crime and professed to have almost no recollection of the assault itself. His testimony, if credited, was sufficient to support a finding of at least one of the statutory mitigating circumstances.

After the jury retired to deliberate, the judge announced that he was going to order a presentence investigation of Gardner. Twenty-five minutes later the jury returned its advisory verdict. It expressly found that the mitigating circumstances outweighed the aggravating circumstances and advised the court to impose a life sentence.

The presentence investigation report was completed by the Florida Parole and Probation Commission on January 28, 1974. On January

30, 1974, the trial judge entered findings of fact and a judgment sentencing Gardner to death. His ultimate finding was that the felony "was especially heinous, atrocious or cruel; and that such aggravating circumstances outweigh the mitigating circumstance, to-wit: none." As a preface to that ultimate finding, he recited that his conclusion was based on the evidence presented at both stages of the bifurcated proceeding, the arguments of counsel, and his review of "the factual information contained in said presentence investigation."

There is no dispute about the fact that the presentence investigation report contained a confidential portion that was not disclosed to defense counsel. Although the judge noted in his findings of fact that the State and Gardner's counsel had been given "a copy of that portion of the report to which they are entitled," counsel made no request to examine the full report or to be apprised of the contents of the confidential portion. The trial judge did not comment on the contents of the confidential portion. His findings do not indicate that there was anything of special importance in the undisclosed portion, or that there was any reason other than customary practice for not disclosing the entire report to the parties. . .expressly recognized by this Court.

. . . Five members of this Court have now expressly recognized that death is a different kind of punishment from any other that may be imposed in this country. . . From the point of view of the defendant, it is different in both its severity and its finality. From the point of view of society, the action of the sovereign in taking the life of one of its citizens also differs dramatically from any other legitimate state action. It is of vital importance to the defendant and to the community that any decision to impose the death sentence be, and appear to be, based on reason rather than caprice or emotion.

. . . It is now clear that the sentencing process, as well as the trial itself, must satisfy the requirements of the Due Process Clause. Even though the defendant has no substantive right to a particular sentence within the range authorized by statute, the sentencing is a critical stage of the criminal proceeding at which he is entitled to the effective assistance of counsel. . . The defendant has a legitimate interest in the character of the procedure that leads to the imposition of sentence even if he may have no right to object to a particular result of the sentencing process.

In the light of these developments we consider the justifications offered by the State for a capital-sentencing procedure that permits a trial judge to impose the death sentence on the basis of confidential information which is not disclosed to the defendant or his counsel.

The State first argues that an assurance of confidentiality to potential sources of information is essential to enable investigators to obtain relevant but sensitive disclosures from people unwilling to comment publicly about a defendant's background or character. The availability of such information, it is argued, provides the person who prepares the report with greater detail on which to base a sentencing recommendation and, in turn, provides the judge with a better basis for his sentencing decision. But consideration must be given to the quality, as well as the quantity, of the information on which the sentencing judge may rely. Assurances of secrecy are conducive to the transmission of confidences that may bear no closer relation to fact than the average rumor or item of gossip, and may imply a pledge not to attempt independent verification of the information received. The risk that some of the information accepted in confidence may be erroneous, or may be misinterpreted by the investigator or by the sentencing judge, is manifest.

If, as the State argues, it is important to use such information in the sentencing process, we must assume that in some cases it will be decisive in the judge's choice between a life sentence and a death sentence. If it tends to tip the scales in favor of life, presumably the information would be favorable and there would be no reason why it should not be disclosed. On the other hand, if it is the basis for a death sentence, the interest in reliability plainly outweighs the State's interest in preserving the availability of comparable information in other cases.

The State also suggests that full disclosure of the presentence report will unnecessarily delay the proceeding. We think the likelihood of significant delay is overstated because we must presume that reports prepared by professional probation officers, as the Florida procedure requires, are generally reliable. In those cases in which the accuracy of a report is contested, the trial judge can avoid delay by disregarding the disputed material. Or if the disputed matter is of critical importance, the time invested in ascertaining the truth would surely be well spent if it makes the difference between life and death.

The State further urges that full disclosure of presentence reports, which often include psychiatric and psychological evaluations, will occasionally disrupt the process of rehabilitation. The argument, if valid, would hardly justify withholding the report from defense counsel.

Moreover, whatever force that argument may have in non-capital cases, it has absolutely no merit in a case in which the judge has decided to sentence the defendant to death. Indeed, the extinction of all possibility of rehabilitation is one of the aspects of the death sentence that makes it different in kind from any other sentence a State may legitimately impose. . . .

Even if it were permissible to withhold a portion of the report from a defendant, and even from defense counsel, pursuant to an express finding of good cause for nondisclosure, it would nevertheless be necessary to make the full report a part of the record to be reviewed on appeal. Because the State must administer its capital-sentencing procedures with an even hand, it is important that the record on appeal disclose to the reviewing court the considerations that motivated the death sentence in every case in which it is imposed. Without full disclosure of the basis for the death sentence, the Florida capital-sentencing procedure would be subject to the defects that resulted in the holding of unconstitutionality in *Furman v. Georgia*. In this particular case, the only explanation for the lack of disclosure is the failure of defense counsel to request access to the full report. That failure cannot justify the submission of a less complete record to the reviewing court than the record on which the trial judge based his decision to sentence Gardner to death.

Nor do we regard this omission by counsel as an effective waiver of the constitutional error in the record. There are five reasons for this conclusion. First, the State does not urge that the objection has been waived. Second, the Florida Supreme Court has held that it has a duty to consider "the total record" when it reviews a death sentence. Third, because two members of that court expressly considered this point on the appeal in this case, we presume that the entire court passed on the question. Fourth, there is no basis for presuming that the defendant himself made a knowing and intelligent waiver, or that counsel could possibly have made a tactical decision not to examine the full report. Fifth, because the judge found, in disagreement with the jury, that the evidence did not establish any mitigating circumstance, and because the presentence report was the only item considered by the judge but not by the jury, the full review of the factual basis for the judge's rejection of the advisory verdict is plainly required. For if the jury, rather than the judge, correctly assessed the Gardner's veracity, the death sentence rests on an erroneous factual predicate.

We conclude that Gardner was denied due process of law when the death sentence was imposed, at least in part, on the basis of information that he had no opportunity to deny or explain. . .

THE CHIEF JUSTICE concurs in the judgment. JUSTICE WHITE, concurring in the judgment. "[W]e believe that in capital cases the fundamental respect for humanity underlying the Eighth Amendment, requires consideration of the character and record of the individual offender and the circumstances of the particular offense as a constitutionally indispensable part of the process of inflicting the penalty of death. This conclusion rests squarely on the predicate that the penalty of death is qualitatively different from a sentence of imprisonment, however long. . . Because of that qualitative difference, there is a corresponding difference in the need for reliability in the determination that death is the appropriate punishment in a specific case.

Here the sentencing judge indicated that he selected Gardner for the death penalty in part because of information contained in a presentence report that was not disclosed to Gardner or to his counsel and to which Gardner had no opportunity to respond. A procedure for selecting people for the death penalty that permits consideration of such secret information relevant to the "character and record of the individual offender," fails to meet the "need for reliability in the determination that death is the appropriate punishment" which the Court indicated was required. . . This conclusion stems solely from the Eighth Amendment's ban on cruel and unusual punishments. . . my conclusion is limited. . . to cases in which the death penalty is imposed. I thus see no reason to address in this case the possible application to sentencing proceedings—in death or other cases—of the Due Process Clause, other than as the vehicle by which the strictures of the Eighth Amendment are triggered in this case. For these reasons, I do not join the plurality opinion but concur in the judgment.

JUSTICE BLACKMUN, concurring in the judgment.

Given the judgments of the Court in *Woodson v. North Carolina,* 428 U.S. 280 (1976), and in *Roberts v. Louisiana,* 428 U.S. 325 (1976), I concur in the judgment the Court reaches in the present case.

JUSTICE BRENNAN. I agree for the reasons stated in the plurality opinion that the Due Process Clause of the Fourteenth Amendment is violated when a defendant facing a death sentence is not informed of the contents of a presentence investigation report made to the sentencing judge. However, I adhere to my view that the death penalty is in all circumstances cruel and unusual punishment prohibited by the Eighth and Fourteenth amendments. I therefore would vacate the death sentence, and I dissent from the Court's judgment insofar as it remands for further proceedings that could lead to its imposition.

JUSTICE MARSHALL dissenting. Last Term, this Court carefully scrutinized the Florida procedures for imposing the death penalty and concluded that there were sufficient safeguards to insure that the death sentence would not be "wantonly" and "freakishly" imposed. *Proffitt v. Florida,* 428 U.S. 242 (1976). This case, however, belies that hope. While I continue to believe that the death penalty is unconstitutional in all circumstances, and therefore would remand this case for resentencing to a term of life, nevertheless, now that Florida may legally take a life, we must insist that it be in accordance with the standards enunciated by this Court. In this case I am appalled at the extent to which Florida has deviated from the procedures upon which this Court expressly relied. It is not simply that the trial judge, in overriding the jury's recommendation of life imprisonment, relied on undisclosed portions of the presentence report. Nor is it merely that the Florida Supreme Court affirmed the sentence without discussing the omission and without concern that it did not even have the entire report before it. Obviously that alone is enough to deny due process and require that the death sentence be vacated as the Court now holds. But the blatant disregard exhibited by the courts below for the standards devised to regulate imposition of the death penalty calls into question the very basis for this Court's approval of that system in *Proffitt.*

JUSTICE REHNQUIST, dissenting. Had I joined the plurality opinion in last Term's *Woodson v. North Carolina,* I would join the concurring opinion of my Brother White in this case. But if capital punishment is not cruel and unusual under the Eighth and Fourteenth Amendments, as the Court held in that case, the use of particular sentencing procedures, never previously held unfair under the Due Process Clause, in a case where the death sentence is imposed cannot convert that sentence into a cruel and unusual punishment. The prohibition of the Eighth Amendment relates to the character of the punishment, and not to the process by which it is imposed. I would therefore affirm the judgment of the Supreme Court of Florida.

{End of Case}

SUMMARY

The death penalty was the most common form of punishment in the 17th and 18th centuries. In England during that period, there were over 200 crimes for which it could be imposed. As of 1995, approximately 77 percent of the people in the United States supported the use of the death penalty. The Death Information Penalty Center, however, contends that when the public is provided with alternative sentences, such as life imprisonment without any possibility of parole, only a minority of people support the death penalty.

Those who contend that the death penalty is unconstitutional typically base their legal argument on the cruel and unusual punishment clause of the Eighth Amendment to the U.S. Constitution. Those who support the death penalty point out that the due process clauses of the Fifth and Fourteenth amendments state: "no person shall be deprived of life without due process of law." Thus, the two amendments imply that the constitution does not forbid the death penalty.

The U.S. Supreme Court has had a tortured experiment in the constitutional regulation of the death penalty. Prior to 1972, the Supreme Court placed virtually no constitutional restrictions on the imposition of the death penalty. Most state legislatures had rejected the automatic death penalty statutes. Juries were generally instructed that if they found the defendant guilty of a capital crime, they must then decide between death and life imprisonment. The juries had virtually unguided discretion. In most cases, little information regarding the defendant's character, background, and previous criminal record was presented.

In 1972, the U.S. Supreme Court decided *Furman v. Georgia,* which held by a 5-4 decision that the capital punishment statute in Georgia was unconstitutional. All nine justices wrote separate opinions. Each of the opinions concluded that juries should not be given unguided discretion in imposing the death penalty. The decision, while providing no guidance regarding the use of the death penalty, clearly established that all states' death penalty statutes were unconstitutional.

DISCUSSION QUESTIONS

1. Should the death penalty be an authorized punishment? Justify your answer.

2. What safeguards may be imposed to prevent the death penalty from being discriminatorily applied?

3. Is the death penalty effective in crime prevention? Explain.

4. What are the general characteristics of individuals on death row?

5. Discuss the legal ramifications of imposing the death penalty.

6. Should executions be televised? Justify your answer.

7. Explain the court's rationale for holding that it was cruel and unusual to execute a person who does not understand the gravity of the punishment.

ENDNOTES FOR CHAPTER 11

1. William Bailey, "Murder, Capital Punishment and Television," *American Sociological Review*, Vol. 55 No.5, 1990, pp. 628-633 and "Public Executions," *Journal of Prison Discipline and Philanthropy*, July 1859, pp.117-123.

2. Neil Walker, "Executive Clemency and the Death Penalty," *American Journal of Criminal Law*, Vol. 22, p. 245, 1994.

3. "Capital Punishment, 1994," NCJ-158023, February, 1996.

4. John N. Ferdico, *Criminal Law and Justice Dictionary,* (St. Paul: West, 1992) p. 200.

5. Harry E. Allen and Clifford E. Simonsen, *Corrections in America,* 7th ed. (Upper Saddle River, NJ: Prentice-Hall) p. 320.

6. *Louisiana ex rel. Francis v. Resweber*, 329 U.S. 459 (1947).

7. 408 U.S. 238 (1976).

CHAPTER 12

PRISONERS' RIGHTS

KEY TERMS

Deference period

"Hands off" period

Rights period

Section 1983 cases

Writ of habeas corpus

Deliberate indifference

Prison Litigation Reform Act

CHAPTER OBJECTIVES

After studying this chapter, the reader will be able to:

☐ List and explain the three periods of court involvement in prisoners' rights.

☐ List and explain the four areas of prisoners' rights.

☐ Explain the importance of the writ of habeas corpus.

☐ Analyze the Prison Litigation Reform Act of 1994.

☐ Explain the "back to the basics" movement regarding prison conditions.

☐ Diagram the historical development of the "cruel and unusual" clause.

☐ List the prisoners' rights that the courts have recognized in court cases.

☐ Define the "deliberate indifference" requirement.

☐ Explain the importance of the *Warner v. Orange County* case.

Prior to the 1960s the courts stayed out of the area of prisoners' rights. In the late 1960s, the U.S. Supreme Court began to involve itself in this area and has since decided more than 30 cases on the subject. The courts' involvement in prisoners' rights can be divided into three periods: the "hands off" period (prior to 1964), the "rights" period (1964-1978), and the "deference" period (since 1979).[1]

During the *hands off period*, the courts rarely accepted a case involving the conditions of confinement or prisoners' rights based on the concept that prison administrators were the ones best qualified to determine the appropriate conditions of confinement. While the courts apparently recognized that prisoners have constitutional rights, the courts felt that it was not their role to intervene to protect those rights.

One theory to explain the reluctance of the courts to intervene during this period was that the courts perceived that intervention would usurp the proper functions of the legislative and executive branches of the government. A second reason given is that the courts felt they lacked the expertise necessary to protect prisoners' rights and therefore ran a risk of interfering with the proper functioning of the prisons. The third popular reason given was that most prisoners were confined in state institutions, and federal courts were hesitant to interfere in state governmental operations.

During the *rights period*, the courts became actively involved in prison administration. The movement started when the lower federal courts demonstrated a willingness to identify prisoners' rights and moved to protect those rights. In addition, the legal profession developed a cadre of public interest lawyers who were more willing to fight the system than in the past.

The present period is marked by the policy of the courts to defer to prison administrators' judgments unless constitutional violations are apparent. The present climate can be described as one in which prisoners will lose on most rights issues, while the courts stress the need to give deference to the expertise of correctional officials. The federal Prison Litigation Reform Act of 1996 is designed to limit federal court intervention into prison administration.[2] This legislation is discussed later in this chapter.

AREAS OF INVOLVEMENT

Prisoners' rights can be divided into four broad areas:

1) Right of access to the courts

2) Individual rights

3) Due process issues

4) Cruel and unusual punishment[3]

The general consensus is that the courts tend to favor inmates when the issue involves the right of access to the courts and favor the prison officials when the other three areas are involved. Included in Appendix A are excerpts from the American Bar Association's *Stan-*

dards for Criminal Justice: Legal Status of Prisoners. The standards are statements regarding what the law is or should be relating to the legal status of prisoners. Appendix B contains the national policies on corrections as ratified by the American Correctional Association. The two appendices should be reviewed by the reader to obtain a better understanding of the legal status of prisoners and our national policies on corrections.

DUE PROCESS RIGHTS

Except for those cases brought by pretrial detainees regarding the conditions of their confinement, most due process rights issues concern procedural protections that must be afforded an inmate. For example, the inmate can not contend that the prison officials cannot take the action that they have taken, only that before taking the action, the officials failed to provide him or her with the procedural protections to which he or she was entitled. In this area, it appears that the Supreme Court generally holds that if a liberty interest is involved, such as the loss of good time, that prior to taking the action the inmate has a right to written notice, an opportunity to be heard, a written statement of the reasons for the decisions and the right to be represented by a representative (not necessarily an attorney).

Torts

In most situations, prisoners challenging actions of prison officials do so by tort actions. A *tort* is a civil wrong or injury, other than a breach of contract, resulting from a violation of a duty. Most tort cases involving prisoners are filed under the *Civil Rights Act, Section 1983.*

Less than two percent of the 1983 cases filed by inmates were successful in obtaining any redress. Despite this low rate of success, the number of cases filed each year continues to increase. It was estimated that approximately 50,000 suits were filed nationwide by prisoners in 1995. In 1993, New York state alone had over 10,000 filed against it.

Conditions of Confinement

Prisoners who are detained in pretrial confinement facilities may challenge the conditions of their confinement under the Fifth or Fourteenth Amendments' due process clause. Prisoners who have been convicted may challenge their conditions under the Eighth Amendment's prohibition against cruel and unusual punishments.

Civil Rights Act
Title 42, Section 1983, U.S. Code

Any person who, under color of any statute, ordinance, regulation, custom, or usage, or any state, or territory, subjects or causes to be subjected, any citizen of the United States or other person within the jurisdiction thereof to the deprivation of any rights, privileges, or immunities secured by the Constitution and laws, shall be liable to the party injured in an action at law, suit in equity, or other proper proceedings for redress.

Habeas Corpus

Traditionally, prisoners have filed *writs of habeas corpus* to attack the state court convictions. This writ, traditionally known as the "Great Writ," is a constitutionally protected writ designed to require the government to justify why the individual is being held in confinement. Under the process, the prisoner can file a writ in federal court alleging that he is being illegally held in confinement because his conviction was in violation of a state or federal constitutional right. If the writ involves only state issues, then the state courts make the final decision. If the writ is based on a federal issue (e.g., his conviction was based on the violation of a federal constitutional right) then the final decision makers are the federal courts. After the prisoner files the writ, the receiving court determines whether a writ should issue. If the court issues a writ, then the warden (actually a representative from the attorney general's office) must come forward and justify the confinement. The justification usually consists of filing proof of the conviction, at which point the burden shifts to the defendant to establish the illegality of the conviction. Less than one percent of the writs filed are successful. The problem is that a vast number of writs flood the court system.

The writ is also the way that the death penalty from state criminal trials is traditionally attacked in federal court. In the past, convictions have been voided years after the defendants were found guilty. The process has also been used to delay the imposition of the death penalty. To eliminate this, in 1976, the U.S. Congress passed the Antiterrorism and Effective Death Penalty Act. This act establishes limitation periods for the bringing of *habeas* actions and requires that federal courts generally defer to state courts' determinations. Under the act, a habeas petitioner will normally have one year in which to seek relief. If the claim has been adjudicated in state court, relief will not be available unless the state court's adjudication resulted in a decision that is either contrary to, or involved an unreasonable application of, clearly established federal law as determined by the U.S. Supreme Court, or was based on an unreasonable determination of the facts in light of the evidence presented in the state court proceedings. The presumption of correctness accorded state courts' factual findings was also strengthened. Second or successive *habeas* actions presenting new claims must be dismissed unless the claim is shown to rely on a new, previously unavailable rule of constitutional law, or the factual predicate for the claim could not have been discovered previously through due diligence, and the new facts would be sufficient to establish by clear and convincing evidence that, except for the error, no reasonable fact finder would have convicted.[4]

Prison Litigation Reform Act

In an attempt to reduce federal involvement in the operation of state correctional systems, the U.S. Congress passed the Prison Litigation Reform Act in 1996. This act was an amendment to the 1994 Crime Bill.[5] Under this act, federal courts are instructed to extend no further than necessary prospective relief in prison overcrowding orders. The act sets two minimum conditions for the entry of prisoner release orders: first, a prior order of less intrusive relief must have failed; second, the prison official must have had a reasonable opportunity to comply with the previous order. One popular method used by federal courts was to order the correction of a problem, or in the alternative, to release the prisoners held under the conditions complained of in the case. In addition, a single judge may not issue a prisoner release order based on overcrowding. Any order issued must be approved by an appellate court or a three judge federal court. The court, before issuing an order for relief, must find by clear and convincing evidence that overcrowding is the primary cause of the violation of a federal right and no relief other than an order releasing prisoners will remedy the violation. Prior to filing for a release order, the prisoner must first exhaust his or her state remedies. In addition, prisoners may not bring federal civil rights actions for mental or emotional injury suffered while in custody without a prior showing of physical injury. The award of attorney fees to successful prisoner litigators was also limited to only that which was directly and reasonably incurred in enforcing the relief.

BACK TO BASICS

Starting in the mid-1990s, legislators have decided that they were tired of "coddling" prison inmates and attempted to make prison conditions harsher for the inmates. A Mississippi state senator stated, "We want a prisoner to look like a prisoner and to smell like one." In 1996, Mississippi banned individual televisions from inmate cells, banned air conditioning, prohibited weight-lifting equipment, and required inmates to dress in striped uniforms with CONVICT stamped on the back. Ohio, Wisconsin, and North Carolina have enacted similar legislation. California is now charging inmates $3 to initiate court actions and has banned R-rated movies. South Carolina has banned conjugal visits for minimum security inmates, ending a 50-year tradition. New Jersey is considering legislation that would require inmates to work 10-hour days with no educational programs, no gyms, and no TVs. The U.S. Congress has eliminated educational grants for federal prisoners. Chain gangs are once again being used in some Southern states.[6] While the above perks may be considered rights by some, it appears that the courts will defer to the prison administrators regarding the new trend in making prison a harsher place. As one judge stated, "It appears that none of these types of measures will deter crime, but they do not infringe on any prisoner's constitutional rights."

HISTORICAL BACKGROUND OF THE "CRUEL AND UNUSUAL" CLAUSE

Included in this section are excerpts for the U.S. Supreme Court case of *Ronald Allen Harmelin, Petitioner v. Michigan* (Decided June 27, 1991). A review of the excerpts will provide the reader with a summary of the historical background of the "cruel and unusual" clause of the Eighth Amendment.

[In this case, the defendant claims that his sentence was disproportionate and therefore in violation of the "cruel and unusual" clause of the Eighth Amendment. The Court denied his claim.]

Justice Scalia announced the judgment of the Court...

...There is no doubt that the Declaration of Rights is the antecedent of our constitutional text. (This document was promulgated in February 1689 and was enacted into law as the Bill of Rights) In 1791, five state constitutions prohibited "cruel or unusual punishments," and two prohibited "cruel" punishments. The new federal Bill of Rights, however, tracked Virginia's prohibition of "cruel and unusual punishments," which most closely followed the English provision. In fact, the entire text of the Eighth Amendment is taken almost verbatim from the English Declaration of Rights, which provided "[t]hat excessive Baile ought not to be required nor excessive Fines imposed nor cruell and unusuall Punishments inflicted."

Perhaps the Americans of 1791 understood the Declaration's language precisely as the Englishmen of 1689 did—though as we shall discuss later, that seems unlikely. Or perhaps the colonists meant to incorporate the content of that antecedent by reference, whatever the content might have been. Solem suggested something like this, arguing

that since Americans claimed "all the rights of English subjects," "their use of the language of the English Bill of Rights
is convincing proof that they intended to provide at least
the same protection,". . .Thus, not only is the original meaning of the 1689 Declaration of Rights relevant, but also the
circumstances of its enactment, insofar as they display the
particular "rights of English subjects" it was designed to
vindicate. . . The Magna Carta provided that "[a] free man
shall not be fined for a small offence, except in proportion
to the measure of the offence; and for a great offence he
shall be fined in proportion to the magnitude of the offence,
saving his freehold. . .

Most historians agree that the "cruell and unusuall Punishments" provision of the English Declaration of Rights
was prompted by the abuses attributed to the infamous Lord
Chief Justice Jeffreys of the King's Bench during the Stuart
reign of James II. . . They do not agree, however, on which
abuses.

Jeffreys is best known for presiding over the "Bloody
Assizes" following the Duke of Monmouth's abortive re-
bellion in 1685, a special commission led by Jeffreys tried,
convicted, and executed hundreds of suspected insurgents.
Some have attributed the Declaration of Rights provision to
popular outrage against those proceedings.

But the vicious punishments for treason decreed in the
Bloody Assizes (drawing and quartering, burning of women
felons, beheading, disembowling, etc.) were common in that
period—indeed, they were specifically authorized by law
and remained so for many years afterwards. Thus, recently
historians have argued, and the best historical evidence suggests, that it was not Jeffrey's management of the Bloody
Assizes that led to the Declaration of Rights provision, but
rather the arbitrary sentencing power he had exercised in
administering justice from the King's Bench, particularly
when punishing a notorious perjurer. Jeffreys was widely
accused of "inventing" special penalties for the King's enemies, penalties that were not authorized by common-law
precedent or statute.

The preamble to the Declaration of Rights, a sort of indictment of James II that calls to mind the preface to our own Declaration of Independence, specifically referred to illegal sentences and King's Bench proceedings. "Whereas the late King James II, by the Assistance of diverse Evill Councellors Judges and Ministers imployed by him did endeavour to subvert and extirpate the Protestant Religion, and the Lawes and Liberties of this Kingdome."

By Prosecutions in the Court of King's Bench for Matters and Causes cognizable onely in Parlyament and by diverse other Arbitrary and Illegall Courses." "[E]xcessive Baile hath beene required of Persons committed in Criminall Cases to elude the Benefit of the Lawes made for the Liberty of the Subjects. And excessive Fines have been imposed. And illegall and cruell Punishments have been inflicted. All which are utterly and directly contrary to the knowne Lawes and Statutes and Freedome of this Realme.

The only recorded contemporaneous interpretation of the "cruell and unusuall Punishments" clause confirms the focus upon Jeffreys' King's Bench activities, and upon the illegality rather than the disproportionality of his sentences. In 1685, Titus Oates, a Protestant cleric whose false accusations had caused the execution of 15 prominent Catholics for allegedly organizing a "Popish Plot" to overthrow King Charles II in 1679, was tried and convicted before the King's Bench for perjury. Oates' crime, "bearing false witness against another, with an express premeditated design to take away his life, so as the innocent person be condemned and executed" had, at one time, been treated as a species of murder, and punished with death. At sentencing, Jeffreys complained that death was no longer available as a penalty and lamented that "a proportionable punishment of that crime can scarce by our law, as it now stands, be inflicted upon him." The law would not stand in the way, however. The judges met, and, according to Jeffreys, were in unanimous agreement that "crimes of this nature are left to be punished according to the discretion of this court, so far as that the judgment extend not to life or member." *Ibid.* Another justice taunted Oates that "we have taken special care of you,"... The court then decreed that he should pay a fine of "1000 marks upon each Indictment," that he should be "stript of [his] Canonical Habits," that he should stand in the pillory annually at certain specified times and places, that on May 20 he should be whipped by "the common hangman" "from Aldgate to Newgate," that he should be similarly whipped on May 22 "from Newgate to Tyburn," and that he should be imprisoned for life. "The judges, as they believed, sentenced Oates to be scourged to death." Oates would not die, however. Four years later, and several months after the Declaration of Rights, he petitioned the House of Lords to set aside his sentence as illegal. "Not a single peer ventured to affirm that the judgment was legal; but much was said about the odious character of the appellant" and the Lords affirmed the judgment. A minority of the Lords dissented, however, and their statement sheds light on the meaning of the "cruell and unusuall Punishments" clause: "1st, [T]he King's Bench, being a Temporal Court, made it a Part of the Judgment, That Titus Oates, being a Clerk, should, for his said Perjuries, be divested of his canonical and priestly Habit . . . ; which is a Matter wholly out of their Power, belonging to the Ecclesiastical Courts only. "2dly, [S]aid Judgments are barbarous, inhuman, and unchristian; and there is no Precedent to warrant the Punishments of whipping and committing to Prison for Life, for the Crime of Perjury; which yet were but Part of the Punishments inflicted upon him. "4thly, [T]his will be an Encouragement and Allowance for giving the like cruel, barbarous and illegal Judgments hereafter, unless this Judgment be reversed. "5thly, ... [T]hat the said Judgments were contrary to Law and ancient Practice, and therefore erroneous, and ought to be reversed. "6thly, Because it is contrary to the Declaration on the Twelfth of February last ... that excessive Bail ought not to be required, nor excessive Fines imposed, nor cruel nor unusual Punishments afflicted."

Unless one accepts the notion of a blind incorporation, however, the ultimate question is not what "cruell and unusuall punishments" meant in the Declaration of Rights, but what its meaning was to the Americans who adopted the Eighth Amendment. Even if one assumes that the Founders knew the precise meaning of that English antecedent, a direct transplant of the English meaning to the soil of American constitutionalism would in any case have been impossible. There were no common-law punishments in the federal system, so that the provision must have been meant as a check not upon judges but upon the Legislature.

Wrenched out of its common-law context, and applied to the actions of a legislature, the word "unusual" could hardly mean "contrary to law." But it continued to mean (as it continues to mean today) "such as [does not] occu[r] in ordinary practice," "[s]uch as is [not] in common use."

The Eighth Amendment received little attention during the proposal and adoption of the federal Bill of Rights. However, what evidence exists from debates at the state ratifying conventions that prompted the Bill of Rights as well as the floor debates in the First Congress which proposed it "confirm[s] the view that the cruel and unusual punishments clause was directed at prohibiting certain methods of punishment."

SIGNIFICANT CASES INVOLVING PRISONERS' RIGHTS

In this section, some of the significant cases involving prisoners' rights are discussed. Most cases are presented in summary form only. Two are presented as abridgements of the actual court opinions. The two opinions should provide the reader with an understanding of the form and substance of court opinions in this area.

Large v. Superior Court of County of Maricopa

This case, decided by the Arizona Supreme Court, held that the forcible administration of anti-psychotic drugs to a prisoner for management and control rather than for treatment violated the prisoner's liberty interest protected by the due process clause. The court stated that the forcible administration of such dangerous drugs to a mentally ill prisoner in nonemergency situations was unconstitutional.[7]

Bounds v. Smith

In *Bounds v. Smith,* the U.S. Supreme Court made it clear that states were required to have law libraries to assist inmates in their efforts to petition the courts unless the states provided legally trained persons to assist the inmates.[8]

Hutto v. Finney

In this case, the Supreme Court held that given the harsh conditions of punitive isolation cells in the Arkansas prison system, inmates could not be placed in those cells for more than 30 days without violating the inmate's constitutional rights against cruel and unusual punishment.[9]

Estelle v. Gamble

The Supreme Court held in this case that an inmate cannot prove that inadequate medical care by the prison staff is cruel and unusual unless the inmate can also establish that the prison officials were deliberately indifferent to a serious medical condition.[10]

Helling v. McKinney

In *Helling*, the Court held that the treatment a prisoner receives in prison, and conditions under which he is confined, are subject to scrutiny under the Eighth Amendment. In this case, the prisoner was seeking an injunction prohibiting prison authorities from subjecting him to environmental tobacco smoke. Apparently, he shared a cell with an inmate who smoked five packs of cigarettes a day. In this case, the court stated that the prisoner should have been permitted to prove that his exposure to secondhand smoke was an unreasonable danger to his future.[11]

Jones v. N.C. Prisoners' Labor Union

In *Jones*, the Supreme Court held that a state may ban meetings of prisoners' unions and prohibit the unions from soliciting members and from making bulk mailings to members who are in prison.[12]

Meachum v. Fano

In the *Meachum* case, the Court held that inmates have no due process rights to avoid transfer to another prison where conditions may be harsher. It appears that the state may transfer the prisoners, and it makes no difference if the transfer is for administrative or disciplinary reasons.[13]

Vitek v. Jones

Unlike the *Meachum* case, the Court held in *Vitek* that a Nebraska state prisoner has a liberty interest to challenge his transfer to a state mental hospital. Accordingly, before the transfer of a prisoner from a correctional institution to a mental hospital, the inmate must be provided with appropriate procedural protections.[14]

Turner v. Safety

In this case, the Supreme Court held that when a prison regulation impinges on an inmate's constitutional rights, the regulation will still be valid if the prison officials can establish that the regulation is reasonably related to legitimate penological interest. This approach is labeled as the "rational basis" approach. In addition, the Court placed the burden on the party (prisoner) whose rights have been violated to demonstrate that the government had no rational basis for doing what it did or did not do. In assessing the actions of the prison officials, the Court stated that four factors should be examined: (1) whether there is a rational connection between the prison regulation and the legitimate governmental interest put forward to justify it, (2) whether an alternative means of exercising the right exists in spite of what the prison has done, (3) whether striking down the prison officials' action would have a significant effect on fellow inmates or staff, and (4) whether there are ready alternatives available to the prison or whether the regulation appears instead to be an exaggerated response to the problem it is intended to address.[15]

Wolff v. McDonnell

In the *Wolff v. McDonnell* case, the U.S. Supreme Court ruled that inmates have a liberty interest in good-time credits, and therefore good-time credits may not be denied without holding a hearing. In addition, the inmate should be (1) given notice of the alleged infraction, (2) given an opportunity to call witnesses, and (3) present documentary evidence, unless allowing these rights would be unduly hazardous to institutional safety or correctional goals. The inmate is also entitled to a written decision of the reasons for the action. The written decision should describe the evidence relied upon to make the decision. [16]

Procunier v. Martinez

The *Procunier v. Martinez* case involved the censorship of outgoing mail. The Court stated that prisons could not censor outgoing mail that was viewed by prison authorities expressing "inflammatory views," unduly complained about prison administration, or was otherwise inappropriate. The court held that these standards were too broad and failed to exclude only material that posed a legitimate threat to the institution. Even restrictions on inmate correspondence that furthers an important or substantial interest of penal administration will nevertheless be invalid if the restriction is too broad. Accordingly, California prison regulations that authorize censorship of statements that unduly complain or magnify grievances, express inflammatory political, racial, religious, or other views is invalid.

The court stated that the decision by prison officials to censor or withhold delivery of a particular letter must be accompanied by minimum procedural safeguards. Accordingly, when mail is censored, the inmate sending the mail must be notified and given an opportunity to appeal to an official who was not involved in the original censorship decision. The court based their decision in this case on the First Amendment rights of the correspondents outside of prison as well as the rights of the inmates.[17]

DELIBERATE INDIFFERENCE

The courts have held that before prison administrators may be held liable for the violation of a prisoner's Eighth Amendment rights, the administrators must have acted with deliberate indifference. In the below case, the U.S. Supreme Court attempts to define *deliberate indifference*.

Farmer v. Brennan

U.S. Supreme Court No. 92-7247

DEE FARMER, PETITIONER v. EDWARD BRENNAN, WARDEN, et al. [June 6, 1994]

Justice Souter delivered the opinion of the Court.

A prison official's "deliberate indifference" to a substantial risk of serious harm to an inmate violates the Eighth Amendment. This case requires us to define the term "deliberate indifference" as we do by requiring a showing that the official was subjectively aware of the risk.

I.

The dispute before us stems from a civil suit brought by petitioner, Dee Farmer, alleging that respondents, federal prison officials, violated the Eighth Amendment by their deliberate indifference to the petitioner's safety. Petitioner, who is serving a federal sentence for credit card fraud, has been diagnosed by medical personnel of the Bureau of Prisons as a transsexual, one who has "[a] rare psychiatric disorder in which a person feels persistently uncomfortable about his or her anatomical sex," and who typically seeks medical treatment, including hormonal therapy and surgery, to bring about a permanent sex change. _American Medical Association, Encyclopedia of Medicine 1006_ (1989); see also American Psychiatric Association, _Diagnostic and Statistical Manual of Mental Disorders,_ 74-75 (3d rev. ed. 1987).

For several years before being convicted and sentenced in 1986 at the age of 18, petitioner, who is biologically male, wore women's clothing (as petitioner did at the 1986 trial), underwent estrogen therapy, received silicone breast implants, and submitted to unsuccessful "black market" testicle-removal surgery. Petitioner's precise appearance in prison is unclear from the record before us, but petitioner claims to have continued hormonal treatment while incarcerated by using drugs smuggled into prison, and apparently wears clothing in a feminine manner, as by displaying a shirt off one shoulder. The parties agree that petitioner projects feminine characteristics.

The practice of federal prison authorities is to incarcerate preoperative transsexuals with prisoners of like biological sex, and over time authorities housed petitioner in several federal facilities, sometimes in the general male prison population, but more often in segregation. While there is no dispute that petitioner was segregated at least several times because of violations of prison rules, neither is it disputed that in at least one penitentiary petitioner was segregated because of safety concerns.

On March 9, 1989, petitioner was transferred for disciplinary reasons from the Federal Correctional Institute in Oxford, Wisconsin (FCI-Oxford), to the United States Penitentiary in Terre Haute, Indiana (USP-Terre Haute). Though the record before us is unclear about the security designations of the two prisons in 1989, penitentiaries are typically higher security facilities that house more troublesome prisoners than federal correctional institutes. See generally _Federal Bureau of Prisons, Facilities 1990._ After an initial stay in administrative segregation, petitioner was placed in the USP-Terre Haute general population.

Petitioner voiced no objection to any prison official about the transfer to the penitentiary or to placement in its general population. Within two weeks, according to petitioner's allegations, petitioner was beaten and raped by another inmate in petitioner's cell. Several days later, after petitioner claims to have reported the incident, officials returned petitioner to segregation to await, according to respondents, a hearing about petitioner's HIV-positive status.

Acting without counsel, petitioner then filed a . . . complaint, alleging a violation of the Eighth Amendment. See *Bivens v. Six Unknown Fed. Narcotics Agents*, 403 U. S. 388 (1971); *Carlson v. Green*, 446 U. S. 14 (1980). As defendants, petitioner named respondents: the warden of USP-Terre Haute and the Director of the Bureau of Prisons (sued only in their official capacities); the warden of FCI-Oxford and a case manager there; and the director of the Bureau of Prisons North Central Region Office and an official in that office (sued in their official and personal capacities). As later amended, the complaint alleged that respondents either transferred petitioner to USP-Terre Haute or placed petitioner in its general population despite knowledge that the penitentiary had a violent environment and a history of inmate assaults, and despite knowledge that petitioner, as a transsexual who "projects feminine characteristics," would be particularly vulnerable to sexual attack by some USP-Terre Haute inmates. This allegedly amounted to a deliberately indifferent failure to protect petitioner's safety, and thus to a violation of petitioner's Eighth Amendment rights. Petitioner sought compensatory and punitive damages, and an injunction barring future confinement in any penitentiary, including USP-Terre Haute.

. . .The District Court denied petitioner's . . . motion and granted summary judgment to respondents, concluding that there had been no deliberate indifference to petitioner's safety. The failure of prison officials to prevent inmate assaults violates the Eighth Amendment, the court stated, only if prison officials were "reckless in a criminal sense," meaning that they had actual knowledge of a potential danger. Respondents, however, lacked the requisite knowledge, the court found. [Petitioner] never expressed any concern for his safety to any of [respondents]. Since [respondents] had no knowledge of any potential danger to [petitioner], they were not deliberately indifferent to his safety....

II.

The Constitution "does not mandate comfortable prisons," *Rhodes v. Chapman*, 452 U. S. 337, 349 (1981), but neither does it permit inhumane ones, and it is now settled that the treatment a prisoner receives in prison and the conditions under which he is confined are subject to scrutiny under the Eighth Amendment. In its prohibition of "cruel and unusual punishments," the Eighth Amendment places restraints on prison officials, who may not, for example, use excessive physical force against prisoners. See *Hudson v. McMillian*, 503 U. S. (1992). The Amendment also imposes duties on these officials, who must provide humane conditions of confinement; prison officials must ensure that inmates receive adequate food, clothing, shelter and medical care, and must "take reasonable measures to guarantee the safety of the inmates." See *Hudson v. Palmer,* 468 U. S. 517, 526-527 (1984).

In particular, as the lower courts have uniformly held, and as we have assumed, "[p]rison officials have a duty . . . to protect prisoners from violence at the hands of other prisoners—the protection [an inmate] is afforded against other inmates" as a "conditio[n] of confinement" subject to the strictures of the Eighth Amendment). Having incarcerated "persons [with] demonstrated proclivit[ies] for antisocial criminal, and often violent, conduct," *Hudson v. Palmer*, supra, at 526, having stripped them of virtually every means of self-protection and foreclosed their access to outside aid, the government and its officials are not free to let the state of nature take its course. . . Prison conditions may be "restrictive and even harsh," *Rhodes*, supra, at 347, but gratuitously allowing the beating or rape of one prisoner by another serves no legitimate penological objectiv[e]. . . any more than it squares with evolving standards of decency. . . Being violently assaulted in prison is simply not part of the penalty that criminal offenders pay for their offenses against society.

It is not, however, every injury suffered by one prisoner at the hands of another that translates into constitutional liability for prison officials responsible for the victim's safety. Our cases have held that a prison official violates the Eighth Amendment only when two requirements are met. First, the deprivation alleged must be, objectively, "sufficiently serious,". . . a prison official's act or omission must result in the denial of "the minimal civilized measure of life's necessities." For a claim (like the one here) based on a failure to prevent harm, the inmate must show that he is incarcerated under conditions posing a substantial risk of serious harm.

The second requirement follows from the principle that only the unnecessary and wanton infliction of pain implicates the Eighth Amendment. To violate the Cruel and Unusual Punishments Clause, a prison official must have a sufficiently culpable state of mind. In prison-conditions cases that state of mind is one of "deliberate indifference" to inmate health or safety, a standard the parties agree governs the claim in this case. The parties disagree, however, on the proper test for deliberate indifference, which we must therefore undertake to define.

Although we have never paused to explain the meaning of the term "deliberate indifference," the case law is instructive. The term first appeared in the United States Reports in *Estelle v. Gamble*, 429 U. S., at 104, and its use there shows that deliberate indifference describes a state of mind more blameworthy than negligence. In considering the inmate's claim in *Estelle* that inadequate prison medical care violated the Cruel and Unusual Punishments Clause, we distinguished "deliberate indifference to serious medical needs of prisoners," from "negligen[ce] in diagnosing or treating a medical condition," holding that only the former violates the Clause. We have since read *Estelle* for the proposition that Eighth Amendment liability requires "more than ordinary lack of due care for the prisoner's interests or safety." While *Estelle* establishes that deliberate indifference entails something more than mere negligence, the cases are also clear that it is satisfied by something less than acts or omissions for the very purpose of causing harm or with knowledge that harm will result. That point underlies the ruling that "application of the deliberate indifference standard is inappropriate" in one class of prison cases: when officials stand accused of using excessive physical force. In such situations, where the decisions of prison officials are typically made in haste, under pressure, and frequently without the luxury of a second chance. An Eighth Amendment claimant must show more than "indifference," deliberate or otherwise. The claimant must show that officials applied force maliciously and sadistically for the very purpose of causing harm.

With deliberate indifference lying somewhere between the poles of negligence at one end and purpose or knowledge at the other, the courts of appeals have routinely equated deliberate indifference with recklessness . . . It is, indeed, fair to say that acting or failing to act with deliberate indifference to a substantial risk of serious harm to a prisoner is the equivalent of recklessly disregarding that risk.

That does not, however, fully answer the pending question about the level of culpability deliberate indifference entails, for the term recklessness is not self-defining. The civil law generally calls a person reckless who acts or (if the person has a duty to act) fails to act in the face of an unjustifiably high risk of harm that is either known or so obvious that it should be known . . . The criminal law, however, generally permits a finding of recklessness only when a person disregards a risk of harm of which he is aware . . . We hold instead that a prison official cannot be found liable under the Eighth Amendment for denying an inmate humane conditions of confinement unless the official knows of and disregards an excessive risk to inmate health or safety; the official must both be aware of facts from which the inference could be drawn that a substantial risk of serious harm exists, and he must also draw the inference. This approach comports best with the text of the Amendment as our cases have interpreted it. The Eighth Amendment does not outlaw cruel and unusual "conditions"; it outlaws cruel and unusual "punishments." An act or omission unaccompanied by knowledge of a significant risk of harm might well be something society wishes to discourage, and if harm does result, society might well wish to assure compensation....

WARNER V. ORANGE COUNTY PROBATION DEPT.

CA 2, No. 95-7055 decided 9/9/96, affirming 870 F.Supp. 69

Question: Can a probation department be held civilly liable for requiring attendance at a religion-based A.A. program as a probation condition?

Holding: Yes. Coerced attendance as condition of probation violated Establishment Clause.

Facts: The U.S. Court of Appeals for the Second Circuit held that a county probation department opened itself up to civil liability under 42 USC 1983 by recommending that a motorist who pleaded guilty to drunk driving be required to attend meetings of Alcoholics Anonymous as a condition of probation. The probation condition constituted coercion of religious activity in violation of the First Amendment's Establishment Clause.

The fact that the sentencing judge made the final decision about probation did not amount to a superseding cause relieving the probation department of liability. The majority also rejected the probation department's assertion of quasi-judicial absolute immunity. Individual probation officers might well be entitled to such immunity, but U.S.

Supreme Court decisions strongly indicate that the department itself is not, the majority said.

Finally, it rejected the department's argument that the probation condition did not actually violate the Establishment Clause. The program had a strongly religious content, and the plaintiff was coerced into participating on pain of being imprisoned, it reasoned.

Judge Winter, dissenting, said the plaintiff waived his claim or consented to the probation condition by voluntarily participating in the program before being sentenced. The dissenter also said that the probation condition did not violate the Establishment Clause, as opposed to the First Amendment's Free Exercise Clause.

Plaintiff Robert Warner pleaded guilty to driving drunk and without a license. The Orange County, N.Y., Department of Probation ("OCDP") prepared a presentence report recommending probation with six special conditions, including the condition that Warner "attend Alcoholics Anonymous at the direction of [his] probation officer." The trial judge sentenced Warner to three years of probation, imposing the special conditions recommended by the OCDP.

Warner then brought suit against OCDP under 42 USC 1983, claiming that the probation condition forced him to participate in religious activity in violation of the First Amendment's Establishment Clause, and that OCDP was responsible, in part because it recommended the A.A. therapy to the sentencing court.

The district court found that the program Warner was required to attend involved a substantial religious component. For example, the "Twelve Steps" included instruction that participants should "make a decision to turn our will and our lives over to the care of God . . . "[a]dmit to God . . . the exact nature of our wrongs," be "entirely ready to have God remove all these defects . . .," and "seek! through prayer and meditation to improve our conscious contact with God .. . ." Meetings frequently began with a religious invocation, and always ended with a Christian prayer. The district court awarded Warner declaratory judgment, nominal damages of one dollar, and attorney's fees, 870 F.Supp. 69, 56 CrL 1318 (DC SNY 1994).

It is clear that Warner's injury resulted from a custom or policy of Orange County, as opposed to an isolated instance of conduct. OCDP's recommendation was one of six standard probation conditions that it routinely submitted to sentencing judges in alcohol cases. OCDP argues that it is nonetheless not legally responsible because it was the judge's sentencing decision, not the Probation Department's recommendation, that caused the harm. Tort defendants, including those sued under Section 1983, are "responsible for the natural consequences of [their] actions." *Malley v. Briggs,* 475 U.S. 335,- 344 n.7 (1986). This includes "those consequences attributable to reasonably foreseeable intervening forces, including the acts of third parties." *Guiterrez-Rodriquez v. Cartagena,* 882 F.2d 553, 561 (CA 1 1989).

Under New York law, the determination of probation terms is a nondelegable judicial task. The probation department therefore argues that its role was purely advisory. *Malley* rejected a similar argument advanced by a state trooper who argued that he was shielded from responsibility for obtaining an allegedly illegal arrest warrant by his entitlement to rely on the judgment of the judicial officer in finding probable cause and issuing the warrant. The court said such reliance was not justified if "a reasonably well-trained officer in [the same) position would have known that his affidavit failed to establish probable cause and that he should not have applied for the warrant." 475 U.S. at 345.

The circumstances in *Malley* were more favorable than those here to the argument of exoneration by reason of the intervening decision of the judge. A police officer applying for an arrest warrant appears in a partisan role, whereas the probation officer is a neutral adviser to the court. The district court noted a high likelihood of court adoption of recommendations by the probation department. We review this determination for clear error, and find none. Given the neutral advisory role of the probation officer toward the court, it is an entirely "natural consequence," *Malley,* 475 U.S. at 344 n.7, for a judge to adopt the OCDP's recommendations as to a therapy provider without careful scrutiny.

Warner, following the advice of his attorney, sampled A.A. sessions prior to sentence and made no objection to their religious content at the time of sentence. However, this does not resolve the true issue of proximate cause, which is whether, when OCDP made its recommendation, it was reasonably foreseeable that the recommendation would result in the harm. Warner's failure to object was entirely foreseeable. Assuming his early visits made him aware of the full extent of the religious content of the A.A. therapy, it was not clear that Warner was aware at the time that the religious content gave him any legal basis to object, or that he had even told his lawyer about the religious content. Furthermore, even if aware of his rights, he might well have been afraid to annoy the sentencing judge by objecting to the standard recommendation of the probation department.

For the same reasons and others, Warner's conduct did not constitute consent. A defendant facing sentence may well undertake daily attendance at mass in the hope of convincing the sentencing judge of his penitence. We do not see how such conduct, without more, could be construed as consent to a sentence of probation conditioned on daily attendance at mass.

Nor can the actions of A.A. be considered to have broken the chain of causation. There can be no question as to the reasonable foreseeability of the religious nature of the program OCDP was recommending for Warner. OCDP is responsible for any resulting injury to Warner's First Amendment rights.

OCDP contends that even if its recommendation to the judge was a proximate cause of Warner's sentence, it is immune from liability. It claims that probation department sentence recommendations are so integral a part of the judicial process as to benefit from an absolute quasi-judicial immunity similar to that enjoyed by prosecutors. Were this suit brought against the probation officer, the claim for absolute immunity would likely have merit. See *Dorman v. Higgins,* 821 F.2d 133 (CA 2 1987), *Shelton v. McCarthy,* 699 F.Supp. 412 (DC WNY 1988). However, Warner sued only the department.

The county also argues that forcing Warner to attend Alcoholics Anonymous did not violate the First Amendment's Establishment Clause. We disagree. The Supreme Court has repeatedly made clear that "at a minimum, the Constitution guarantees that government may not coerce anyone to support or participate in religion or its exercise, or otherwise act in a way which 'establishes a [state] religion or religious faith, or tends to do so." *Lee v. Weisman,* 112 S.Ct. 2649, 2655 (1992), quoting *Lynch v. Donnelly,* 465 U.S. 668, 678 (1984). The A.A. program had a substantial religious component; we have noticed that the meetings were intensely religious events. Neither the probation recommendation, nor the court's sentence, offered Warner any choice among therapy programs. If Warner had failed to attend A.A., he would have been subject to imprisonment for violation of probation.

Orange County argues that even if Warner was forced to attend the meetings, he was not required to participate in the religious exercises that took place. The county argues that, as a mature adult, Warner was less susceptible to such pressure than the children who were required to stand in respectful silence during a school prayer in *Lee v. Weisman,* 112 S.Ct. at 2658-59; it points out that the Supreme Court expressly questioned whether the obligation imposed by the school in *Lee* might have been constitutionally tolerable "if the affected citizens had been mature adults." *Id.* at 2658.

We do not find this argument convincing. Warner's exposure was more coercive than the school prayer in *Lee.* The plaintiff in *Lee* was subjected only to a brief two minutes of prayer on a single occasion. Warner, in contrast, was required to participate in a long-term program of group therapy that repeatedly turned to religion as the basis of motivation. And when he appeared to be pursuing the program with insufficient zeal, the requirement that he attend "Step meetings" to probation officer reintensify his motivation. Warner was also paired with another member of A.A. as a method of enhancing his indoctrination into the group's approach to recovery from alcoholism. Failure to cooperate could lead to incarceration. The trial judge found that Warner's success in remaining aloof diminished his damages to a token of one dollar, the fact that Warner managed to avoid indoctrination despite the pressure he faced does not make the county's program any less coercive, or nullify the county's liability.

Dissent: Warner either waived his claim or consented to A.A. attendance because he voluntarily began attendance before any involvement by the probation office. Further, the sentence by the trial court was an independent, superseding cause. The invocation of the Establishment Clause, rather than the Free Exercise Clause, puts into play a principle that portends changes in our penal system that are not required. - Winter, J.

SUMMARY OF PRISONERS' RIGHTS

The constitutional rights of prisoners are summarized below:

Conjugal Visitation: No federal court has yet to hold that prisoners have a constitutional right to enjoy conjugal visits (family visits).

Mail: The courts have been active in protecting the rights of prisoners to receive and send mail, as noted in the *Martinez* case. Although access to mail is a "right," the courts have held that correctional administrators can place reasonable restrictions on prisoners in the exercise of that right if there is a compelling state need. Note: prison officials may not read mail addressed to, or received from, attorneys or government officials. They may, however, check that mail to ensure that it contains no contraband.

Religion: Prisoners have the right, within limitations, to exercise their religious customs or duties. The courts have, however, upheld restrictions on the exercise of the religious practices based on reasonable and substantial justification. The burden of justifying the restrictions is placed on the prison administrators.

Access to Courts: As noted earlier, the courts have continued to stress the right of prisoners to free access to the courts. Note: federal legislation discussed earlier in this chapter has attempted to limit the access. It will be interesting to observe whether the courts will uphold those laws.

Right to Medical Treatment: The courts have held that prisoners have a right to adequate medical treatment.

DISCUSSION QUESTIONS

1. Explain the different periods of involvement by the courts in prison adminstration.

2. Classify prisoners' rights into four areas.

3. Explain the purposes of the Prison Litigation Reform Act of 1996.

4. Explain the importance of prohibition against cruel and unusual punishment.

5. What are the differences between the rights of prisoners who are in pretrial confinement and those who have been convicted?

6. Under what conditions may a prisoner sue for lack of health care?

7. Explain the significance of the *Warner* case.

ENDNOTES FOR CHAPTER 12

1. Jack E. Call, "The Supreme Court and Prisoners' Rights,", *Federal Probation,* Vol. 59, No. 1, March, 1995, pp. 36-46.

2. 28 U.S.Code 3626, as amended.

3. Call, 1995: p. 41.

4. 18 U.S.Code 3663A.

5. 28 U.S. Code 3626.

6. *Time*, September 4, 1995, p.31 and *Newsweek*, October 17, 1994 p.87.

7. 714 P2d 399 (1986).

8. 97 S.Ct. 1491 (1977).

9. 98 S.Ct. 2565 (1978).

10. 97 S.Ct. 285 (1976).

11. 113 S.Ct. 2475 (1993).

12. 97 S.Ct. 2532 (1977).

13. 96 S.Ct. 2532 (1976).

14. 100 S.Ct. 1254 (1980).

15. 107 S.Ct. 2254 (1987).

16. 94 S.Ct. 2963 (1974).

17. 94 S.Ct. 1800 (1974).

A client on an electronic monitoring device checking in.

CHAPTER 13

INNOVATIONS IN CORRECTIONS

KEY TERMS

Curfew

Curfew Parole Program

Day-reporting centers

Electronic monitoring

Home confinement

"Lock them up" policy

Supervised release

CHAPTER OBJECTIVES

After studying this chapter, the reader will be able to:

☐ Explain the present "lock them up" policy.

☐ Analyze the use of electronic house arrest.

☐ Explain the advantages and disadvantages of home confinement.

☐ List the sanctions involved with the use of home confinement.

☐ Explain the history and present use of electronic monitoring.

☐ Analyze the controversy involving the duration of home confinement.

☐ List the legal issues involved in electronic monitoring and home confinement.

☐ Analyze the concept of using day-reporting centers as alternatives to jail.

☐ Explain the history of day-reporting centers.

☐ Explain the concept involved in "intensive supervision."

☐ Analyze the concept of "self-governance" in prisons.

PAYING FOR CRIMES

In a growing trend that indicates how politically charged the crime problem has become, more and more states are trying to make prisoners pay for everything from filing lawsuits to their room and board. The number of inmates in state prisons has tripled since 1980. Our present "lock them up" policy is very expensive and robs the local communities and states of funds needed for schools, roads, etc. Presently, there are over one million state prisoners. This increase in population and the political pressures to tighten the budgets has led state officials to claim they are justified in going after even token payments from inmates, most of whom have little or no resources. In 1995, more than two dozen states passed laws intended to regain some of the costs of incarceration. For example, Arizona requires inmates to pay a utility fee if they have a television or other "major electrical appliance." Connecticut and Missouri have laws that force inmates to pay the expenses of their confinement. New Hampshire compels prisoners to repay the cost of state-provided lawyers. Texas takes part of an inmate's wages earned from any work program outside the prison.[1]

ELECTRONIC HOUSE ARREST

Electronic surveillance technology was first developed in the mid-1960s. It was not used with offenders until the 1980s. Since then, however, it has developed into one of the most popular intermediate sanctions used in the United States.[2] It is estimated that more than one million people in the United States will ultimately be placed on some form of electronic monitoring. Not only is the number of offenders placed on electronic monitor house arrest increasing, but the types of offenders are becoming more diverse. At first, it was used for offenders awaiting trial or sentencing and offenders released from institutional correctional facilities. In addition, it was first traditionally used for property offenders. The growing popularity of electronic monitoring has been due, in large measure, to the increasing demands to supervise offenders and protect communities effectively. Public support for the use of monitoring as an alternative to imprisonment is probably based on the public knowledge regarding the high cost of incarceration.

Pagers

The Texas Department of Criminal Justice is using pagers on a test program. Approximately 100 parolees were given pagers and were required to check in by calling a computer that confirms their identities using voice verification. This system allows the parolees to leave their homes to go to work, job training, or substance abuse counseling

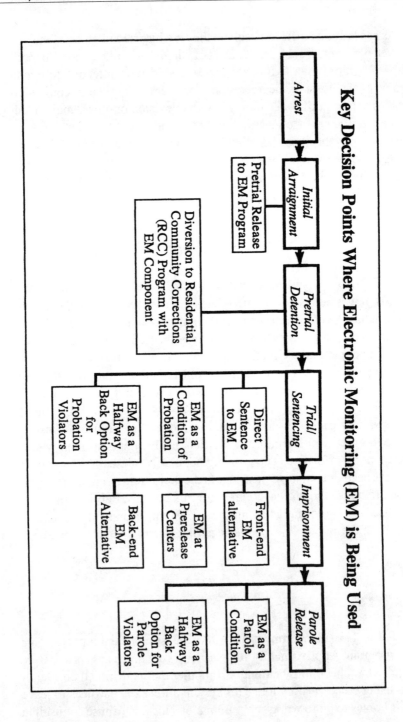

Key Decision Points Where Electronic Monitoring (EM) is Being Used

while still being monitored. The parolees must call the computer at scheduled times and in response to random pages. The computer determines the location of the parolee at certain times by identifying the telephone number that the parolee is calling from.

This program is scheduled to be used on parolees requiring higher levels of supervision. Under this system, the parolees are monitored continuously. The system costs the state approximately $3.21 per day per prisoner.[3]

Article

AN ANALYSIS OF HOME CONFINEMENT AS A SANCTION[4]

In 1988, in Addison County, Vermont, the Honorable Frances McCaffrey stunned an already cynical public when he imposed an innovative but controversial sentencing sanction on a convicted cocaine peddler who stood before him for punishment. The defendant, at 26, had been a student at Middlebury College and was known on campus as the "pharmacist" in view of his drug-dispensing capabilities. What made this defendant unique was that John Zaccaro, Jr., was the son of the 1984 Democratic Vice Presidential candidate, Geraldine A. Ferraro, and the product of an affluent, influential background. With his defense lawyers at his side, defendant Zaccaro was sentenced to serve four months of a one-to-five-year suspended prison term under house arrest rather than behind bars.

Within a short time, the media discovered that Zaccaro was serving his period of house arrest in a $1,500-a-month luxury apartment in Burlington, Vermont, which included cable television, maid services, and privileges at the neighboring YMCA. When interviewed, the prosecutor, John Quinn, stated that house arrest is a joke and concluded that Zaccaro was, for the most part, not being punished but grounded for 90 days. Expressing the view that Zaccaro's incarceration under an experimental program was making a mockery of the jail sentence, a spokesperson for Vermont's then Governor, Madeline M. Kunin, stated,

"We will take a look and maybe we will make some changes." In spite of the protestations, Zaccaro successfully completed the program without incident.

In a recent, celebrated case, arms dealer Adnan Khashoggi was placed under house arrest after posting $10 million bail following an indictment on charges of mail fraud and obstruction of justice for allegedly helping Ferdinand and Imelda Marcos plunder the Philippine Treasury. The decision to place Khashoggi under house arrest caused substantial controversy:

> In July, Mr. Khashoggi traded a 75 square foot cell at the Metropolitan Correctional Center in Manhattan for his 30,000 square foot, luxury Fifth Avenue apartment overlooking the spires of St. Patrick's Cathedral complete with a swimming pool. The Saudi arms dealer wears the band on his right ankle according to officials in the U.S. Marshal's Office. The 54-year-old defendant was originally restricted to the court's jurisdiction—New York City and surrounding northern suburbs—which apparently affords him access to many of the city's posh watering holes. His hours are loosely restricted, too. He must remain home from 1:00 a.m. to 8:00 a.m. He received the court's permission to make holiday trips to Aspen, Colorado, and his family home in Ft. Lauderdale, Florida, one of the 12 residences he owns throughout the globe.

In this era of increasing public outrage concerning the growing crime problem, and a presidential commitment to wage a war on drugs, were the court's controversial dispositions in these two cases merely anomalies or were they balanced attempts to find suitable alternatives to incarceration? In sentencing jurisdictions throughout the country, judges are being faced with balancing such competing objectives as public safety, humaneness, and the assurance of offender accountability, while confronting accelerating increases in prison overcrowding and a political commitment to incapacitation and retributive justice.

The Probation and Pretrial Services Division of the Administrative Office of the United States Courts points out that the use of house arrest and electronic monitoring equipment is increasing as an alternative to pretrial detention. During 1989, 185 defendants were placed on electronic monitoring in the federal system. Judicial officers are beginning to use house arrest and curfew as mechanisms to release offenders who otherwise may be confined to local jail.

In discussing the rationale for home confinement for pretrial defendants, the Administrative Office of the United States Courts makes the following declaration:

> The purpose of home confinement is to provide, in concert with pretrial services supervision, an alternative to detention for those persons whose nonappearance or danger to community safety cannot be controlled by less restrictive release conditions. Punishment is not appropriate for persons presumed innocent; therefore, home confinement is not used to punish, only to assure appearance and community safety.

In addition to providing cost-effective alternatives to incarceration at the pretrial and sentencing stages of the process, home confinement programs are being used at the federal level as a method to release inmates from custody before their scheduled release date. On March 3, 1986, the United States Parole Commission implemented an experimental program to provide an alternative to community correction center residence during the 60-day period before the parole release date. This "Curfew Parole Program" . . . is designed for prisoners who would otherwise qualify for community treatment center residence, but who have acceptable release plans and do not require the support services provided by the community treatment center. Under this program, qualified and approved prisoners have their release date advanced for up to 60 days on the condition that they remain at their place of residence between the hours of 9 p.m. and 5 a.m. every night unless they are given permission in advance by those supervising the offender, even visiting hours may be restricted.

On November 1, 1987, the United States Sentencing Commission implemented sentencing guidelines that allowed for the imposition of home confinement as an alternative to probation and supervised release (*supervised release* is a post incarceration period of community supervision implemented by the probation service under court jurisdiction). Also, in November 1990, Congress enacted legislation to provide a mechanism to allow the Federal Bureau of Prisons to release inmates up to six months earlier than scheduled under a term of home confinement.

Based upon the foregoing, it is apparent that home confinement is being used as a viable pretrial release and sentencing option as well as a condition of early post-incarceration release. With this backdrop, this article explains what home confinement is and how electronic monitoring is used in conjunction with it. The article discusses the cost advantages of home confinement and analyzes legal issues that have been raised regarding this sentencing option. Practical matters are also addressed, including criteria for selecting offenders to participate in home confinement, the appropriate duration for home confinement, and requirements for staffing home confinement programs.

Defining Home Confinement

The concept of home confinement is relatively ambiguous. *Home confinement* may range from evening curfew to detention during all nonworking hours to continuous incarceration at home. Monitoring techniques may range from periodic visits or telephone calls to continuous monitoring with electronic equipment. Home confinement options produce various degrees of offender control, and jurisdictions vary in the manner in which they implement these programs.

Curfew has been described as a type of home confinement requiring subjects to remain at home during specific time frames, generally in the evening. *Home detention* is more severe than curfew, requiring offenders to remain at home at all times except for certain specified periods. Exceptions allow travel for religious services, work, education, correctional treatment, shopping for food, and medical emergencies. Home detention tends to be strictly enforced and provides significant control over an offender's movement.

The most severe home confinement sanctions may be characterized as *home incarceration*, in which offenders are required to remain in their homes with even more limited exceptions for such fundamental needs as religious services or medical care. Because the major objective of this form of detention is to punish, given current prison overcrowding, this intermediate sanction has been well-accepted. It contains aspects of rehabilitation within the framework of punishment and specific deterrence. Asserted to be a cost-effective alternative to imprisonment, its use has been expanded by the development of electronic monitoring programs.

Electronic Monitoring

Technologically, electronic monitoring dates back to 1964, when an electronic telemetry system based on a triangulation process using radio signals to locate vessels was modified for possible criminal justice applications. This technology was refined by Ralph Schwitzgebel and described in *Behavioral Science.* During the mid-1960s, electronic monitoring systems were used to determine the location of parolees, mental patients, and research volunteers in Boston, Massachusetts. The initial systems were set up using multiple receivers to trace movement throughout specified areas. The number of receivers used and transmission characteristics of the environment were based upon the size of the monitored area.

Two more current monitoring systems require telephone lines to communicate between an offender's residence and a central location. The first type is described as an *active system* and consists of a transmitter, a receiver-dialer unit, and a central computer or receiver. In this system, the transmitter is strapped to the offender and broadcasts an encoded signal to a receiver situated in the offender's home. The receiver is connected by telephone to the central computer or receiving unit. When the transmitter, worn by the offender, is within range of the receiver, the system indicates the offender's location. When the offender leaves the range of the unit, the signal from the transmitter is not received, which indicates an absence. The absence is then transmitted to the central computer telephonically. An attendant at the central computer station monitors the signals, comparing them to the offender's prearranged schedule and reporting breaches to the correctional agency.

A second type of unit using telephone lines consists of a central office computer, an encoder device, and a verifier box. In this type of system, referred to as a *passive system,* the offender wears the encoder device on either the wrist or ankle. A remote computer is programmed to generate random telephone calls to the offender, who is required to provide voice identification and then insert the encoder device into the verifier box to confirm the offender's identity. The verifier box tests the encoder for a specific code implanted in the bracelet that positively identifies the offender. The system provides a report when the phone is not answered or if a busy signal is received for an extended period. It also signals a default if an offender fails to insert the encoder device into the verifier box properly. Electronic analysis of offender voice samples stored in the central computer detects impostors.

Essentially, the difference between the two systems is that the active system operates continuously, monitoring the offender from the time the offender arrives home until his or her departure. The passive system verifies the offender's presence only at selected times when random telephone calls are made from the central office.

Since 1984, 20 states have placed 45 electronic monitoring programs in operation, and the number continues to mushroom as equipment manufacturers aggressively market their goods and services while simultaneously refining their products. The technology is regularly revised in order to ensure report validity and minimize equipment malfunctions.

Cost Effectiveness of Home Confinement

From a cost-benefit perspective, home confinement has advantages. Assuming the officers in charge had a limit of 10 cases to monitor, building in a pay differential for what would clearly be an irregular schedule of hours, the cost per offender on an annual basis might well be $2,500 as compared to an average of 10 times that amount for a year of imprisonment.

Moreover, indirect savings result from the offender's ability to support his or her family while on home confinement. Wide-scale implementation of home detention affects welfare costs in that tax revenues collected by the state can also offset costs if the offender is capable of maintaining employment.

House arrest is cost-effective because government not only saves the yearly cost of housing an offender ($10,000-$15,000 per year) but also the construction costs of new prison space at approximately $50,000 per bed. Petersilia points out, however, that the initial cost of an electronic monitoring program may not necessarily be inexpensive. Because firms are attempting to recoup development costs, initial equipment purchases are quite expensive. The following is an assessment of the electronic monitoring experience in Kenton, Kentucky:

> Kentucky spent about $30,000 to purchase 12 electronic monitors. A cost evaluation of the program after six months concluded that the electronic monitoring had cost the county $10,000-$20,000 more than it would have spent

$20,000 more than it would have spent if the 23 persons monitored had been sent to jail instead. However, if the system is used for 12 persons for an entire year, the cost comparisons reverse, and the county would save about $65,000.

It is also extremely important to recognize that this analysis relates to expenditures during the mid-1980s. Since then, based upon my observations as a probation administrator, the cost of equipment has significantly decreased due to extensive competition among vendors.

In more than two-thirds of the jurisdictions that use electronic monitoring, costs are reduced because fees are charged to offenders capable of meeting payment schedules. The fees vary, with half of the programs charging between $100 and $300 per month. A quarter of the programs charge fees less than $100, and another quarter charge in excess of $300. The highest fee was $450 per month for the lease of electronic monitoring equipment.

Often, fees based upon sliding scales are charged offenders, and such fees have financed entire house arrest programs. According to the San Diego Probation Department, fees covered the purchase of 85 bracelets, as well as the cost of the computer used to monitor offenders and the salary of two probation officers assigned to oversee the program.

In contrast, it costs $28.00 daily to house a person in the county work-furlough detention center with about half of that fee being paid by the offender and $43.00 per day to feed, clothe and guard jail inmates, according to probation and sheriff's department figures. That latter figure, moreover, does not include the jail's multimillion-dollar construction costs which dramatically widens the price differential.

The Eastern District of New York Probation Department submits that house detention, instead of prison, is cost-effective from the perspective of governmental expenditures. In 1986, the average annual cost of imprisoning an individual was $15,468.70. Estimating that one officer could monitor a specialized caseload of 25 house detainees who would otherwise be imprisoned, the annual savings would be $386,717, less the probation officer's $50,000 salary. This produces a net savings of $336,717 per year on costs to the government. (These data did not incorporate expenses that would be incurred if electronic monitoring equipment were used.) During fiscal year 1993, the Administrative Office of the United States Courts awarded a national electronic monitoring contract to a vendor at substantially reduced costs for these services.

Criteria for Selecting Offenders

Based upon a variety of traditional sentencing factors, jurisdictions have developed varied selection criteria for assessing offender eligibility for home confinement programs. Various jurisdictions have screening programs geared to assess risks that usually preclude certain categories of serious or repeat offenders from entering the programs. Some programs have used objective, risk-scoring mechanisms that consider factors such as violence, substance abuse, unstable interpersonal relations, immigration issues, extensive prior records, and unstable employment histories.

The Probation Department of the United States for the Eastern District Court of New York offers the following general criteria for selecting offenders for home confinement:

> House detention should be used very selectively. It should never be used for defendants involved in crimes of violence or crimes using firearms. It would not be suitable for defendants with a history of current heroin or cocaine usage. It would be inappropriate for drug sellers. In general, house detention should not be used with any defendant who could be considered a danger to the community (i.e., one offering substantial risk of further criminal activity).

In selecting individuals for early parole into an electronic monitoring program, the United States Parole Commission set the following criteria:

> The program was restricted initially to individuals paroled by the commission, but was later expanded to include individuals who were originally denied parole but who were not classified poor risks (as measured by the salient factor score) and had at committed a drug distribution offense rated as category six or higher in accordance with the commission's offense severity rating)

Although some propose the use of house arrest as an alternative measure for offenders perceived to be nonviolent, researchers strongly recommend that serious violent offenders and predatory property offenders never be placed in house arrest programs.

Duration of Home Confinement

There has been a good deal of controversy concerning the length of time an offender should be required to stay at home. This affects the length of the sentence if the court is attempting to equate the home-confinement punishment to a 24-hour-a-day traditional period of incarceration.

Researchers have determined that long sentences can lead to "cabin fever." A survey of probation personnel led to the conclusion that a six-month limit on home incarceration was appropriate. The survey revealed that in home confinement situations, often, living with others created problems and family conflicts when offenders were required to remain at home all day and evening. Probation personnel believed that when offenders were allowed to leave for specific time frames, scheduling became critical, and problems developed when scheduling was vague and ambiguous. Officers stressed the need to ensure the integrity of the home confinement program by setting specific schedules with periodic verification. The planning enabled officers to develop individualized supervision programs accommodating the assorted needs and life-styles of the diversified offender populations they serviced. Generally, there was a good deal of telephone contact between offenders and the probation department, to ensure effective communication and eliminate potential problems arising from scheduling changes and deviations.

In the Probation Department for the District of New York, offenders are provided with special conditions of probation detailing their obligations while under house detention. Offenders are allowed to work but must return home promptly at the end of the workday. They are permitted to leave home for necessary medical and dental services as well as for weekly religious observance and for food shopping, if no other family member is available for this function. Offenders are permitted to have visitors and obviously are permitted to leave the residence in a life-threatening emergency such as a fire in the dwelling.

The conditions point out that the offenders must at all other times be restricted to the confides of the home. Their presence is checked through an electronic monitoring system, frequent unannounced home visits, and telephone calls by probation personnel. In order to maintain the integrity of the supervision process, the offenders are required to provide detailed data relating to employment schedules and their routes to and from work, as well as a daily log which is reviewed periodically by the Probation Department. Thus, all movements outside the home must be cleared in advance by the Probation Department. The offenders are also made fully aware of their responsibility to answer the phone. Additionally, they are not permitted call forwarding service and are advised to secure call waiting service. This enables the offender to place one call on hold while answering another in order to ensure easy access by the Probation Department.

Pre-approved schedules are submitted to the central computer location in electronic monitoring cases, and the central station audits the transmission reports 24 hours per day, seven days per week. The procedures for violations usually require the central station to attempt to establish contact with the offender. If it confirms an unauthorized absence, the central station notifies a probation officer who is on call and required to investigate the breech further. Offenders may, in fact, be home. Field trips to homes have occasionally revealed that the breeches were the result of either a power surge or equipment malfunction.

Staffing Requirements

Implementing home detention and electronic monitoring programs generally requires significant administrative changes, affecting personnel policy, revocation procedures, and relationships with other components of the criminal justice system. A major issue concerning implementation is the procedure required in the event a violation is reported. The following are among the administrative options to be considered in the event of a violation: a simple computer record of the violation, a follow up with a phone call to determine the offender's presence, and personal verification via a home visit in order to determine whether the report is accurate. Taking into consideration the possibility of a false alarm, the last alternative is the most appropriate but is costly and creates significant personnel problems.

Probation officers are not traditional law enforcement officers and do not provide a 24-hour-a-day service. Because violations frequently occur during the evening and on weekends, officers must be on call throughout the week in order to respond in a timely manner. Morale problems may result if officers are not compensated for working extra hours. Personnel policies and employee attitudes have to be significantly modified in order to enforce the conditions of supervision effectively. These issues can also become a source of problems if highly educated and trained probation officers eventually begin to perceive themselves as performing only surveillance functions. They frequently may be responding to false alarms, and these activities can become extremely dangerous if officers are visiting high crime areas during off-hours without proper training and equipment. In assessing staffing needs and community protection, one writer submits:

> Community protection, however, can be facilitated only by maintaining a pool of well-trained probation officers operating at a low detainee-to-supervisor ratio. In the Florida Community Control Program, the maximum caseload for a team of a surveillance officer and one supervising officer is 40 offenders. Even for arrest programs that have enough supervisory personnel, training presents another potential obstacle. House arrest surveillance involves assuring strict compliance with severe limitations to offenders' freedom of movement. Hence, supervising probation officers will have to assume a greater policing function than those assigned to ordinary probation duty. Whether probation departments have the financial and human resources to train and maintain staffs for home confinement programs on a broad scale remains to be seen.

In conjunction with staffing issues, administrators are required to work with the court and prosecutors to develop uniform standards for reporting violations of home confinement. Budget cuts in programs and the increasing number of individuals on supervision have made careful planning by administrators and support by judges and prosecutors crucial. Unless administrators plan properly, set clear criteria for the selection of offenders and the duration of surveillance, and adopt appropriate procedural guidelines, the benefits of the technology may be significantly reduced.

Legal Issues

Home confinement symbolizes public disapproval and provides a form of social stigmatization. This is consistent with current criminological precepts of deterrence, retribution, and proportionality between offense and appropriate punishment. The purposes of home confinement are diverse, and the specific restrictions imposed through it determine how intrusive and punitive the sanction is. Without explicit statutory authority to impose home confinement as a condition of supervision, appellate courts may determine that such a sentence constitutes an abuse of judicial discretion:

> Although house arrest is a less severe and less punitive restriction than probationary detention in a prison setting, it remains a unique and controversial deprivation of liberty. By its very nature, the house arrest sanction imposes a regime of intrusive confinement. Unless a broader view of probation becomes widespread, the implementation of this novel sanction will be facilitated by the enhanced credibility and recognition that may derive from explicit statutory endorsement.

It has been recognized that probationers and parolees have diminished rights. Courts nevertheless have established that probationers do have a number of constitutionally protected rights that can possibly be violated by the state's coercive power. Generally, the authority to grant probation has led to broad discretion in determining conditions. Restrictions have included warrantless searches by probation officers, restrictions on travel and association, and regulation of employment and choice of residence. Courts have upheld these restrictions as reasonable. The general elements for establishing the validity of a probation condition are clarity, reasonableness, and institutional requirements aimed at either rehabilitating the offender or ensuring the protection of society. Additionally, without a showing of a reasonable relationship between a condition of release and the purpose of release, the abridgement of a fundamental right will not be tolerated:

> Arguably, the wearing of an electronic device protects society and rehabilitates the individual. Setting a curfew for a convicted offender might protect society and instill a sense of discipline that can be rehabilitative for the probationer. Clarity of conditions poses no problem in electronic surveillance cases because the client obviously knows what is happening and how the condition might be breached. Where the practice may run into probable difficulties is in the rea-

sonableness and constitutionality requirements. Reasonableness is closely linked to the equal protection provision of the Fourteenth Amendment, basically meaning that the requirement be fair and just. There is nothing inherently unfair or unjust with electronic surveillance when viewed in isolation, but when applied to an aggregate where financial capability becomes a determinant to obtaining probation, equal protection considerations might arise, particularly when no provisions are made for accommodating indigent defendants.

With regard to electronic surveillance infringing upon an offender's right to privacy, rulings have determined that this form of monitoring does not breach this right. To argue that the electronic device would violate the right against self-incrimination is refutable with the recognition that the use of an electronic device is not testimonial self-incrimination but physical in nature. Additionally, the use of an ankle device is not a form of cruel and unusual punishment, and the user is not subjected to any significant humiliation or degradation. Upon analysis, compared to incarceration, home detention would be perceived as much less restrictive and more humane. There are, however, unclear equal protection issues. A challenge could be made that an indigent offender may be considered ineligible for a period of probation with electronic surveillance due to his inability to defray the costs. Seemingly, jurisdictions would have to provide funding in order to ensure that eligibility for participation was universal and not predicated upon an offender's ability to pay. When courts assess challenges to conditions of house arrest, they must adopt a stance that cautiously balances the state's interest in imposing home confinement against the liberty interests of the offender as they relate to constitutional safeguards. Thus, sentencing courts must consider First Amendment rights and conditions. If they do not provide opportunities for offenders to gain permission to travel for religious purposes, this might constitute an abridgement of religious freedom and could be considered unconstitutional. Offenders who suddenly develop religion upon an order of house arrest should be suspect and supervised cautiously to determine if they are violating travel restrictions. Deprivation of association has generally been held as a consequence of the restrictive nature of probation as long as it is related to rehabilitation and the prevention of recidivism. There have been several recent cases concerning credit for jail time for periods spent in home confinement as part of a probation sentence or pretrial condition. In New York, a court held that home confinement, as a condition of probation, does not entitle the defendant to jail time for the period of probation spent in home confinement. This decision was reached after the court analyzed Section 70.30(3) of the New York State Penal Law pertaining to the term "in custody," which relates to jail credit entitlements credited to penal sentences. In an Alaskan case, a court held, "We think that under certain circumstances, the restraints imposed as conditions of probation may be so substantial that the defendant is, in legal effect, 'in custody' although on probation confinement need not be penal in nature to be custodial."

A recent federal case challenging jail credit while on house detention held that an offender should not be granted credit for time spent confined to his residence prior to self-surrender, because it would be contrary to statutory law and "fly in the teeth of common sense." Additionally, conditions imposed on a defendant's appeal bond, which included electronic monitoring home confinement, were determined not to constitute official detention for subsequent jail-time credit. In another New York case, the court concluded that the computer report in conjunction with a defendant's admission was adequate in establishing a violation of be a need for more scientific and technical testimony in the event an offender does not admit the violations. This view could require probation personnel to make home visits when breaches are reported electronically. This would ensure that computer-generated reports are not subject to challenges for possible technological malfunctions if the violation action is contested.

Conclusions and Unresolved Issues

A number of issues have been addressed in this article concerning the concept and implementation of home confinement. Renzema and Skelton submitted that home confinement is cost-effective. However, these programs have a number of indirect costs that have not been quantified with specificity. In mid-1987, there were 826 offenders on monitoring devices. As of February 1989, the number had grown to 6,490 nationwide. With the programs proliferating in jurisdictions throughout the country, numerous offenders placed on electronic monitoring have committed more serious offenses than those of previous years. These researchers further inform that typical offenders are burglars, drug offenders, and major traffic violators. Most noticeably, the proportion of offenders who have committed violent crimes nearly doubled between 1987 and 1989 from 5.6 percent to 11.8 percent. A survey disclosed that the median age in 1989 was 29.1 years with women representing 10.4 percent of the monitored population. Finally, in assessing the success of the programs, when evaluating risk-assessments on electronic monitoring, there was very little difference among offense categories with the exception of traffic offenders. A National Institute of Justice study concluded that this group generally committed fewer technical violations and new offenses than other individuals under electronic monitoring supervision. Their supervision terms were, however, shorter than the others, which may have minimized their risk for technical and new-offense violations.

The study found no significant difference in outcomes among programs that primarily supervise probationers, inmates or offenders on parole or in community corrections. All had successful termination rates of between 74.3 percent and 76.0 percent.

When electronic monitoring was used for pretrial offenders in the federal system during fiscal year 1989, only nine cases out of 168 failed to appear, for a failure rate of 5.4 percent. This compares to a 2.8 percent failure rate for all other offenders; however, those placed on electronic monitoring were presumably perceived as presenting a greater risk of flight or danger to the community. The rearrest rates for the electronic monitoring cases were 3.6 percent for felonies and 2.4 percent for misdemeanors compared with the national rates of 1.9 percent and 1.0 percent for unmonitored cases. Once again, the issue of greater risk may be the variable that resulted in the increased rearrest rates. House arrest may compromise public safety, because offenders have the capacity to continue their criminal activity while at home. The sanction cannot guarantee crime-free living. This often depends upon an offender's willingness to comply with the conditions of supervision and the capabilities of the supervising service. It has also been proposed that house arrest may widen the correctional net, since it could be used as an adjunct to the sentences normally imposed, thereby increasing the intensity of the sanction and costs. Conversely, the punishment may not have a deterrent effect, because its crime preventive effects do not achieve the same objectives as total incarceration. Bias

and racial issues may be other concerns, as there could be a disproportionate number of affluent white-collar offenders participating in these
innovative programs.

The Administrative Office of the United States Courts reports
that the average annual per capita cost of housing an inmate in a federal penal facility was $20,803 during fiscal year 1992. This amount
does not include collateral expenses such as defendants' public assistance cost, tax losses, and prison construction expenses to house these
offenders. By the end of 1991, there were 823,414 individuals under
penal jurisdiction. The growth rate represents an increase in prison
populations of 150 percent since 1980 and translates into a need for
approximately 1,000 new prison bed spaces weekly. It was reported
that in mid-1991, local jails held 422,609 people, 101 percent over the
rated capacity of the nation's jails.

With these issues in mind, it can be concluded that a strong commitment must be made to combat the problem of prison overcrowding.
This can only be done by exploring other methods that will safely control eligible offenders within the community. As U.S. District Court
Judge Jack Weinstein stated: "long prison terms, and imprisonment for
more and more persons, cannot be borne indefinitely. Other controls to
prevent crime, social policies to avoid criminality, and alternative punishments are essential." In order to accomplish these objectives, community correctional agencies must be adequately staffed, funded, and
provided with state-of-the-art equipment and technological assistance.
An unwillingness to allocate adequate resources will result not only in
continued cynicism toward innovative alternatives but will also create
the possibility of compromising public safety due to poor planning and
fiscal short-sightedness. In this regard, an organizational inability to
use this option judiciously became the subject of negative publicity
when federal prosecutors in the Southern District of New York de-
nounced electronic monitoring devices used to track defendants on bail
after two reputed high-profile organized criminals fled. Authorities later
contended that if defendants pose a risk of flight or community danger,
the use of this alternative was extremely problematic and subject to
abuse.

Similarly, under mounting political pressure from the New Jersey legislature following several highly publicized negative experiences
that compromised community safety, the embarrassed commissioner
of the state department of corrections abandoned the early release pro-

gram of electronic monitoring in spite of the beneficial budgetary implications.

Presently, probation supervision accounts for approximately 60 percent of the 4.3 million adults serving a sentence. About half of these probationers were convicted of felonies. Researchers determined that within three years, two of three of these offenders were either arrested for a new felony or charged with violating their supervision conditions.

Innovative correctional programming requires extremely careful screening of participants, uncompromising resource allocation, sophisticated program design, and a total willingness to withstand adverse media exposure and political pressure. Without these ingredients, the future of widespread house detention as a true alternative to prison is bleak, as far too many are still haunted by the memory of Willie Horton and his impact upon the political arena.

Taking into consideration the many unresolved issues raised in this article, it is submitted that further research is necessary under strict methodological standards to evaluate the effectiveness of home confinement. Only then can decision makers truly determine the feasibility of this correctional alternative and its total impact and consequences.

{End of Article}

Article

USING DAY REPORTING CENTERS AS AN ALTERNATIVE TO JAIL[5]

Growing prison populations, court-ordered capacity limits on jails and prisons, and tight government budgets have forced a return to correctional innovation and a renewed interest in community-based corrections programming. Among the newer innovations are several intermediate sanctions that serve as steps between the security and punishment of prisons and jails and the supervision without security offered by probation and parole. Intensive supervision, house arrest, and electronic monitoring are becoming accepted alternatives to incarceration.

Another intermediate sanction gaining popularity is day reporting. *Day reporting* can be defined as "a highly structured nonresidential program utilizing supervision, sanctions, and services coordinated from a central focus." Day reporting offers the punishment of confinement combined with the rehabilitative effects of allowing the offender to continue employment and receive treatment.

Offenders committed to day-reporting centers live at home and report to the center regularly, often daily. While at the center, the participant submits an itinerary that details his or her daily travels, destinations, and purposes. This schedule allows the supervision staff to monitor and control the client's behavior and is also a valuable tool for teaching responsibility to offenders. Clients are normally required to call in several times a day, and center staff also call the clients to verify their whereabouts. While at the center, the participants may be required to submit to drug testing and participate in counseling, education, and vocational placement assistance. Offenders are normally required to be employed in the community or be full-time students.

Day-reporting centers are a fairly recent innovation in community corrections programs, but like intensive supervision, house arrest, and other recent intermediate sanctions, they borrow from elements of more traditional correctional programming. Office visits, client interaction in a group setting, drug screening and treatment, and field work are all components of day reporting that have been used in probation and parole for years.

History of Day-Reporting Centers

Day-reporting centers started in Great Britain in the early 1970s as an alternative to incarceration for older petty criminals who were chronic offenders. The British Home Office originally asked Parliament to create the first day-treatment centers in 1972. At the same time, there was an independent movement by individual local probation agencies to open centers to provide group services to probationers. George Mair, the principal research officer of the Home Office Research and Planning Unit, traced the spread of day centers in England and Wales to prison overcrowding in the United Kingdom and to the interest of probation officials in supervising offenders in a group setting. Frustrated by the inability to manage effectively the behavior of probationers in a traditional setting, officers were anxious to try working with groups of offenders. The Criminal Justice Act of 1982 formalized the existence of day treatment centers, and by the mid-1980s there were more than 80 centers in England and Wales. These programs differed greatly in staffing, target populations, programs and services offered, and hours of operation.

The first day-reporting center in America was opened in 1986 by the Hampden County, Massachusetts, Sheriff's Department. The center was implemented as an early release program for selected county jail inmates. This and other early day-reporting centers in the United States drew upon the 10 years of experience of the British centers. Day-treatment programs in use for juvenile offenders and deinstitutionalized mental patients also contributed to the accumulated knowledge about the concept. Additionally, day reporting was similar to a "living out" release option used by the Federal Bureau of Prisons that allowed inmates to spend prison time at home, after they had finished a residential phase of treatment at community correction centers.

Day-Reporting Center Operation

Like their British forerunners, American day-reporting centers are organized and operated in a variety of ways. Day-reporting centers differ in the offenders targeted to participate, criteria for selecting participants, operating agencies, services offered, violation policies, and even the goals of the center.

Day reporting is a concept that is adaptable to a number of different populations. Day-reporting centers are used to offer enhanced treatment and supervision to probationers or sentenced offenders not on probation, to monitor inmates released early from jail or prison, to monitor arrested people prior to trial, as a halfway-out step for inmates who have shown progress in community corrections or work release centers, and as a halfway-in step for offenders who are in violation of probation or parole.

Whatever the population selected, day reporting allows the treatment and supervision of arrested individuals and convicted offenders in a setting that is more secure than ordinary probation but less inhibiting and less expensive than incarceration. In performing this task, day-reporting centers fulfill three separate and distinct purposes: 1) enhanced supervision and decreased liberty of offenders; 2) treatment of offenders' problems; and 3) reduced crowding of incarceratory facilities.

Corbett asserted that this multiplicity of purpose also serves to satisfy goals of various correctional philosophies. The reduction of offender mobility and liberty supports a punishment philosophy and may act as a specific deterrent to future criminal activity. These restrictions also allow for a certain amount of incapacitation and, therefore, protection of the public. The ability to offer needed treatment to offenders assists in the correction or rehabilitation of offenders. Lastly, day reporting is significantly cheaper to operate the correctional institutions, allowing for greater cost effectiveness.

Differences in eligibility criteria are attributable to a variety of factors including the following: the orientation of the agency operating the center, the available population of offenders, the support of elected officials and judges, and the political climate of the community. Some programs place limits on the offenders they will accept based on type of offense, usually rejecting violent offenders. Besides the instant offense for which the offender is responsible, other eligibility variables may include the offender's gender, legal status, treatment needs, prior record, and residential stability. Program administrators must also ensure that the selected population exists in sufficient quantity to allow for program feasibility. If the desired population is too small, or unavailable for placement, the administration is faced with changing its eligibility criteria and selecting a different segment of offenders, thereby redefining the mission of the day-reporting center.

In discussing the effects of differing eligibility criteria, one cannot overlook the possible deleterious and costly effects of using day reporting, or any correctional program or sanction, when a less severe and less expensive alternative would be effective. The concept of net widening in corrections is a widely recognized and well-documented phenomenon. John Larivee, executive director of the Crime and Justice Foundation, which operates day-reporting centers in Massachusetts, lists three reasons that can account for the net-widening effect: unclear program goals, a mistaken belief that community corrections is soft on criminals, and a lack of support from public officials.

Judges and other involved decision makers must be convinced of the effectiveness of day-reporting centers and be willing to support them. If this support is not present, the center can expect continuing difficulty in securing participants, which may lead to taking inappropriate offenders who are easier to enroll, rather than serving the appropriate population that was originally identified. Corbett warned against the possible misuse of day-reporting centers to overtreat or widen the net and also the danger of overusing centers to maximize cost savings. This can lead to a loosening of standards and may damage programs that are required to accept clients who are dangers to the community or do not possess the motivation towards correction that is needed.

A day-reporting center's mission is often dependent on the type of agency that is offering the services. Day-reporting centers are operated by a wide range of government, public, and private agencies including residential community corrections centers, work release programs, jails, and treatment programs. These agencies obviously have different missions which, in turn, translate into diverse goals.

Day reporting is frequently operated on the site of a residential corrections facility such as a halfway house or work-release facility. The advantage to this arrangement is that facility staff members can use their normal down time to perform day-reporting duties. This sharing of staff between programs allows for a more cost-effective use of experienced, trained personnel. Among the services commonly provided by day-reporting centers are support, treatment, or referral for treatment, for offenders in such areas as substance abuse, mental health, education, vocational training, and job placement. In addition to these treatment services, most centers employ several tools of supervision to help monitor offenders' behavior. Centers commonly screen for use of intoxicants and illegal drugs and impose curfews and control over offenders' whereabouts and associates. Field work is normally less stringent and less frequent than with other intermediate sanctions, such as house arrest, but is still used along with telephone calls to monitor offenders' travel and verify employment and schooling. Additionally, centers normally enforce court-ordered fines, restitution, and family support and often assign community service.

Besides these common supervision and treatment services, some centers offer specialized services. Day-treatment centers in England frequently provide recreational and social services to their clientele, making the center not just a place of supervision but also a sort of offenders' club, where clientele can join with their peers, relax, and engage in socially acceptable pastimes. It is less common for American centers to provide this type of service, but some centers do provide recreational activities on site or in the community. Emergency or transitional housing is also provided by some programs. It would seem that providing housing to center clients would violate one of the key tenets of day reporting and could serve to blur further the line separating day reporting clients from residential services clients such as work releasees. One program that serves female offenders, who may be in a day reporting center program for child abuse, provides on-site day care for its clientele.

The goals of the day-reporting center and the philosophy of its parent agency will normally dictate the amount of flexibility in the center's violation policy. Centers that act as extensions of prisons or jails and espouse a philosophy of community protection will likely be less tolerant of program violations, such as using drugs or losing employment. Programs that place a priority on the rehabilitation and treatment of participants will be more likely to exercise a range of disciplines for violations of rules, rather than simply depending on incarceration of offenders. Jail and prison overcrowding may also affect violation policy, because many day-reporting centers operate to relieve overcrowding. Larivee warned against falling into the "more is better" trap: the more supervision, sanctions, and services imposed on the offender, the better the program. This results in an expensive, rigid program that no offender can successfully complete and no agency can possibly deliver.

Orange County's Experience

The Orange County, Florida, metropolitan area is one of the fastest growing areas in the country. Unfortunately, this growth has also led to growth in the jail population. Orange County has implemented a number of alternatives to incarceration to help control overcrowding. The jail has had a traditional pretrial release program for a number of years, which released selected offenders prior to their court obligations and also has administered a federally mandated population capacity release program. The Community Corrections Department of the Corrections Division has operated a work-release center for over 10 years. This 165-bed minimum security facility is primarily for sentenced county jail inmates but does service a small population of pretrial inmates. In 1989, the Community Corrections Department opened the Community Surveillance Unit, an electronically monitored home confinement program that currently monitors 150 pretrial and sentenced county inmates.

The latest attempt to help control overcrowding and provide treatment and community reintegration for inmates is a day-reporting center for 25 offenders. The center operates out of the existing work-release center and provides supervision and treatment to offenders who have been successfully complying with the work release or community surveillance programs. Participants are required to physically check in daily at the center and submit daily itineraries. Whereabouts are monitored by daily telephone calls and regular, random field checks. Clients are prohibited from using any illegal substances, and the center conducts drug and alcohol testing. All participants must be employed or be full-time students and must continue any treatment begun in work release or community surveillance. Failure to follow program conditions can cause the day-reporting center client to be returned to work release, community surveillance, or jail. The day-reporting center, which opened in May 1991, is staffed by a correctional surveillance officer who is assisted by work-release center staff.

Although it is too soon to know the long-term effects day reporting will have on the offenders who have participated in the program, the following statistics demonstrate that the program is meeting its goal to offer cost-effective treatment and reintegration into the community for selected offenders without endangering the community.

As of January 31, 1994, 224 offenders have participated in day reporting. The program has a success rate of 84 percent, and only one client has been rearrested while in the program. The new arrest was for a nonviolent misdemeanor offense. Over $136,000 in supervision fees were collected from clients to help offset the cost of the center. A study of the clients that successfully finished the day-reporting center program showed that eight percent of them were rearrested after completing the program. The amount of time between completing the program and rearrest averaged 7.5 months, with the shortest period being one month and the longest, 17 months. Of the seven re-offenders, four were arrested for new misdemeanors and three were accused of committing felony offenses. None of the seven were first-time offenders when accepted to the day-reporting center, and they had an average 7.2 prior arrests. Six of the seven committed the same offense for which they were in the day reporting center program. This may indicate that these individuals' criminal behavior was more deeply rooted and that the day-reporting center was not able to alter their criminality significantly. Future recidivism studies performed after a longer period of time will be needed to verify these results.

Preliminary indications are that Orange County's day-reporting center is an effective alternative to incarceration. Day reporting has helped relieve jail overcrowding and has provided treatment and supervision of offenders and at less cost to the community.

Discussion and Recommendations

In evaluating the effectiveness of day-reporting centers, it is important to consider not just program success rates but how day-reporting centers compare with incarceration in accomplishing treatment goals and in cost efficiency. English centers are operating effectively and are becoming a recognized aspect of probation supervision, evidenced by the continued spread of centers there. American centers in Massachusetts are reporting successful completion rates of 66 percent to 81 percent. These programs are also experiencing success in serving a population of prison-bound offenders and therefore saving tax dollars that would have been needed for prison beds. An important measure of success for any correctional program is the decreased recidivism of former participants. Unfortunately, because day reporting is a relatively recent development in community corrections programming, recidivism studies have not been conducted or at least not published in the professional journals.

Until recidivism is studied more comprehensively, two measures of success can be used to analyze day reporting: cost effectiveness and protection of the community. In assessing cost effectiveness, it is critical that the cost of centers is compared with the cost of incarceration. It is, therefore, equally important that day-reporting center clients be individuals that were incarceration bound. Day reporting, being an intermediate sanction that uses smaller caseloads than would be found in probation, will naturally not compare favorably with probation's costs. If offenders that would have been sentenced to probation are instead selected to be supervised by day reporting, the end result would be the costly widening of the net of social control. If, however, the offender was prison or jail-bound, the effect is to modify the offender's behavior at less cost than is required for incarceration.

Of course, cost effectiveness is a secondary concern to the safety of the community. No program will last long, no matter the cost savings, if it seriously threatens the well-being of the citizens. Community corrections is inherently political, and its very existence dependent on the approval, or at least the tolerance, of the community. Because community protection is of paramount importance to community corrections, a great deal of attention needs to be given to those treated in the community. Violent offenders and criminals whose crimes were particularly notorious are a significant risk to the operation of day reporting.

If not the violent or serious offender, then which of the offenders that populate our institutions should be selected? Perhaps we should take advice from the original English centers. These first programs were operated for petty criminals who were in danger going to prison not for the heinousness of their crimes but rather from the sheer number of nonviolent crimes that they committed. Day reporting should be reserved for the offender whose behavior has not been corrected by probation and who has evidenced a need for greater structure in his or her treatment. This is the niche that day reporting will fill in a correction continuum that endeavors to apply the proper amount of control and treatment to ensure the correction of the individual.

{End of Article}

Article

Intensive Supervision: A New Way to Connect With Offenders[6]

The essential challenge of supervision is to obtain sufficient knowledge about offenders' activities to be able to affect those activities. Even under the best of staffing circumstances, there will always be one probation officer to many offenders. More often than not, these offenders do not wish the officer to know what they are doing. How can a probation officer maximize his or her ability to track offender whereabouts and activities in a cost-effective manner?

Enter intensive supervision, Southern Florida style. Four years ago we were looking for a significant, immediate sanction for drug use in the occasional drug-user population. Dade County had the highest rate of cocaine use in the Southern District. Drug use was one of the most frequent violations leading to revocation and imprisonment. We believed an immediate consequence would deter occasional users from further use and would screen for drug-dependent users who could not stop using drugs on their own. Available consequences were inadequate; modifications of release conditions to add electronic monitoring or drug abuse treatment took too long. We also believed drug abuse treatment was not always indicated for occasional users, most of whom were not drug dependent, were unmotivated for treatment, or were often involved in drug trafficking. What else could we do with the resources we had?

We tried a new idea with a few offenders. We believe over the past four years we have developed this idea into a powerful method to control risk, a method which has many applications across populations and behaviors.

Intensive Supervision in Southern Florida

Offenders in the general supervision population in Dade County who test positive for cocaine or marijuana, the drugs of choice in the district, are placed in what we call intensive supervision. The case transfer occurs within 48 hours of a positive Emit test result. Because the Southern District of Florida has its own drug testing lab, in most cases offenders are transferred within four days of testing or within a week of the actual drug use.

Drug Use Issues

The offender is instructed to report to the office twice a week for drug testing. Networking with employers when necessary has revealed a surprising level of cooperation to allow the offender to report for testing. To our knowledge, not one single person has lost a job as a result of reporting.

Offenders are also required to report for a 16- to 20-hour drug abuse education program. This service is provided free of charge by two local hospitals to the community at large. It is available during evenings and weekends. The education program is not treatment. It is presented to the offender as information to use in making an informed decision about drug use and treatment. It differs from the traditional approach in which the probation officer tells the offender, "You have used drugs while under supervision, you have a drug problem." Or, "You need treatment."

Occasional, non-dependent drug users unmotivated for treatment are given an incentive: if they complete the education program, show no further drug use, and comply with intensive supervision instructions, they will not be required to enter treatment. Offenders who show continued drug use are referred for treatment. The Substance Abuse Subtle Screening Inventory (SASSI) is used as a screening tool in conjunction with behavioral observations.

Intensive Reporting

Offenders are told that, because of their positive drug test, they have been placed in intensive supervision. They are further informed that they will remain under intensive supervision for an unspecified period of time, depending on their future performance.

A detailed interview is conducted as to the circumstances surrounding the drug use, with the goal of obtaining an admission of drug use from the offender. The offender is informed that his or her reporting instructions are now changed: henceforth, the offender is to page the probation officer before every move from one location to another and upon arriving home. He or she is instructed to wait 15 minutes after paging the probation officer. If the officer does not respond within the 15 minutes, the offender is to call the officer's answering machine and leave a detailed message including name, time, present location, destination, and estimated time of return. Offenders are instructed that they are not to have caller ID or call return. By prohibiting caller ID and call return, the officer can return calls from home or any other location. Call forwarding is not allowed.

Incoming offenders are coached on how to report and conditioned to the procedure by initially returning pages and calls at an almost one-to-one frequency. Gradually, the frequency of response is dropped for those offenders who are employed, have no positive tests, and are otherwise stable. Sufficient response frequency is sustained to maintain the reporting behavior.

Supervision Advantages

The officer monitors the pager and the answering machine. Field contacts are made to verify location and activities. No longer is the probation officer looking for offenders who may or may not be where they are supposed to be. By recognizing the numbers on the pager and listening to the answering machine, the officer can pinpoint an offender's location any time and see the offender in the community. If the offender is not located at the last reported location, the officer immediately contacts significant others, locates the offender, and confronts him or her regarding inaccurate reporting. Failures to report are not charged as violations. Instead, they are used to inquire as to the offender's activities and reiterate the necessity of compliance. Failures to report also provide leads for further investigation.

Intensive reporting has a number of benefits for the officer and the offender:

1. Listening to messages gives us an unprecedented look at an offender's life-style: where the offender spends free time, how much time the offender spends at home. Subtle, and sometimes not so subtle, voice changes detectable in messages tell us the offender may be having a problem or may be under the influence of drugs or alcohol. Answering machines with date/time features provide immediate verification of the actual time of the message. Discrepancies between actual time and the time the offender reports are brought to the offender's attention every time they occur.

2. The procedure extends our presence in the offender's life. No longer can the offender easily predict when the officer will contact him or her. The combination of telephone and field contacts serves to reinforce the officer's presence. The probation officer can now multiply the opportunities for contact through use of the telephone,

while remaining in control as to how much supervision to apply in each case.

The extension of the officer's presence in the offender's life is not always negative; it is also positive. When an offender is complying, the officer responds to a message and positively reinforces the offender's adherence to a constructive schedule. We have found many offenders react positively to this kind of individualized attention. The rapport developed in this manner serves to increase cooperation on the part of the offender.

3. The intensity of reporting is not reduced when the officer is off duty. Daily, the officer chooses when to respond to pages or messages. When the officer is on leave, offenders continue to report as usual. During extended leave periods and on weekends, a secretary transcribes the messages. The officer reviews the transcribed records upon return, and the records provide valuable information as to offenders' schedules and patterns of movement.

4. The procedure makes the offender take notice of his or her activities. Those who are involved in criminal activity have the most difficulty reporting and can be easily targeted for investigation. Impulsive offenders have to practice discipline: make a phone call, wait for an answer, leave a detailed message. Most offenders comply with the reporting instructions.

5. Depending on the offender's motivation to change, the reporting procedure either coerces or assists in the cessation of criminal associations. In either case, intensive reporting is a way to increase the probability that the offender will avoid the "people, places, and things" that trigger drug use and other dysfunctional behaviors.

Administrative Advantages

In a time of reduced resources, intensive supervision offers considerable advantages:

1. Whereas reporting demands are significantly increased, no action by a releasing authority is required, because the instructions are covered by the standard conditions of release. District judges

were briefed before we began using this method and have extended their full support. There are significant savings in time and resources. No paperwork to modify release conditions need be prepared, mailed, handled, or signed by probation office staff, judges, or parole commission staff. No appointment of counsel, involvement by attorneys, or court time is involved in situations in which the offender might oppose a modification. Inquiring attorneys are advised that increased reporting instructions are based on probable cause of drug use as shown by a presumptive drug test. In four years, only one offender has formally, and unsuccessfully, challenged the instructions.

2. Intensive supervision also saves treatment funds and maximizes treatment resources. The testing protocol serves to screen offenders able to control their drug use from those who are drug dependent. Those whose drug use continues under the increased restrictions are placed in treatment. Offenders in denial are more likely to accept treatment when their failure to remain abstinent in intensive supervision is clearly remonstrated.

3. No outside contractor is involved. Equipment costs are minimal. There are no fees to collect. Virtually no additional paperwork is generated.

Requirements

In order to be effective, intensive supervision requires support in the following areas of personnel and equipment:

1. Intensive supervision requires probation officers who are attuned to field supervision. Willingness to insist consistently on compliance is crucial. Investigative training is important in that intensive reporting often uncovers information that requires follow-up. Unexplained assets or income, assets obtained by fraudulent means, and multiple identities are but a few examples of leads that are uncovered.

2. Intensive supervision requires management support. Any supervision program that demands a significant change in offender

behavior patterns will, generate complaints. Offenders will attempt to evade instructions by appealing to supervisors and top management. Positive supervisor involvement in the process increases the probability that the offender will remain compliant.

3. The third personnel requirement is caseload size not to exceed 25 offenders if the entire caseload is on intensive reporting. Because the program has no set duration, caseload size can be maintained by returning stable cases to general supervision to allow for incoming, unstable cases.

4. Equipment requirements are a 15-memory pager and an answering machine with remote message retrieval and date-time feature. A cellular phone for field work is highly desirable, but not essential.

Where Do We Go From Here?

At this time we do not know whether intensive supervision results in significant reductions in risk and noncompliant behaviors. When we began using this procedure, we did not simultaneously institute research to measure effectiveness. We have attempted to go back and examine some indicators, such as drug use, during and after intensive supervision. Uncontrolled variables (e.g., a lack of control groups matched or other characteristics or a lack of standardization in testing schedules after intensive supervision) preclude any conclusions. Prospective, controlled research is needed to determine whether this intensive supervision method makes a significant difference in compliance.

In a search for effective supervision, this procedure merits further examination and development. One obstacle to such development is lack of resources. Because intensive supervision does not require a special condition of release, it does not qualify for additional personnel. Its efficiency is its Achilles' heel.

In the technological area, the procedure can be improved in many ways. While we used the very limited technology we had, new voice-mail systems can increase effectiveness. Features such as ability to save messages can aid the officer in managing an intensive supervision caseload or even a few offenders placed under the reporting procedure.

We will be exploring new telephone technology in the near future and welcome exchange of information in this area.

Intensive supervision can be successfully applied to other groups of high-risk offenders in addition to occasional drug users. Offenders placed in drug abuse treatment can certainly benefit. After all, what is the point of providing drug abuse counseling a few hours per week if the offender spends the rest of the time engaged in activities that are incompatible with treatment? The activities of offenders unwilling to obtain employment can be tracked. Too often we instruct offenders to "get a job," but fail to interfere with the job they already have: criminal activity. Follow-up on social service referrals can be improved by requiring immediate feedback from offenders as to whether they report for referral appointments. Activities of re-released supervision violators and violent offenders can be tracked from the first day of their release. This method can be used in conjunction with electronic house arrest to track the offender outside the home. Similarly, it can be used by halfway houses to track offender activities outside the facility.

Finally, although we do not supervise juveniles, we have discussed this method of intensive reporting with juvenile justice professionals. They see potential for improvement in the supervision of the juvenile population through this procedure. Juveniles, who are still amenable to adult direction, can be given such direction through this method. All of the supervision advantages discussed in the case of adults apply to juveniles.

Finding methods to provide improved, cost-effective supervision must be a priority if community corrections is to meet taxpayers' risk control demands. We believe this method offers a significant improvement over supervision techniques currently in use and welcome inquiries and ideas for improvement.

{End of Article}

For those of us who have been involved in corrections for more years than we care to admit, it is difficult to think of a prison run by inmates. The basic concept discussed in the following article is controversial. However, in our search for a better method of dealing with crime, we cannot afford to overlook any possible solution.

Article

INMATE INVOLVEMENT IN PRISON GOVERNANCE[7]

Few oxymorons sound to most people as silly and naive as that of prison democracy, and for good reasons. For one, one wants offenders punished, and democracy sounds like a reward. For another, few citizens are enchanted with what passes for democracy elsewhere, and one can conceive of the liabilities of representative governance enhanced, corrupted, and caricatured in prison settings.

How do we see democracy misfiring?

- We may feel the wrong people dependably get elected.

- To get elected, we see them making promises that we believe are not seriously intended.

- We feel that when political candidates get elected they start looking out for themselves and their sponsors instead of those who elected them.

- These perceptions make many of us cynical about politics.

- As people lose interest they stop participating, which one suspects makes it easier for the wrong people to get themselves elected.

Time and again, prison politicians have been blamed for the demise of prison governance experiments, and with unseemly delight. Carefully documented worst-case scenarios have made it possible for penologists to indulge in 20/20 hindsight and discouraging extrapolations. Their jaundiced accounts, however, are only one side of the story. History can supply, if need be, scenarios that show that prisoner involvement can work. It need not create vehicles for the ascendance of self-appointed subcultural spokespersons who are oily, smooth, and psychopathic, or loud and angry and unconstructively obnoxious, or need participatory management widen the gap between prisoners and staff or corrections and the public.

Prisoner involvement, constructively envisaged, can be the very opposite of cynicism-enhancing game playing. It can be, as one Scottish prisoner put it to me, about becoming active instead of passive. It can be about creating community. It can be about prisoners having sound and practical ideas about improving life in the prison, about proposing these ideas and working hard to implement them. It can be about staff and prisoners working together, or as closely together as possible, about prisoners working together, and staff working together, to solve problems.

Prisoner involvement can enhance prison regimes by reducing the dependency of dependent prisoners, the alienation of alienated ones, and the ambivalence to authority of most others. It can help to motivate constructive involvements in civilian life through experiences in which the prisoner sees improvements as a result of actions he or she has taken in the quality of his or her institutional life and that of other prisoners.

Commitment and Trust

Prisons gain from prison democracy when prisoners become committed to the improvement of prisons. The development of this commitment, of course, hinges on the degree to which we can provide the prisoners with opportunities for involvement that make sense to them from their perspective, as well as making sense to us from ours.

Commitment also varies with the degree to which opportunities permit each prisoner to successfully display and rehearse skills along areas of his or her interest. For all participants, including prisoners, mindful activity is preferable to mindless activity, and it is satisfying to do something that one feels qualified to do. The same holds for the benefit of collaborative activity. Working with others allows for the exercise of interpersonal skills and can enhance the competence in the exercise of these skills. This, many prisoners and staff find useful. Collaborative activity also provides a respectable setting for people to interact with people they would ordinarily avoid. One can sneak up on offenders and subject them to constructive staff and peer influence at work. Persons who are sources of prison problems can even be enlisted in this way in the solution of prison problems. At minimum, those who have been enlisted to help solve a problem will be less likely to resist the implementation of solutions. Where prisoners and staff collaborate, problems can be solved in ways that are acceptable to prisoners and staff, and the resulting actions will make sense to prisoners and staff. But no one can argue that any of this is easy.

The principal impediment to initiating any experiment in prisoner involvement is the "them versus us" culture of prisons, which is shared, or rather, reciprocated, by prisoners and staff. Where a group of prisoners is convoked to consider involvement, one hears variations on themes such as "they don't trust us," and "we don't trust (expletives to taste)," and "we don't trust them to let us do anything," meaning, to trust us. Counterpart issues for staff are: "Can we trust offenders to behave responsibly without constant monitoring and supervision?"

Trust issues are related to the fact that even in the most benevolent prisons—there are such institutions—transactions between staff and prisoners are essentially parental. Prisoners request, demand, or protest. Staff members concede or refuse, circumscribe, delimit, monitor, and order prisoners about.

The transition from these sorts of transactions to adult-adult transactions is unbelievably difficult and strangely painful for both prisoners and staff. Among other things, prisoners must give up structure, the support inherent in dependence, and the luxury of blaming staff for every conceivable adversity; staff members must give up structure and prized assumptions about the immaturity, incapacity, and intrinsic untrustworthiness of prisoners.

To threaten to violate these vested assumptions of prisoners and staff invites expressions of anxiety from both groups to varying degrees. Anxiety is also evoked by the prospect of unknown challenges with which one feels one might be unable to cope. Then there is the prospect of hard work, which may not be unambivalently welcomed by some.

Anxiety, unfortunately, can be expressed in a variety of ways, and none of these is delicate, civilized, or attractive. This is especially true where anxiety translates into anger, and the change agent is at the receiving end of this anger. Such are stormy seas, and interventionists must reliably weather them at early stages of implementation. They must also deal with the next stage of the process, in which staff and prisoners wake up in the cold light of morning from their initial commitment and ask, "How can we undo it?"

A Prison Constitutional Convention

In the remainder of this article, I will summarize efforts to stimulate the inception of democracy in two Scottish prisons. One of these interventions was an intensive two-day convocation in an open prison, a prison without walls for prisoners who are on the last lap of long sentences. The prison contained some 70 prisoners and 37 staff members.

The person who designed the convocation in this prison was the regional director of the Scottish Prison Service responsible for the region in which the prison is located. Also involved was the prison's warden. Half the prisoners in the institution were present for the 2-day meeting and participated in it. So did 12 staff members—mostly uniformed officers.

The first day opened with a session in which the results of an opinion survey of staff and prisoners were presented to the group. A discussion of these findings was led by the head of the Research Branch of the Scottish Prison Service. The discussion highlighted perceived problems in the prison that could hypothetically benefit from remedial action. It also pointed out the fact that the climate of the prison is seen as a relaxed one, which would make it conducive to corroborative relationships.

The convocation was divided into task forces after a second presentation by the regional director about the Prison Service's commitment to the empowerment of officers and prisoners. The director stressed the opportunity offered to the prison to become a pioneering experiment in self-governance.

A staff group and three prisoner groups were first formed around the issue of assigning and taking responsibility. The officers dealt with the question, "What do we do that they can and should do for themselves?," while the prisoners considered, "What do they do that we can and should do for ourselves?"

During an ensuing plenary session, spokespersons for the groups explained their suggestions, which decorated the front of a dining hall and varied considerably in legibility. The reports also varied in content. The staff manifesto ranged from justificatory statements, (such as, "Why all the boundary rules? [Answer:] Protection of residents.") through cautious bids (such as, "Don't you trust us? [Answer:] Yes, given trust.") and concessions varying in generosity from making residents responsible for cleanliness and tidiness to letting them allocate the recreation budget and coordinate visiting arrangements.

One prisoner group brought a roster of requests for autonomy or discretion, and a second included new privileges in a laundry list. The third group, by contrast, offered several detailed, constructive proposals, some of which implied a strong task-oriented outlook and an uncompromising commitment to the Protestant ethic.

The group suggested that educational trips be organized by prisoner committees. It proposed a meeting between a town committee and a prisoner committee every month to improve relationships between prisoners and town folk with a view to enhancing (work and volunteer activity) placement schemes. It recommended a system of work allocation (for work on prison grounds) by a prisoner committee made up of skilled or experienced prisoners. The group also asked that "people with work or recreation skills (be) given the opportunity to pass on experience to others who are interested" and that "prisoners be consulted about job creation within the prison." They requested that prisoners be permitted to organize their own lunches for outside placements by being given a budget for the week to organize and supervise their own visits, by committee, and that they be allowed to run the inmate canteen with accounts available for inspection at all times.

The prisoners emphasized that all committees would have to be democratically elected, and they added a proposal for an open day for town folk to visit the prison and talk to prisoners and staff about the aim of the prison to improve relations, with the possibility of having town folk visit any time to see the jail working.

An idiosyncratic element in the report was mention of a vote of no confidence in the prison social worker, but not much was made of this passing reference in the discussion of the group's report. A concluding talk dealt with the need for meticulous detail and careful documentation in proposals to be drafted.

The second day opened with a speech by the prison's warden, who emphasized his receptivity to responsible proposals. The warden extended this offer to include proposals for the allocation of portions of the prison budget. The regional director also spoke, enjoining the group to be productive and offering support.

The next set of subgroups were asked to consider "the other side's" perspective, with officers considering the prisoners' views, and prisoners, those of the staff. The officers responded valiantly to this mandate, reviewing the impact on the inmates of minor rules and redundant security rituals and discussing the need for greater flexibility and open communication. Several of the staff showed remarkable empathy in characterizing prisoner reactions to frustrating prison routines.

No such empathy was forthcoming from the three prisoner groups, whose summarized reports were discursive and off the point. The discussion was similarly tangential and degenerated into attacks on the prison social worker. The rest of the reporting period was taken up with demands that the social worker be fired and the director's rejection of this demand. This dialogue sounded like a parent-child exchange, in which limits are tested and parents have to react to set boundaries.

The juncture proved to be a turning point in the intervention: a transmutation into attentiveness to business occurred in the next session, during which prisoners and staff dealt with the question, "What's in it for us?," presuming that the program were implemented.

The group of officers indicated that if they were freed of surveillance obligations and permitted to expand human service activities, this would make their jobs more interesting and worthwhile. They welcomed the opportunity to change from a custody role to a facilitator-counseling role and of enhanced "opportunity for interaction." They also recognized that their jobs would become more demanding and that training might be in order to ensure that they were qualified to do what was expected of them.

The officers discussed the risks and benefits of the impending changes for themselves as a group. To participate in a pioneering venture could advance one's career, but less so if the institution were seen as unrepresentative. Officers in other prisons might subject them to derision, and the public might become concerned about safety issues. A single escape could damage the program.

In response to the question, "What's in it for us?" the officers listed the following:

- Job satisfaction

- Free the staff to do other more worthwhile productive tasks

- The opportunity for more interaction

- A more demanding role for staff

- Because it is a pioneering project, (it can) further individual careers

- Gives staff opportunity to change from conventional role

One of the prisoner groups answered the same question with a counterpart list of benefits:

- The chance to get rid of the "them vs. us" attitude

- More relaxed community atmosphere

- More integration with staff (i.e., joint ventures with staff)

- Less boredom

- Less paranoia about release

- More rehabilitation factor

- Less bitterness against system on release

It should be obvious that the roster reflects commitment to collaborative activity and reintegration. The prisoners said they wanted to multiply joint activities with staff, including recreational activities. They saw the possibility of a useful bridging experience from the prison to the community. They saw activities as a way to reduce boredom and acquire and rehearse coping skills. The groups also saw value in improving the prison for future generations of prisoners.

Creating An Organization

To this point we had experienced dramatic movement, which included all night debates in prisoners' dormitories. It was now necessary to capitalize on this enthusiasm by designing the structure of the new governance machinery. To this end, prisoner groups were tasked with listing desired interest groups or committees; a mixed prisoner-staff group was asked to deal with the overall organization and structure of governance.

The products of the groups turned out to be remarkably congruent. Joint staff-inmate committees were envisaged by the prisoners, except for groups representing housing units. These committees were envisaged as having responsibility for various functions, such as advising on culinary matters, running the commissary, coordinating visiting arrangements, and disbursing recreational funds. Each drafting group also suggested setting up a public relations committee to cement relations between the prison and the public.

In the overall structure, the committees were seen reporting to a council of six officers and four inmates, who in turn were to report to a managerial group comprising the warden and two senior officers. This system was set up to deal with budgetary and policy decisions at various levels. Also envisaged was a monthly community meeting that would include all prisoners and staff of the institution.

The convocation ended with the appointment of a prisoner-staff coordinating group charged with implementing the design, which was to begin at once. The prisoner representatives to this group were chosen among those who had played leading roles in the convocation.

The coordinating group went on to define its mission to include drafting a constitution. In this constitution, the prisoners and staff streamlined the organization that had been suggested, consolidating proposals from the various groups. The constitution also spelled out procedures for elections and committee deliberations. Excerpts from the documents read as follows:

1) The community council will consist of one executive committee and four subcommittees. The executive committee will be known as the council committee and will consist of four residents, one senior officer and one officer who have been duly elected to serve.

The four subcommittees will be known as:

1) House Committee
2) Visits and Family Welfare Committee
3) Sports and Recreation Committee
4) Public Relations Committee

Each subcommittee will consist of two residents and one officer who have been duly elected to serve. The executives reserve the right to increase the size of any subcommittee to look into different aspects of any changes or problems that may arise and also to co-opt anyone who has specialized knowledge to help to solve problems in the field.

Subcommittees

- Each subcommittee will meet at least once per week. Relevant time is to be allowed.

- Any issues that cannot be resolved at subcommittee level will be forwarded to the council committee.

- It will be the responsibility of each subcommittee to put forward reasoned arguments backed by relevant documentation, where appropriate, when forwarding issues to the council committee.

Council Committee

- It will be the duty of the council committee to review all proposals put forward by the subcommittees and to try to resolve all issues at council level. Any issues that cannot be resolved at council level will be forwarded to the governor (warden).
- The council committee will have access to relevant documentation, stationery and equipment in order to put forward properly formulated issues to the Governor. The council committee will meet once every two weeks to discuss and resolve any issues put forward by the subcommittees.
- The council committee will meet once per month with the governor to update him on any relevant decisions taken and to put forward to him any issues they could not resolve.

Election of Committee

All officers and residents will be eligible to serve on the council committee or any of the four subcommittees.

- Notice for forthcoming elections and for willing candidates will be posted on the notice board at least seven days prior to the election. Anyone interested will put their names on the posted sheet. All candidates will be subject to a ballot with those attaining the highest number of votes being elected into office. If any positions are not filled from the notice board, then proposals will be accepted from the body of the hall. All officers and residents are eligible to vote.

- All committee members will serve for a period of three months, when they will be subject to re-election. If, during a term of office, anyone decides to drop out, the candidate with the next highest vote (relevant to the specific committee) will be co-opted until the end of that term.

- Any alterations or additions to the constitution can only be passed by a majority vote at an election.

- The council committee will have the right to call an extraordinary election by giving the appropriate notice.

Coordinator/Record Keeper

It was decided at the inaugural meeting that an election should take place for a coordinator/record keeper, whose post will include the duties of keeping the flow of information between the various subcommittees and the council. And also be responsible to the council for the preparation of proposals from all the committees to the governor. And of course the keeping of the records and decisions made for future reference. The post will be on the same terms as the posts on the council and subcommittees.

A month later the prison's newsletter reported results of elections to the committees and the council. The paper reported that "the Community Council held their first meeting last week" and pointed out that "the subcommittees meet every week and report to the Council who assemble on a fortnightly basis. . . Minutes of each meeting are taken, then submitted to the coordinator who will keep a record of them."

Of course, this does not end the change process, and problems could still develop. The governance structure could be deemed superfluous and become underutilized. Fresh trust tests could be devised in the shape of proposals and demands that invite rejection. Personality conflicts could also arise that preempt serious business. New political entities in prisons are at first vulnerable, and they must be monitored and nurtured to ensure their survival.

A Grass Roots Mission Statement

It remains for me to describe a briefer experiment, which proved instructive but less conclusive. The target in this instance was a prison cellblock in a multipurpose prison, which functions as a detention facility for the west coast of Scotland. The cellblock contained long-term inmates and lifers in the midstage of their careers and is relatively new.

Twenty prisoners and three staff members participated in an afternoon meeting presided over by the principal officer of the cell block who was serving as acting warden. This officer is a respected staff member who volunteers as coordinator for the prison religious fellowship and has a loyal following among inmates.

Given the time available for the intervention, I proposed that the group draft a mission statement for the cellblock. Mission statements are taken seriously in Scotland, where quality management strategies are popular. The Prison Service has a mission statement, as do all prisons and autonomous special units. But no cellblock, in Scotland or elsewhere, has drafted a mission statement, and none has originated with a group of prisoners and officers.

I started the session noting that mission statements had traditionally been vapid public relations ploys, but that they have in recent times become embodiments of the central concerns of organizations, which guide and inform what they do and serve as reminders of what they stand for. This proved to become a problem when I cited the Prison Service mission statement, and the prisoners questioned whether this statement guided the agency's actions. (Rumors had circulated about impending cutbacks in furlough arrangements.)

Other objections from the group took familiar forms. One inmate reviewed a long and checkered prison career to document his reluctance to place trust in new initiatives. Another prisoner cited societal and systemic constraints to make a case for the proposition that local reform was futile. Other prisoners opined that mission statements should be drafted after more fundamental concerns had been addressed.

Eventually, the discussion drifted to mission statement planks that appeared to have some group support. Among these, one dealt with the desire to have the cell block operate as a community. Another dealt with the involvement of prisoners in decisions. A third suggested that rules be enforced with "flexible consistency." A fourth proposed that a climate be created to make family visits pleasant and profitable. Others dealt with the use of time, the planning of prison careers, and the control of serious drugs in the prison. This topic proved especially controversial and sparked a spirited debate.

The debate next turned to issues of a housekeeping nature and focused on assignments to double and single cells. The ostensible issue was the prioritizing of single-cell assignments, but the concern revolved around a specific individual and his assignment, with pressure to exact a decision in this matter becoming quite intense. The senior officer resisted the concerted campaign to force this issue, which presupposed the eviction of an inmate who was not present at the meeting.

At this stage the mission statement had to be tabled, but the group expressed satisfaction at the opportunity for what they saw as an open and honest exchange. This satisfaction was somewhat tempered when the prisoner on whose behalf cell assignment pressure had been exercised exploded in anger and left the meeting in a huff. It was subsequently resolved that the mission statement project would be resuscitated at a more strategic juncture.

I relay the second account with the first to point up the difficulties one encounters in pursuing the task of making prisons more normalized, humane, and participatory environments. Inmate cultures, and sometimes staff cultures, are obdurate, and having learned to fear, resent, and mistrust members of other groups, are apt to respond to trust bids with reluctant misgivings. The process of facing, surfacing, and disarming such resistances is slow, painful, and emotional. But given skilled and committed allies, such as my friends in the Scottish Prison Service, reform can eventually be achieved, and prisoners and officers can learn to work together to improve the settings in which they live and work.

Postscript

Whether American corrections is ready for this challenge is a difficult question. U.S. prisons are larger than those in Scotland. Our public appears more retributive. But inmate councils exist in American jurisdictions, and their role can be expanded, so can the involvement of prison staff in working with inmate councils. And in the U.S., functional prison units exist, which can serve as a setting in which community can be fostered.

Both American and Scottish correctional philosophies presuppose that offenders can be challenged to take responsibility for their lives upon release. This challenge, if it is taken seriously, is better met if prisoners are provided with opportunities to undertake responsibilities while in prison than if they are deprived of such opportunities. The point is to find acceptable ways for prisoners to shoulder and discharge responsibilities in the prison.

{End of Article}

SUMMARY

In a growing trend that indicates how politically charged the crime problem has become, more and more states are trying to make prisoners pay for everything from filing lawsuits to their room and board. The number of inmates in state prisons has tripled since 1980. Presently, there are over one million state prisoners. This increase in population and the political pressures to tighten the budgets has led state officials to claim they are justified in going after even token payments from inmates, most of whom have little or no resources. In 1995, more than two dozen states passed laws intended to regain some of the costs of incarceration.

Electronic surveillance technology was first developed in the mid-1960s. It was not used with offenders until the 1980s. Since then, however, it has developed into one of the most popular intermediate sanctions used in the United States. It is estimated that more than one million people in the United States will ultimately be placed on some form of electronic monitoring. Not only is the number of offenders placed on electronic monitoring house arrest increasing, but the types of offenders are becoming more diverse. At first, it was used for offenders awaiting trial or sentencing and offenders released from institutional correctional facilities.

In sentencing jurisdictions throughout the country, judges are being faced with balancing such competing objectives as public safety, humaneness, and the assurance of offender accountability, while confronting accelerating increases in prison overcrowding and a political commitment to incapacitation and retributive justice.

Growing prison populations, court-ordered capacity limits on jails and prisons, and tight government budgets have forced a return to correctional innovation and a renewed interest in community-based corrections programming. Among the newer innovations are several intermediate sanctions that serve as steps between the security and punishment of prisons and jails and the supervision without security offered by probation and parole. Intensive supervision, house arrest, and electronic monitoring are becoming accepted alternatives to incarceration.

DISCUSSION QUESTIONS

1. Describe some of the programs that states are attempting to use to reduce the high cost of prisonization.

2. Explain the advantages and disadvantages of home confinement.

3. What are the advantages to the use of electronic monitoring?

4. Explain the concepts behind the use of day-reporting centers.

5. Should inmates have a role in prison governance? Explain your answer.

ENDNOTES FOR CHAPTER 13

1. *New York Times*, July 9, 1996.

2. Michael P. Brown and Preston Elrod, "Electronic House Arrest: An Examination of Citizen Attitudes," *Crime and Delinquency*, July 1995, pp. 332-346.

3. *Houston Chronicle*, June 9, 1996, p.2D

4. Stephen J. Rackmill, Chief United States Probation Officer, Eastern District of New York, *Federal Probation*, Vol. 58, No.1, (March 1994). Footnotes omitted.

5. David W. Diggs and Stephen L. Pieper, *Federal Probation*, Vol. 58, No. 1 (March 1994) pp. 9-14. Mr. Diggs is manager of the direct supervision Department Orange County Corrections Division. Mr. Pieper is the Senior Superior of the Community Surveillance Unit in the Community Corrections Department of the Orange County, Florida Division. Footnotes omitted.

6. Carol Freburger and Marci B. Almon, *Federal Probation*, Vol. 58, No., Sept. 1994.

7. Hans Touch, *Federal Probation*, Vol. 59, No. 3 (June 1995). Footnotes and citations omitted. Mr. Touch is a Distinguished Professor of Criminal Justice at the State University of New York at Albany.

CHAPTER 14

CORRECTIONS AS A CAREER FIELD

CHAPTER OBJECTIVES

After studying this chapter, the reader will be able to:

☐ Analyze the corrections field as a career choice.

☐ Explain the meaning of the phrase "corrections is a growth industry."

☐ Explain the types of positions available in the corrections field.

☐ Describe the working conditions of correctional officers.

☐ Explain the training requirements for the various types of correctional officers.

☐ Analyze the employment outlook for the corrections field.

☐ Explain the multifaceted role of juvenile probation officers.

☐ List and explain the codes of ethics that apply to the corrections field.

☐ Analyze the requirements to be successful in the corrections field.

In this chapter, we will look at corrections as a career field. Included are discussions on parole and probation officers, the government occupational outlook for correctional officers, and the multifaceted role of juvenile probation officers. In addition, included in the chapter are the codes of ethics and a primer for probation (and parole) officers seeking upward mobility.

It is estimated that approximately 400,000 individuals are employed by correctional systems at the federal, state, and local levels. The demand for correctional employees has been increasing and probably will continue to increase in the foreseeable future. It is often stated that "corrections is a growth industry." Correctional employees represent both sexes and all ethnic groups. Since the work in corrections is varied, there are opportunities available for all types of skills and academic disciplines. Most researchers divide correctional employment

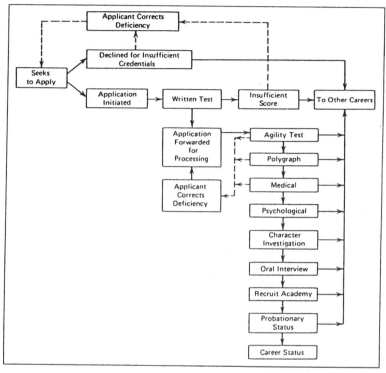

Corrections employment application procedure.

into four main categories which cover a wide range of occupations and professions. They are:

- Custodial
- Treatment
- Administrative
- Support

Most individuals enter into corrections as *correctional officers* (COs). The correctional officers generally perform custodial roles in jails, prisons, and other institutions. The correctional officer position is not known for high-entry-level pay. The typical correctional officer's entry pay is traditionally in the low $20,000.

PAROLE AND PROBATION OFFICERS

There are approximately 60,000 parole officers in the United States. Most are employed by state or county correctional departments. Probation officers generally work for the courts. Halfway houses and work-release centers also hire probation and parole officers.

The average starting salaries for probation and parole officers in 1995 was about $28,000 per year. The average salary for a probation or parole officer was about $36,000. Those working for the federal government generally receive the highest salaries. Like most government employees, parole and probation officers are given good benefits packages, which include health insurance and a pension plan.

The regulations concerning requirements for parole or probation officers vary from state to state. Generally, the minimum educational requirement for becoming a parole or probation officer is a bachelor's degree in criminal justice, criminology, corrections, social work, or a related subject. A master's degree, as well as previous experience in the criminal justice system, is required in many cases. Some parole officer positions require fluency in a foreign language, especially Spanish. Personal qualities for parole or probation officers include patience, good communication skills, and the ability to work well with and motivate people.

One good method to gain the necessary experience for entry into the profession is by volunteer service with a rehabilitation center or some other social service organization. Many of the agencies offer internships for students interested in a career in corrections. It is also helpful to contact local governmental agencies handling parole or probation and arrange informational interviews with parole or probation officers.

Generally, an individual enters the profession as a parole officer trainee before assuming the title of parole officer. New employees receive a majority of their training via on-the-job training. Advancement opportunities for parole officers are good. There are opportunities as supervisors, administrators, and department heads. Some parole officers assume supervisorial positions as directors of specialized units.

The parole officer tries to help the parolee find housing, employment, job training, or formal education. In addition, the officer may try to help by referring the parolee to other specialists, such as a psychologist or a drug rehabilitation counselor, or to a halfway house. An officer is generally required to contact and talk with businesses that employ parolees. A great part of a parole or probation officer's job is directed toward ensuring that the defendant is upholding the parole or probation agreement.

Parole and probation officers usually work out of a government building, court house, social service agency, or correctional institution. Often they are required to travel to various settings, such as private homes, businesses, or schools, in order to conduct interviews and investigations. Typically their work week is 40 hours, but overtime, as well as evening and weekend work may be necessary. Because of potential emergencies, some may be on seven-day, 24-hour recall status for part of their time. For more information regarding this career field, you may contact the American Correctional Association, 8025 Laurel Lakes Court, Laurel, MD. 20707.

CORRECTIONAL OFFICERS[1]

(D.O.T. 372.3b7-014,.567-014,.667-018, and .677; and 375.367-010)

Nature of the Work

Correctional officers are charged with overseeing individuals who have been arrested, are awaiting trial or other hearing, or who have been convicted of a crime and sentenced to serve time in a jail, reformatory, or penitentiary. They maintain security and observe inmate conduct and behavior to prevent disturbances and escapes. Many correctional officers work in small county and municipal jails or precinct station houses as deputy sheriffs or police officers with wide ranging responsibilities. Others are assigned to large state and federal prisons where job duties are more specialized. A relatively small number supervise aliens being held by the Immigration and Naturalization Service before being released or deported. Regardless of the setting, correctional officers maintain order within the institution, enforce rules and regulations, and may supplement whatever counseling inmates receive from psychologists, social workers, or other mental health professionals.

To make sure inmates are orderly and obey rules, correctional officers monitor inmates' activities, including working, exercising, eating, and bathing. They assign and supervise inmates' work assignments. Sometimes it is necessary to search inmates and their living quarters for weapons or drugs, to settle disputes between inmates, and to enforce discipline. Correctional officers cannot show favoritism and must report any inmate who violates the rules. A few officers hold staff security positions in towers, where they are equipped with high-powered rifles. Other, unarmed officers are responsible for direct supervision of inmates. They are locked in a cellblock alone, or with another officer, among the 50 to 100 inmates who reside there. The officers enforce regulations primarily through their communications skills and moral authority.

Other correctional officers periodically inspect the facilities. They may, for example, check cells and other areas of the institution for unsanitary conditions, weapons, drugs, fire hazards, and any evidence of infractions of rules. In addition, they routinely inspect locks, window bars, grille doors, and gates for signs of tampering.

Correctional officers report orally and in writing on inmate conduct and on the quality and quantity of work done by inmates. Officers also report disturbances, violations of rules, and any unusual occurrences. They usually keep a daily record of their activities. In the most modern facilities, correctional officers can monitor the activities of prisoners from a centralized control center with the aid of closed circuit television cameras and a computer tracking system. In such an environment, the inmates may not see anyone but officers for days or weeks at a time.

Depending on the offender's classification within the institution, correctional officers may escort inmates to and from cells and other areas and admit and accompany authorized visitors to see inmates. Officers may also escort prisoners between the institution and courtrooms, medical facilities, and other destinations. They inspect mail and visitors for contraband (prohibited items). Should the situation arise, they assist law enforcement authorities by investigating crimes committed within their institution and by helping search for escaped inmates.

Correctional officers may arrange a change in a daily schedule so that an inmate can visit the library, help inmates get news of their families, or help inmates in other ways. In a few institutions, officers receive specialized training, have a more formal counseling role, and may lead or participate in group counseling sessions.

Correctional sergeants directly supervise correctional officers. They usually are responsible for maintaining security and directing the activities of a group of inmates during an assigned watch or in an assigned area.

Working Conditions

Correctional officers may work indoors or outdoors, depending on their specific duties. Some indoor areas of correctional institutions are well-lit, heated, and ventilated, but others are overcrowded, hot, and noisy. Outdoors, weather conditions may be disagreeable (e.g., when standing watch on a guard tower in cold weather). Working in a correctional institution can be stressful and hazardous: correctional officers occasionally have been injured or killed by inmates.

Correctional officers usually work an eight-hour day, five days a week, on rotating shifts. Prison security must be provided around the clock, which often means that junior officers work weekends, holidays, and nights. In addition, officers may be required to work overtime.

Employment

Correctional officers held about 310,000 jobs in 1994. Six of every 10 worked at state correctional institutions such as prisons, prison camps, and reformatories. Most of the remainder worked at city and county jails or other institutions run by local governments. About 9,000 correctional officers worked at federal correctional institutions, and about 4,000 worked in privately owned and managed prisons.

Most correctional officers work in relatively large institutions located in rural areas, although a significant number work in jails and other smaller facilities located in law enforcement agencies throughout the country.

Training, Other Qualifications, and Advancement

Most institutions require that correctional officers be at least 18 or 21 years of age, have a high school education or its equivalent, have no felony convictions, and be a United States citizen. In addition, correctional institutions increasingly seek correctional officers with postsecondary education, particularly in psychology, criminal justice, police science, criminology, and related fields.

Correctional officers must be in good health. The federal system and many states require candidates to meet formal standards of physical fitness, eyesight, and hearing. Strength, good judgment, and the ability to think and act quickly are indispensable. Other common requirements include a driver's license, and work experience that demonstrates reliability. The federal system and some states screen applicants for drug abuse and require candidates to pass a written or oral examination, along with a background check.

Federal, state, and local departments of corrections provide training for correctional officers based on guidelines established by the American Correctional Association, the American Jail Association, and other professional organizations. Some states have special training academies. All states and local departments of correction provide informal on-the-job training at the conclusion of formal instruction. On-the-job trainees receive several weeks or months of training in an actual job setting under an experienced officer.

Academy trainees generally receive instruction on institutional policies, regulations, and operations; constitutional law and cultural awareness; crisis intervention, inmate behavior, and contraband control; custody and security procedures; fire and safety; inmate rules and legal rights; administrative responsibilities; written and oral communication, including preparation of reports; self-defense, including the use of firearms and physical force; first aid including cardiopulmonary resuscitation (CPR); and physical fitness training. New federal correctional officers must undergo 200 hours of formal training within the first year of employment. They must complete 120 hours of specialized correctional instruction at the Federal Bureau of Prisons residential training center at Glynco, Georgia, within the first 60 days after appointment. Experienced officers receive in-service training to keep abreast of new ideas and procedures.

Entry requirements and on-the-job training vary widely from agency to agency. For instance, correctional officers in North Dakota need two years of college with emphasis on criminal justice or behavioral science, or three years as a correctional, military police, or licensed peace officer. The department then provides 80 hours of training to start, and follows up with 40 hours of training annually. On the other hand, Connecticut requires only that candidates be 18 years of age, have a high school diploma or GED certificate, and pass a medical/physical examination, including drug screening. It then provides 520 hours of initial training, and follows up with 40 hours annually.

Correctional officers have the opportunity to join prison tactical response teams, which are trained to respond to riots, hostage situations, forced cell moves, and other potentially dangerous confrontations. Team members often receive monthly training and practice with weapons, chemical agents, forced entry methods, and other tactics.

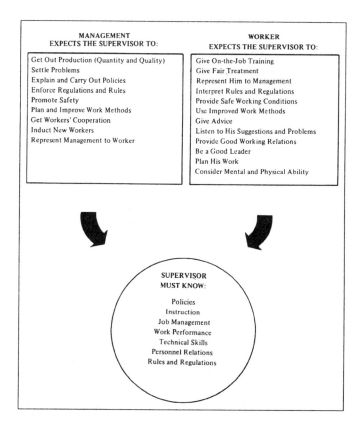

MANAGEMENT
EXPECTS THE SUPERVISOR TO:

Get Out Production (Quantity and Quality)
Settle Problems
Explain and Carry Out Policies
Enforce Regulations and Rules
Promote Safety
Plan and Improve Work Methods
Get Workers' Cooperation
Induct New Workers
Represent Management to Worker

WORKER
EXPECTS THE SUPERVISOR TO:

Give On-the-Job Training
Give Fair Treatment
Represent Him to Management
Interpret Rules and Regulations
Provide Safe Working Conditions
Use Improved Work Methods
Give Advice
Listen to His Suggestions and Problems
Provide Good Working Relations
Be a Good Leader
Plan His Work
Consider Mental and Physical Ability

SUPERVISOR
MUST KNOW:

Policies
Instruction
Job Management
Work Performance
Technical Skills
Personnel Relations
Rules and Regulations

With education, experience, and training, qualified officers may advance to correctional sergeant or other supervisory or administrative positions. Many correctional institutions require experience as a correctional officer for other corrections positions. Ambitious correctional officers can be promoted to assistant warden. Officers sometimes transfer to related areas, such as probation or parole officer.

Job Outlook

Job opportunities for correctional officers are expected to be plentiful through the year 2005. The need to replace correctional officers who transfer to other occupations or leave the labor force, coupled with a rising employment demand, will generate many thousands of job openings each year. Some local and a few state correctional agencies have traditionally experienced difficulty in attracting qualified applicants, largely due to relatively low salaries and unattractive rural locations. This situation is expected to continue, ensuring highly favorable job prospects.

Employment of correctional officers is expected to increase much faster than the average for all occupations through the year 2005 as additional officers are hired to supervise and control a growing inmate population. Expansion and new construction of correctional facilities also are expected to create many new jobs for correctional officers, although state and local government budgetary constraints could affect the rate at which new facilities are built. Increasing public concern about the spread of crime and illegal drugs, resulting in more convictions, and the adoption of mandatory sentencing guidelines calling for longer sentences and reduced parole for inmates also will spur demand for correctional officers.

Layoffs of correctional officers are rare because security must be maintained in correctional institutions at all times.

Earnings

According to a 1994 survey in *Corrections Compendium,* a national journal for corrections professionals, starting salaries of state correctional officers averaged about $19,100 a year, ranging from $13,700 in Kentucky to $29,700 in New Jersey. Professional correctional officers' salaries, overall, averaged about $22,900 and ranged from $17,000 in Wyoming to $34,100 in New York.

At the federal level, the starting salary was about $18,700 to $20,800 a year in 1995 (supervisor), correctional officers starred at about $28,300 a year. Starting salaries were slightly higher in selected areas where prevailing local pay levels were higher. The 1995 average salary for all federal non-supervisory correctional officers was about $31,460; for supervisors, about $57, 100.

Correctional officers usually are provided uniforms or a clothing allowance to purchase their own uniforms. Most are provided or can participate in hospitalization or major medical insurance plans; many officers can get disability and life insurance at group rates. They also receive vacation and sick leave and pension benefits. Officers employed by the federal government and most state governments are covered by civil service systems or merit boards. Their retirement coverage entitles them to retire at age 50, after 20 years of service, or at any age with 25 years of service. In the federal system and some states, correctional officers are represented by labor unions.

Related Occupations

A number of related careers are open to high school graduates who are interested in protective services and the field of security. Bailiffs supervise offenders and maintain order in local and state courtrooms during legal proceedings. Bodyguards escort people and protect them from injury or invasion of privacy. House or store detectives patrol business establishments to protect against theft and vandalism and to enforce standards of good behavior. Security guards protect government, commercial, and industrial property against theft, vandalism, illegal entry, and fire. Police officers and deputy sheriffs maintain law and order, prevent crime, and arrest offenders.

Other corrections careers are open to people interested in working with offenders. Probation and parole officers monitor and counsel offenders, process their release from correctional institutions, and evaluate their progress in becoming productive members of society. Recreation leaders organize and instruct offenders in sports, games, arts, and crafts.

{End of Article}

Article

THE MULTIFACETED ROLE OF THE
JUVENILE PROBATION OFFICER[2]

An organization can, and should, set standards for ethical and professional conduct for all of the various aspects of the juvenile probation officer role. These standards represent a framework for the ideal juvenile probation officer. Only the juvenile probation officer can "flesh out" the established framework and, through his actions and demeanor fulfill this complex, multifaceted role. The probation officer is expected to fulfill many different roles, often "taking up the slack" after judges, attorneys, social agencies and parents and so on, have met what they see as their own clearly defined responsibilities in the case, and have expressed an unwillingness to extend themselves beyond these limits. Probation officers are all different in their individuality, but they share a strong, common concern for youth and the community.

A probation officer must balance many and sometimes conflicting roles, often within the same time frame. He or she must understand personal priorities, values and biases and how they coincide or conflict with those of the agency, resolving any conflicts in a manner that maintains credibility and effectiveness. The more the probation officer can be proactive in these roles, the less he or she will have to be reactive.

A short list of roles has been generated to stimulate thinking. Types of roles include diagnostician, agent of change, peace officer, and coordinator.

The Complete Juvenile Probation Officer [Many roles listed below.]

Cop—Enforces judge's orders

Prosecutor—Assists D.A./conducts revocations

Father Confessor—Establishes helpful, trustful relationship with juvenile

Rat—Informs court of juvenile's behavior/circumstances

Teacher—Develops skills in juveniles

Friend—Develops positive relationship with juveniles

Surrogate Parent—Admonishes, scolds juveniles

Counselor—Addresses needs

Ambassador—Intervenes on behalf of juvenile

Problem Solver—Helps juvenile deal with court and community issues

Crisis Manager—Deals with juvenile's precipitated crises (usually at 2 a.m.)

Hand Holder—Consoles juvenile

Public Speaker—Educates public re: tasks

P.R. Person—Wins friends/influence people on behalf of probation

Community Resource Specialist—Service broker

Transportation officer—Gets juvenile to where he has to go in a pinch

Recreational Therapist—Gets juvenile to use leisure time well

Employment Counselor—Gets kids jobs

Judge's Advisor—Court service officer

Financial Advisor—Monitors payment, sets payment plan

Paper Pusher—Fills out myriad of forms

Sounding Board—Listens to irate parents, kids, police, teachers, etc.

Punching Bag—Person to blame when anything goes wrong, such as when a kid commits a new crime

Expert Clinician—Offers or refers to appropriate treatment

Family Counselor/Marriage Therapist—Keeps peace in juvenile's family

Psychiatrist—Answers question: why does the kid do it?

Banker—Juvenile needs car fare money

Tracker—Finds kid

Truant officer—Gets kid to school

Lawyer—Tells defense lawyer/prosecutor what juvenile law says

Sex Educator—Facts of life, AIDS, & child support (Dr.Ruth)

Emergency Foster Parent—In a pinch

Family Wrecker—Files petition for abuse/neglect

Bureaucrat—Helps juvenile justice system function

Lobbyist—For juvenile, for department

Program Developer—For kid, for department

Grant Writer —For kid, for department

Board Member—Serves on a myriad of committees

Agency Liaison—With community groups

Trainer—For volunteers, students

Public Information Officer— "Tell me what you know about probation"

Court Officer/Bailiff—In a pinch

Custodian—Keeps office clean

Victim Advocate—Deals with juvenile's victim

CODES OF ETHICS

Every profession has its code of ethics. Accordingly, the codes of ethics of the American Correctional Association and the American Probation and Parole Association are set forth below. *Codes of ethics* serve as guidelines for professionals in the field. Because codes of ethics are not legislative enactments, there are no disciplinary actions associated with their violations. The codes provide us with a set of standards that we should strive to meet in our professional life.

American Correctional Association Code of Ethics

Preamble: The American Correctional Association expects of its members unfailing honesty, respect for the dignity and individuality of human beings and a commitment to professional and compassionate service. To this end, we subscribe to the following principles:

• Members will respect and protect the civil and legal rights of all individuals.

• Members will treat every professional situation with concern for the person's welfare and with no intent of personal gain.

• Relationships with colleagues will be such that they promote mutual respect within the profession and improve the quality of service.

• Public criticisms of colleagues or their agencies will be made only when warranted, verifiable and constructive in purpose.

• Members will respect the importance of all disciplines within the criminal justice system and work to improve cooperation with each segment.

• Subject to individual's right to privacy, members will honor the public's right to know and will share information with the public to the extent permitted by law.

• Members will respect and protect the right of the public to be safeguarded from criminal activity.

• Members will not use their positions to secure personal privileges or advantages.

• Members will not, while acting in an official capacity, allow personal interest to impair objectivity in the performance of duty.

• No member will enter into any activity or agreement, formal or informal, which presents a conflict of interest or is inconsistent with the conscientious performance of his or her duties.

• No member will accept any gift, service, or favor that is, or appears to be, improper or implies an obligation inconsistent with the conscientious performance of his or her duties.

• In any public statement, members will clearly distinguish between personal views and those statements or positions made on behalf of an agency or the Association.

• Each member will report to the appropriate authority any corrupt or unethical behavior where there is sufficient cause to initiate a review.

• Members will not discriminate against any individual because of race, gender, creed, national origin, religious affiliation, age or any other type of prohibited discrimination.

• Members will preserve the integrity of private information: they will neither seek data on individuals beyond that needed to perform their responsibilities, nor reveal non-public data unless expressly authorized to do so.

• Any member who is responsible for agency personnel actions will make all appointments, promotions, or dismissals in accordance with established civil service rules, applicable contract agreements and individual merit, and not in furtherance of partisan interests.[3]

American Probation and Parole Association Code of Ethics

1. I will render professional service to the justice system and the community at large in effecting social adjustment for the offender.

2. I will uphold the law with dignity, displaying an awareness of my responsibility to offenders while recognizing the right of the public to be safeguarded from criminal activity.

3. I will strive to be objective in the performance of my duties, recognizing the inalienable right of all persons, appreciating the inherent worth of the individual, and respecting those confidences which can be reposed in me.

4. I will conduct my personal life with decorum, neither accepting nor granting favors in connections with my office.

5. I will cooperate with my co-workers and related agencies and will continually strive to improve my professional competence through the seeking and sharing of knowledge and understanding.

6. I will distinguish clearly, in public, between my statements and actions as an individual and as a representative of my profession.

7. I will encourage policy, procedures and personnel practices which will enable others to conduct themselves in accordance with the values, goals, and objectives of the American Probation and Parole Association.

8. I recognize my office as a symbol of public faith and I accept it as a public trust to be held as long as I am true to the ethics of the American Probation and Parole Association.

9. I will constantly strive to achieve these objectives and ideals, dedicating myself to my chosen profession.

Article SUCCESS IN THE ORGANIZATION: A PRIMER FOR PROBATION OFFICERS SEEKING UPWARD MOBILITY[4]

Each year a number of young college graduates, many quite talented, enter the probation profession eager to serve the courts, further the cause of justice, and help redirect the competent lives of errants. Some are successful and make significant contributions in the community corrections field. Still others, however, bring with them unrealistic expectations and unclear goals. As a result, they find the work unsatisfying and their careers blocked by a lack of opportunity for advancement. What is it that separates these two groups? Why is one group successful in finding satisfaction and opportunities for greater challenges while the other experiences burnout and disillusionment?

The difference between the successful and those less so in the field of community corrections is the same as it is in any other occupation. The successful possess certain traits that employers are seeking and that cause others in the field to look to them for leadership.

On occasions too numerous to recall we have been asked what characteristics we look for in candidates when filling supervisory and management positions in our respective organizations. Our responses, while not identical, tend to focus on several common characteristics which, for the purpose of this article, we have entitled *The Twelve "Cs"*. These qualities or characteristics, while applicable in community corrections, could apply in any organization or enterprise.

The Twelve "Cs"

Competent	Clear and Curious Mind	Composed
Committed	Compulsive	Competitive
Considerate	Cooperative	Consistent
Courageous	Communication Skills	Character

We hasten to add that these 12 characteristics are by no means inclusive of all the qualities we desire in employees, but they certainly are those we prioritize when we are engaged in the hiring process and selecting employees for promotions.

Competent

One of the first characteristics employers seek is competence. In addition to meeting the academic and experience requirements, people desiring greater responsibility must possess the intelligence and the heart for the job. Likewise, because the new position will require them to learn new techniques in dealing with people and will call upon them to use talents they did not fully exploit as a line officer, new supervisors must be trainable and willing to learn. The skills that made them competent frontline employees may not meet the demands of the new position.

Being competent includes having a vision, and that vision should be consistent with that of the organization to which they belong. In addition, they must be able to communicate that vision to their subordinates.

Finally, competent supervisors are those who exhibit control, particularly self-control. Charles Gandy, a prominent Texas attorney living in the Brazos Valley, is wont to say, "Don't start a fight you don't need to win." While it is it frequently difficult to adhere to this admonition, good supervisors, nevertheless, should be expected to practice sufficient self-control to avoid unnecessary conflict.

Clear and Curious Mind

Supervisors must be endowed with clear and inquisitive minds— minds driven by common sense that are not only capable of recalling relevant data but analyzing it as well. They must be able to ferret out the wheat from the chaff and distinguish the minor issues from the big picture.

They must possess active minds that continue to absorb new information and subsequently translate that information into problem-solving strategies. Many years ago, far more than we wish to remember, International Business Machines, commonly known as IBM, initiated a practice of placing signs on the desks of its employees, and these signs contained a single word— "Think." The company's motive was obvious: it wanted its employees to be creative, to develop new strategies, and, as a consequence, to make the company more profitable. While this practice was implemented in a corporate setting, it is one which may be fittingly applied to entities in the criminal justice system. The ability to think strategically—considering an issue from different perspectives—is an essential quality for supervisors and managers.

Far too many employees attempt to attain advancement within their organization by working harder. Although hard work is admirable and should not be discouraged, those who work smarter rather than harder and are viewed as problem solvers tend to rise faster within the organization. Imagination and creative conceptualization are essential qualities sought in managers and supervisors. Management expert and prominent industrial leader Clarence B. Randall wrote of the importance of imagination in an administrator:

> He must be able to foresee what is likely to happen before it does. He must sense the significance of the forces that work about him and be able to evaluate their probable impact upon his decisions. Half a poet at heart, he must dream dreams and see visions. He must have the gift of building castles in the air without waiting for brick and mortar.

Evaluating the probable impact of forces around them requires supervisors to view problems in a variety of ways. Marlene Wilson points out:

> Too much valuable time goes into solving the wrong problems, and dealing with things that should have never been allowed to become problems, or dealing with the results rather than the causes of problems.

In addition, James Adams suggests:

> Few people like problems. Hence the natural tendency in problem solving is to pick the first solution that comes to mind and run with it. The disadvantage of this approach is that one may either run off a cliff or into a worse problem than the one started

with. A better strategy in solving problems is to select the most attractive path from many ideas and concepts.

The key to problem solving is the ability to conceptualize as many solutions as possible from which to choose. Adams stresses:

> A good conceptualizer must be a creative conceptualizer. The mental characteristics which seem to make one creative not only are valuable in idea-having, but also better equip one to find and define problems and implement the resulting solutions.

It is also critical that supervisors be decisive. After analyzing available data from a global perspective, they must possess the ability to make a decision and be prepared to stick with it. In addition, the action plan they adopt should include incremental steps that will lead to the successful fulfillment of their objective.

Finally, a necessary and complementary component of a clear mind is good judgment, and particularly the exercise of good judgment under pressure. Academic achievement is a poor substitute for good judgment. During our careers we have seen many who appear academically suited for increased responsibility fail because of their inability to exercise sound judgment in decision-making situations.

Composed

Composure is an essential ingredient for success in an organization. Supervisors and managers must be self-assured and assertive, balanced with a good demeanor. This balance is important, for many people in supervisory positions, particularly those early in their careers, tend to become enamored with a sense of self-importance, and this can easily cause their downfall in an organization and with the external environment. Jesse E. Clark, who served as an assistant warden with the Texas Department of Corrections, a U.S. probation officer, and, at the time of his untimely death, U.S. district clerk for the Southern District of Texas, once told a group of young probation officers, "Don't take yourself too seriously because no one else does." A healthy sense of humor—even humor that at times is self-deprecating—can serve supervisors and managers well. In addition, supervisors must exhibit a mature demeanor. No one, and particularly subordinates, respects or likes people who appear to be immature.

Finally, a part of composure is appearance, and persons in supervisory positions should dress as well as their financial circumstances permit. Steve Robinson, director of the Texas Youth Commission, once made the observation that a well-dressed person with average intelligence will likely enjoy better career opportunities than a highly intelligent person who dresses poorly. While this may not be fair, it is, nonetheless, a fact of life: persons who dress well tend to command a greater degree of respect, and opportunities for advancement will come easier to them.

Committed

One of the more important qualities supervisors must possess is commitment—commitment to the employer, the agency, and the agency's mission. Truly committed supervisors, particularly those in agencies that deliver human services as probation departments do, view their position as their life's work, not just as a job. Former President Woodrow Wilson once said:

> You are not here merely to make a living. You are here in order to enable the world to live more amply, with greater vision, with a finer spirit of hope and achievement. You are here to enrich the world and you impoverish yourself if you forget the errand.

Commitment is also demonstrated through a sense of loyalty to the employer. A particularly favorite admonition used by Dr. George J. Beto, a clergyman, educator, and correctional administrator, which he drew from the writings of Edmund Burke, was "Don't bite the hand that feeds you." Found in that brief sentence is the message that one should be loyal to one's employer. This is particularly true of supervisors in an organization who are charged, to a great degree, with carrying out the agency's mission.

Probably one of the greatest correctional administrators was the late Joseph E. Ragen, who, while serving as warden of the Stateville and Joliet prisons in Illinois, presented his employees with the following homily:

If you work for a man, in Heaven's name work for him. If he pays you wages that supply you bread and butter, work for him, speak well of him, and stand by him, and stand by the institution he represents.

If put to a pinch, an ounce of loyalty is worth a pound of clearness; if you must vilify, condemn, or eternally disparage, resign your position.

But as long as you are part of the institution, do not condemn it. If you do, you are loosening the tendrils that hold you to the institution, and with the first high wind that comes along, you will be uprooted and blown away, and probably you will never know why.

Warden Rageri's admonition is one that should be totally embraced by frontline employees who hope to succeed as supervisors and managers.

Finally, commitment is demonstrated through professional involvement. It is axiomatic that people who excel are usually involved in organizations that promote their profession. A cursory examination of community corrections leaders throughout the United States will show that most are active and contributing members of professional organizations. In addition to making a contribution to their profession and developing a sense of ownership, people in professional organizations establish relationships that, with time, serve to further their careers.

Compulsive

While this particular characteristic has some negative connotations, for the purpose of this article the term "compulsive" refers to the desire and ability to bring closure to an assignment, project, or issue. All too frequently supervisors have difficulty bringing closure to a particular initiative, and their inability to do so can cause irreparable harm to an organization. People who demonstrate that they can get things done, and done right, are a valuable asset to an organization.

Competitive

High energy and a competitive spirit are qualities sought after in supervisors. No supervisors will be successful if they are satisfied with the status quo, become just another member of a group, or lack the desire to be the very best. Another saying of Dr. Beto's was, "If you are not the lead cow, the scenery never changes." Supervisors should strive to see that the scenery always changes, not only for themselves but for their subordinates as well.

Two essential components of a competitive spirit are patience and perseverance. A perfect example of this is Abraham Lincoln, who sought public office on a number of occasions only to suffer disappointment. Because he never gave up hope and never lost sight of his objective, he persevered and was eventually elected President of the United States.

Cooperative

Competitiveness should not lead to a "win at all cost" mentality. Successful leaders are those who cooperate with others, negotiate compromise when necessary, and constantly seek mutual benefits in their interaction with others. They seek a balance between competition and cooperation. According to Stephen R. Covey:

> Competition has its place in the marketplace or against last year's performance—perhaps even against another office or individual where there is no particular interdependence, no need to cooperate. But cooperation in the workplace is as important to free enterprise as competition in the marketplace.

For an organization to be effective, its employees must cooperate with one another. Supervisors who can generate cooperation among employees will contribute significantly to the success of the organization and will quickly gain the attention of management. Too, people who consistently seek win/win relationships in all situations will realize the support of subordinates, peers, and management, and this support may well serve as the vehicle for advancement in the agency.

Considerate

People employed in probation and community corrections deal daily with people with problems. In addition to providing services to offenders and their families, probation personnel are called upon to address the needs of victims, law enforcement officers and court officials, colleagues, and employees of agencies charged with delivering human services. Many of these people are ill-equipped to handle their duties and responsibilities effectively, lack vision, are frustrated and unhappy with their stations in life, and feel overwhelmed by the demands of our complex society. Supervisors should be considerate when dealing with these people and should be sensitive to their problems. Consideration of the plight of others and a firm yet charitable nature will enhance the effectiveness of supervisors and managers.

Consistent

It is imperative that supervisors be consistent with those whom they supervise. According to Randall, when dealing with people and in making decisions, supervisors must "have one eye on what has gone on before and the other on what lies ahead." Hersey and Blanchard write:

> To be really consistent (in our terms) managers must behave the same way in similar situations for all parties concerned. Thus, a consistent manager would not discipline one subordinate when the person makes a costly mistake but not another staff member and vice versa. It is also important for managers to treat their subordinates the same way in similar circumstances even when it is inconvenient—when they don't have time or when they don't feel like it.

Supervisors and managers who fail to be consistent will not be able to provide clear direction to their staff. Equally important as being consistent in the manner we relate to others is that our actions be consistent with what we say. Kotter stresses:

> Few things can undermine the credibility of communication faster than a problem with consistency. People usually assume that actions do speak louder than words. As a result, one regularly finds in an effective leadership process a remarkable degree of congruence between the actions of key players and the messages they communicate.

Courageous

Closely related to consistency is courage, a quality that all successful supervisors possess. Quoting from Randall:

Good ideas are not self-executing. They become effective only when there is behind them the driving force of a man who believes in them so fervently that he accepts all risks and surmounts all obstacles. Such high courage, upon which all industrial leadership must rest, has two sources: one is humility, the other is insight.

Courageous supervisors are driven by principles and are willing to take stands on critical issues, regardless of their popularity. In addition, courage is required of new supervisors because their role in the organization will have changed in that they will be responsible for directing people who formerly were their peers. This newly assumed role will prove to be very challenging and frustrating to the supervisor. In *The Prince,* a treatise on power written in 1513 and printed posthumously in 1532, Niccolo Machiavelli provided the following words of caution to new administrators:

It ought to be remembered that there is nothing more difficult to take in hand, more perilous to conduct, or more uncertain in its success than to take the lead in the introduction of a new order of things. Because the innovator has for enemies all those who have done well under the old conditions and lukewarm defenders among those who may do well under the new.

While Machiavelli's cautionary advice was written for Renaissance nobility, it is applicable today to anyone assuming a position of authority. New supervisors and managers in community corrections would do well to remember the potential pitfalls envisioned by this Italian political philosopher and statesman and act accordingly. They should also be prepared to develop new friends among their co-workers because their relationships will change within the organization.

Communication Skills

A key ingredient in the formula for successful supervision and management is the ability to communicate, both in the written and spoken word. It has been our observation that far too many people entering the probation profession cannot compose a decent sentence. In most cases, this inability to write is not entirely their fault. They are the products of a generation where reading is not stressed in the home, where the television, with its inane programs, dominates leisure time, and where our educational institutions place insufficient emphasis on the importance of reading and writing.

Effective leaders are able to communicate their vision in a way that it is easily and immediately understood and translated into action. People with good communications skills are able to develop consensus on issues, and this is particularly important for managers and supervisors. As Covey points out:

> When you can present your own ideas clearly, specifically, visually, and most important, contextually, in the context of a deeper understanding of their paradigms and concerns, you significantly increase the credibility of your ideas.
>
> There is no substitute for a good command of the English language.
>
> Finally, essential to communication skills is knowing when not to speak. Most problems encountered by people are caused by quick and ill-considered responses.

Character

Probably the most important quality supervisors can possess is character, or what James Q. Wilson refers to as a "moral sense" and what Sam S. Souryal simply calls "ethics." It is this quality that all ethical employers seek in candidates for management and supervisory positions. Again, quoting from Randall:

> Character—one of the greatest words in the English language—defies both analysis and definition. Yet, no talent for administration, however brilliant, can long endure in a man without it. The fine executive invariably possesses a code of values which he himself has established. They sprang from his ethical and spiritual life and hold him staunchly true. In the face of each new challenge which he inspires in his associates, he issues few commands. They will obey, but that is the not the relationship, They follow, with enthusiasm and zeal.

According to Covey, "Character is the foundation of win/win, and everything else builds on that foundation." If, in responding to those who have asked what characteristics we look for in a candidate for a supervisory or management position in our organization, we were able to mention one quality, it would be character. It is all-important because the person with character is the person with integrity, credibility, and a moral sense, and whose presence in an organization can do nothing but enhance it.

In summary, probation officers possessing the qualities described in this article are in an excellent position to become the future leaders of the criminal justice system and are the type of leaders that are solely needed. [Footnotes omitted.]

{End of Article}

SUMMARY

It is estimated that approximately 400,000 individuals are employed by correctional systems at the federal, state, and local levels. The demand for correctional employees has been increasing, and probably will continue to increase in the foreseeable future. It is often stated that "corrections is a growth industry." Correctional employees represent both sexes and all ethnic groups. Because the work in corrections is varied, there are opportunities available for all types of skills and academic disciplines. Most researchers divide correctional employment into four main categories: custodial, treatment, administrative, and support. These categories cover a wide range of occupations and professions.

Most individuals enter into corrections as correctional officers (C.O.s). The correctional officers generally perform custodial roles in jails, prisons, and other institutions. The correctional officer position is not known for high entry level pay.

Correctional officers are charged with overseeing individuals who have been arrested, are awaiting trial or other hearing, or who have been convicted of a crime and sentenced to serve time in a jail, reformatory, or penitentiary. They maintain security and observe inmate conduct and behavior to prevent disturbances and escapes. Many correctional officers work in small county and municipal jails or precinct station houses as deputy sheriffs or police officers with wide ranging responsibilities. Others are assigned to large state and federal prisons where job duties are more specialized. A relatively small number supervise aliens being held by the Immigration and Naturalization Service before being released or deported.

There are approximately 60,000 parole officers in the United States. Most are employed by state or county correctional departments. Probation officers generally work for the courts. Halfway houses and work release centers also hire probation and parole officers.

The average starting salaries for probation and parole officers in 1995 was about $28,000 per year. The average salary for a probation or parole officer is about $36,000. Those working for the federal government generally receive the highest salaries. Like most government employees, parole and probation officers are given good benefits packages which include health insurance and a pension plan.

The juvenile probation officer is expected to fulfill many different roles, often "taking up the slack" after judges, attorneys, social agencies and parents and so on, have met what they see as their own clearly defined responsibilities in the case, and have expressed an unwillingness to extend themselves beyond these limits. Juvenile probation officers are all different in their individuality, but they share a strong, common concern for youth and the community.

A probation officer must balance many and sometimes conflicting roles, often within the same time frame. He or she must understand personal priorities, values and biases and how they coincide or conflict with those of the agency, resolving any conflicts in a manner that maintains credibility and effectiveness. The more the probation officer can be proactive in these roles, the less he or she will have to be reactive.

DISCUSSION QUESTIONS

1. Explain what a new correctional employee can expect during his or her first year on the job.

2. What types of duties can career correctional personnel expect to encounter during their careers in the field?

3. What steps may be taken to enhance corrections as a career field?

4. Explain the role that professional codes of ethics should play in our professional career.

5. What is the difference between those who are successful in corrections and those who are not?

ENDNOTES FOR CHAPTER 14

1. *U.S. Government's Occupational Handbook* (1996).

2. National Center for Juvenile Justice, *Juvenile Probation Officer's Deskbook* U.S. Department of Justice.

3. *Code,* adopted August 1975 at the 105 Congress of Correction and revised August 1990 at the 120th Congress of Correction.

4. Dan Richard Beto and Elvin Brown, JR., *Federal Probation*, Vol. 60, No. 1, pp. 50-56 (March, 1996). Mr. Beto is the Director of the Correctional Management Institute of Texas at Sam Houston State University in Huntsville, Texas. Dr. Brown is the Director of the Montgomery County Department of Community Supervision and Corrections in Conroe, Texas.

APPENDIX A

National Policies on Corrections as Ratified by the American Correctional Association

CORRECTIONAL POLICY ON CLASSIFICATION

Introduction:

Classification is a continuing process basic to identifying and matching offender needs to correctional resources. This continuing process involves all phases of correctional management.

Statement:

Classification should balance the public's need for protection, the needs of offenders, and the efficient and effective operation of the correctional system, In developing and administering its classification system, a correctional agency should:

A. Develop written classification policies that establish criteria specifying different levels of security, supervision, and program involvement; establish procedures for documenting and reviewing all classification decisions and actions; describe the appeal process to be used by individuals subject to classification; and specify the time frames for monitoring and reclassifying cases;

B. Develop the appropriate range of resources and services to meet the identified control and program needs of the population served;

C. Base classification decisions on rational assessment of objective and valid information, including background material (criminal history, nature of offense, social history, educational needs, medical/mental health needs, etc.) as well as information regrading the individual's current situation, adjustment, and program achievement;

D. Train all personnel in the classification process and require specialized training for those directly involved in classification functions;

E. Use the classification process to assign individuals to different levels of control on the basis of valid criteria regarding risk (to self and others) and individual needs, matching these characteristics with appropriate security, level of supervision, and program services;

F. Involve the individual directly in the classification process;

G. Assign appropriately trained staff to monitor individual classification plans for progress made and reclassification needs;

H. Objectively validate the classification process and instruments, assess on a planned basis the degree to which results meet written goals, and, as needed, refine the process and instruments; and

L. Provide for regular dissemination of classification information to all levels of correctional staff and to involved decision-makers outside of corrections as an aid in the planning, management, and operation of the correctional agency.

CORRECTIONAL POLICY ON HEALTH CARE FOR OFFENDERS

Introduction:

Correctional facilities and other correctional agencies that, either by law or as part of their stated mission, provide health care to accused and adjudicated offenders must provide health services that are appropriate and that reflect contemporary standards for health care. To ensure accountability and professional responsibility, these services should meet the policy guidelines set forth below and the health care standards of the American Correctional Association.

Statement:

Health care programs for offenders include medical, dental, and mental health services. Such programs should:

A. Be delivered by qualified health care professionals;

B. Provide to offenders, upon their arrival at a facility or at the beginning of their participation in a correctional program or service, both oral and written information concerning access to available health services;

C. Provide continuous, comprehensive services commencing at admission, including effective and timely screening, assessment and treatment, appropriate referral to alternate health care resources where warranted, and, if necessary, referral at discharge for continuing health problems;

D. Establish a system to identify and treat emergencies quickly and effectively;

E. Establish a formal program to treat and manage inmates with communicable diseases;

F. Provide appropriate health care training for all correctional staff and continuing education opportunities for professional health care providers;

G. Establish health education programs to encourage offenders to participate in their own health maintenance and in the prevention of communicable disease; and

H. Provide a medical records system for documentation of care and information sharing, consistent with privacy, confidentiality, and security concerns, to enhance continuity of service and professional accountability.

CORRECTIONAL POLICY ON EMPLOYMENT OF WOMEN IN CORRECTIONS

Introduction:

The American Correctional Association has a long-standing commitment to equal employment opportunity for women in adult and juvenile corrections.

Statement:

Women have a right to equal employment. No person who is qualified for a particular position/assignment or for job-related opportunities should be denied such employment or opportunities because of gender. Therefore, correctional agencies should:

A. Ensure that recruitment, selection, and promotion opportunities are open to women;

B. Assign female employees duties and responsibilities that provide career development and promotional opportunities equivalent to those provided to other employees;

C. Provide all levels of staff with appropriate training on developing effective and cooperative working relationships between male and female correctional personnel; and

D. Conduct regular monitoring and evaluation of affirmative action practices and take any needed corrective actions.

PUBLIC CORRECTIONAL POLICY ON EMPLOYMENT OF EX-OFFENDERS

Introduction:

Obtaining and maintaining employment is a primary step toward assuring the successful transition of offenders to law-abiding citizens in the community. The cooperation of government, business, industry, and volunteer agencies and organizations is essential in making employment opportunities available. In helping to implement this philosophy, correctional agencies should demonstrate their willingness to employ qualified ex-offenders.

Statement:

Ex-offenders should be given equitable consideration for employment. Correctional agencies should:

A. Implement and promote programs that will help offenders to prepare for, seek, and bold gainful employment in the community;

B. Develop and implement policy permitting qualified ex-offenders to be employed in correctional agencies in capacities that preserve the security and public safety mission of those agencies; and

C. Support legislation that will ensure that equal employment opportunities for ex-offenders are restored.

CORRECTIONAL POLICY ON CORRECTIONAL RESEARCH AND EVALUATION

Introduction:

Research and evaluation, and the use of the findings that result from such efforts, are essential to informed correctional policy, program development, and decision-making.

Statement:

Correctional agencies have a continuing responsibility to promote, initiate, sponsor, and participate in correctional research and evaluation efforts, both external and internal, in order to expand knowledge about offender behavior and enhance the effectiveness and efficiency of programs and services. To encourage and support these research and evaluation efforts, correctional agencies should:

A. Establish clearly defined procedures for data collection and analysis that ensure the accuracy, consistency, integrity, and impartiality of correctional research projects;

B. Conduct regular and systematic evaluation of correctional management, programs, and procedures and implement necessary changes;

C. Review and monitor correctional research to ensure compliance with professional standards, including those relating to confidentiality and the protection of human rights;

D. Prohibit the use of offenders as experimental subjects in medical, psychological, pharmacological, and cosmetic research except when warranted and prescribed for the diagnosis or treatment of an individual's specific condition in accordance with current standards of health care;

E. Make available to others the information necessary for correctional research and evaluation, consistent with concerns for privacy, confidentiality, and security;

F. Involve and train appropriate correctional staff in the application of correctional research and evaluation findings; and

G. Encourage the dissemination of correctional research and evaluation findings.

CORRECTIONAL POLICY ON LEGAL ISSUES AND LITIGATION

Introduction:

Adherence to law is fundamental to professional correctional practice. This entails avoiding litigation through sound management, effective use of the adversarial process to resolve issues that are litigated, and professional compliance with judicial orders.

Statement:

Problems addressed through litigation, such as inadequate and insufficient facilities, services, procedures, and staffing, can often be remedied through professional correctional practice, supported by government officials and the public with the necessary capital and operational resources. To achieve sound management of legal issues, correctional agencies should:

A. Use the standards and accreditation process of the American Correctional Association and the Commission on Accreditation for Corrections as a method to develop and maintain professional practice;

B. Consult frequently with legal counsel to remain informed of current developments in the law and to anticipate and avoid emerging legal problems;

C. Train staff about legal issues and responsibilities and provide them with legal representation when appropriate;

D. Attempt to resolve potential legal problems through dispute resolution techniques such as administrative grievance procedures;

E. Negotiate and settle litigation when agreements can be developed consistent with professional correctional practice;

F. Litigate, when no professionally reasonable alternative is possible, with the best legal and correctional expertise available and with full preparation and development of the case; and

G. Implement court orders in a professional manner.

CORRECTION POLICY ON INFORMATION SYSTEMS

Introduction:

Timely and accurate information is a basic requirement for effective management of organizations. Such information forms a basis for sound decision-making and provides for accountability in operations and program results.

Statement:

For correctional managers to function effectively, they must have accurate and timely information. The design of correctional information systems must reflect combined efforts of both correctional professionals and information system specialists. To meet the diverse needs of a correctional agency, information systems should be designed that will support the management processes of the agency as their primary function, support service delivery functions by providing data relevant to their efficiency and outcome, and provide sufficient flexibility to support relevant research and evaluation.

To promote development of effective information systems, correctional agencies should:

A. Clearly define the desired scope of the systems consistent with a realistic assessment of anticipated resources and technologies;

B. Involve and train correctional managers in all stages of system development and operation to ensure managers' needs are met;

C. Prepare detailed and carefully monitored development plans to ensure systems are designed and implemented in a timely and cost-effective manner;

D. Require that the system include formal evaluation procedures to ensure the quality of system input and output;

E. Cooperate with correctional, law enforcement, and other public agencies to provide for mutual sharing of information, consistent with legitimate concerns for privacy, confidentiality, and system security;

F. Ensure appropriate information needs of the public are met, consistent with legal requirements; and

G. Advocate provision of resources to implement and update advanced information system technologies.

CORRECTIONAL POLICY ON DESIGN OF CORRECTIONAL FACILITIES

Introduction:

The effectiveness and efficiency of correctional staff in maintaining security and delivering services can be either enhanced or limited by the physical plants in which they operate. Quality design has long-term cost and program advantages in assisting a correctional system to accomplish its mission.

Statement:

Correctional architecture is unique, involving the design of facilities that are functionally and environmentally supportive of the needs and activities of a confined society. The design of such facilities is a multi disciplinary process. To improve the design quality and operational adequacy of new and renovated correctional facilities, correctional agencies should:

A. Define operations of correctional facilities prior to design, including written specifications of the facility's mission and functional elements, basic operating procedures, and starting patterns so the design can fully support intended correctional operations;

B. Select architects and engineers on merit, as demonstrated by either successful completion of prior correctional projects, or by successful completion of other projects combined with access to recognized correctional expertise;

C. Design correctional facilities through a multi disciplinary process that directly involves correctional professionals, criminal justice planners, architects and engineers, and that also seeks the contribution of other groups and disciplines who have an interest in the facility's design, including those involved in the facility's day-to-day operations;

D. Ensure that facility designs conform to applicable codes and nationally approved professional standards and that they encourage direct interaction in supervision of offenders, consistent with staff safety;

E. Ensure facility design is sufficiently flexible to accommodate changes in offender population and in the facility's mission, operating procedures, and staffing;

F. Maintain project oversight to assure that design objectives are met;

G. Recognize the need for early selection of key staff who will be responsible for initial operation of the facility so they can participate in the design and construction process; and

H. Engage in an ongoing process of research and evaluation to develop, improve, and recognize the most successful design features, equipment technologies, and operating procedures.

CORRECTIONAL POLICY ON PURPOSE OF CORRECTIONS

Introduction:

In order to establish the goals and objectives of any correctional system, there must be a universal statement of purpose that all members of the correctional community can use in goal setting and daily operations.

Statement:

The overall mission of criminal and juvenile justice, which consists of law enforcement, courts, and corrections, is to enhance social order and public safety. As a component of the justice system, the role of corrections is:

A. To implement court-ordered supervision and, when necessary, detention of those accused of unlawful behavior prior to adjudication;

B. To assist in maintaining the integrity of law by administering sanctions and punishments imposed by courts for unlawful behavior;

C. To offer the widest range of correctional options, including community corrections, probation, institutions, and parole services, necessary to meet the needs of both society and the individual; and

D. To provide humane program and service opportunities for accused and adjudicated offenders that will enhance their community integration and economic self-sufficiency and that are administered in a just and equitable manner within the least restrictive environment consistent with public safety.

CORRECTIONAL POLICY ON PRIVATE SECTOR INVOLVEMENT IN CORRECTIONS

Introduction:

Although most correctional programs are operated by public agencies, there is increasing interest in the use of profit and nonprofit organizations as providers of services, facilities, and programs. Profit and nonprofit organizations have resources for the delivery of services that often are unavailable from the public correctional agency.

Statement:

Government has the ultimate authority and responsibility for corrections. For its most effective operation, corrections should rise all appropriate resources, both public and private. When government considers the use of profit and nonprofit private sector correctional services, such programs must meet professional standards, provide necessary public safety, provide services equal to or better than government, and be cost-effective compared to well-managed governmental operations. While government retains the ultimate responsibility, authority, and accountability for actions of private agencies and individuals tinder contract, it is consistent with good correctional policy and practice to:

A. Use in an advisory and voluntary role the expertise and resources available from profit and nonprofit organizations in tire development and implementation of correctional programs and policies;

B. Enhance service delivery systems by considering the concept of contracting with the private sector when justified in terms of cost, quality, and ability to meet program objectives;

C. Consider use of profit and nonprofit organizations to develop, fund, build, operate, and/or provide services, programs, and facilities when such an approach is cost-effective, safe, and consistent with the public interest and sound correctional practice;

D. Ensure the appropriate level of service delivery and compliance with recognized standards through professional contract preparation and vendor selection is well as effective evaluation and monitoring by the responsible government agency; and

E. Indicate clearly in any contract for services, facilities, or programs the responsibilities and obligations of both government and contractor, including but not limited to liability of all parties, performance bonding, and contractual termination.

CORRECTIONAL POLICY ON OFFENDERS WITH SPECIAL NEEDS

Introduction:

The provision of humane programs and services for the accused and adjudicated requires addressing the special needs of certain offenders. To meet this goal, correctional agencies should develop and adopt procedures for the early identification of offenders with special needs. Agencies should also develop a plan for providing the services that respond to those needs and for monitoring the delivery of services in both confined and community settings.

Statement:

Correctional systems should assure provision of specialized services and programs to meet the special needs of offenders. To achieve this, they should:

A. Identify the categories of offenders who will require special care or programs. These categories include:

1. Offenders with severe psychological needs, mental retardation, significant psychiatric disorders, behavior disorders, multiple handicaps, neurological impairments, and substance abuse;

2. Offenders who are physically handicapped or chronically or terminally ill;

3. Offenders who are elderly;

4. Offenders with severe social and/or educational deficiencies, learning disabilities, or language barriers; and

5. Offenders with special security or supervision needs, such as protective custody cases, death row inmates, and those who chronically exhibit potential for violent or aggressive behavior.

B. Provide specialized services or programs for those offenders who arc identified as being in need of special care or programs. Such services and programs may be provided within the correctional agency itself, or by referral to another agency that has the necessary specialized program resources, or by contracting with private or voluntary agencies or individuals that meet professional standards;

C. Maintain specialty trained staff for the delivery of care, programs, and services;

D. Maintain documentation of the services and programs provided;

E. Institute carefully controlled evaluation procedures to determine each program's effectiveness and the feasibility of its continuation or the need for adjustments; and

F. Provide leadership and advocacy for legislative and public support to obtain the resources needed to meet these special needs,

CORRECTIONAL POLICY ON USE OF APPROPRIATE SANCTIONS AND CONTROLS

Introduction:

In developing, selecting, and administering sanctions and punishments, decision makers must balance concern for individual dignity, public safety, and maintenance of social order. Correctional programs and facilities are a costly and limited resource; the most restrictive are generally the most expensive. Therefore, it is good public policy to use these resources wisely and economically.

Statement:

The sanctions and controls imposed by courts and administered by corrections should be the least restrictive consistent with public and individual safety and maintenance of social order. Selection of the least restrictive sanctions and punishments in specific cases inherently requires balancing several important objectives-individual dignity, fiscal responsibility, and effective correctional operations, To meet these objectives, correctional agencies should:

A. Advocate to all branches of government-executive, legislative and judicial-and to the public at large the development and appropriate use of the least restrictive sanctions, punishments, programs, and facilities;

B. Recommend the use of the least restrictive appropriate dispositions in judicial decisions;

C. Classify persons under correctional jurisdiction to the least restrictive appropriate programs and facilities; and

D. Employ only the level of regulation and control necessary for the safe and efficient operation of programs, services, and facilities,

CORRECTIONAL POLICY ON COMMUNITY CORRECTIONS

Introduction:

Correctional programs operating in a community setting are an integral part of a comprehensive correctional system. These include community residential facilities, probation, parole, and other programs that provide supervision and services for accused or adjudicated juveniles and adults. Responsiveness to the needs of victims and offenders and to protection of the public is essential to the success of community programs and services.

Statement:

The least restrictive sanctions and controls consistent with public and individual safety and maintenance of social order require that the majority of offenders receive services in a community setting. It is the responsibility of government to develop, support, and maintain correctional programs and services in the community. A screening process to select offenders who can be safely maintained in the community is critical for placement in these programs. Those responsible for community corrections programs, services, and supervision should:

A. Seek statutory authority and adequate funding, both public and private, for community programs and services;

B. Develop and ensure access to an array of services, residential or nonresidential, that adequately address the identifiable needs of offenders and the community;

C. Inform the public and offenders of the reasons for community programs and services, the criteria used for selecting individuals for these programs and services, and that placement in such a program is a punishment;

D. Ensure the integrity and accountability of community programs by establishing a reliable system for monitoring and measuring performance in accordance with accepted standards and professional practice;

E. Recognize that public acceptance of community corrections is enhanced by victim restitution and conciliation programs; and

F. Seek the active participation of a well-informed constituency, including citizen advisory boards and broad-based coalitions, to address community corrections issues.

CORRECTIONAL POLICY ON
CORRECTIONAL INDUSTRY

Introduction:

Correctional industry programs, whether operated by the public or private sector, aid correctional systems in reducing idleness, lowering costs, and providing opportunities for offenders to gain job skills, training, and economic self-sufficiency and to participate in programs of victim compensation and institution cost-sharing.

Statement:

Correctional industry programs. Operating under sound management principles and effective leadership, should:

A. Be based on statutes and regulations that support the development, manufacturing, marketing, distribution, and delivery of correctional industry products and services;

B. Be unencumbered by laws and regulations that restrict access to the marketplace, competitive pricing, and fair work practices except as necessary to protect the offender and the system from exploitation.

C. Provide evaluation and recognition of job performance to assist in promoting good work habits that may enhance employability after release;

D. Provide training and safe working conditions, for both staff and offenders, similar to those found in the community at large;

E. Assure that the working conditions in industry operated by public or private organizations are comparable with those in the industry at large, and that compensation to inmates is fair;

F. Recognize that profit-making and public service are both legitimate goals of an industry program;

G. Support reinvestment of profits to expand industrial programs, improve overall operations, maintain and upgrade equipment, and assist in the support of inmate training programs that enhance marketable skills, pre-release training, and job placement services; and

H. Integrate industry programs, public or private, with other institutional programs and activities under the overall leadership of the institution's chief administrator.

CORRECTIONAL POLICY ON USE OF FORCE

Introduction:

Correctional agencies administer sanctions and punishments imposed by courts for unlawful behavior. Assigned to correctional agencies involuntarily, offenders sometimes resist authority imposed on them, and may demonstrate violent and destructive behaviors, use of legally authorized force by correctional authorities may become necessary to maintain custody, safety, and control.

Statement:

Use of force consists of physical contact with an offender in a confrontational situation to control behavior and enforce order. Use of force includes use of restraints (other than for routine transportation and movement), chemical agents, and weapons. Force is justified only when required to maintain or regain control, or when there is imminent danger of personal injury or serious damage to property. To assure the use of force is appropriate and justifiable, correctional agencies should:

A. Establish and maintain policies that require reasonable steps be taken to reduce or prevent the necessity for the use of force, that authorize force only when no reasonable alternative is possible, that permit only the minimum force necessary, and that prohibit the use of force as a retaliatory or disciplinary measure;

B. Establish and enforce procedures that define the range of methods for and alternatives to the use of force, and that specify the conditions under which each is permitted. The procedures must assign responsibility for authorizing such force, assure appropriate medical care for all involved, and provide the fullest possible documentation and supervision of the action;

C. Establish and maintain procedures that limit the use of deadly force to those instances where it is legally authorized and where there is an imminent threat to human life or a threat to public safety that cannot reasonably he prevented by other means;

D. Maintain operating procedures and regular staff training designed to anticipate, stabilize, and defuse situations that might give rise to conflict, confrontation, and violence;

E. Provide specialized training to ensure competency in all methods of use of force, especially in methods and equipment requiring special knowledge and skills such as defensive tactics, weapons, restraints, and chemical agents; and

F. Establish and maintain procedures that require all incidents involving the use of force be fully documented and independently reviewed by a higher correctional authority. A report of the use of force, including appropriate investigation and any recommendations for preventive and remedial action, shall be submitted for administrative review and implementation of recommendations when appropriate.

CORRECTIONAL POLICY ON CONDITIONS OF CONFINEMENT

Introduction:

Correctional systems must administer the detention, sanctions, and punishments ordered by the courts in an environment that protects public safety and provides for the safety, rights, and dignity of staff, accused or adjudicated offenders, and citizens involved in programs.

Statement:

Maintaining acceptable conditions of confinement requires adequate resources and effective management of the physical plant, operational procedures, programs, and staff. To provide acceptable conditions, agencies should:

A. Establish and maintain a safe and humane population limit for each institution based upon recognized professional standards;

B. Provide an environment that will support the health and safety of staff, confined persons, and citizens participating in programs. Such an environment results from appropriate design, construction, and maintenance of the physical plant as well as the effective operation of the facility;

C. Maintain a professional and accountable work environment for staff that includes necessary training and supervision as well as sufficient staffing to carry out the mission of the facility; and

D. Maintain a fair and disciplined environment that provides programs and services in a climate that encourages responsible behavior.

CORRECTIONAL POLICY ON CROWDING AND EXCESSIVE WORKLOADS

Introduction:

Overpopulation of correctional programs and facilities can negate the effectiveness of management, program, security, and physical plant operations and can endanger offenders, staff, and the public at large. High Population density within correctional facilities has been associated with increased physical and Rental problems, more frequent disciplinary incidents, higher rates of assault and suicide, and decreased effectiveness of programs and services. When the population of a correctional program or facility exceeds capacity, maintaining safe and reasonable conditions of confinement and supervision becomes increasingly difficult, and may become impossible, Excessive workloads in institutional and community corrections dilute effectiveness of supervision and support services and threaten public safety.

Statement:

The number of offenders assigned to correctional facilities and community services should be limited to levels consistent with recognized professional standards. Correctional agencies should:

A. Establish and maintain safe and humane population and workload limits for each institution and service program based on recognized professional standards;

B. Develop, advocate, and implement, in coordination with the executive, legislative, and judicial branches of government, emergency and long-term processes by which offender populations can be managed within reasonable limits;

C. Anticipate the need for expanded program and facility capacity by using professional population projection methodologies that reflect both demographic and policy-related factors influencing correctional population growth;

D. Advocate the full development and appropriate use of pretrial/adjudication release, probation, parole, community residential facilities, and other community services that are alternatives to assigning offenders to crowded facilities or that reduce the duration of assignment of offenders to such facilities; and

E. Develop, advocate, and implement plans for necessary additional facilities, staff, programs, and services.

CORRECTIONAL POLICY ON OFFENDER EDUCATION AND TRAINING

Introduction:

Many accused and adjudicated juvenile and adult offenders lack basic educational, vocational, and social skills necessary to enhance community integration and economic self-sufficiency. These deficiencies may interact with other socioeconomic and psychological factors to affect the life choices, made by offenders and may limit the legitimate financial and social opportunities available to these individuals.

Statement:

Education and training are integral parts of the total correctional process. Governmental jurisdictions should develop, expand, and improve delivery systems for academic, occupational, social, and other educational programs for accused and adjudicated juvenile and adult offenders in order to enhance their community integration and economic self-sufficiency. Toward this end, correctional agencies should:

A. Provide for assessment of academic, vocational, and social skills deficiencies of those under their jurisdictions;

B. Make available opportunities to participate in relevant, comprehensive educational, vocational, and social skills training programs and job placement activities that are fully coordinated and integrated with other components of the correctional process and the community as a whole;

C. Ensure programs provided are taught by certified instructors in accordance with professional standards and relevant techniques;

D. Provide incentives for participation and achievement in education and training programs;

E. Maximize use of public and private sector resources in development, implementation, coordination, and evaluation of education and training programs and job placement activities; and

F. Evaluate the efficiency and effectiveness of program performance based on measurable goals and objectives.

CORRECTIONAL POLICY ON JUVENILE CORRECTIONS

Introduction:

The juvenile corrections system must provide specialized care for young offenders in our society. Juvenile corrections, although sharing the same overall purpose as adult corrections, has significant different processes and procedures and requires specialized care, services, and programs.

Statement:

Children and youth have distinct personal growth and developmental needs and should be secure from any harmful effects of association with adult offenders. Juvenile corrections must provide a continuum of programs, services, and facilities for accused and adjudicated juvenile offenders that arc separate from those for adult offenders. Services and care for the individual youth must be a primary concern, consistent with protection of the public and maintenance of social order. To achieve these goals, juvenile corrections officials and agencies should:

A. Establish and maintain effective communication with all concerned with the juvenile justice system-executive, judicial, and legislative officials, prosecution and defense counsel, social service agencies, schools, police, and facilities-to achieve the fullest possible cooperation in making appropriate decisions in individual cases and in providing and using services and resources;

B. Provide a range of community and residential programs and services to meet individual needs, including education, vocational training, recreation, religious opportunities, family, aftercare, medical, dental, mental health, and specialized programs and services such as substance abuse treatment;

C. Involve the family and community as preferred resources and use the least restrictive appropriate dispositions in program planning and placement for juveniles;

D. Exclude from correctional systems all status offenders (those whose behavior would not be considered criminal if committed by adults);

E. Operate a juvenile classification system to identify and meet the program needs of the juvenile offender, while actively considering the public's need for protection; and

F. Support limitations on the use of juvenile records according to approved national standards, recognizing that the need to safeguard the privacy and rehabilitative goals of the juvenile should be balanced with concern for the protection of the public, including victims,

CORRECTIONAL POLICY ON
FEMALE OFFENDER SERVICES

Introduction:

Correctional systems must develop service delivery systems for accused and adjudicated female offenders that are comparable to those provided to males. Additional services must also be provided to meet the unique needs of the female offender population.

Statement:

Correctional systems must be guided by the principle of parity. Female offenders must receive the equivalent range of services available to other offenders, including opportunities for individualized programming and services that recognize the unique needs of this population. The services should:

A. Assure access to a range of alternatives to incarceration, including pretrial and post-trial diversion, probation, restitution, treatment for substance abuse, halfway houses, and parole services;

B. Provide acceptable conditions of confinement, including appropriately trained staff and sound operating procedures that address this population's needs in such areas as clothing, personal property, hygiene, exercise, recreation, and visitation with children and family;

C. Provide access to a full range of work and programs designed to expand economic and social roles of women, with emphasis on education; career counseling and exploration of nontraditional as well as traditional vocational training; relevant life skills, including parenting and social and economic assertiveness; and prerelease and work education release programs;

D. Facilitate the maintenance and strengthening of family ties, particularly those between parent and child;

E. Deliver appropriate programs and services, including medical, dental, and mental health programs, services to pregnant women, substance abuse programs, child and family services, and provide access to legal services; and

F. Provide access to release programs that include aid in establishing homes,economic stability, and sound family relationships.

CORRECTIONAL POLICY ON STAFF RECRUITMENT AND DEVELOPMENT

Introduction:

Knowledgeable, highly skilled, motivated, and professional correctional personnel are essential to fulfill the purpose of corrections effectively. Professionalism is achieved through structured programs of recruitment and enhancement of the employee's skills, knowledge, insight, and understanding of the correctional process.

Statement:

Correctional staff are tire primary agents for promoting health, welfare, security, and safety within correctional institutions and community supervision programs. They directly interact with accused and adjudicated offenders and are the essential catalysts of change in the correctional process. The education, recruitment, orientation, supervision, compensation, training, retention, and advancement of correctional staff must receive full support from the executive, judicial, and legislative branches of government. To achieve this, correctional agencies should:

A. Recruit personnel, including ex-offenders, in an open and accountable manner to assure equal employment opportunity for all qualified applicants regardless of sex, age, race, physical disability, religion, ethnic background, or political affiliation, and actively promote the employment of women and minorities;

B. Screen applicants for job-related aspects of physical suitability, personal adjustment, emotional stability, dependability, appropriate educational level, and experience. An additional requisite is the ability to relate to accused or adjudicated offenders in a manner that is fair, objective, and neither punitive nor vindictive;

C. Select, promote, and retain staff in accordance with valid job-related procedures that emphasize professional merit and technical competence. Voluntary transfers and promotions within and between correctional systems should be encouraged;

D. Comply with professional standards in staff development and offer a balance between operational requirements and the development of personal, social, and cultural understanding. Staff development programs should involve use of public and private resources, including colleges, universities, and professional associations;

E. Achieve parity between correctional staff and comparable criminal justice system staff in salaries and benefits, training, continuing education, performance evaluations, disciplinary procedures, career development opportunities, transfers, promotions, grievance procedures, and retirement; and

F. Encourage the participation of trained volunteers and students to enrich the correctional programs and to provide a potential source of recruitment.

CORRECTIONAL POLICY ON PROBATION

Introduction:

The vast majority of adjudicated adult and juvenile offenders remain in the community. Probation is a judicial decision that assigns the responsibility for supervision and control of these offenders to community corrections.

Statement:

Probation is a frequently used and cost-effective sanction of the court for enhancing social order and public safety, Probation may be used as a sanction by itself or, where necessary and appropriate, be combined with other sanctions such as fines, restitution, community service, residential care, or confinement. Agencies responsible for probation should:

A. Prepare disposition assessments to assist the court in arriving at appropriate sanctions. The least restrictive disposition consistent with public safety should be recommended;

B. Establish a case management system for allocating supervisory resources through a standardized classification process;

C. Provide supervision to probationers and, with their input, develop a realistic plan to ensure compliance with orders of the court;

D. Monitor and evaluate, on an ongoing basis, the probationers's adherence to the plan of supervision and, when necessary, modify the plan of supervision according to the changing needs of the offender and the best interests of society;

E. Provide access to a wide range of services to meet identifiable needs, all of which arc directed toward promoting law-abiding behavior;

F. Assure any intervention in an offender's life will not exceed the minimal amount needed to assure compliance with the orders of the court;

G. Initiate appropriate court proceedings, when necessary, if the probationer fails to comply with orders of the court, supervision plan, or other requirements so the court may consider other alternatives for the protection and well-being of the community;

H. Oppose use of the probation sanction for status offenders, neglected or dependent children, or any other individuals who arc neither accused nor charged with delinquent or criminal behavior;

I. Establish an educational program for sharing information about probation with the public and other agencies; and

J. Evaluate program efficiency, effectiveness, and overall system accountability consistent with recognized correctional standards.

CORRECTIONAL POLICY ON PAROLE

Introduction:

Parole is the conditional release of air offender from confinement before expiration of sentence pursuant to specified terms and conditions of supervision in the community. The grant of parole and its revocation are responsibilities of the paroling authority. Supervision of the parolee is provided by a designated agency that ensures compliance with all requirements by the release, through a case management process. Because the vast majority of those incarcerated will eventually be released into the community, the public is best protected be a supervised transition of the offender from institutional to community integration. Parole offers economic advantages to the public, the offender, and the correctional system by maximizing opportunities for offenders to become productive, law-abiding citizens.

Statement:

The parole component of the correctional system should function under separate but interdependent decision-making and case supervision processes. Paroling authorities should seek a balance in weighing the public interest and the readiness of the offender to reenter society under a structured program of supervisory management and control. Paroling systems should be equipped with adequate resources for administering the investigative, supervisory, and research functions. Administrative regulations governing the grant of parole, its revocation, case supervision practices, and discharge procedures should incorporate standards of due process and fundamental fairness. To achieve the maximum cost-benefits of parole supervision, full advantage should be taken of community-based resources available for serving offender employment and training needs, substance abuse treatment, and other related services. The parole system should:

A. Establish procedures to provide an objective decision-making process incorporating standards of due process and fundamental fairness in granting of parole that will address, at a minimum, the risk to public safety, impact on the victim, and information about the offense and the offender;

B. Provide access to a wide range of support services to meet offender needs consistent with realistic objectives for promoting law-abiding behavior;

C. Ensure any intervention in an offender's life will not exceed the minimum needed to ensure compliance with the terms and conditions of parole;

D. Provide a case management system for allocating supervisory resources through a standardized classification process, reporting parolee progress, and monitoring individualized parolee supervision and treatment plans;

E. Provide for the timely and accurate transmittal of status reports to the paroling authority for use in decision-making with respect to revocation, modification, or discharge of parole cases;

F. Establish programs for sharing information, ideas, and experience with other agencies and the public; and

G. Evaluate program efficiency, effectiveness, and overall accountability consistent with recognized correctional standards.

CORRECTIONAL POLICY ON STANDARDS AND ACCREDITATION

Introduction:

Correctional agencies should provide community and institutional programs and services that offer a full range of effective, just, humane, and safe dispositions and sanctions for accused and adjudicated offenders. To assure accountability and professional responsibility, these programs and services should meet accepted professional standards and obtain accreditation. The use of standards and the accreditation process provides a valuable mechanism for self-evaluation, stimulates improvement of correctional management and practice, and provides recognition of acceptable programs and facilities. The American Correctional Association and the Commission on Accreditation for Corrections have promulgated national standards and a voluntary system of national accreditation for correctional agencies. The beneficiaries of such a process are the administration and staff of correctional agencies, offenders, and the public.

Statement:

All correctional facilities and programs should be operated in accordance with the standards established by the American Correctional Association and should achieve and maintain accreditation through the Commission on Accreditation for Corrections. To fulfill this objective, correctional agencies should:

A. Implement improvement as necessary to comply with the appropriate standards specified or referenced in the following manuals and supplements:

1. Standards for Adult Parole Authorities

2. Standards for Adult Community Residential Services

3. Standards for Adult Probation and Parole Field Services

4. Standards for Adult Correctional Institutions

5. Standards for Adult Local Detention Facilities

6. Standards for Juvenile Community Residential Facilities

7. Standards for Juvenile Probation and Aftercare Services

8. Standards for Juvenile Detention Facilities

9. Standards for Juvenile Training Schools

10. Standards for the Administration of Correctional Agencies

B. See and maintain accreditation through the voluntary process developed by the Commission on Accreditation for Corrections in order that, through self-evaluation and peer review, necessary improvements are made, programs and services come into compliance with appropriate standards, and professional recognition is obtained.

CORRECTIONAL POLICY ON VICTIMS OF CRIME

Introduction:

Victims of crime suffer financial, emotional, and/or physical trauma. The criminal justice system is dedicated to the principle of fair and equal justice for all people. Victims' rights should be pursued within the criminal justice system to ensure their needs are addressed.

Statement:

Victims have the right to be treated with respect and compassion, to be informed about and involved in the criminal justice process as it affects their lives, to be protected from harm and intimidation, and to be provided necessary financial and support services that attempt to restore them to their former position before the crime was committed. Although many components of the criminal justice system share in the responsibility of providing services to victims of crime, the correctional community has an important role in this process and should:

A. Support activities that advocate the rights of the victims;

B. Promote local, state, and federal legislation that emphasizes victim rights and the development of victim service programs in local communities;

C. Advocate funding and technical assistance to develop and expand victim service programs;

D. Promote and advocate the development of programs in which offenders provide restitution to victims, and compensation and service to the community;

E. Promote active participation of victims in the criminal justice process, including the opportunity to be heard;

F. Promote the use of existing community resources and community volunteers to serve the needs of victims;

G. Cooperate in the development of training programs, designed for criminal justice officials, that promote sensitivity to victims' rights and identify community services; and

H. Operate those victim assistance programs that appropriately fall within the responsibility of the field of corrections.

NATIONAL CORRECTIONAL POLICY ON EMPLOYEE ASSISTANCE PROGRAMS

Introduction:

The most valuable resource in any correctional agency is the staff employed by that agency. Corrections is a service delivery enterprise with people as its most important product. The employees who deliver those services should be afforded all reasonable assistance to allow them to do the best job possible.

Statement:

Employee assistance programs should be made available to all employees. The programs should address employee needs and requirements that will help ensure a high level of on-the-job performance. Correctional agencies should:

A. Establish employee assistance programs based on appropriate assessment of employee needs and desires;

B. Publicize program availability regularly and frequently in a variety of ways to ensure that all employees know not only what is available to them, but also how to access and participate in them;

C. Provide programs at no cost to the employee where possible. Where the employee must pay some or all of the cost of the program/service, it should be an amount that does not exceed what that person could reasonably be expected to pay;

D. Provide an employee in the central/main office of the agency who would be responsible for coordinating all employee assistance programs, Each facility or major organizational unit should have one person designated as the coordinator of employee assistance programs;

E. Ensure programs and services are provided either directly by the agency or by other public or private agencies to which the employee is referred for assistance;

F. Require the Employee Assistance Program Coordinator to report at least quarterly on the level of activity that has occurred. That information should be used to assess the needs for adding, deleting, or modifying specific employee assistance programs;

G. Ensure employee requests or referrals for assistance remain confidential, unless the employee expressly elects to waive confidentiality.

APPENDIX B

AMERICAN BAR ASSOCIATION
LEGAL STATUS OF PRISONERS[1]

Standard 23-2.1. Access to the judicial process

(a)　Prisoners should have free and meaningful access to the judicial process; governmental authorities should assure such access. Regulations or actions should not unduly delay or adversely affect the outcome of a prisoner's claim for relief or discourage prisoners from seeking judicial consideration for their grievances. Interests of institutional security and scheduling may justify regulations that affect the manner in which access is provided.

(b)　To implement the principles in paragraph (a), the following standards should apply:

(i) Access should not be restricted by the nature of the action or the relief sought. Prisoners should be entitled to present any judicially cognizable issue, including:

(A) Challenge to the legality of their conviction or confinement;

(B) Assertions against correctional or other governmental authorities of any rights protected by constitutional, statutory, or administrative provision or the common law;

(C) Civil legal problems; and

(D) Assertions of a defense to any action brought against them.

(ii) Judicial procedures should be available to facilitate the prompt resolution of disputes involving the legality, duration, or conditions of confinement. The doctrine of exhaustion of remedies should apply unless past practice or other facts have demonstrated the futility of the available process. An administrative process unable to reach a decision within [thirty] working days is presumptively unreasonable.

(iii) When directed by a court, prisoners' attendance at legal proceedings directly involving their interests should be assured by correctional authorities.

(iv) Prisoners should be allowed to prepare and retain legal documents. The time, place, or manner of their preparation may be regulated for purposes of institutional security and scheduling. Retention of legal documents may be regulated only for purposes of health and safety. Regulations covering the preparation or retention of legal documents should be the least restrictive necessary.

(v) Legal documents should not be read, censored, or altered by correctional authorities, nor should their delivery be delayed.

(vi) Prisoners' decisions to seek judicial relief should not adversely affect their program, status within a correctional institution, or opportunity for release.

Standard 23-2.2 Access to legal services

(a) Prisoners should have access to legal advice and counseling, and, in appropriate instances, will have a right to counsel, in connection with all personal legal matters, including but not limited to:

(i) Court proceedings challenging conditions of confinement, correctional treatment, or supervision;

(ii) Parole grant and revocation proceedings;

(iii) Hearings to determine the length of sentences to imprisonment;

(iv) Civil matters, to the same extent as provided to members of the general public who are financially unable to obtain adequate representation; and

(v) Institutional disciplinary, classification, grievance, and other administrative proceedings. This standard does not limit existing rights to representation in parole revocation proceedings or in cases arising under subparagraph (a)(i) or

(vi) Neither, however, does it require correctional and parole authorities to allow the representation by legal counsel of prisoners at parole grant and other institutional hearings except as provided by law.

(b) Legal assistance for postconviction proceedings challenging the legality of a prisoner's conviction or confinement should conform to the requirements of standard 22-3.1.

(c) Prisoners should be entitled to retain counsel of their choice when able to do so and, when financially unable to obtain adequate representation, to have legal assistance provided for them by responsible governmental authorities to the same extent that such assistance is made available to members of the general public with comparable legal needs. Governmental authorities should establish programs to assure that adequate legal services are reasonably available to prisoners.

(d) Legal assistance for prisoners should be rendered by persons authorized by law to give legal advice or provide representation. When legal assistance is rendered by a person who is not an attorney, such counsel substitute should be trained by an attorney or educational institution and should receive continuing supervision by an attorney. Prison regulations should not restrict a prisoner's attorney in the selection of those assisting him or her.

(e) The relationship between a person providing legal assistance under paragraph (d) and a prisoner should be protected by the attorney-client privilege. Correctional authorities should facilitate confidential contact and communication between prisoners and persons providing legal assistance to them.

(f) Correctional and parole authorities should regulate by rule the roles of all persons who participate in institutional hearings.

Standard 23-2.3 Access to legal materials

(a) Correctional authorities should make available to prisoners educational services pertaining to their legal rights even when they have access to legal services. Printed materials outlining the recognized grounds for postconviction relief and the resources available to any person to pursue legal questions, specially prepared for prison inmates and written in terms understandable to them, are most desirable. Alternatively, an adequate collection of standard legal reference materials related to criminal law and procedures and cognate constitutional provisions should be part of a prison library.

(b) Prisoners should be entitled to acquire personal law books and other legal research material. Any regulation of the storage of legal material in personal quarters or other areas should not unreasonably interfere with access to or use of these materials. The retention of personal legal materials may be regulated and restricted in accordance with standard 23-1.1.

Standard 23-3.1. Rules of conduct

(a) Correctional authorities should promulgate clear written rules for prisoner conduct.

These rules and implementing criteria should include:

(i) A specific definition of offenses, a statement that the least severe punishment appropriate to each offense should be posed, and a schedule indicating the minimum and maxim possible punishment for each offense, proportionate to offense; and

(ii) Specific criteria and procedures for prison discipline and classification decisions, including decisions involving security status and work and housing assignments.

(b)   A personal copy of the rules should be provided to each prisoner upon entry to the institution. For the benefit of illiterate and foreign-language prisoners, a detailed oral explanation of the rules should be given. In addition, a written translation should be provided in any language spoken by a significant number of prisoners.

Standard 23-3.2. Disciplinary hearing procedures

(a)   At a hearing where a minor sanction is imposed, the prisoner should be entitled to:

(i)   Written notice of the charge, in a language the prisoner understands, within [seventy-two] hours of the time he or she is suspected of having committed an offense; within another [twenty-four] hours the prisoner should be given copies of any further written information the tribunal may consider;

(ii)   A hearing within [three] working days of the time the written notice of the charge was received;

(iii)   Be present and speak on his or her own behalf;

(iv)   A written decision based upon a preponderance of the evidence, with specified reasons for the decision. The decision should be rendered promptly and in all cases within [five] days after conclusion of the hearing; and

(v)   Appeal, within [five] days, to the chief executive officer of the institution, and the right to a written decision by that officer within [thirty] days, based upon a written summary of the hearing, any documentary evidence considered at the hearing, and the prisoner's written reason for appealing. The chief executive officer should either affirm or reverse the determination of misconduct and decrease or approve the punishment imposed. Execution of the punishment should be suspended during the appeal unless individual safety or individual security will be adversely affected thereby.

(b) At a hearing where a major sanction is imposed, in addition to the requirements of paragraph (a), the prisoner should be entitled to have in attendance any person within the local prison community who has relevant information, and to examine or cross-examine such witnesses except when the hearing officer(s):

 (i) Exclude testimony as unduly cumulative; or

 (ii) Receive testimony outside the presence of the prisoner pursuant to a finding that the physical safety of a person would be endangered by the presence of a particular witness or by disclosure of his or her identity.

(c) Disciplinary hearings should be conducted by one or more impartial persons.

(d) Unless the prisoner is found guilty, no record relating to the charge should be retained in the prisoner's file or used against the prisoner in any way.

(e) Where necessary, in accordance with standard 23-1.1(b) or (c), pending the hearing required by paragraph (b), correctional authorities may confine separately a prisoner alleged to have committed a major violation. Such preheating confinement should not extend more than [seven) days unless necessitated by the prisoner's request for a continuance or by the pendency of criminal investigation or prosecution as provided in standard 23-3.3(b).

(f) In the event of a situation requiring the chief executive officer to declare all, or a part, of an institution to be in a state of emergency, the rights provided in this standard may be temporarily suspended for up to [twenty-four] hours after the emergency has terminated.

Standard 23-3.4. Classification

(a)   The initial classification of a prisoner according to security risk status and job or other assignment should be accomplished informally within [thirty] days of the prisoner's arrival at the place of classification.

(b)   The prisoner should meet with a properly trained representative of the classification committee. The committee representative should:

  (i) Explain the classification process, the options the prisoner may have, and the relevant criteria; and

  (ii) Seek to develop a classification consistent with the needs of the prisoner and the institution; and

  (iii) Submit such classification to the classification committee and the prisoner.

(c)   The classification of a prisoner should be reviewed by the classification committee at least every [six]-month period.

(d)   Each decision of the classification committee should explain the considerations and factors that led to the committee's decision. The prisoner should receive a copy of the committee's written decision.

(e)   If the classification committee or the prisoner rejects a classification (or if the prisoner is dissatisfied with the committee's periodic review), the prisoner should be given a prompt hearing before the classification committee if a request is made within [five] days of receipt of the classification decision.

(f) At a classification hearing, the prisoner should be entitled to:

  (i) Timely discovery of any written information the committee may consider, and

  (ii) Be present and speak on his or her own behalf.

(g)   In any classification decision, the presence of a detainer based on a charged, but as yet unproven, criminal offense or parole violation should not be considered if the detainer has been pending for more than [six] months without formal action by the responsible authority after demand by the prisoner. All other detainees may be considered by the committee, but the mere presence of any detainer should not be given conclusive weight in deciding the prisoner's security classification.

Standard 23-5.1. Care to be provided

(a)   Prisoners should receive routine and emergency medical care, which includes the diagnosis and treatment of physical, dental, and mental health problems. A prisoner who requires care not available in the correctional institution should be transferred to a hospital or other appropriate place for care.

(b)   Personnel providing medical care in the correctional institution should have qualifications equivalent to medical care personnel performing similar functions in the community.

(c)   If an institution operates a hospital, it should meet the standards for a licensed general hospital in the community with respect to the services it offers.

Standard 23-5.3. Medical examinations

(a)   Upon admission to a correctional institution a prisoner should receive an examination by a person trained to ascertain visible or common symptoms of communicable disease and conditions requiring immediate medical attention by a physician.

(b)   A sentenced prisoner should receive a thorough physical (including an appropriate evaluation of apparent mental condition) and dental examination in accordance with accepted medical practice and standards:

(i) Within two weeks of admission to the correctional institution;

(ii) Not less than every two years thereafter; and

(iii) Upon release from confinement if the most recent examination was given more than one year earlier.

(c) A person detained in a correctional institution who is not a sentenced prisoner should be afforded a thorough physical and dental examination upon request when the person is confined for more than two weeks.

Standard 23-6.2. Visitation; general

(a) Home furlough programs should be established, giving due regard to institutional and community security, to enable prisoners to maintain and strengthen family and community ties.

(b) Subject to the provisions of standard 23-1.1, correctional authorities should accommodate and encourage visiting by establishing reasonable visiting hours, including time on weekends and holidays, suited to the convenience of visitors.

(c) Subject to the provisions of standard 23-1.1, institutional visiting facilities should promote informal communications and afford opportunities for physical contact. Extended visits between prisoners and their families in suitable accommodations should be allowed for prisoners who are not receiving home furloughs.

(d) Prisoners should be able to receive any visitor not excluded by correctional authorities for good cause. A prisoner may have the exclusion of a prospective visitor reconsidered through a grievance procedure. All visitors may be subjected to nonintrusive forms of personal search.

(e) Visitation periods should be at least [one] hour long, and prisoners should be able to cumulate visitation periods to permit extended visits. Visits with attorneys, clergy, and public officials should not be counted against visiting periods, and should be unlimited except as to time and duration.

(f) Where resources and facilities permit, correctional authorities are encouraged to facilitate and promote visitation by providing transportation or by providing guidance, directions, and assistance as to available travel to visitors arriving in local terminals.

Standard 23-6.5. Religious freedom

(a) Prisoners' religious beliefs should not be restricted or inhibited by correctional authorities in any way.

(b) Prisoners should be entitled to pursue any lawful religious practice consistent with their orderly confinement and the security of the institution.

(c) Correctional authorities should provide prisoners with diets of nutritious food consistent with their religious beliefs. Prisoners should be entitled to observe special religious rites, including fasting and special dining hours, on major holidays generally observed by their religion, subject to standard 23-1.1.

(d) Prisoners should not be required to engage in religious activities.

(e) Correctional authorities should not maintain any information (other than directory information) concerning a prisoner's religious activities.

(f) Modes of dress or appearance, including religious medals and other symbols, should be permitted to the extent they do not interfere with identification and security of prisoners.

(g) Even while being punished, prisoners, should be allowed religious counseling.

(h) Resources and facilities made available for religious purposes should be equitably allocated according to the proportions of prisoners adhering to each faith.

Standard 23-7.1. Resolving prisoner grievances

(a) Correctional authorities should authorize and encourage correctional employees to resolve prisoner grievances on an informal basis whenever possible.

(b) Every correctional institution should adopt a formal procedure to resolve specific prisoner grievances, including any complaint arising out of institutional policies, rules, practices, and procedures or the action of any correctional employee or official. Grievance procedures should not be used as a substitute appellate procedure for individual decisions reached by adjudicative bodies, for example, parole, classification, and disciplinary boards, although a complaint involving the procedures or general policies employed by any correctional adjudicative body should be subject to grievance procedures.

(c) Correctional authorities should make forms available so that a grievant may initiate review by describing briefly the nature of the grievance, the persons involved, and the remedy sought.

(d) The institution's grievance procedure should be designed to ensure the cooperation and confidence of prisoners and correctional officials and should include:

   (i) Provision for written responses to all grievances, including the reasons for the decision;

   (ii) Provision for response within a prescribed, reasonable time limit. A request that is not responded to or resolved within [thirty] working days should be deemed to have been denied;

   (iii) Special provision for responding to emergencies;

   (iv) Provision for advisory review of grievances;

    (v) Provision for participation by staff and prisoners in the design of the grievance procedure;

    (vi) Provision for access by all prisoners, with guarantees against reprisal;

    (vii) Applicability over a broad range of issues; and

    (viii)Means for resolving questions of jurisdiction.

ENDNOTE

[1]. Selected Standards from the American Bar Association's *Standards for Criminal Justice: Legal Status of Prisoners* (formally approved, February 1981). Reprinted by permission of the American Bar Association.

GLOSSARY

Accreditation: A process by which correctional institutions are determined to have met the minimum professional standards of the professional organization.

Acquitted: Found not guilty.

Adjudicatory hearing: The juvenile court proceeding that is equivalent to a trial in adult court.

Aftercare: The term used in lieu of parole for juvenile cases.

Age of majority: The legal age at which individuals are no longer considered juveniles.

Aggravating circumstances: Those circumstances that tend to make the crime more serious (i.e., use of a deadly weapon, committing an offense against a law enforcement officer, taking advantage of a position of trust to commit an offense, etc.

Amnesty: Agreement of protection against prosecution.

Argot: The language of the prison subculture.

Bailiffs: Officers who supervise offenders and maintain order in local and state courtrooms during legal proceedings.

Banishment: The practice of forcing someone to leave a group. Used as a punishment in primitive societies.

Blood feuds: Blood feuds are actions taken by the victim's family or tribe as revenge on the offender's family or tribe.

Booking: The initial point of entry in the jails, also known as intake, and involves the transfer of responsibility for the arrestee from the law enforcement officer to the jail.

Boot camp programs: Rehabilitative programs based on the military boot-camp routine.

Building tenders: System that involved some of the most violent and physically intimidating inmates being chosen as "building tenders" by officers who then controlled their tier or work group by intimidation and fear.

Capital cases: Those cases in which the government seeks the death penalty.

Career criminals: Those persons who make, or attempt to make, a living committing crime.

Case law: Court decisions that are used to regulate similar future cases.

Child saving movement: A movement which was directed at children in need or trouble and attempted to save children by using houses of refuge and reform schools.

Classification: a process for determining the needs and requirements of individuals confined and for assigning them to housing units and programs in light of individual needs and existing correctional resources.

Classification process: That portion of jail procedure that is concerned with the identification, categorization, and assignment of the inmate to various levels of security, programs, and work.

Cleared count: As the result of a head count, the precise location of all prisoners are accounted for.

Co-correctional institution: An institution that houses both male and female offenders.

Code of Hammurabi: Early code of laws involving criminal punishments.

Code of Draco: Early Greek code that used the same penalties for both citizens and slaves and incorporated many of the concepts used in primitive societies (e.g., vengeance, outlawry, and blood feuds).

Codes of ethics: Guidelines for professionals in the field which are not legislative enactments, and there are no disciplinary actions associated with their violations. The codes provide us with a set of standards that we should strive to meet in our professional lives.

Collateral consequence: Loss of privileges and rights because of a felony conviction.

Collateral costs: The costs involved related to the disruptions to the lives of those related to offenders and the economic impact on offenders and their families that result from being involved in the criminal justice system.

Commissaries: Stores within the prison where prisoners are allowed to make purchases.

Community service programs: A sentencing alternative that allows the defendant to stay in the community and use community services as rehabilitative tools.

Community corrections: Correctional programs that exist within the local community.

Community service: A form of community corrections, usually accompanying other forms of sentences, in which offenders are required to participate in volunteer work to repay some of the harm/costs they imposed on the community.

Community treatment centers: Low-level security institutions designed to house offenders which allows them interactions in free society.

Conditions of confinement: The institution's actual physical conditions and the positive or negative impacts they have on inmates.

Congregate work: The bringing of inmates together to work in a common location on a common job.

Conjugal visits: Visits where the inmates are allowed to spend time with family and spouses in private; usually thought of as opportunities for spouses to visit inmates and to engage in sexual activity.

Contact visits: Visits in a setting where inmates and visitors are not separated by a partition.

Contraband: Items possessed by prisoners or detainees that are prohibited by program policy and regulations.

Corporal punishment: Physical punishments such as whipping, stoning, or burning.

Correctional institutions: Facilities designed to hold and control convicted criminal offenders; including prisons and jails.

Correctional officers: Officers who generally perform custodial roles in jails, prisons, and other institutions.

Court liaison: The jail process that is responsible for the safe and timely delivery of jail residents to court.

Curfew: A type of home confinement requiring subjects to remain at home during specific time frames, generally in the evening.

Custody designation: The designation that tells how much supervision the inmate needs and with whom and where he will live.

Day-reporting centers: Highly structured non-residential programs utilizing supervision, sanctions, and services coordinated from a central focus.

Deference period: The period of time (since 1979) when the courts were more conservative in getting involved with prison administration.

Deferred adjudication: A form of probation that is used without a finding of guilt in which the defendant pleas guilty and agrees to defer further proceedings.

Depersonalization: The results of living in a total institution where individuals lose their sense of individuality and identify themselves as members of a set of similar individuals.

Detainer: A warrant placed against a person in a federal, state, or local correctional facility notifying the holding authority of the intention of another jurisdiction to take custody of that individual when he or she is released from custody.

Detention center: A facility for the temporary placement of juvenile offenders. A place where juveniles can be held and provided treatment.

Determinate sentences: Fixed periods of confinement that convicted offenders must serve in a correctional institution.

Deterrence: A punishment viewpoint that focuses on future outcomes rather than past misconduct and is based on the theory that creating a fear of future punishments will deter crime.

Diagnostic centers: The centers that first receive and process inmates who are confined in state penal institutions.

Disenfranchisement: Loss of the right to vote.

Disposition hearing: The proceeding in juvenile court that is similar to the sentencing phase of an adult criminal trial.

Diversion centers: Institutions where offenders live in a facility for a few months and are supervised 24 hours per day but can leave for work and other forms of necessary activity.

Double-celling: The housing of two inmates in a cell designed for only one inmate.

Due process: The required legal process that the legal system must follow in any action to fully protect the rights of citizens, including convicted criminal offenders.

Electronic monitoring: Use of electronic devices to signal supervising probation departments when offenders on home incarceration leave their premises which violate the conditions of their sentence.

Flat time: When an offender serves his or her sentence day for day with no early release.

Gang associates: "Wannabe" gang members or individuals who actively support gang activity without being gang members.

Good-time laws: Statutes that give prison administrators the power to release inmates prior to the expiration of their sentences based on the administrator's judgment that the inmate had shown good behavior and thereby deserved early release.

Group counseling: A planned activity with three or more offenders present in a counseling session for the purpose of solving personal and social problems.

Group home: A community correctional facility where small groups of juveniles live in a home-type setting.

Halfway houses: Group homes that are non-secure facilities that are used to help integrate the youths back into the community.

Juvenile detention centers: Short-term, secure facilities that hold juveniles awaiting adjudication, disposition, or placement in an institution.

"Hands off" period: The period of time (prior to 1964) when the courts rarely accepted a case involving the conditions of confinement or prisoners rights based on the concept that prison administrators were the ones best qualified to determine the appropriate conditions of confinement.

Hands-off policy: Practice of the courts to avoid involvement in correctional matters.

Holy Inquisition: A court set up by the Church of Rome to inquire into cases of heresy.

Home incarceration: A sentence where individuals are required to remain in their homes, except for special reasons (work, school, medical care); purpose is to incapacitate offenders from recommitting their offenses.

Home confinement: The concept of home confinement is relatively ambiguous, it may range from evening curfew, to detention during all nonworking hours, to continuous incarceration at home.

Ideology: The belief system adopted by a group and consists of assumptions and values.

Incapacitation: A punishment viewpoint that holds that while the prisoner is in confinement, he is unlikely to commit crimes on innocent persons outside of prison.

Incorrigible: A person who is unmanageable or uncontrollable.

Indeterminate sentences: Sentences that impose a minimum and maximum period of time that offenders will serve in a correctional program; the actual length of each sentence is determined by the offender's behavior and rehabilitative progress.

Indigent: A person with no funds and source of income. In determining indigency for purposes of ability to retain an attorney, the general test is "financially unable to obtain adequate representation without substantial hardship to themselves or their families."

Informal probation: A form of probation whereby the defendant agrees to comply with the terms of the probation, but no formal court order or court action is taken nor is a finding entered in the case. If the defendant completes the terms of the probation, then the case is dismissed.

Institutionalized personality: The personality type developed by prisoners that is characterized by moving like a robot according to a routinized pattern, losing any initiative, living on a day-to-day basis, forgetting the past, and avoiding the future.

Intensive supervision probation: Probation for offenders who are too antisocial for the relative freedom afforded by regular probation, yet not so seriously criminal as to require incarceration.

Jail therapy: The act of placing the probationer in jail and without holding a hearing, releasing the probationer after a short stay.

Jailhouse lawyers: Inmates who are knowledgeable, or claim to be, about the law and how to work in the judicial system and who use their skills and knowledge to assist other inmates in preparing and submitting legal paperwork.

Jails: Confinement facilities that are used to punish persons convicted of minor offenses and who are sentenced to confinement for a year or less, and to detain individuals awaiting trial.

Judicial intervention: Review by the courts to determine whether the actions of correctional officials are legal and within constitutional boundaries.

Judicial review: The process whereby an appellate court reviews a trial court decision and determines whether the decision is legally correct.

Just deserts model: The belief that criminal offenders should receive punishments in amounts equal to the degree of harm they caused to other individuals and society.

Line officers: Those officers who directly supervise the inmates of a correctional institution; also referred to as correctional officers.

Lock down: A condition where all prisoner movement is stopped.

Lockstep: The practice of requiring inmates to walk/ march in unison while holding the shoulder of the inmate in front of them.

Lockups: A temporary holding facility that is generally operated by the police and is located in a police station or headquarters.

Long-term incarceration: Serving a sentence of more than seven or eight years in a correctional institution.

Mandatory early release programs: The procedures in correctional systems that require inmates to be released prior to the expiration of their sentences to maintain legal limits on institutional populations.

Mandatory supervision: The release of an offender from prison with supervision when he or she completes a prescribed portion of his or her sentence.

Megan's Laws: Sex offender registration laws.

Mitigating circumstances: Those circumstances that tend to reduce the severity of the crime (i.e., cooperation with the investigating authority, surrender, good character).

Orientation process: The process of providing inmates with information regarding the department's policies, programs, educational services, rules, classification procedures, disciplinary procedures, and other inmate activities and programs.

Overcrowding: The housing of more inmates in a facility that is not designed or legally approved to house more than a set maximum number of inmates.

Pardon: An executive act of clemency that legally clears an offender from the consequences of conviction for a criminal offense.

Parens patriae: A legal doctrine that says the state must provide parental-like protections to those who are unable to care for themselves; applied to convicts when popular ideology holds that criminals have shown themselves unable to act like adults.

Parole officers: Officers who supervise offenders who are released from prison on parole or on mandatory supervision. Parole officers generally work under the supervision of the state parole board.

Parole guidelines: Procedures designed to limit or structure parole release decisions based on measurable offender criteria.

Parole: The discretionary release of an inmate from prison when he or she completes a prescribed portion of his or her sentence and the parole board agrees that the release will not increase the likelihood of harm to the public.

Penal servitude: The use of hard labor as punishment which was generally reserved for the lower classes of citizens.

Presumptive sentence: A sentence suggested by the legislative body based on certain factors regarding the crime and the criminal.

Pretrial diversion: A form of probation that is granted prior to trial in which the defendant agrees to waive time and to complete a program or process.

Prison tactical response teams: Teams which are trained to respond to riots, hostage situations, forced cell moves, and other potentially dangerous confrontations.

Prisonization: The process by which prisoners learn the rules of socialization into the prison culture and is seen by many as a criminalization process whereby a criminal novice is transformed from a prosocial errant to a committed predatory criminal.

Privatization: The delivery of correctional services by a private organization, usually a for-profit corporation.

Probation: The conditional release of a defendant based on a promise by the defendant to abide by certain rules.

Probation officers: Officers who supervise probationers and generally work under the supervision of the court system.

Professional criminals: Persons of respectability and high social status who commit crime in the course of their occupations.

Proportionality of punishment: The concept of punishment that the penalty be proportional to the crime.

Put down: The emotional effect of being put in a prison.

Recidivism: The repeating of criminal behavior.

Regular probation: The release of a convicted offender under conditions imposed by the courts for a specified period of time.

Rehabilitation: The view that punishment should be directed toward correcting the offender.

Restitution: A sanction imposed by an official of the criminal justice system requiring an offender to make a payment of money or service to either the direct or a substitute crime victim.

Restorative justice: A concept of justice whose primary goal is to restore the victim to his or her original position and then take corrective action against the offender.

Retribution: Based on the ideology that the criminal is an enemy of society and deserves severe punishment for willfully breaking its rules.

Rights period: The period of time (1964-1978) when the courts became actively involved in the administration of prisons.

Scrip: Items or goods used as currency in a prison.

Section 1983 cases: Those cases where officials sue for violations of individual rights under the provisions of 42 U.S. Code 1983.

Security: The degree of restriction on prisoner activity within a correctional institution. Generally, security is maximum, medium, or minimum levels.

Segregation: The confinement of a prisoner to an individual cell that is separated from the general population. There are three types of segregation: administrative segregation, disciplinary segregation, and protective custody.

Segregative classifications: Assignments of inmates based on age and previous incarceration.

Sentence: An authorized judicial decision that places some degree of penalty on a guilty person.

Sentencing guidelines: Guidelines designed to structure sentences based on the offense severity and the criminal history of the defendant.

Shelters: Short-term facilities that are operated like detention centers, but are non-secure with a physically unrestricted environment.

Shock probation: Probation that is designed to give defendants a "taste of the bars" before placing them on probation.

Shock incarceration: Sentencing offenders to short periods of time in prison with following periods of time on community supervision; the idea is to make offenders realize what prison is like and to avoid their future return to prison.

Specific deterrence: The belief that punishing criminals will reduce their desire to commit other crimes.

Split sentences: Sentences that include both time in an institution and a period of time on community corrections.

Stare decisis: The rule that when Courts decide cases, decisions are based on precedents; counseling, basic and advanced education, and behavioral modification and job-training programs.

State jail felony: A relative new crime classification that is more serious than a misdemeanor and less serious than a felony.

Technical violations: Those probation condition violations that do not involve criminal misconduct.

"Three strikes law": Law that states that an individual receives a life sentence after committing any three felonies.

Train: The bus network used by states to transfer prisoners from one external unit to another.

Trials by ordeal: Practices used by the early churches as substitutes for trials, whereby the accused was subjected to dangerous or painful tests in the belief that God would protect the innocent and the guilty would suffer agonies and die.

UNICOR: The Federal Prison Industries, Inc. which is wholly owned by the federal government with the mission to support the Federal Bureau of Prisons through the gainful employment of inmates in work programs.

Values: Beliefs about what is moral and desirable.

Wergeld: The acceptance of money or property as atonement for wrongs.

White-collar criminals: The traditional name for professional criminals.

Work release: A formal arrangement, sanctioned by law, whereby a prisoner is permitted to leave confinement to maintain approved and regular employment in the community, returning to custody during nonworking hours.

Work-release programs: Programs where inmates are allowed to attend and leave a correctional facility for jobs on the outside.

Writ of habeas corpus: The writ, traditionally known as the "Great Writ" that is constitutional protected writ designed to require the government to justify why the individual is being held in confinement.

INDEX

America's Most Popular
Practical Police Books